Object-Oriented
Software Engineering

Object-Oriented Software Engineering

The Professional Developer's Guide

George Wilkie

The Institute of Software Engineering

 Addison-Wesley Publishing Company

Wokingham, England · Reading, Massachusetts · Menlo Park, California
New York · Don Mills, Ontario · Amsterdam · Bonn · Sydney · Singapore
Tokyo · Madrid · San Juan · Milan · Paris · Mexico City · Seoul · Taipei

Cover designed by Pencil Box Ltd, Marlow, Buckinghamshire
and printed by The Riverside Printing Co. (Reading) Ltd.
Typeset by Meridian Phototypesetting Ltd. Pangbourne
Printed in Great Britain by the University Press, Cambridge
ISBN 0–201– 6276– 1

First printed 1993. Reprinted 1994.

British Library Cataloguing in Publication Data
A catalogue record for this book is available from the British Library.

Library of Congress Cataloging in Publication Data
Wilkie, George.
    Object-oriented software engineering: the professional developer's guide/George Wilkie.
        p.   cm.
    Includes bibliographical references and index.
    ISBN 0-201-62767-1:
    1. Object-oriented programming (Computer science)   2. Software Engineering.   I. Title.
QA76.64.W54   1993   93-13625
005.1'1--dc20   CIP

The Institute of Software Engineering is a division of the MARI Group of high technology companies – a group with a wide range of skills in the information and telecommunications technologies, and specializing in research and development, technology transfer and training. It is a research and consultancy division with an emphasis on the technology transfer of leading edge software engineering and systems development techniques and technology to industry. It regularly produces reports on significant trends and technologies impacting software development and is involved in consultancy, awareness programmes and applied research.

About the author

George Wilkie is a widely recognized consultant and speaker on object-oriented software engineering. He holds BSc and PhD degrees in physics.

Dr Wilkie joined The Institute of Software Engineering in January 1990 as Project Leader with responsibility for all the Institute's activities in the area of object-oriented software engineering. He has provided consultancy and training to many organizations on the introduction and application of object-oriented techniques, and the analysis, design and construction of software systems. He is the Institute's representative in the Object Management Group (OMG) and is a member of the OMG subgroup tasked with evaluating existing object-oriented analysis and design methods.

Prior to joining the Institute, Dr Wilkie spent several years as a software engineer with British Telecom where he was involved in a range of projects and gained software engineering experience in most areas of the traditional software development life cycle.

He is currently at the University of Ulster where he is continuing his research into object-oriented software development.

Foreword

Object orientation – something better but not necessarily new!

Object orientation is an important approach to analysing problems, designing systems and building solutions. If the reader hadn't already found that statement in the literature, this tome wouldn't be under consideration for the reading ahead. And it certainly is the case that the object-oriented approach to general systems analysis (and in particular software systems) is a better approach.

Nevertheless, the press and experts in the field pay too much attention to the words 'new' and 'better.' An aura of mystery and speciality has surrounded object technology, and not necessarily to the betterment of the field of software or any other endeavours.

As to being 'better,' we concur. As to being 'new' – well, it is instructive to look at a bit of history in the field. As early as the late 1970s special object-oriented languages (notably Smalltalk) were in development and use; in the early 1970s object-oriented extensions to languages such as LISP were in simultaneous development at various sites. Expert system tools of the early 1960s, seeking a general approach to the representation of human knowledge, used what are now called 'objects' to represent bits of knowledge and relationships between those bits. The idea isn't new, and isn't mystical.

That the idea is better is traced to its relationship with the 'real world'. All software systems are basically simulations of some real systems. Though an automated airline reservation system might not use the same procedures as the old paper-and-pencil approach (we'd like to think that's the case!), the automation still simulates the process of assigning seats and flights as did the older approach, albeit somewhat faster and with potentially global view.

What brings object orientation to the fore today is the better match between real human systems, which rely upon tenuous, shifting relationships between agents and information (that is, for example, written communication between people with specific expertise) and object-oriented software development, which models communications (requests, or messaging) between objects (active agents comprising embedded data, or information).

This book illuminates the approach, and makes a somewhat better case for its utility. Even more important, the fog of mystery surrounding the subject is burned off by the rising sun of clarity. While discussing the general specialities of the subject, Dr Wilkie explores the categories of use of object technology today, and their application to specific problem domains. As expert a compendium isn't to be found elsewhere.

Richard Mark Soley, PhD
Technical Director
The Object Management Group
Framingham
Massachusetts, USA
July 1992

OBJECT MANAGEMENT GROUP

Preface

Why should you bother with this over-hyped subject? Are there any *real* advantages to be had – or is this approach just flavour-of-the moment? Let's face it, there have been a few notable disasters in the area. But maybe, just maybe, there's more to it than the superficial hype. You are reading this text so perhaps you are one of those people who feels (or hopes) that object orientation might answer some of your software development problems.

Object-Oriented Software Engineering – The Professional Developer's Guide addresses the critical software engineering problems and shows how an object-oriented approach can provide much-improved solutions over previous methods. It is designed as a technology transfer vehicle, helping you decide if object orientation is right for you, and how to approach its introduction.

Over the past two or three years I have been asked the same questions by literally dozens of interested people:

- What? What makes a software development method object-oriented? What are the concepts behind an object-oriented approach?
- How? How are these concepts applied in the development of software?
- Why? Why should I consider an object-oriented development method?
- When? When should I consider using object orientation? When is it appropriate and under what circumstances should I retain existing traditional approaches to software development?
- Who? – Who is using object-oriented software development techniques and to what advantage?

In the following chapters of this book it is my intention to answer all of these questions and to clarify both the terminology and use of the concepts through individual techniques and processes embodying many such techniques.

Different parts of the book will appeal to different types of staff involved in the software development process. It should be read by software developers and managers considering the use of object-oriented software development methods in their organization. It does not assume a prior understanding of object-oriented techniques. It presents the techniques and some tools supporting an object-oriented approach and is directed at both the novice and those with a deeper understanding of object orientation.

Managers should use the book as a vehicle for understanding the concepts of object orientation and to evaluate the merits of the approach with a view to migrating towards an object-oriented software development method.

The book dispels the mystery and confusing claims made about object-oriented techniques by describing the main programming languages, analysis and design methods and database management systems available today. It also predicts future trends in the industry at large. Where possible, explanations are backed up with examples and graphical illustrations to clarify the issues.

Through several user case-studies, presented in Chapter 8, this book consolidates the information presented in preceding chapters with accounts from real-life projects. It illustrates the applicability of an object-oriented approach to both large and small organizations for a wide range of application types from typical commercial DP systems to real-time technical applications.

It has been my intention from the outset to discuss the pros and cons of the technology, and I believe this has been achieved. Where advantages are cited, you will find the disadvantages are also presented. The final decision rests with you, the reader. If you believe that the pros outweigh the cons for your organization then object orientation may be the right method for you. If you don't, then perhaps you've saved a great amount of money by purchasing this book!

The objectives of this book can therefore be summarized as:

- To present the principles behind object-oriented software engineering.
- To show which areas of the software development life cycle these principles can be applied within.
- To illustrate how current object technology supports these principles.
- To illustrate how other developers are using object-oriented software development techniques, through the use of case-studies.
- To help the reader decide if and how object orientation might be applied in his or her software development environment.

Acknowledgements

I am particularly indebted to the following people who provided constructive comments and valuable material during the preparation of this book:

Peter Maxwell (Glockenspiel Ltd), Sean Kempton (Valbecc Ltd), Nick Parsons (Applied Logic Computers), Enrico Bauer (Winter Partners – Switzerland) and Dr Patrick McParland (The Queen's University of Belfast), as well as the staff involved in the user case-studies from British Airways, Praxis, Winter Partners, British Aerospace, Applied Logic Computers, Satellites International Ltd and IBM Ireland Information Services Ltd. Thanks are also due to Mr K Thompson, Mr J Vernon, Mr P Corrigan and Mr A Frazer, all from The Institute of Software Engineering, for their helpful contributions and practical assistance.

Special thanks is due to Dr Richard Soley from the Object Management Group for supplying the foreword and for many discussions and helpful suggestions during the early stages of this book.

I thank my colleagues in the Analysis and Design subcommittee of the Object Management Group (OMG) for the many useful discussions we have had on the subject: Dr Andrew Hutt (ICL), Kevin Murphy (James Martin & Co.), Peter Thomas (Oracle UK) and John Dodd (James Martin Associates). I especially acknowledge the help of Geir Høydalsvik (Norwegian Institute of Technology) for his help and contributions to the analysis and design reference model in Chapter 4 and with the OORASS method.

Finally, and most importantly, I wish to thank my wife Caroline and my parents Donald and Iris for their support and encouragement always.

George Wilkie
The Institute of Software Engineering
Belfast, Northern Ireland
April 1993

Publisher's acknowledgements

The publisher wishes to thank the following for permission to reproduce figures in this book. R.G.G. Cattell (1991), K. Beck and W. Cunningham (1989), Brian Henderson-Sellers (1990), Figures 8 and 9: reproduced with permission of the Association for Computing Machinery, Inc.; William Stubblefield, personal communication; Figure from Course 323 reproduced with permission of Learning Tree International; ODI (1990) reproduced with permission of Object Design, Inc.; M.S. Jackson (1991) reproduced with permission of Butterworth-Heinemann; P. Lyngbaek (1991) reproduced with permission of Hewlett-Packard Company; P. Wegner (1990) reproduced with permission of Peter Wegner; New Science Associates, Inc. (1989), New Science Associates, Ltd (1992); B. Meyer (1988); Versant Object Technology (1990); A.D. Brown (1991) reproduced by permission of McGraw-Hill Book Company Europe; J.A. Purchase and R.L. Winder (1991) reproduced with permission of SIGS Publications.

The publisher wishes to apologize for failing to give due acknowledgement to the above for the use of their material in the first printing of this book.

The author and publisher wish to acknowledge that Figure 4.9 on page 89 and several passages on pages 90–1 of this book were in large part reproduced from 'An Iterative-Design Model for Reusable Object-Oriented Software' Proceedings of the International Conference on Object-Oriented Programming Systems, Languages and Tools, pp. 12–27, Ottawa, Canada, 1990, by Sandjiv Gossain and Bruce Anderson, © 1990 Association for Computing Machinery, Inc. The author and publisher apologize for the omission of a specific reference to this paper within the book. The correct reference has been added in this reprint and will be added in all future reprints of the book.

Brief contents

Contents

5   Object-oriented programming languages   164

8   User case-studies   **287**

Trademark notice

Actor™ is a trademark of Symantec Incorporated
Ada™ is a trademark of the Ada Joint Program Office, DoD, US Government
AM/ST™ is a trademark of Coopers and Lybrand
C++/Views™ is a trademark of CNS Incorporated
COBOL/2™ is a trademark of Micro Focus Incorporated
CodeBase++™ is a trademark of Sequiter Software Incorporated
CommonView™ is a trademark of Glockenspiel Ltd
Dataflex™ is a trademark of Data Access Corporation
dBase™ is a trademark of Ashton Tate Incorporated
DEC™ and Trellis™ are trademarks of Digital Equipment Corporation
Eiffel/S™ is a trademark of SIG Computers GmbH
Eiffel™, EiffelVision™, EiffelBuild™, EiffelStore™ are trademarks of Interactive Software Engineering
Enfin/2™ is a trademark of Enfin Software Corporation
Gemstone™ is a trademark of Servio Corporation
GUI Master™ is a trademark of Vleermuis Software Research b.v.
HOOD™ is a trademark of HOOD Working Group
IBM™, OS/2™, PS/2™ and RS6000™ are trademarks of International Business Machines Corporation
Informix 4GL™ is a trademark of Informix Software Incorporated
Ingres™ is a trademark of Ingres Corporation
LogicAL™ is a trademark of The Applied Logic Group Ltd
MacApp™, Macintosh™ and Macos™ are trademarks of Apple Computer Incorporated
Motif™ is a trademark of Open Software Foundation Incorporated
MS-DOS™ and Windows™ are trademarks of Microsoft Corporation
NeWS™ and SPARCStation™ are trademarks of Sun Microsystems Incorporated
NewWave™ and Iris™ are trademarks of Hewlett-Packard Company
NeXTStep™ is a trademark of NeXT Corporation
O_2™ is a trademark of O_2 Technology
Object Craft™ is a trademark of ObjectCraft Incorporated
Objective-C™, ICPak101™, ICPak201™ and ICPak301™ are trademarks of Stepstone Corporation
Objectivity/DB™ is a trademark of Objectivity Incorporated
ObjectMaker™ is a trademark of Mark-V Systems
Objectory™ is a trademark of Objective Systems SF AB
ObjectStore™ is a trademark of Object Design Incorporated
OMTool™ is a trademark of Martin Marietta Advanced Concepts Center
Ontos™ is a trademark of Ontos Incorporated
OOA*Tool*™ and OOD*Tool*™ are trademarks of Object International Incorporated
Oracle™ is a trademark of the Oracle Corporation
OSMOSYS™ is a trademark of Winter Partners
PostScript™ is a trademark of Adobe Systems Incorporated
Rose™ is a trademark of Rational Incorporated
Sapiens™ is a trademark of Sapiens Corporation
Simula™ is a trademark of Simula AS
SMALLTALK™, SMALLTALK-78™ and SMALLTALK-80™ are trademarks of Xerox Corporation
Smalltalk-V/PM™ and Smalltalk-V/Windows™ are trademarks of Digitalk Incorporated
Software through Pictures™ is a trademark of Interactive Development Environments
System Architect™ is a trademark of Popkin Software and Systems Incorporated
Team*work*™ and SM/OODLE/IM/RT/SA™ are trademarks of Cadre Technologies Incorporated
Turbo Pascal™ is a trademark of Borland International Incorporated
UNIX™ is a trademark of AT&T Corporation
Versant™ is a trademark of Versant Object Technologies
Win++™ is a trademark of Blaise Computing Incorporated
X-Windows™ and CLU™ are trademarks of MIT
Zinc™ is a trademark of Zinc Software Incorporated

1 Introduction

INTENDED READERSHIP   This chapter is applicable to all readers.

CONTENTS

Preamble
1.1 How to use this book
1.2 Technology transfer
1.3 Level of genuine interest
1.4 Current problems in software development
1.5 The advantages of an object-oriented technique
1.6 The disadvantages of an object-oriented approach

CHAPTER PRE-REQUISITES   None.

CHAPTER OVERVIEW

This chapter provides an overview of the book and introduces the reader to the format used throughout the remainder of the text. It identifies the categories of reader and provides a route map suggesting those chapters which will be of most relevance to particular categories of reader.

The chapter considers the problems with current software development approaches and how an object-oriented approach addresses these problems. The main advantages and disadvantages of an object-oriented approach are highlighted.

Saving money on software development is a goal of all software development managers. Important reasons why project costs are high relate to a lack of software and specification reuse, an inability to adapt software developments to changing requirements, a lack of modularity and unnecessarily complex designs. These factors affect the development phases of the life cycle, but their effect is most pronounced in the maintenance phase. Continually we hear of maintenance costs consuming 60, 70 or even 80% of overall development budgets! Object orientation addresses all these issues and, managed properly, can significantly reduce the costs involved in both developing and maintaining software.

Central to any engineering discipline is the concept of reuse – building upon well-understood concepts and modules. For example, an electrical engineer designing a new circuit starts with resistors and transistors. Similarly a mechanical engineer designing a new car may start with an existing gear box. All these components are available off the shelf, or can be derived from well-understood phenomena in a modular way, building on existing products.

So what about software engineering? Many attempts have been made to develop reusable libraries of functions at the programming level. The NAG libraries are perhaps one of the most successful attempts at developing off-the-shelf reusable libraries of functions for the scientific community. However, few attempts have been made to develop reusable system or subsystem specifications.

Reuse can bring benefits at the design stage, the programming stage, and at the testing and maintenance stages by reducing effort through the use of well-tried and tested components. There is no doubt that reuse is as much a cultural issue as a technical one. However, the right technical framework is important in realizing the goal of better reuse. Through classes, inheritance, dynamic binding and polymorphism, object orientation provides technical mechanisms for promoting and encouraging reuse as never before. Eventually object-oriented (**OO**) methods will provide management mechanisms for promoting reuse. The rest will be up to you – the software development professional – to stimulate and adhere to a suitable culture which encourages reuse.

What is object orientation all about?

Object-oriented software systems are composed of objects. An **object** can be a tangible entity such as a person or it can be a less tangible element such as an event. For example, a pilot called Joe may be an object, and a flight number BA2357 might also be an object. An object has certain properties that can be used to describe it – such as a state, and a relationship to other objects. An object also behaves in a certain manner in response to a given stimulus. An object therefore has both data (**state**) and functional (**behavioural**) components.

Objects communicate with one another via **messages**. These messages are analogous to the concept of a procedure or function call in a traditional programming language. A received message may cause an object to behave in a prescribed manner which might result in a change to that object's state.

Objects are categorized into **classes** with similar properties. For example, if we have two people called Sally and Jack, who both work for the Acme Computer Company, then Sally and Jack could be employees of that company. They would be categorized as belonging to the class EMPLOYEE. We say that Sally and Jack are *objects* (or *instances*) of the *class* EMPLOYEE.

Finally, classes of objects are themselves related in a hierarchy. They can inherit general features from classes that are above them in the hierarchy, known as 'superclasses'. For example, employees in a company may fall into several categories such as general employees, managers and directors. A manager can inherit general employee characteristics such as an 'employee number' and a 'salary', while defining additional characteristics such as a 'car allowance'.

The benefits of object orientation

Through the use of objects, classes and message passing, object orientation provides a more modular way of modelling problems. This translates into clearer designs and ultimately leads to clearer implementations enabling better control of complexity with resultant reductions in maintenance costs.

Inheritance provides a powerful means of reusing information by inheriting and creating specializations as necessary. By designing and building systems from existing reusable class hierarchies, software engineers can benefit from tried and tested classes perfected through use in previous developments. Systems are designed in a more modular and extensible way enabling them to evolve more readily as user requirements change.

Object-oriented software life cycles

Chapter 3 presents several ways to introduce object orientation into traditional software life cycles, but concludes that a fully object-oriented software life cycle should be the ultimate goal for all practitioners.

Object-oriented analysis and design

The use of objects with state and behaviour at the analysis stage improves the process of analysing the problem domain because real-world objects such as a bank account can be more accurately modelled. A bank account may have both data, as in an available balance, and behaviour in so far as it may be an interest-bearing account, for example.

Object-oriented design leads on naturally from OO analysis. Experiences with OO design suggest that some developers have difficulty identifying abstract classes. This has led many developers to concentrate on object orientation for the user interface component of a system, where the classes of objects are more easily identified, with the remaining parts of such systems being developed using traditional structured techniques.

Methodologies are appearing for analysis and design. These are still immature and the rich suite of facilities provided by the paradigm leads inevitably to complicated notations for representing design information. As can be expected with any emerging technology, some methods are fully object-oriented while others are pragmatic approaches – building upon well-founded traditional structured techniques. Unfortunately, some methods such as hierarchical object-oriented design (HOOD) are not object-oriented, contrary to the name!

A similar picture is emerging with the CASE tools to support these methods. Some of the proprietary methods such as Objectory and OSMOSYS come packaged in a CASE tool while other methods currently enjoy only partial CASE tool support.

Object-oriented programming

The main object-oriented programming languages are C++, Eiffel, Smalltalk and Objective-C. These fall into two categories: pure and hybrid object-oriented programming languages, depending on whether they enforce object orientation or not (pure OO programming languages enforce OO). C++ and Objective-C are hybrid languages while Eiffel and Smalltalk represent pure OO languages.

Object-oriented programming languages add one extra concept to those already mentioned – namely **dynamic binding**. This process facilitates additional flexibility by enabling the programmer to defer identifying the exact function to be called until run-time. While dynamic binding has definite advantages, it incurs a run-time penalty since the specific function to be called must be computed at run-time rather than being resolved at compile-time. This penalty may be unacceptable in certain time-critical applications.

Objective-C is a proprietary language as was Eiffel until SIG Computers GmbH announced its Eiffel compiler for the MS-DOS environment. Smalltalk continues to have a significant following although it is best suited to rapid prototyping applications. The book concludes that C++ is emerging as the industry standard, although other languages (notably Eiffel) provide important new features such as pre- and post-conditions. Several other object-oriented languages are emerging, including Actor, Trellis, CLOS and Object Pascal, and an object-oriented form of Cobol is promised during early 1993.

To make the best use of these languages, programmers need additional products such as class libraries and integrated programming environments including class browsers and powerful debuggers. Such facilities are starting to appear in products such as ObjectWorks\C++ from ParcPlace Systems.

There are outstanding problems, especially with the current lack of standardization for C++ class libraries which leads to incompatibilities between different third party classes. There are also problems associated with debugging dynamically bound software and badly designed inheritance can lead to unmanageable software. These problems underline the importance of good training for object-oriented development staff.

Experiences from the user case-studies in the book suggest that although several languages provide support for multiple inheritance, this is often not used, developers preferring to use only single inheritance. Furthermore, many developers are only using object-oriented methods for graphical user interfaces, preferring to build the application core using traditional techniques.

Object-oriented DBMSs

Although object-oriented database management systems (**OODBMS**) are still in their infancy, the book presents six commercially available products which are gaining some degree of market acceptance. These are Ontos, GemStone, Objectivity, Object Store, Versant and O_2. The principal advantage of OODBMSs is in their ability to store and manipulate complex information.

The book suggests that many relational users will seek object-oriented extensions to relational systems, while pure OODBMSs have settled into niche technical markets which relational systems cannot satisfy. An OODBMS user case-study concludes that for some users, OODBMSs represent an enabling technology – in so much as they make functionality possible which was hitherto technically infeasible.

Migrating to object orientation

The object-oriented bandwagon is rolling on with increasing numbers of companies adopting the object-oriented paradigm. This book describes how to migrate to an object-oriented regime: what you need to know; how you should go about assessing your suitability for OO; how you go about evaluating an object-oriented programming language, database management system, and so on. The book suggests comprehensive lists of questions to ask vendors, and provides pointers to many of the answers throughout the text.

One of the problems for potential object-oriented developers has been the lack of applications to justify their belief in this paradigm. The user case-studies in Chapter 8 illustrate that object-oriented software development is being successfully applied to both large and small software development projects by large national organizations and small software houses alike.

Object orientation is a winner with software developers. The user case-studies conclude that developers are very enthusiastic about the new techniques. They are well motivated and this certainly helps with the introduction of new techniques into any organization. By harnessing this motivation, together with the object-oriented principles, and tempered by an understanding of the potential problems with the techniques, developers can derive significant benefits from an object-oriented approach.

Key issues for the future include:

- The formation of standards throughout the whole area;
- Better support through CASE tools;
- More sophisticated methods for managing class libraries;
- The availability of class libraries for a given programming language.

1.1   How to use this book

The book consists of a series of chapters which address the various areas of the software development life cycle to which object orientation is applicable. Each chapter begins with a short section which details the chapter content and indicates the required level of understanding to appreciate fully its contents. Particular sections will be of interest to managers, analysts, designers and programmers from both real-time and information-systems backgrounds. Determine the category that best describes your role, then follow the chapters in the order indicated. (Roles are not presented in any particular order.)

Role	Motivation/recommended chapter order
Executive, manager	Executives and managers need an understanding of the overall theory. Therefore they should carefully read the concepts (Chapter 2) first. Other chapters that will be of particular interest are:
	Chapter 3: The OO life cycle
	Chapter 7: Migrating to an OO regime

Chapter 8: User case-studies
Chapter 9: Summary, conclusions and
future trends

MIS managers While most of the book applies equally to
information systems and real-time systems
Chapter 2: Concepts
Chapter 3: OO software life cycles
Chapter 4: OO analysis and design
Chapter 6: OO databases
will be of particular interest to MIS managers.

Technology The person charged with evaluating and
'gatekeeper' introducing new technology into an organization will find this book particularly useful.
These people must understand the theory as
well as appreciate the general state of maturity of existing tools. Therefore they should
carefully read all of this book.

Programmer Programmers should first understand the
concepts (Chapter 2). They should have an
awareness of the analysis and design techniques (Chapter 4), but should concentrate
on the languages chapter (Chapter 5).

Systems Systems analysts should concentrate on:
analyst Chapter 2: Concepts
Chapter 3: OO software life cycles
Chapter 4: Analysis and design

Project leader Project leaders should read this book as
written.
Chapter 3: The OO software life cycle
will be of particular interest.

To summarize:

Chapter		**Intended readership**
2	(Concepts)	All persons interested in object-oriented techniques
3	(Life cycle)	Executives, managers and project leaders
4	(Analysis/design)	Systems analysts and systems architects/designers
5	(Programming)	Systems designers and programmers
6	(Databases)	Information systems personnel

7	(Migrating to OO)	Executives, managers and project leaders
8	(User case-studies)	Executives, managers and persons responsible for introducing new technology
9	(Conclusions)	Executives, managers and persons responsible for introducing new technology.

The details presented represent a compilation from international conference attendance, the British Computer Society special interest group on OOPS, tutorials by respected proponents such as Grady Booch and Mary Loomis, the US-based Object Management Group and discussions with people who have implemented object-oriented systems as well as knowledge gained from a wide range of texts on the subject, and the author's own experience.

1.2   Technology transfer

The underlying theme of the book is one of migration to an object-oriented regime. The book is intended to aid the process of technology transfer. Therefore, particular sections are directed at the senior technical management and the 'technology gatekeeper' within the organization. Buxton (Buxton and Malcolm, 1991) describes the general process and problems associated with technology transfer and concludes:

> 'any technology to be transferred must be clearly visible and it must be possible to estimate its value in the client organisation. If it is not possible to measure the value, the technology is unlikely to be taken up. Secondly, the client organisation must be in a state of maturity which enables it to receive, to understand and to put to use this technology'.

The book provides the reader with a thorough understanding of object orientation so he or she will be in a better position to estimate its value within their organization. Technology transfer is a multi-faceted process involving a number of different areas, as shown in Figure 1.1. Each of these areas is addressed. The management issues applied to the technology transfer process and to the object-oriented software development life cycle are discussed in Chapter 7 which is devoted to the process of technology transfer. A good general account of the issues associated with the technology transfer process is given in Pressman (1988).

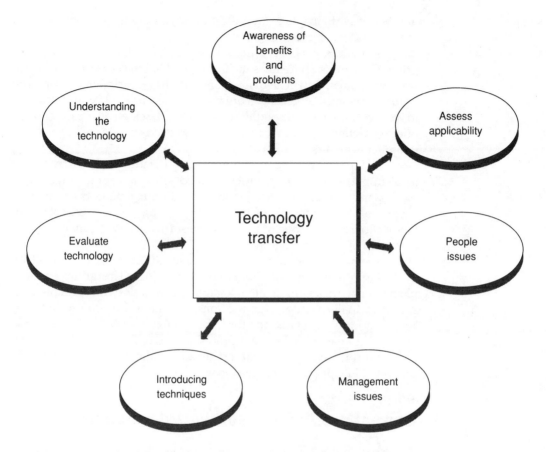

Figure 1.1 Multi-facets of technology transfer.

1.3 Level of genuine interest

During the past five years the computer industry has witnessed an upsurge in the interest and adoption of object-oriented techniques. This so-called paradigm is fuelled by the multitudes of vendor hype directed at selling more products regardless of the real benefits and problems associated with the technology.

Worldwide conferences on object-oriented systems now regularly draw 1000 to 3000 participants, from both industry and academia. The number of participants is an indication of how seriously the computer industry views object orientation.

In the UK the Object Interest Group (OIG), formed in 1990, comprises 15 member companies including the National Westminster Bank, British Airways, British Aerospace and the UK Department of Trade and Industry amongst others. Each organization seconded several employees to work for three months with the OIG. They assessed all areas of object-oriented technology, met with vendors and end users, as well as entering into pilot evaluation projects.

In Japan, the Ministry of International Trade and Industry (MITI) is to support research into object-oriented software engineering. This is particularly interesting since Japan as a nation has built its commercial success on the principles of the manufacturing process. Object orientation provides a means of pushing the software development process towards a manufacturing process.

In the US, the Object Management Group (OMG) was set up in 1989 to promote standards in object technology. This group has seen phenomenal growth in its membership which now stands at more than 250 (principally vendor organizations). Its main direction to date has been in addressing standards for a distributed application architecture, which will enable cooperative processing across heterogeneous hardware and software platforms (more details on the work of the OMG are presented in Appendix D to this book).

1.4   Current problems in software development

Before moving on to Chapter 2, let us consider the current problems related to software development in the industry at large.

In the information systems world the emphasis is on analysing the data associated with a particular application or business need, with the analysis of processing requirements taking second place. A team of developers might produce a data design for the system, taking data redundancy into consideration through the use of 1st, 2nd and 3rd normal form (for example, Codd, 1972). The processing required within the system is developed around these tables of data. While data duplication is discouraged, programs can contain duplicated code. Later, inconsistencies between programs can appear if changes are made to some, but not all, modules that contain duplicate code. This results in reduced quality and reliability of the final system. Furthermore, processes often make assumptions about the implementation of data and this can result in strong coupling between modules in a system, leading to unnecessary complexity. As a result systems become inflexible and unresponsive to change.

In the real-time applications development world the opposite is true. Processing is the primary consideration, with any associated data being generally of less interest. Typically, top-down functional decomposition is employed. It is a logical well-organized discipline, encouraging the orderly development of systems. However, the method suffers from several flaws – it does not take account of the evolutionary nature of software systems, it often neglects the data structure aspect, and a top-down procedure does not promote reusability.

Top-down design prematurely binds the temporal relations between functions and this limits system evolution and reusability. For example, if three functions A, B and C are the result of a top-down functional decomposition then the output of function A forms the input to function B, and the output of function B forms the input to function C. In such circumstances, if function B must change, then it is likely that either or both of functions A and C will also have to be modified. It is unlikely that functions A, B and C could be used in another application independently of one another.

Key to the current problems in software development is the time-to-market. Many modern systems require development effort of between 10 and 200 man-years over an elapsed period of perhaps 1–3 years. However, in the meantime requirements are changing and becoming more fully understood (by both the end user and the systems analyst), businesses merge and objectives change. To be successful, the software development process must accommodate the dynamics of a changing environment. Current structured techniques struggle with changing environments and final systems rarely satisfy the needs of the user at the time of delivery.

The effects of these problems are:

- High production and maintenance costs;
- Loss of competitive advantage through the inability to adapt quickly to a changing market;
- Low return on investment as system evolution diverges from business progression.

Therefore, the objectives of a better software development method are:

- To increase the quality and reliability of the system, minimizing maintenance costs;
- To enable the software developer to react quickly to change, minimizing the impact of change on the system under development or maintenance;
- To protect investment by reusing existing components to evolve new systems.

Object orientation seeks to address these issues by providing a framework which encourages extensibility, reusability and the easier management of complexity. Following chapters of this book describe the concepts, design methods, programming languages and database management systems. This information is related back to these prime objectives for a better software development method.

1.5   The advantages of an object-oriented technique

The most fundamental advantage of object-oriented techniques, compared to traditional structured techniques, is in creating a more modular approach to the analysis, design and implementation of software systems. Modularity has always been recognized for its importance in communicating ideas and in reducing complexity to a comprehensible level (Myers, 1978; Yourdon and Constantine, 1979).

At the analysis stage object-oriented analysis provides a single, unified approach – which traditional structured systems analysis lacks. All the modelling techniques apply to the same fundamental elements of the system, that is, the classes of objects, whereas structured systems analysis views different aspects of a system using different fundamental elements – data entities are considered in entity relationship modelling and processes in data flow diagrams. This leads to loosely associated views of the final system which makes the job of delegating modules of work to individual software developers difficult. Chapter 4 discusses these issues in more detail.

Through the use of inheritance, polymorphism and dynamic binding, object orientation provides mechanisms which support software reuse and extensibility as never before. This helps reduce development times, enables systems to adapt more readily to changing requirements and cuts maintenance bills significantly. The support for extensibility also makes object orientation particularly useful in areas where the software requirements are not well understood. The incremental development cycle promotes evaluation and re-evaluation from analysis through to implementation in a short cycle, enabling the product requirements to evolve along with the software product under development. Chapter 3 presents a design process incorporating both class design and application design as two distinct activities within the object-oriented design process. In such an overall process, applications are constructed from individual classes in a bottom-up manner which encourages extensibility.

1.6 The disadvantages of an object-oriented approach

The single biggest disadvantage at present is the immaturity of the techniques and tools. However, this situation is changing rapidly. Many programming languages are now sufficiently mature for commercial use. However, analysis and design techniques are still evolving and the whole area of object-oriented database management systems is a long way from commercial maturity.

The lack of a standard notation for expressing object-oriented design properties is one of the more significant impediments to the widespread use of such techniques. There should be a set of symbols that anyone familiar with object concepts can understand. Only when such a standard emerges will people be able to communicate reliably about object-oriented design decisions.

Programming language development environments have a long way to go in providing the required levels of sophistication for managing class hierarchies, especially to expose the available classes so reuse can be exploited to its maximum potential.

The very concept which brings many benefits to an object-oriented approach, namely inheritance, also brings problems associated with increased coupling (or linkage) between classes. Furthermore, polymorphism and dynamic binding are complex concepts and they make testing resultant software more difficult. Chapter 5 discusses these problems in more detail.

The highly incremental prototyping life cycles encouraged by some object-oriented programming environments such as Smalltalk bring problems associated with the management of software developments, which can lead to wandering designs causing poor overall quality.

With an awareness of these shortcomings, and good management, most of these problems can be reduced to an acceptable level. Remember, all technologies (both old and new) have their problems. The first stage in overcoming them is in knowing about them!

2 Concepts

CONTENTS

CHAPTER PRE-REQUISITES

There are no specific prerequisites for this chapter. Readers should be computer literate and have a basic understanding of the main elements used in traditional structured software engineering, such as procedures, functions and data.

CHAPTER OVERVIEW

This chapter introduces the basic building blocks upon which the object-oriented methodology is based. The chapter deals with all the main principles, however some of these concepts are not available in all so-called object-oriented programming languages, design methodologies or database management systems. Later chapters will detail specific characteristics of the various products and languages available. This chapter contains many examples to illustrate the concepts.

By the end of the chapter you will be aware of the main concepts and how they provide benefit to the software development process. You will be able to decide which concepts are of most use in your development environment. This will help when deciding on vendor-supplied tools and techniques which claim to be 'object-oriented'.

2.1 Introduction

Object orientation is derived from
the following key concepts:

    Objects
    Classes
    Inheritance
    Message passing
    Polymorphism

2.2 Objects

The traditional view of software systems is as a composition. There is a
collection of *data* that represents some information and a set of *procedures*
which manipulates the data. Things happen in the system by invoking
procedures and giving them some data to manipulate. The data and procedural logic are separate components which comprise the overall software system.

    In the object-oriented view of software systems there is a single
entity called an object which represents both the data and the procedures.
Like pieces of data, objects can be manipulated. However, like procedures, objects can describe the manipulation as well.

    Objected-oriented systems revolve around these objects.
Anything can be an object; some examples are shown in Figure 2.1.

    An **object** is a collection of data (**attributes** or **properties**) and
functional logic (**methods**). The data defines the state of the object and
the methods define the behaviour of the object. There are two kinds of
methods, firstly interface methods which provide a means of communicating with the object. The second kind of methods are internal methods
which create object behaviour but are not accessible from outside the
object. These two kinds of methods are very important. The interface
methods provide a clearly defined way of communicating with an object.
The internal methods need only be known to the designer of that object.
Users of the object ONLY need to know about the interface methods. This
limits the number of assumptions made about a module of software: the
user can only make assumptions about the interface methods, that is,
what methods are available, what information they expect to be passed
and what information they return to the caller. A *contract* is established
between the caller (or user) and the called object. This contract describes
the dialogue between caller and called objects.

    Figure 2.2 shows the fundamental constituents of an object.

    As an example, consider an object representing the electrical

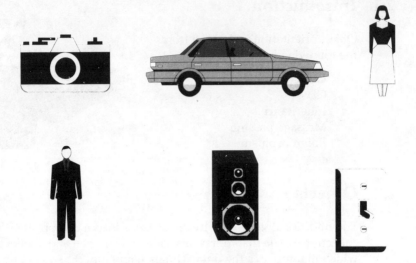

Figure 2.1   Some common everyday objects.

switch shown in Figure 2.1. A switch has some data – it has a state, either on or off. It also has a unique identity which identifies it from all other like objects. It has some interface methods – Switch_on to turn a light bulb on, and Switch_off to turn the light off again. These interface methods alter the *state* data within the object, changing the value to either on or off as appropriate. A switch might also have an internal method such as Activate_Relay which would be used to make an electrical connection from a power supply to the light bulb.

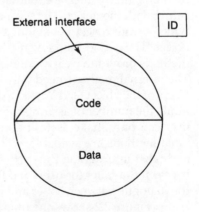

Figure 2.2   An object.

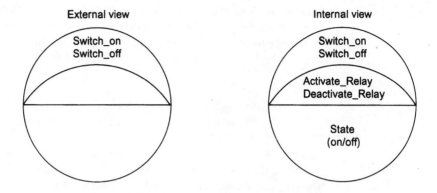

Figure 2.3   The external and internal views of the switch object.

The external and internal views of the switch object are shown in Figure 2.3. The external view is the view as seen by users of this object. That is, the 'black box' view where another object would have access to the Switch_on and Switch_off methods only, and would not understand anything of the internal mechanics. The internal view, on the other hand, is the 'glass box' view, where all details of the object's composition are observable.

A call (by another object) to the Switch_on interface method causes the switch object's State to change from off to on and also causes the Activate_Relay method to be invoked. This, in turn, causes an electrical connection between the power supply and the actual light bulb. Conversely a call to the Switch_off method causes State to change from on to off and the Deactivate_Relay method to be invoked.

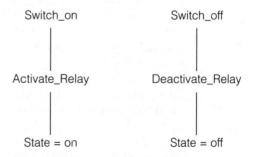

As another example involving concepts more normally encountered in typical information systems, consider an object called An_Employee. This object contains details about a company employee such as name, address, salary, grade, and so on (the attributes). It also contains a number of interface methods used to manipulate this infor-

mation, such as Alter_Salary, Alter_Address, and so on. Suppose that altering an employee's salary requires validation to ensure that the
new salary lies within the accepted range for the given grade. Then
the method Alter_Salary might contain the following internal method
calls:

Validate_Salary	check salary is within range
Update_Salary	update salary ATTRIBUTE

Validate_Salary and Update_Salary would be hidden from the outside
world as they are unnecessary detail; they only need to be known within
the employee object, hence they are internal methods.

This ability of an object to hide internal methods from the users of
that object is a powerful feature. It has the benefit of enabling better control (and limiting) of the knock-on effects when implementation detail
within an object has to change. Knock-on effects are caused when
changes to one module cause changes to be required in other modules. It
is a manifestation of the coupling between modules. The reader is
referred to Yau *et al.*, 1978 for an account of the knock-on effects that can
occur when one change gives rise to a series of forced changes.

In object-oriented systems the principal cause of knock-on effects
is from changes to an object's interface, and NOT from changes to the
internal details of an object. Keeping an object's interface as simple as
possible is therefore important in reducing knock-on effects. The objective should always be to hide as much detail as possible from users (or
clients) of an object.

Returning to Figure 2.2, each object is uniquely identified by its
identity (ID). Object identity enhances the notion of pointers in conventional programming languages, foreign keys in databases, and file names
in operating systems. Object identity is a semantic concept associated
with objects, however the simplest implementation is to use the hardware memory address of an object as its identity. This is the main option
used to reference objects in languages such as C++ or Eiffel. An object's
identity is separate from its state. Two objects could have the same state
but would have different identities. For example, two switch objects
could be in the ON state, but they are nevertheless separate switches with
separate identities.

An attribute can be a primitive type such as an integer, string, and
so on, or it can be another object. Figure 2.4 illustrates the situation where
the variable called value holds the number 4, the variable called string
holds a character string and the variable obj holds either a reference to
another object or an actual object.

Object-oriented systems enable objects to possess attributes which
are themselves objects. This is achieved through **abstract data types**

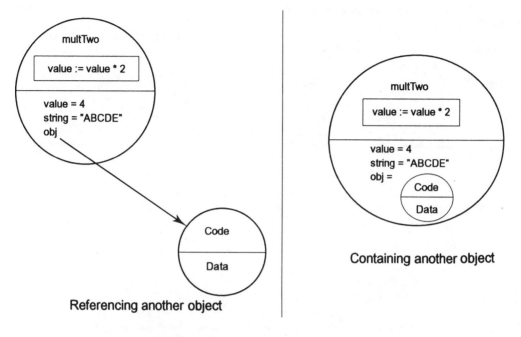

Figure 2.4   Details of an object.

(ADTs), where objects are constructed from existing data structures. An ADT hides the physical storage of information from the user but provides a public set of methods that the user may invoke to manipulate the attributes of the object. This is a very powerful technique which encourages clearly defined modules and helps reduce the overall complexity in software systems.

Here we see the data inside an object being hidden from users of that object. Again this limits the knock-on effects when changes are made to an existing system. For example, an object's data may be held in a number of ways. It may be held in a flat-file structure or in a set of relational database tables. In both cases the data may be accessed externally through an interface method such as Query_name which returns the names of all employees whose salary is greater than £20 000. In one case the Query_name interface method would call an SQL statement to perform the query, while in the other case a series of internal methods may be used to determine the answer. In both cases the structure of the data is hidden from the users of the object – hence the term abstract data type. Figure 2.5 illustrates this scenario.

An object can be composed of other objects – this is known as **aggregation** and it is particularly useful in object-oriented database systems where groups of objects are held within a container object for manipulation and management. For example, cars are stored in a car

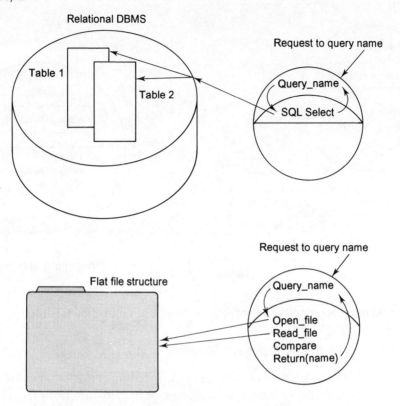

Figure 2.5   Different object implementations, but the same object interface.

park. Modelling this situation using OO techniques can be achieved using two objects: a Car_Park object and a Car object. The Car_Park holds (or contains) Cars.

The act of combining data and methods is called **encapsulation**. No object can directly read or change the state of any other object (where all the data in an object defines its state). Accessing any part of an object's state (that is, data) is accomplished through its interface methods. However, such access is only possible if the object itself permits it. This concept of **data hiding** or **data abstraction** leads to weak coupling (refer to glossary) between objects.

The state of an object persists, so the result of the next operation may depend on the result of the last operation carried out by that object. In the example of a switch used earlier, if the switch is in the on state, then the command Switch_off will cause a state change to off and a relay will be deactivated. However, if the switch was already in the off state then the command Switch_off will have no effect on the relay.

Two final terms to introduce in this section are **fine** and **coarse grain** as applied to objects. These terms refer to the amount of information held within the object. For example, a fine grain object might be an integer and a coarse grain object might be a complete document. As another example, a coarse grain object might be a car and a fine grain object might be a switch. A car would contain many switches, therefore in this case a car is an aggregate object. The term object can therefore apply to anything, no matter what the size. In this way, developers can build coarse grain objects from fine grain objects in a similar way to the composition of matter in the physical world, where, for example, animals are composed of molecules, molecules are composed of atoms, atoms are composed of a nucleus and electrons, nuclei are composed of protons and neutrons. . . . Here we see that object orientation provides a natural way to model real-world phenomena within a computer system.

2.3 Classes

Whilst objects are themselves the basic entities describing an application, they are not the fundamental elements of the system. Many similar objects can be specified by the same general description. The description of an object is called a **class**. Every object is an **instance** of a class.

A class defines the methods used by an object and declares the data types which define the allowable states an object can be in. The class is a blueprint used to create objects as instances of that class type. For a given class type, at run-time there can be many instances of that class – these are the objects. The situation can be likened to that for garden gnomes. The mould or cast used to create the gnome shape is analogous to the class, and the actual gnomes are object instances cast from the mould (or class).

Each instance contains the information that distinguishes it from the other instances (such as the object ID discussed in the previous section). Taking the garden gnome analogy, we could have gnomes painted different colours, one from another. The colours would represent values of attributes associated with the gnomes.

Individual objects populate their data (often called **instance variables**) to satisfy their own needs, however the class is used to define the data. A class is therefore generally (but not exclusively) a compile-time concept. The 'code' associated with an object resides in the class, while the 'data' resides in the instance of the class, that is, the object. In this way, objects of the same type share the methods of the class rather than duplicating code for each object instance. Figure 2.6 illustrates this situation.

Thus classes provide a means of defining and managing the structure of objects.

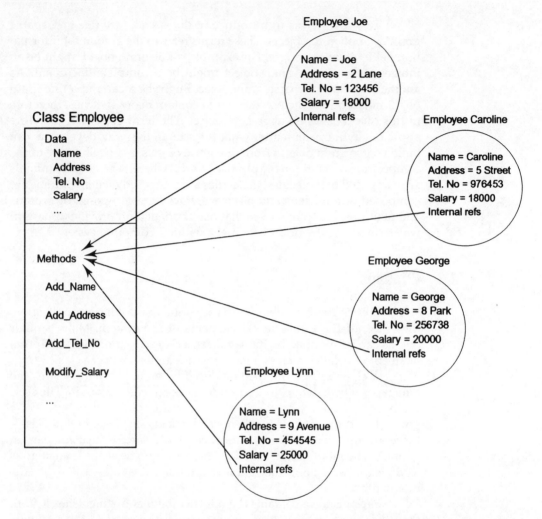

Figure 2.6 Relationship between classes and objects. The 'Internal refs' in each object refer to the addresses of the methods. The diagram depicts the shared nature of the methods while the values associated with the class data are private to the particular object.

2.4   Inheritance

Often, objects may have similar but not identical attributes and methods. In this situation it is useful to have the ability to inherit properties. **Inheritance** provides a mechanism for managing classes and for sharing commonalty. Inheritance comes in several forms, namely **single inheritance** and **multiple inheritance**. Multiple inheritance often leads to a form called **repeated inheritance**. Both multiple and single inheritance can exhibit **selective inheritance**. The following example will clarify these terms.

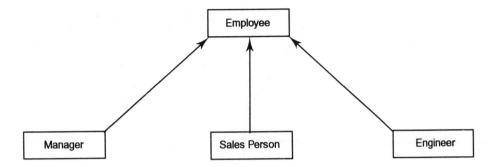

Figure 2.7   An example of single inheritance.

A company has employees. Employees could be managers, sales people or engineers. But all of these people have certain properties in common (such as an employee number, a recruitment date, and so on). Therefore managers, sales persons and engineers can all inherit general properties from a class called employee.

In Figure 2.7, Managers, Sales Persons and Engineers are subclasses of a common superclass called Employee in this example. Subclasses inherit attributes and methods from their superclasses. The arrows (or in some cases just lines) indicate a superclass/subclass inheritance relationship. In this example, Managers, Sales Persons and Engineers inherit characteristics from the Employee class. For example, they all have an employee number, a name, address, date when current employment commenced, and so on. All of these attributes could be inherited from the Employee class. This type of inheritance is called single inheritance because each of the subclasses inherits from no more than one superclass.

Superclasses such as Employee in Figure 2.7 can, themselves, inherit from super-superclasses. For example, Employee could inherit from a class called Person. In turn, Person could inherit from a class called Living_Organism. In this way an inheritance hierarchy of classes can be constructed.

If an employee could be both a manager and a sales person then multiple inheritance may provide the most succinct way to represent this situation, as shown in Figure 2.8. **Multiple inheritance** allows a class to inherit from more than one immediate superclass. The rules for defining multiple inheritance must handle any conflicts which may arise. For example, naming conflicts can arise, where the same name may be used to represent different attributes or methods in two different parents, and both these attributes or methods are inherited into the same child class. A programming language must resolve this kind of conflict. This illustrates that although multiple inheritance does provide a powerful mech-

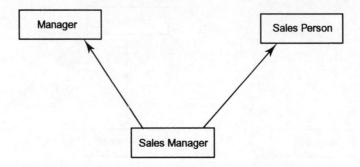

Figure 2.8   An example of multiple inheritance.

anism for organizing ideas, it introduces increased complexity.

Different languages provide varying levels of support for the complicated situations which can arise through inheritance, such as naming conflicts. The degree of programmer support for inheritance should be an important consideration when choosing an object-oriented programming language, and not simply the type of inheritance supported (that is, single or multiple). How does the programming language manage naming conflicts caused by multiple inheritance? Does it show the programmer how the conflict arose?

Class inheritance hierarchies can become complicated by repeated inheritance where a sales manager may exhibit some characteristics of a manager and other characteristics of a sales person, both of which in turn exhibit characteristics of an employee. This scenario is shown in Figure 2.9. **Repeated inheritance** results from a child class (for example, Sales

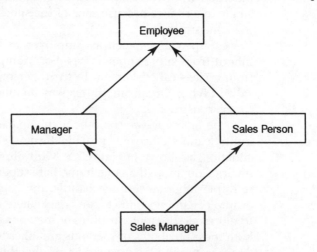

Figure 2.9   An example of repeated inheritance.

Manager) inheriting from two parents (for example, Manager and Sales Person) which in turn inherit from the same grandparent (Employee). The child therefore could potentially inherit everything from the grandparent twice. The programming language, or analysis/design CASE tool must resolve this problem.

Subclasses (for example, Sales Manager) inherit methods and attributes from superclasses (for example, Manager). However, a subclass can redefine any of the methods or attributes inherited from the superclass as well as defining additional methods and attributes of its own. This is an extremely powerful feature when combined with polymorphism which is discussed in a later part of this chapter.

In **selective inheritance**, the subclass inherits only some of the methods from the superclass. This feature can be useful when trying to limit the information a user has access to. For example, in a banking system there might be several views of a bank account including one for the clerk, manager and the customer. All would have access to some aspects of the same bank account as depicted in Figure 2.10.

The customer has access to only the very basic details of the account. The bank clerk has access to some additional information related to any other account that customer may hold. The manager has access to all the information in the bank account, including the attribute Credit_Risk – relating to the credit history of the account holder.

Classes combine into class libraries with many classes in a given library linked through an inheritance relationship. Developing an application consists of developing a class library and using the constituent classes in the construction of the application. Experiences with OO programming indicate that multiple inheritance leads to less redundancy in the final code produced. Inheritance reduces code duplication (or the temptation to duplicate code) and this represents one of the major benefits from the concept. Developers arrange classes into hierarchies with more generic classes towards the top of the hierarchy, and increasing specialization towards the bottom of the hierarchy. This arrangement promotes the development of 'new' code rather than the development of 'all' code regardless of whether it is new or not.

An inheritance example

The following example is used extensively in Chapter 5 to illustrate the syntax of several object-oriented programming languages.

Consider the analysis of the personnel in a small company. There are general employees, then there are managers and there is one director. All personnel have a name, age, address, salary and employee number. Managers additionally have a car allowance. The director has a car allowance and a bonus. These three classes of personnel could be defined independently of one another. However by defining the generic attributes and methods, which are common to all personnel, in the Employee

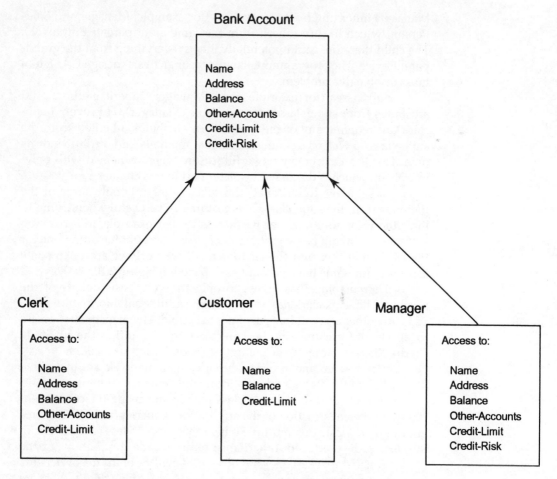

Figure 2.10   Implementing views of an object through selective inheritance.

class, and using the properties of inheritance, the Manager and Director classes can inherit this generic information and behaviour (that is, the methods). The Director class can inherit attributes and methods from both the Manager and the Employee. Thus an inheritance hierarchy builds with the more general classes higher up and increasing special-ization towards the bottom as shown in Figure 2.11.

The director or manager classes can redefine data types or methods previously defined higher in the inheritance hierarchy (although object-oriented programming languages generally only allow dervied classes to redefine methods and not data types). The book returns to this notion in a later section when dynamic binding and polymorphism are discussed.

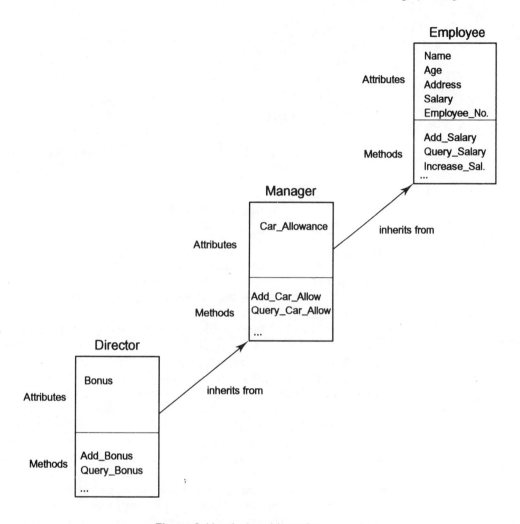

Figure 2.11   A class hierarchy.

2.5   Message passing

Objects communicate with one another by passing messages. A **message** contains a name which identifies its destination, and may also contain some arguments or parameters. This is similar to a traditional function or procedure call. The message, when received, will cause the invocation of an appropriate method within the receiving object. For example, building on the scenario in Figure 2.11, at a particular time each year a manager may be responsible for increasing the salaries of his or her subordinate employees. This would involve an object of the class Manager

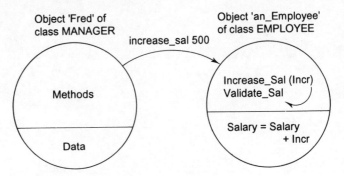

Figure 2.12   Message passing.

sending a message Increase_Sal to each object of class Employee for which that manager has responsibility. Figure 2.12 depicts the situation. Before the employee salary is increased a Validate_Sal internal method might be called to check the salary increment is within the allowable range, for example.

In its simplest form, a message is the same as a function or procedure call in a traditional sense, since the net effect is the same. However, a message can involve a more complicated path from sender to receiver than normally associated with a traditional function call. In a traditional programming language such as C or Pascal the sender knows the address of the receiver. A function or procedure call causes the program counter to jump from the current execution statement to the address of the called function or procedure. So the *binding* of the message to the function being called is achieved at compile-time. Achieving all bindings at compile-time eases consistency checking and helps to bring any type-related problems to the user's attention at the earliest opportunity.

In an object-oriented language, passing a message from one object to another can involve more processing because it is not always possible to assume that the sender knows the address of the receiver. This is referred to as *dynamic binding*. The detailed mechanics will be discussed later. However, for the meantime it is sufficient to say that dynamic binding delays the final association of a message name with a function until run-time. It can increase the speed of compilation, at the expense of run-time efficiency, and enhances the flexibility of a language by enabling it to be fundamentally changed without recompilation. At the logical level, some kind of a central message handler determines the destination address for a given message. The type of object being accessed and the method within that object determine the message destination address.

When a message is sent, the sender object may stop processing and pass control to the receiver object. When the receiver completes processing it may send a response to the originator – this is a synchronous response. However, where there are multiple threads of control, as in a parallel processing system, responses are normally asynchronous, with messages queued at the receiver for processing. The sending object is often referred to as the **client** and the receiving object as the **server**. A contract exists between the client and server describing what services a server offers and what responses a client expects to receive for a given request.

A client's request is performed by transforming it into a **method invocation**. This transformation is called the **binding** process. A method invocation identifies a method, a collection of method parameters and an execution engine. The execution engine interprets the method in a dynamic context containing the method parameters. A result is returned to the client upon completion of the method invocation. For example, consider the message used in Figure 2.12, which would be coded as:

An_Employee Increase_Sal 500

The message originates within one of the methods in an object called A_Manager (of class type Manager – refer to Figures 2.11 and 2.12). The message is destined for another object called An_Employee (this is one of the method parameters). Here the message name is Increase_Sal – perhaps to increase the salary of a company employee. The salary is to be increased by 500 (this is the other method parameter).

Normally the method name corresponds to the message name. In the above example the method to be invoked is Increase_Sal, associated with the class defining the object An_Employee. The method is invoked by *binding* the message name to the object's method. The situation is depicted in Figure 2.13.

In this example the client is the manager object and the server is the employee object. At program run-time, the message from the manager called Fred is intercepted by a message handler which firstly identifies the destination object and then the destination method within that object. At this point the message is bound to the appropriate method and the method is executed.

Different classes of object can respond to the same message in different ways. If different classes of object are referred to with the same method name then message-sending **polymorphism** is possible. An example would be the message Add applied to a numerical object and a string object. For numbers the Add message causes addition of numbers, while for strings, concatenation results (see Section 2.6 on polymorphism for more details).

As a practical example of the concept of polymorphism in

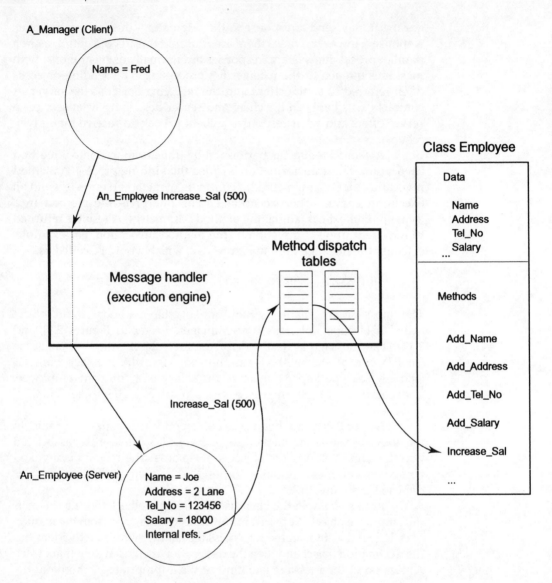

Figure 2.13   Message binding.

message passing, consider an object-oriented operating system which holds all information in an object form, so, for example, a file would become an ObjectFile with both data and behaviour. The operating system acts, in part, as an exchange for routing messages between objects. Now consider that a user of this system wishes to print out the contents of a particular ObjectFile called readme. The user issues the command print readme. Sending the message print to the ObjectFile called readme causes an invocation of the print method associated with that ObjectFile. This print method (which is part of the behaviour of an ObjectFile) sends the appropriate control sequences to the physical printer and the file gets printed out. The user did not need any prior knowledge about the file type, that is, it is an ASCII file, a PostScript file, or a file in the format of a particular word processor. That information is implicit in the type of the object being printed. This is another example of the usefulness of polymorphism.

2.6 Polymorphism

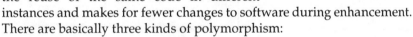

This is the ability of an object to assume different types or manipulate objects of different types. (The word polymorphic means 'having many forms'.) Polymorphism facilitates the reuse of the same code in different instances and makes for fewer changes to software during enhancement. There are basically three kinds of polymorphism:

(1) Inclusion
(2) Operation
(3) Parametric.

2.6.1 Inclusion polymorphism

This form of polymorphism applies to so-called strongly typed languages such as Eiffel, Trellis and C++. Programming languages in which the type of every expression is determined at compile-time are **statically typed** languages. The requirement that all variables and expressions are bound to a type at compile-time is often too restrictive. Imposing a weaker requirement that expressions are guaranteed to be *type-consistent* reduces this restriction and leads to more flexibility. Strongly typed languages make use of type-consistent expressions.

Inclusion polymorphism is implemented through a concept in type theory. A single name may represent objects of many different classes that are related by some common superclass. Inheritance is therefore key to the use of this form of polymorphism. Suppose that class Dog inherits from class Animal. If the language treats Dog as a subtype of Animal, then the compiler will allow an instance of a Dog wherever it expects an instance of an Animal. This is **dynamic typing**. The Static type of an identifier (see glossary) is the type with which the identifier is

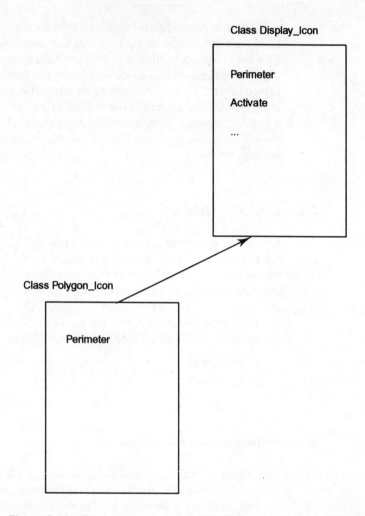

Figure 2.14   The interplay between inheritance and polymorphism.

initially declared. If, at run-time, the entity becomes associated with an object of another type, this type becomes the dynamic type of the reference. For type compatibility the dynamic type must be a descendant of the static type. The following example illustrates this concept.

Inclusion polymorphism example

The following example and Figure 2.14 illustrate the interplay between inheritance and polymorphism. Consider an application which includes a graphical user interface (GUI). The GUI is composed of many objects including a class of objects called Display_Icon. This class defines a number of methods applicable to the operation of icons. Consider further that a particular type of icon called Polygon_Icon has some specific properties but also has many general properties by virtue of being a subclass of Display_Icon. In this case the developer uses inheritance so Polygon_Icon inherits from Display_Icon and defines/redefines those methods particular to the polygon icon as depicted in Figure 2.14.

The Polygon_Icon inherits from Display_Icon and is therefore a subclass of Display_Icon. The methods defined in the Display_Icon class are available to users of objects of class Polygon_Icon. Consider a message Activate in Figure 2.14 being sent to an object of class Polygon_Icon. If no match to the message exists in the local class, the methods of the superclass are searched until a match is found or all methods in the line of inheritance are exhausted – in which case a run-time error occurs (in object-oriented programming languages employing static type checking this would be a compiler error). Some systems use complex searching algorithms which do not suffer performance degradation as the depth of the inheritance hierarchy increases.

If there are two identifiers called D and P such that:

D = object of class Display_Icon
[List of general methods including the Activate method]

P = object of class Polygon_Icon
[Specific Perimeter method]

then sending an Activate command to Object P will cause Object P to 'activate' using the method Activate which its class (Polygon_Icon) inherited from the class Display_Icon. However, sending the command Perimeter to Object P will cause the locally defined version of the Perimeter method to be invoked. The Perimeter message is said to be polymorphic – the same message can be sent to different classes of object and results in different actions being taken. This example is illustrated by the following code segments.

If an identifier called Shape is declared as an object of type Display_Icon, and if the following assignment is made:

Shape := P where ":=" denotes a logical assignment

so that Shape becomes a reference to a polygon_icon (that is, it assumes the dynamic type of Polygon_Icon), then sending a message Perimeter to the object referenced by the variable Shape:

Shape.Perimeter

causes the Perimeter method in class Polygon_Icon to be invoked (as opposed to the Perimeter method in class Display_Icon).

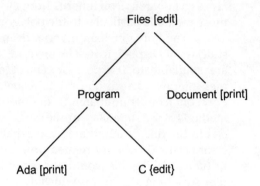

Figure 2.15   Inclusion and operation polymorphism (adapted from Blair, 1990).

This is an example of **inclusion polymorphism**. The same identifier (Shape) can represent (that is, point to) objects of different types (such as Polygon_Icon or Display_Icon) which have a common superclass (Display_Icon). Operations (such as Perimeter) defined in one class apply to any subclass.

The example also illustrates **dynamic binding,** where the dynamic form of the object (referred to by the identifier Shape) determines which version of the method (Perimeter in this example) to apply. Dynamic binding requires binding of functions to function calls at run-time. This contrasts with traditional programming languages where the binding of function calls to functions occurs at compile/link-time (**static binding**).

2.6.2   Operation polymorphism

In this kind of polymorphism behaviour is shared between objects of different classes which bear no relationship by subclassing. The differences between inclusion and operation polymorphism are more clearly understood from the following example.

Consider Figure 2.15. This shows one possible class hierarchy for representing files in an operating system. According to Blair (1990), objects of type *file* are either *document* or *program* files. *Program* files are either *Ada* or *C* programs. An edit operation is defined for all files. Hence through subtyping *edit* will apply to document files and to Ada or C programs. This is inclusion polymorphism. In Figure 2.15 a print operation is explicitly defined for Ada programs and Document files. There is no concept of subtyping between Ada programs and Document files for the print method. Therefore the print operation is interpreted in the context of each call. This is **operation polymorphism**, sometimes called **unconstrained polymorphism**.

Function overloading is another form of operation polymorphism. The type of the parameters in the message dictates this form of polymorphism. It applies where there are several definitions of the same method within a single class. Consider the following C++ skeleton definition of a class called Window:

```
class Window
  {
  (Attribute List here)
  (Method definitions follow...)
  write(char *st) ;
  write(char c) ;
  write(int i) ;
  }
```

This class defines the same method name write three times – each version will be slightly different since it has to contend with a different type of input data. When sending a message containing the method write to an object of type Window, the type of the message parameters dictates which form of the write method to invoke. There is nothing new in this form of overloading, most languages use the arithmetic operators '+', '–' and '*' to add, subtract and multiply integers or floating-point numbers. These operators work even though the underlying machine implementations of integer and floating-point arithmetic are different. The compiler generates object code to invoke the appropriate implementation based on the type of the operands (integer or floating-point).

2.6.3   Parametric polymorphism

This form of polymorphism is often called **genericity**. It uses types as parameters in generic type (or class) declarations. For example if you need a class to handle the queuing of various types of object then the following code segment depicts such an implementation:

```
class queue [t_obj]
private:
        que_arr: array[1..10] of t_obj ;
public:
        add_item (new_obj:t_obj) ;
end class
```

This declaration uses a parameter [t_obj], and refers to the generic type t_obj within. In a specific application, the type t_obj is replaced with a specific type. The definition is basically a template, providing a general way to handle certain types of objects. For example, if the queue was used to hold objects of type car then the programmer would declare the class queue as follows:

```
queue [car] car_park ;
```

where car_park is the name of the queue of cars.

This simple example illustrates the most important advantage of parametric polymorphism – code sharing. In languages which do not support parametric polymorphism the user would have to replicate code for each different type of queue required.

2.7 Reuse

Reusability can be justified both economically because of increased productivity and intellectually because it simplifies the understanding of phenomena.

Software reusability has many different forms, each with a different economic payoff. Wegner (1990) identifies four discrete kinds of reuse:

- Inter-application reusability.
- Development reusability.
- Program reusability.
- Code reusability.

Inter-application reusability involves the reuse of software components in a variety of applications. For example, as Wegner (1990) suggests, 'compilers and operating systems provide much economic benefit through inter-application reusability'. Libraries such as NAG for mathematical and scientific applications have also been very successful. Reuse of analysis and design specifications from one application to another is an important facet of reuse. Often developers consider only the reuse of software, but analysis and design information may also be reused in many situations. This is discussed further in Chapter 4 on analysis and design.

Development reusability involves the reuse of components in successive versions of a given program. Wegner (1990) suggests that: 'components written for a given application are rarely reused in other programs but may be reused many times during the development and enhancement of a given program. Reusability of application software is one of the most important forms of reusability. It should be distinguished from interapplication reusability since its goal is to support an integrated collection of special-purpose software components rather than general-purpose components reusable in other contexts.'

Program reusability involves the reuse of programs in successive executions with different data. Wegner (1990) argues that 'this form does not benefit from modularity to the same extent as development reusability. Program reusability is enhanced by the use of user-friendly interfaces.'

Code reusability involves the reuse of code during the single execution of a program. This form of reusability benefits from modularity, where a module performs some pre-described function and is called wherever this functionality is required.

In object-oriented systems, the mixture of inheritance with dynamic binding and polymorphism creates extremely powerful facilities to support reuse of software. This is illustrated in the polymorphic array example which follows.

Meyer (1988) refers to the example of a polymorphic array where the array elements can be references to instances of any of the heir classes. For example, an array could be defined as:

a: ARRAY[COORD]

where COORD (a coordinate on a map, for example) could be defined as class Point. The Point class could have two child classes Complex and Vector, representing two ways of describing a point in space. Then the polymorphic array a can contain elements which are references to objects of class Point, Complex or Vector. This has advantages for software reuse since the same array can now be used to hold information on objects of more than one class (or type). A polymorphic array is shown in Figure 2.16.

The design and development of object-oriented systems specifically addresses the areas of **development reusability** and **inter-application reusability** through the class hierarchy which is a direct product of the design process and supported through implementation using an object-oriented programming language.

Inter-application reusability is also addressed within the area of object orientation through higher-level application objects which may be

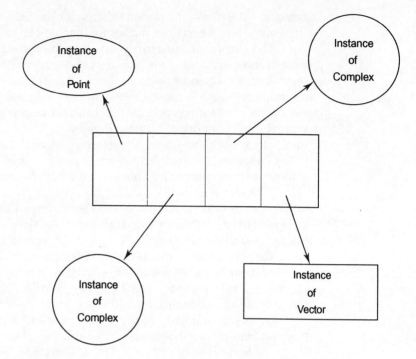

Figure 2.16   A polymorphic array (adapted from Meyer (1988) with permission).

combined to form more complete composite application objects. These application objects will present an interface through which the outside world can communicate with them, in a similar manner to the way more fundamental objects, discussed in earlier sections of this chapter, provide interfaces for communication. An application object is composed of many more fundamental objects. For example, in the future it may be possible to purchase application objects such as a spell-checker and a thesaurus from one vendor. These application objects may be dynamically combined with a basic word-processor object from another vendor to provide a more highly functional composite application object. Thus the end user benefits from the ability to choose the best components from different vendors, while at the same time, the composite application object makes good reuse of existing components.

Inheritance provides a means of reusing generic analysis and design specifications from one application to another. Generic class specifications, such as those for a pay roll, sales ledger, stock control system and so on, may be created from the analysis phase of a development life cycle. These classes can then be reused through inheritance. For example, a specific stock control system might inherit the generic properties and add specific details required for a given end user.

Although an object-oriented approach encourages reuse, there is no doubt that reuse is as much a cultural issue as a technical one. The right management framework and rewards system is required to make reuse work!

2.8   Potential benefits

The normalization of logic as represented in object-oriented programming by the development of class hierarchies with generic classes towards the top of the tree and increasing specialization towards the bottom produces a number of benefits. These benefits include:

- **Easier management of complexity.** By defining logic at the object level the overall complexity of a total application is broken down in a manner which is conceptually easier to understand because it more accurately reflects the real world in so far as real-world 'things' generally have both attributes and behavioural characteristics.

- **Reliability and ease of change.** Reliability and ease of change affect the time-to-market and maintenance issues in software development. The inherent modularity created by an object reduces the 'knock-on' effects caused by changes to software. Since the only information available to a programmer is the list of messages which can be sent to an object and a list of the responses from the object, it is possible to change the logic within an object without fear of a ripple effect to any logic in another object. Abuse of data in an object and illegal access is also prevented since it is only possible to access the data through messages. Polymorphism creates a more flexible system since changes can be accommodated by producing a new object which inherits from a parent and adds some additional methods. Messages which are already in use for other objects in the same collection can automatically be used with the new object. Furthermore, high-level object identification at relatively early stages of information systems design allows programmers to begin work while analysis of the system continues. This cycle lends itself to rapid prototyping.

- **Software reuse.** The modularity of objects combined with the abstraction stage in the design process where generic characteristics of a set of objects are extracted leads to much more reusable software modules. Furthermore, inheritance provides a means by which a new subclass can be derived from an original superclass, with additional properties as required. This entails writing only the code to support the added features of the new subclass. The AT&T Bell Labs experience with object-oriented technologies is illustrative of the potential benefits. During a three year period, Bell moved new development from C to C++. Their analysis of C programs showed that typically 80 % of the code for a given application was new code, written explicitly for that application; only 20 % of the code came from pre-existing libraries. In contrast, analysis of C++ programs showed that by the third year of C++ use, only 20 % of the code was new code written explicitly for the application; 80 % of the code was inherited from object types already defined in the class library. This represents a 4:1 reduction in the lines of new code that had to be written to implement a new application. After accounting for design and debugging time, total development time was often decreased by 60 %.

2.9 Summary

This chapter has introduced the fundamental components upon which the object-oriented approach to software development is based. Those components are:

- **Objects** which embody both functionality and data through the process of encapsulation;
- **Classes** which provide a way to categorize objects;
- **Inheritance** which provides a means of managing classes and encourages a reuse approach to software development through selection, addition and redefinition of parts of existing classes;
- **Messages** which provide a means of communication between objects through clearly defined interfaces;
- **Polymorphism** which provides added flexibility to software systems, making them more extensible.

It must be stressed that the concepts presented here represent the main features of an object-oriented approach. Not all of these concepts are applicable at the analysis, design or programming stages. Most object-oriented techniques and programming languages define their own terms which may not match the names used here. Some people say that standardization is essential, but personally I feel that understanding the underlying concepts is the most important thing. You only have to look at existing structured analysis and design techniques and programming languages to realize that there are few standard naming conventions in use there – what hope for a standard nomenclature in the object-oriented arena?!

The following chapter describes the fundamentals of an object-oriented software development life cycle. Subsequent chapters present the object-oriented concepts as applied to specific areas of the life cycle, viz. analysis, design, programming and OODBMSs. These chapters discuss the techniques and technology used to support object orientation in each area.

3 The OO software engineering life cycle

CONTENTS

3.1 The traditional life cycle
3.2 OO techniques in the software life cycle
3.3 Conclusions

CHAPTER
PRE-
REQUISITES

The reader should also be familiar with a traditional software development life cycle, and understand the significance of the distinct stages in a software life cycle, such as analysis, design, coding and testing.

CHAPTER
OVERVIEW

This chapter discusses how and where object-oriented techniques can be applied in the software development life cycle. It introduces an object-oriented software development life cycle, detailing the steps required and the advantages which result.

The chapter also presents hybrid life cycles, composed of part traditional and part object-oriented techniques. The merits of such life cycles are examined and the advantages and disadvantages of various combinations are discussed.

The details will help you decide on the allocation of resources and to plan for an object-oriented software development project. Subsequent Chapters 4, 5 and 6 expand on particular stages in the object-oriented software life cycle introduced here.

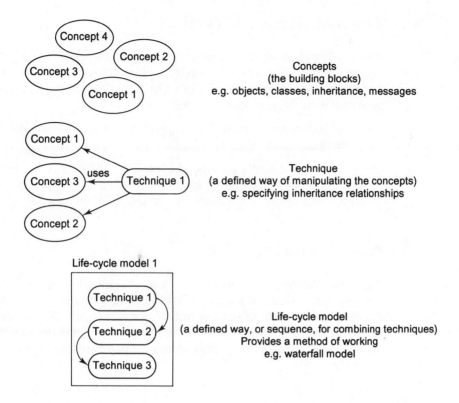

Figure 3.1 The relationship between concepts, techniques and life-cycle models.

The preceding chapter introduced the concepts, or basic building blocks, upon which the object-oriented approach is based. Chapters 4 and 5 will address the *techniques* used in manipulating the basic concepts. This chapter deals with the overall framework practitioners use when developing systems in an object-oriented way. It discusses ways to thread *techniques* together to form overall procedures or *life-cycle models*. Figure 3.1 illustrates the relationship between concepts, techniques and life-cycle models.

Full life-cycle models are generally composed from sub-life-cycle models. A sub-life cycle involves a number of techniques threaded together in a prescribed way. For example, the design stage in an overall life cycle is a sub-life cycle. Design involves several techniques which combine in a particular way to enable a developer to design systems.

3.1   The traditional life cycle

A life-cycle model is a description of the overall shape of a systems development project. The life-cycle model captures the management control and iteration strategies for a project. Ould (1990) explains that the purpose of the life-cycle model is:

> 'to give a risk-reducing structure to a software development project'.

Many life-cycle models assume the project will be subdivided into phases. An underlying model commonly called the 'waterfall' model (Boehm, 1981) provides the basis for one software life cycle.

3.1.1   The waterfall model

This model attempts to separate the life cycle into discrete activities. It creates a linear series of actions, each of which must be completed before the next is started. A refinement to this model is to consider the process is rarely linear, being more iterative (with management reviews) between the various stages. At the most general level there are three phases to the life cycle:

(1) Analysis

(2) Design

(3) Implementation.

The analysis phase covers project initiation, feasibility and analysis of the problem domain. The design phase covers architectural design, detailed component design, logical and physical design. Implementation covers the coding and testing of the program. The model is illustrated in Figure 3.2.

Analysis of the requirements of current and future users defines the scope of the work. The analyst achieves this through questioning sessions with appropriate representatives from the user/customer organization. Following this the analyst writes a user requirements definition and a software requirements specification. The user requirements definition is *in the language of the user.* It can be understood by both the analyst and the software user. It forms an agreement between both parties. The software requirements specification is written *in the language of the software developer.* The software developers use this document.

Satisfying the user requirements definition involves moving from the problem domain to the solution space. That is, to the software development team charged with formulating a solution to the stated problem.

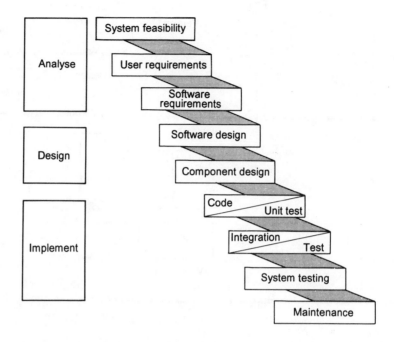

Figure 3.2   A traditional 'waterfall' life cycle for software development.

The project enters the design stage. This stage is the most loosely defined since it is essentially a creative rather than a mechanistic process. It is a phase of progressive decomposition towards more and more detail.

System construction takes place according to the design. System testing is carried out against various test specifications relating to (i) the components (from the design); (ii) the integration (where the components are brought together for testing in a systematic fashion) and (iii) the system (from the requirements specification).

3.1.2   The evolutionary model

The evolutionary model is a deliberate development strategy producing successively better versions of a production system. Different life-cycle submodels may be used for the development of each version. The first version might be built using rapid development tools, with successive versions being refinements to the system in terms of application performance, or extending the limits of data storage and so on. Essentially, the

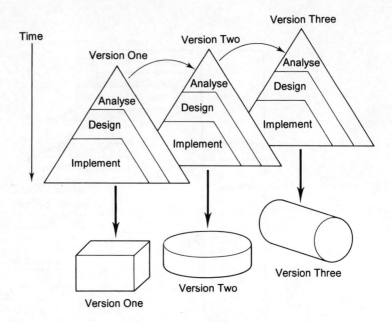

Figure 3.3   An evolutionary model for software development (adapted from OMG, 1992b).

process is one of moulding and shaping the software system to meet the end user's needs. Figure 3.3 illustrates the evolutionary model.

3.1.3   The incremental delivery model

This model addresses the need to develop production-quality software in small, manageable components called **increments**. The model is particularly useful in situations where the software requirements may be unstable such as for large, long-term developments (Charette, 1990). It reduces the risk and improves management confidence by producing new 'assets' at regular intervals. Figure 3.4 illustrates the incremental delivery model.

Rapid prototyping techniques may be introduced into either the evolutionary or incremental delivery models, the resultant prototypes becoming part of the final system.

There are many other life-cycle models including *exploratory models*, *spiral models* and *knowledge-based models*. All these models are simplifications. Various life-cycle models may be blended together on one project. This is also true for object-oriented software development where many object-oriented techniques can be slotted into a traditional software life-cycle model such as those described in the preceding sections.

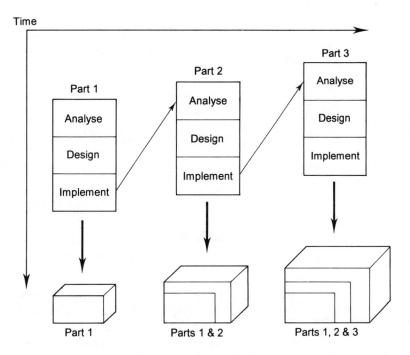

Figure 3.4   An incremental delivery model (adapted from OMG, 1992b).

However there can be problems and complications if traditional structured techniques are applied along with object-oriented techniques within some given life-cycle model. This topic is discussed in the following sections.

3.2   Object-oriented techniques in the software life cycle

Some of the ideas presented in this section are derived from Henderson-Sellers (1990, 1991). In particular, Sections 3.2.1, 3.2.2 and 3.2.3 uses the structure and ideas of Henderson-Sellers (1991), which the author gratefully acknowledges.

Henderson-Sellers (1991) proposes that an important question concerning the introduction of an object-oriented methodology into commercial environments is whether to use the techniques throughout the whole life cycle, or to 'mix and match' with traditional techniques. Mixing traditional structured and object-oriented techniques is used to create some kind of hybrid development life cycle. As Henderson-Sellers (1991) suggests: 'The arguments for proposing a mixed approach consider the reality of the large current investment in traditional structured

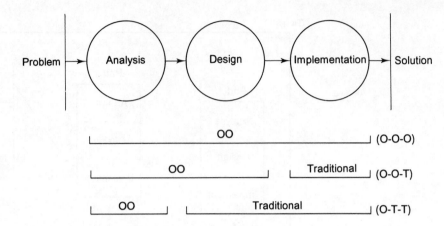

Figure 3.5   Problem to solution: OO versus traditional
structured techniques.

techniques.' There is a significant amount of software already developed using a traditional approach, and expertise is high in such techniques. Furthermore, many organizations have ploughed large investments into CASE tools supporting traditional techniques, such as entity relationship and data flow diagramming.

There are various routes open to the development manager. Figure 3.5 depicts the road from the problem to the solution.

One route is the move to a completely object-oriented life cycle. However, combinations of traditional and object-oriented techniques are possible. The permutations are listed below:

	Analysis	**Design**	**Implementation**
(1)	O	O	O
(2)	O	O	T
(3)	O	T	O
(4)	T	O	O
(5)	T	T	O
(6)	T	O	T
(7)	O	T	T
(8)	T	T	T

where 'O' represents using an object-oriented approach and 'T' indicates the use of traditional techniques.

Option 8 is the fully traditional approach and is inappropriate for discussion in this book.

Options 3 and 6 are very unlikely candidates. In a hybrid approach, there will always be a need to translate between the OO and

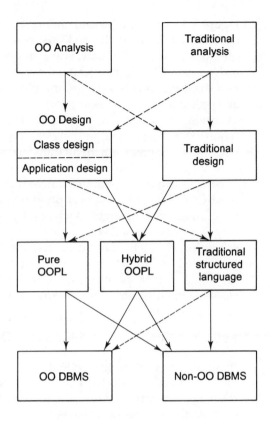

Figure 3.6   OO versus structured techniques (adapted from Henderson-Sellers, 1991b).

traditional representations. *Translations are difficult.* Options 3 and 6 present two traditional/OO boundaries and therefore involve two translations. For this reason these are not good options and should be discounted.

This leaves the following five options:

- To adopt object-oriented methods throughout the complete development (O-O-O);
- To adopt an OO design and implementation while retaining traditional analysis methods (T-O-O);
- To adopt OO analysis and design while retaining traditional implementation in a procedural language (O-O-T);
- To adopt an OO analysis method with a traditional design and implementation (O-T-T);
- To adopt an OO implementation with a traditional analysis and design (T-T-O).

Figure 3.6 shows the possible interplay between traditional and object-oriented methods at the analysis, design and implementation levels. Methods exist for OO analysis and design. OO programming languages implement OO designs. OO database management systems exist to support the need for objects (or information) to persist beyond the lifetime of an application, as well as supporting the usual database functions such as concurrency, security, and so on. The dotted arrows indicate routes requiring a transformation between representations. The solid arrows indicate direct paths where no transformation is necessary.

Figure 3.6 indicates that both pure and hybrid object-oriented languages can use currently available object-oriented DBMSs. However, most OODBMSs also support programmatic interfaces from traditional programming languages such as C. Object-oriented programming languages can be used with non-object-oriented DBMSs. There are many examples of such configurations, for example the OSMOSYS tool (discussed in Chapter 4) can produce Smalltalk code to interface with relational databases. In such cases the OO application must include classes with attributes which map onto the relational database schema.

3.2.1   Full object-oriented development (O-O-O)

In an object-oriented life cycle the three stages of analysis, design and implementation still exist. These stages can be bound together in any of the ways currently used to support traditional software development – such as the sequential waterfall model, the incremental model or the evolutionary model as described in Section 3.1. To capitalize on the inherent modularity of objects, and to realize maximum extensibility, the object-oriented software life cycle should resemble the evolutionary model in Section 3.1.2. An object-oriented software development life cycle should be more incremental and iterative in nature compared with traditional structured life cycles.

For information systems development the traditional life cycle has distinct stages for logical data design and logical process design. However, these two stages are now merged into one as classes include both data and process. High-level analysis and design are accomplished using objects which contain:

- Data
- Services

Objects provide services using a client/server model in which they interact via messages. The use of a client/server model leads to the system being described as 'responsibility-driven'. There is a form of 'contract' between interacting objects. One object (the client) knows what services another object (the server) can provide. The server knows what corresponding responses it must reply with. Responsibilities are a way to apportion work amongst objects which make up the application.

The strength of a fully integrated OO life cycle comes from the use of the same object model (the concepts defined in Chapter 2) at each stage from problem to solution. Many of the same techniques apply at analysis, then again during design and yet again in implementation. The difference is that in analysis the techniques are applied to high-level objects which model business procedures, roles and rules within organizations; whereas in design such objects are refined and rigour is introduced by adding objects to manage user dialogues, relationships, referential integrity, transactions and so on. These objects are then implemented directly using object-oriented programming languages. It should therefore be possible to trace objects right through from a high-level analysis to the actual software produced.

Object-oriented analysis provides a slightly different way of viewing the problem domain compared with traditional structured analysis. A class logically contains both data and function. This replaces the old notion of an entity which defines only data. Inheritance replaces entity relationship subtyping. Transaction analysis diagrams, depicting the messages passing between instances of various classes, replaces data flow diagramming. The traditional entity relationship diagrams are replaced by class relationship diagrams and class hierarchy diagrams.

Support for analysis and design is available through so-called 'soft' technology – that is, through methods. There is now CASE tool support for some

Individual cogs are important, but it is the effects from combining them which yield the desired result.

methods. Such support is directed at the techniques which the method prescribes. Few tools actually impose a life-cycle model. Generally the user must refer to the accompanying documentation for life-cycle guidance. There is an important message here for those about to purchase a CASE tool. I firmly believe that the method, life-cycle model and individual techniques should be fully understood and evaluated BEFORE any CASE tool is bought. All too often organizations buy into CASE in an effort to force some semblance of structure or procedure on an ill-defined software development process. Sometimes this works, but more often little attention is given to the life-cycle (or sub-life-cycle) model and the CASE introduction fails because the tools are used to aid techniques and the overall life-cycle process is lost because no one took the associated documentation too seriously!

Support for the implementation phase is through the various language offerings from many vendors (see Chapter 5 for details). Implementation is also supported through several object-oriented DBMS vendors. An OODBMS provides similar facilities to an OO programming language with the addition of object persistence and the normal database management system facilities such as security, querying and sharing.

True OO support in each of these areas entails the use of objects, classes, message passing, inheritance and polymorphism.

Henderson-Sellers (1991), Booch (1990) and Bailin (1989) have developed methods for a complete object-oriented systems development. They all recognize the need to encompass both top-down decomposition and bottom-up system building.

Analysis is accomplished in a top-down manner. The result is a set of fairly high-level classes and the interactions (both inheritance and message passing) between these classes. As the analysis stage merges into design, lower-level class diagrams can be drawn to illustrate more internal detail of the classes. These class diagrams decompose into *n* levels – each level decomposing classes into their parts and describing their behaviour. The class design also involves defining additional classes required to map the solution into the target hardware/software environment, and abstracting common features to produce generic, abstract data/function types (that is, the classes) which form into a class hierarchy. It is necessary to periodically re-evaluate the class hierarchy as more objects are identified within the detailed design stage. Consequently, inheritance diagrams will be further developed and refined.

For example, at the analysis stage, a class might represent a complete *department* within an organization. The class incorporates both information and behaviour relating to that department. The analysis might further decompose the *Department* class to produce several classes such as *Rooms*, *Furniture* and *Employees*. The design stage might develop the *Rooms* class further by adding functionality for representing a room graphically on a user interface, for example. The design stage would also involve extracting the generic properties of this *Department* class which could be applied to other departments in the organization through inheritance.

From this stage onwards bottom-up techniques are taken into consideration. A bottom-up approach is aimed at composing applications by using existing collections of classes.

The main differences between a structured and an object-oriented life cycle are to be seen in the design phase. OO design is a two-stage process:

- Class design
- Application design

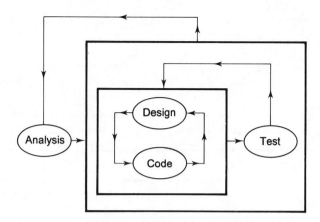

Figure 3.7   Overview of an OO life cycle (OMG, 1992a).

Class design involves developing functionality associated with specific classes and developing class hierarchies through abstraction of common data and function – creating more generic classes. Class design involves both bottom-up and top-down procedures. Much of the application design is achieved bottom-up after the constituent class design is complete, although application design will inevitably uncover additional classes which must be refined via class design. Coding of individual classes is often done before the application design is complete. So the distinction between application design and coding is much less than in a traditional life cycle. Chapter 4 describes both class and application design in more detail. Figure 3.7 illustrates the evolutionary development life cycle which is recognized as providing the best basis for object-oriented analysis and design.

   The main feature of this model is that the design and code loop in the centre provides a basis for fast innovative code creation. This produces versions of the development application which can be evaluated quickly and fed back into the cycle for further design – the essence of an evolutionary or prototyping life cycle. Such iterative processes tend to reduce risk in software development. Maude and Willis (1991) show how rapid prototyping (a highly iterative process) can be used to reduce risk.

   In his OO method – object-oriented software engineering (OOSE) – Jacobson (1992) suggests using an iterative life cycle which is similar to that presented in section 3.1.3. Jacobson states, however, that the analysis phase of the next increment can overlap with the implementation phase of the current increment. This life cycle is illustrated in Figure 3.8. Jacobson suggests that each increment should involve essentially 5–20 additional business-level objects (identified from the analysis phase).

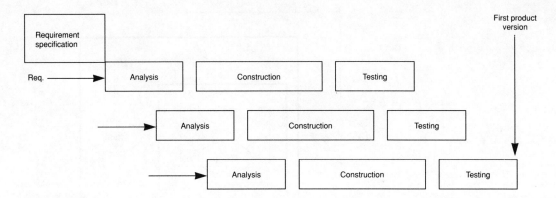

Figure 3.8   An iterative life cycle for OOSE [Jacobson *et al.*, 1992]. Note: The term 'construction' used in this figure and also by Jacobson *et al.* is equivalent to the term 'implementation' as used throughout this book.

Each increment should cover a limited period of time such as 3–6 months.

Class design, as already mentioned, is done before completion of the application design. To a large extent the two design processes (class and application) run in parallel, with the application design having an influence on the class design. If a class hierarchy already exists, from a previous project, then additional work would be done to identify existing reusable classes, before

Only artists should have the right to start with a clean sheet!

embarking on any new class design. Reuse is a thorny subject in most organizations. You only have to mention the subject and the excuses start coming in – the *'not invented here'* syndrome, or *'I don't have confidence that this module will do the job correctly'*, or *'It won't run fast enough'*. Existing tools offer very little help in identifying reusable material. But reuse of analysis, design and software material should be an important part of any **engineering** discipline.

Cox (1990, 1992a, 1992b) discusses the issue of software reuse and the software industrial revolution where software development will move from a fabrication-based industry, where monolithic teams *fabricate* monolithic products from first principles, to an assembly-based industry, where there will be many smaller projects and users at higher levels will solve their own problems by *assembling* components that were fabricated by the lower levels of a specialized labour hierarchy. This is a radical move. There is no doubt that during an interim period this specialized labour force could benefit from assembling the components which they themselves created.

Life cycles need to address these issues, and meld reuse with new development. When you mention reuse to software development staff they immediately think of code reuse. This is important but as Jacobson (1992) suggests, reuse of code increases productivity, but increasing productivity even further requires the reuse of larger modules. This can be accomplished by introducing reuse in earlier phases of the life cycle when the system is being structured.

Individual classes are implemented during the class design stage. For a particular abstract data type there will be many implementation options. For example, a queue could be implemented using linked list schemes or by using an array. Memory limitations, response times and so on are the basis for implementation decisions. Each class is tested individually before it becomes a *bona fide* component of the ultimate class library.

Testing an object-oriented system involves the same basic approach as testing a traditionally developed system. Testing starts at the object level. Individual objects can be tested initially in isolation to verify that the output agrees with the supplied stimulus. Both black-box (testing inputs and outputs) and glass-box (testing internal methods) testing may be required at this stage to ensure that objects behave as they are supposed to. Many classes in a hierarchy may be purely abstract classes – that is generalized classes used as conveniences in the development of specialized classes through inheritance. It is vital to test such abstract classes, however, it is important to note that many methods inherited from abstract classes may be redefined further down a hierarchy and cannot necessarily be trusted in more specialized classes just because they were tested elsewhere! Here again we see the distinction between software development for a specific application and that for generic components to be used in any number of future projects.

In many applications, classes are interrelated. A class may use facilities provided by several other classes, which in turn use facilities provided by yet more classes. These classes combine logically to form class clusters. The context of individual classes (or objects) must be tested to ensure that they perform correctly in combination with cooperating objects. It is the interrelations between classes which are being tested at this stage. It is necessary to perform integration testing on a class cluster before submitting the component classes to the library. The

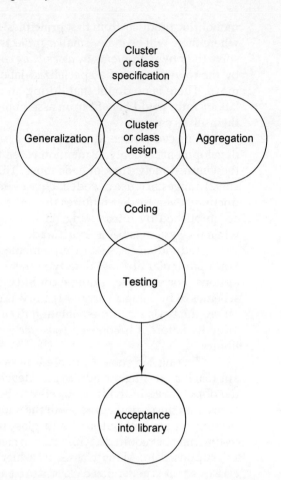

Figure 3.9   A typical class life cycle (adapted from Henderson-Sellers 1990: Copyright 1990, Association for Computing Machinery, Inc.).

integration strategy is decided at the class design stage. Within the over-all system development life cycle there is a sub-life cycle for each imple-mented class. Figure 3.9 shows the life cycle for a class or class-cluster development and is adapted from work by Henderson-Sellers (1990). The overlap between the circles in the figure indicates the iterative process that goes on between the various stages.

Partial system integration is possible at various stages of the development. Here, parts of the overall application are combined from the class library. These subsystems can be used in a feedback loop to verify user requirements. This process illustrates the incremental nature of the object-oriented life cycle. Object-oriented programming languages and their associated development environments can encourage incre-mental development to a greater or lesser extent (see Chapter 5). Careful choice of software development environment and programming language is therefore important.

Henderson-Sellers (1990) discusses how, 'Through aggregation (to form clusters) and generalization, case-specific classes are revised to make them sufficiently generic. This increases the chances that they will be of use in a wider range of applications than the single one for which they were originally developed'. They argue that such a philosophy 'requires a greater effort than one-off design/implementations in the short term, but, in the long term, can lead to a significant reduction in overall systems development time and effort.' OO programming offers excellent possibilities to reuse and modify existing classes in subsequent application developments.

Construction of the application is based around the class hierarchy and uses a 'shopping list' approach where the developer picks classes from here and there to produce the application.

Finally, integration and system testing verify that the classes work harmoniously and that the end application meets the users' requirements.

Figure 3.10 summarizes the preceding text. It depicts a possible object-oriented software life cycle. There is no one software life cycle that has gained universal acceptance. However, the life cycle presented here illustrates the main features of the process which involves both class and application design as distinct activities.

Figure 3.11, adapted from Henderson-Sellers (1990), illustrates the effect of changing requirements on the whole development process. According to Henderson-Sellers (1990), 'The requirements, design and implementation stages grow and iterate over time, while individual classes or class clusters (groups of classes) undergo their own life cycle. Characteristics of a software system, which evolves dynamically as the users' and analysts' knowledge grows, can be readily incorporated in the overall life cycle model. '

Figure 3.11 shows expanding software requirements and a correspondingly expanding software design over time. The global design leads to new classes and class aggregates (or clusters) which are implemented, tested and submitted to the class library. The final application is constructed from this class library.

Users' needs continually change and specifications are rarely fixed for the duration of a software development project. Methods are only now being developed which can incorporate such characteristics within the overall systems development. Classes and class aggregates can undergo detailed design and implementation in isolation from the overall software system. As the requirements expand in time, some of the resulting classes may have to change and new classes (or class clusters) may have to be added. The inherent modularity created through encapsulation and a client/server interaction process, between objects, limits the knock-on effects on classes which have already been implemented.

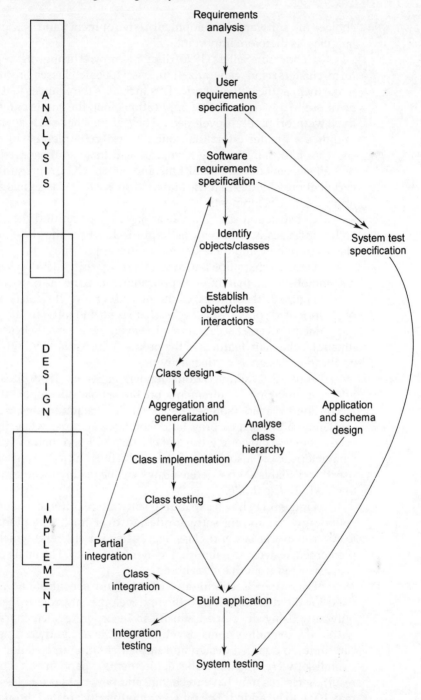

Figure 3.10   An object-oriented development model.

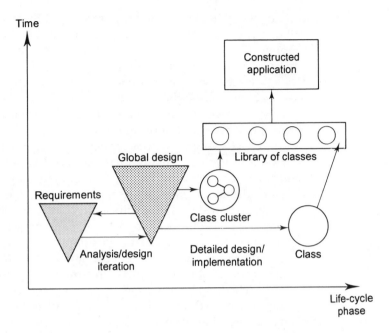

Figure 3.11   Effect of requirements evolution on the OO development process (adapted from Henderson-Sellers, 1990: Copyright 1990, Association for Computing Machinery, Inc.).

The classes and class aggregates are incorporated into the final application in a bottom-up fashion at a much earlier stage than components in a traditional development would be. This results from the incremental nature of the life cycle, encouraging partial application construction at the earliest opportunity.

Development team skills and allocation

The OO software life cycle differs somewhat from a traditional life cycle as discussed in the previous section. These differences suggest different roles for staff within a development team. Analysis is still done by a systems analyst. However, if the project is sufficiently large as to involve, say, 12–20 developers then according to Booch (1991) the following team roles can be envisaged. Design requires two types of designer: class designers and system architects. The system architects 'are the most senior developers, best qualified to make strategic decisions'. They will have overall responsibility for the system design. Booch (1991) suggests that 'the class designers are responsible for creating the class structure of a system' and the groups of cooperating objects. Each class designer maintains the interface to some major class library. Booch (1991) identifies two categories of implementor: class implementors and application programmers. The class implementor 'works under the supervision of the class designer'. The application programmers 'take the products of the class implementors and put them together'. They can be thought of as system integrators. They are oriented towards the end application whereas class implementors are oriented towards providing services to the application programmers.

If the development project is large enough there are also class and application testers who look after testing classes and applications respectively. However, often class and application testing is performed by the respective class and application implementors (I accept that there are sound psychological reasons for using different resources for implementation and testing). Finally there is a need for an overall class library manager. This person is responsible for managing class libraries and for ensuring that system architects make good use of existing classes in their application-level design specifications. The class library manager spans many separate application development projects. This should be a permanent job with a suitable position of influence and responsibility within the organization. It requires a person with sound technical and organizational abilities, along with strong interpersonal skills.

Scheduling the various types of resource is another important issue. The preceding software life cycle suggests that the resource spent on analysis will not change. However, Booch (1991) suggests that 'more resources are required at the design phase because there is more work than usual in this stage'. Class implementors are required earlier than programmers would be in a traditional life cycle. This is because much class implementation can be accomplished before the final application design is complete.

Figure 3.12 illustrates that the class library manager should be involved from an early stage of analysis to help identify potentially reusable classes. As the project progresses, the class designer gets involved and class implementation starts before the class or application design is complete. Application design begins sometime during class design. Application implementation begins during application design but is not complete until sometime after class and application design have been completed.

The blurred boundaries between analysis, design and implementation present problems for project management. Chapter 4 suggests a definition for the boundary between the analysis and design stages. The boundary between design and implementation is in two parts: class design/implementation and application design/construction. More resource will normally be required for class implementation than for application implementation, although the proportions will depend on the size of the application and the number of reusable classes available. The proportions will also depend on whether a pure or hybrid OO programming language (**OOPL**) is used. Using a pure OOPL there will be little implementation work separate from class implementation. However, there may still be a need to have some implementors with an overall view

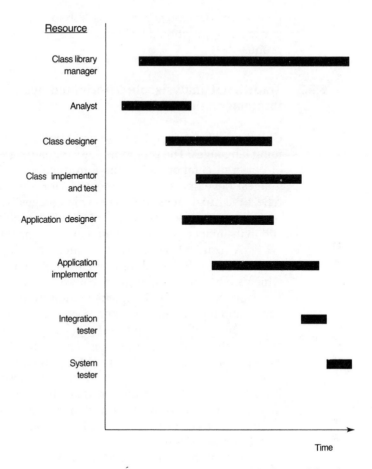

Figure 3.12   A possible resource schedule for an OO software development. Note that the bars denote involvement in the project but are not intended to imply any specific degree of commitment.

of the end application rather than the more blinkered views which the class implementors have. These resources perform the role of system integrator. They oversee the combining of progressively larger components to build the final application. They also perform integration testing.

In situations where a highly evolutionary life cycle (such as rapid prototyping) is used, many of the specific roles discussed here will be merged into one. For example, the person specifying a set of objects at the analysis stage may be made responsible for developing such objects further during design and ultimately implementing the resultant objects. This management structure avoids much of the communication overhead between different team members, but it is more difficult to ensure that sufficient time is spent making classes truly reusable. Ideally the people who develop generic classes should not become too involved in a particular application development, otherwise their impartiality is compromised.

3.2.2 Traditional analysis, object-oriented design and implementation (T-O-O)

Object-oriented principles were first applied through several programming languages. The programming languages are the most mature area of object orientation. After the introduction of OO programming languages, developers needed methods for software design that could reflect the capabilities of these new languages. The design phase represents the next most mature area of OO. Today, object-oriented analysis is still in its infancy and is the least mature of the three areas.

A prudent company wishing to adopt an object-oriented approach to software development might consider only those areas which are sufficiently mature for commercial use. Such a company could adopt an OO design and implementation strategy while continuing with a tried and tested traditional approach to analysis.

This strategy requires techniques for translating the results of the analysis phase into object designs. This translation can be difficult! For example, as Henderson-Sellers (1991) suggests, OO analysis involves different aggregation principles from traditional structured analysis. Wasserman *et al.* (1990) formulated an object-oriented structured design method which performs this translation. Alabiso (1988) also proposed a method for transforming from a traditional structured analysis to an object-oriented design.

For information systems developers, traditional structured analysis produces as a minimum :

(1) Entity relationship diagrams (ERDs) and
(2) Data flow diagrams (DFDs).

DFDs normally use bubbles to represent processes and arrows to represent the flow of data between processes. ERDs normally use rectangles to represent entities which contain data, and lines to represent the relationships (one:one, many:one, and so on) between entities. Appendix A shows the popular traditional analysis diagrams and techniques.

Object-oriented analysis and design uses class relationship diagrams, class hierarchy diagrams and transaction analysis diagrams (see Chapter 4 for details). The transformation from traditional analysis to OO design involves identifying classes from DFD data stores and ERD entities; and identifying class methods from DFD processes. The DFD data flows become messages between objects of given classes and define client/server relationships. The relationship information on the ERDs maps onto the relationships between classes. It can also help determine some of the inheritance relationships between classes. (Refer to Ward (1989) for more details.) Chapter 4 includes an example showing the relationship between ERDs/DFDs and class diagrams. It must be emphasized that the translation can be difficult because ERDs and DFDs represent different aspects of a system whereas class diagrams and transaction diagrams are two views of the same information. Chapter 4 discusses this subject further.

For real-time systems developers, the traditional analysis stage tends to produce DFDs and process state diagrams (refer to Appendix A). Translating these diagrams into class diagrams is more difficult because the concept of a data entity, which translates to a class, will not have been considered. However, event-driven process state diagrams are a natural concept for modelling using OO design. Process state diagrams identify some entities. They also identify the state data and processing associated with the class.

In general the translation from traditional analysis to OO design adds further complexity to an already difficult design process. Classes contain both data and functional logic bound together. ERDs can bear strong similarity to classes. However, it is more difficult to relate DFDs to the functionality of a particular class. Classes may overlap more than one DFD and one DFD process bubble may relate to more than one class of object. In the translation some classes appear to have no functional behaviour while others appear to have no data. In these cases the developer must partially re-analyse the requirements using an object-oriented approach. Some classes will merge with others and some additional classes will be created. The net result is that some work has to be redone!

3.2.3   Object-oriented analysis and design with a traditional implementation (O-O-T)

Many companies are unlikely to migrate from procedural to object-oriented code because of the large current investments they have in procedural code, such as COBOL, and associated coding tools. As Henderson-Sellers (1991) suggests, 'A further concern is the lack of current standards and the evolving nature of object-oriented programming languages.'

The main benefits from this hybrid approach involving OO analysis and design (OOA&D) coupled with a traditional implementation relate to being able to model the problem domain using OO analysis. OO analysis promises a more natural medium for communication between the end user and the analyst than current structured analysis techniques provide.

Object-oriented analysis and design complement one another. The analysis-to-design transition is therefore straightforward and amounts to progressively adding more objects required at the base level of object aggregates. More services and attributes may also be added to a class as a result of the design process.

A full object-oriented design will consist of a generalized and optimized class hierarchy design, along with an application design based on the class design. Figure 3.6 depicts these two stages of object-oriented design. Structured programming languages do not support all the principles of object orientation (encapsulation, inheritance, message passing and polymorphism). It is therefore difficult (at best!) to implement a *full* object-oriented design using a traditional structured programming language. Some form of translation between the OO and traditional representations must take place. Chapter 5 contains a section describing the use of a traditional structured programming language (Fortran) in an object-oriented manner. After reading this section, the reader will appreciate the difficulties in trying to implement an object-oriented design using a traditional programming language.

Procedural languages generally support only procedural abstraction. Data abstraction and encapsulation are feasible, but it is the responsibility of the programmer to ensure their implementation. Inheritance cannot be explicitly implemented, so it is not possible to take full advantage of reuse and extensibility which are at the heart of object-oriented concepts. Some of the commonality can be factored out into individual routines, but the possibilities for later reuse are limited.

Henderson-Sellers (1991) indicates that the modular structure of an object-oriented design should cause no problems when coded as a suite of subroutines using a procedural language. This will enforce a modularity into the procedural code produced.

The translation from an object-oriented design to a procedural language implementation is not very gratifying because traditional programming languages are not at all well suited to object-oriented techniques (Chapter 5 illustrates this by using an example of Fortran code written in an object-oriented manner). However, Coad and Yourdon (1990, 1991a) indicate that several organizations are currently using this approach.

Chapter 4 contains a section on an OOA&D method and associated CASE tool called OSMOSYS which enable an analyst to perform object-oriented analysis and design. The tool then produces a relational database schema and software to interface with a relational database. The tool can export design information in an external source format for use with IBM's Cross Systems Product (CSP) to produce CICS applications in COBOL. The tool addresses a market sector where development managers are reluctant to dismiss the large investments they have made in relational technology. These managers are, however, keen to take advantage of any benefits to be derived at the front end of the life cycle from an object-oriented approach.

3.2.4 OO analysis, traditional design and implementation (O-T-T).

The main benefits from this hybrid approach involving OO analysis coupled with a traditional design and implementation relate to being able to model the problem domain using OO analysis. OO analysis promises a more natural medium for communication between the end user and the analyst than current structured analysis techniques provide.

If a developer insists on retaining a traditional programming language then this flavour of hybrid life cycle is possibly better than O-O-T discussed in a preceding section. The reason is that the more work done up front using object-oriented techniques, then the more will have to be redone in the resulting translation to a non-object-oriented representation for implementation. Analysis provides high-level business objects representing business procedures and so on. By the time design is complete many more objects will have been introduced and the commitment to using an object-oriented programming language will be greater. The main exception to this statement is where an application generator CASE tool will be used to cut the code. But in this situation the paradigm used for code generation is not so important.

Such a life cycle requires a translation between the analysis and design phases. The translation is essentially the reverse of that discussed in Section 3.2.2. The developer must translate class diagrams back into structured diagrams such as data flow diagrams and entity relationship diagrams for information systems, and to functional (or process) decomposition and state transition diagrams for real-time systems (see Appendix A for details). The process information can be extracted from the identified classes and likewise the data aspects can be used to create data entities. The translation from object-oriented analysis to structured design should be easier than the reverse (that is, from a structured analysis to an object-oriented design).

3.2.5 Traditional analysis and design with an object-oriented implementation (T-T-O).

This life cycle makes little sense. The use of a pure OO programming language (such as Eiffel or Smalltalk) forces the developer to use an object-oriented design method. Figure 3.6 indicates that implementing a structured design using a pure object-oriented programming language requires a translation to be performed. However, hybrid OO programming languages such as C++ provide OO constructs on top of a procedural language. The developer is at liberty to use either OO or traditional techniques, or any mixture of the two. Using a hybrid OO programming language, a structured design can be implemented directly…but the implementation is NOT object-oriented!

Hybrid OO programming languages allow object orientation to be introduced in an evolutionary manner. As Ramackers (1989) suggests: 'Programmers can continue using procedural code next to OO code. The OO code can gradually grow in percentage as programmers get used to the new approach.' The hybrid OO languages also offer more compatibility with existing hardware and software environments, because they are based on existing technologies.

3.3 Conclusions

Object-oriented methods for analysis and design are supported by object-oriented programming languages and object-oriented database management systems. This provides a unified object-oriented approach to software development with a full object-oriented software life cycle.

The object-oriented software life cycle introduces more iteration between the various stages. The mixture of top-down and bottom-up design for classes with predominantly bottom-up implementation of applications encourages interactions leading to more robust and flexible designs. The resulting classes can be more generic and exhibit more potential for reuse both within a given project and in future software development projects.

Implementation of classes can take place in parallel with much of the design work. This means that coding starts much earlier compared with a traditional life cycle. More personnel are required earlier in the project. The final application implementation phase should be completed faster than in a traditional development since the investment in time and effort occurs earlier rather than later.

The significant dependence on class libraries introduces a new job category to an object-oriented software development team – namely the class library manager. The class library manager's job is to keep class libraries up to date and ensure that all classes submitted to such libraries are adequately tested beforehand. The class library manager ensures that all changes to a class library are communicated to all members of the development team. The class library manager should be responsible for ensuring that software professionals make good use of the available classes in their designs and implementations. The class library manager should therefore be a job description for a permanent employee rather than simply a role within a team for the duration of one project. The class library manager may also have to improve the reusability of existing classes and search for new classes or class libraries, within and from outside the organization, which may be potentially reusable within the company.

The chapter has also considered a number of hybrid software life cycles. These 'compromise' solutions might be considered by project managers in an attempt to offset the cost of starting with a completely new set of methods and tools. The hybrid approaches may be more pragmatic, but there is likely to be more effort required to complete a project using a hybrid life cycle. This results from the need to translate between OO and traditional representations of data and process.

The best approach is to adopt OO throughout the life cycle. Only by this approach can the output of one stage be optimized to the input of the next. The reason for adopting a new technique is to achieve better performance. It may be better productivity, or better management of user requirements, or better reuse of analysis, design or source code. Whatever your motivation for migrating to a new methodology, you will limit the potential benefits if you adopt a hybrid approach. The hybrid approach will also make it more difficult to measure (or even perceive) any benefits.

Hybrid life cycle approaches can only be considered a temporary stage while developers are coming to terms with new techniques in a gradual fashion. To this end, the use of hybrid object-oriented programming languages provides programmers with a more gradual introduction to object orientation.

4 Analysis and design

**INTENDED
READERSHIP**
Systems analysts and software designers should read this chapter. Much of the information will also be useful to project leaders. The chapter contains information on techniques for both real-time and information systems analysis and software design professionals.

**CHAPTER
PRE-
REQUISITES**
The reader should be familiar with the object-oriented principles as detailed in Chapter 2. It is assumed that the reader is also familiar with the methods used in traditional structured analysis and design, such as entity relationship diagrams and data flow diagrams. For completeness, popular techniques used in structured analysis are summarized in Appendix A.

**CHAPTER
OVERVIEW**
This chapter introduces you to the ideas, techniques and procedures involved in object-oriented analysis and design. Using a framework for OOA&D, the chapter presents the salient features of an OOA method. The chapter discusses the principal problems with traditional structured analysis and design methods and shows how an object-oriented approach addresses these problems.

A reference model identifies the main concepts and techniques to look for in an OOA&D method.

Several object-oriented analysis and design methods are summarized and their degree of support for the object-oriented concepts (presented in Chapter 2) is discussed. These methods illustrate widely differing approaches to OOA&D – from the evolutionary approaches by proponents like Shlaer and Mellor, whose method exhibits strong influences from traditional structured techniques, to responsibility-driven design by Rebecca Wirfs-Brock which exemplifies a purist view of OOA&D.

The goal of this chapter is not to say which method is best, but rather to show the differences between methods and to allow conclusions to be drawn as to their applicability for developing different kinds of software applications.

Some readers may prefer to skip over the reference model and method summary sections on first reading. A later section discusses the issues to consider when choosing a method and provides a list of questions to ask a method vendor. This section relies heavily on the reference model. It presents tables of features for a number of methods. These tables provide many answers to pertinent questions related to selecting an OOA&D method.

Graphical examples illustrate the concepts and augment the text. References are cited for further reading.

4.1 Why should I consider OO analysis and design?

There is no point in considering OOA&D unless you think it is an improvement on traditional structured analysis and design methods. Before you start into this chapter in earnest, consider some of the problems with structured analysis and design which the object-oriented approach seeks to resolve.

The main objective in analysing a system is to provide an accurate approximation to the real world which can be converted into an accurate model of the world in software. This requires good communication between the analyst and the ultimate system's end users. Structured analysis, where a problem is divided into separate processing and data components, does not provide a good way to communicate with a (possibly) naive end user. By comparison, *the objects modelled in OOA&D provide a more realistic representation, which an end user can more readily understand.*

The structured analysis and design methodology uses **entity relationship** and **data flow diagrams** (ERDs and DFDs) as the main vehicles for communicating analysis and design information (see Appendix A). ERDs relate to data entities in the system while DFDs relate mainly to the processing in the system. The main connection between the DFDs and ERDs is through the DFD data stores which should correspond to the data entities in the ERDs. Often the processes specified in DFDs relate to several data stores or entities and several processes may use the same data store. This results in DFDs specified at the logical level not translating directly into modules in the physical design. The physical design becomes abstract and does not map clearly onto the user requirements. Thus designs become difficult to understand, particularly for staff newly assigned to on-going projects. By comparison, *OOA&D provides a consistent approach which maps cleanly onto a physical design and implementation.*

Structured analysis and design does not provide a good framework for encouraging the reuse of specifications. Reuse, of whatever kind, speeds system development. System requirements change and evolve over time. A suitable framework for reuse can help to limit the ramifications of changing requirements on systems under development. Furthermore, traditional techniques for design, such as functional decomposition, do not support evolving end-user requirements. Designs tend to bind the temporal relationships between functions prematurely, leading to strongly coupled systems which are less extensible. By comparison, *OOA&D provides a framework which supports reuse and extensibility.*

The following sections in this chapter discuss these fairly provocative statements in more detail, and show how an object-oriented approach addresses these issues.

The chapter summarizes a number of OO analysis and design methods:

(1) Booch (1990)

(2) Responsibility-driven design (RDD) – incorporating class responsibility collaboration (CRC) (Beck and Cunningham, 1989; Wirfs-Brock *et al.*, 1990)

(3) Hood (1989a, 1989b)

(4) Object-oriented analysis and design (Coad and Yourdon, 1991a, 1991b)

(5) OSMOSYS (Winter Partners)

(6) Object-oriented systems analysis (Shlaer and Mellor, 1988)

(7) OOSE (Jacobson, 1992)

(8) Object-oriented structured design (Wasserman *et al.*, 1990)

(9) Object modelling technique (OMT) (Rumbaugh *et al.*, 1991)

(10) Object-oriented role analysis, synthesis and structuring (OORASS) (Reenskaug *et al.*, 1991)

(11) Object-oriented software development (Colbert, 1989).

Later sections of this chapter discuss these methods and show how they support the areas of analysis and/or design.

4.2   OO analysis

We live in a very complex world. Even simple tasks would be confusing without some techniques for abstracting out the essential features from the world around us and classifying these into hierarchies of generalizations and patterns. In addition, complex objects can be composed from simpler objects which interact to form the more complex behaviour. Such mechanisms of analysis are a part of our mental ability, enabling us to grasp and understand the world in which we live.

During the initial phase of software development, analysis, the essence of some domain within the real world is abstracted to provide a model from which a software system can ultimately be developed. The analyst determines what the system must do to meet the needs of the customer. The resultant requirements specification should clearly describe WHAT the software's external behaviour should be, without any prejudgement about HOW the software will produce this exact behaviour. This initial phase of software development is crucial because it is the basis for everything that comes after it. If the software requirements specification is ambiguous, inconsistent or incomplete, then, at worst, all the project's succeeding phases are doomed to failure. At best, the project is headed for costly rework when specification problems are realized. Figure 4.1 shows the road from specification to delivery.

Object-oriented analysis can be performed on two levels. At the highest level it can be used to analyse large domains such as:

- A complete industry
- A complete enterprise
- A major business unit
- A group sharing common concepts
- A subset of an organization's activities

At this level the objective is to understand an enterprise and the domain in which it exists. It is concerned with understanding the motivation behind, and planning to provide, a set of systems solutions within that domain. The models developed will be a complete, but not detailed, description of the domain – sufficient to understand the opportunities that exist. The exercise may expose the possibilities for the partitioning of coordinated projects to achieve integrated systems.

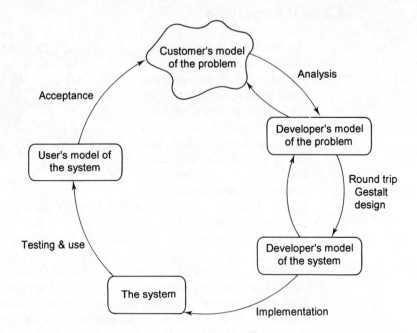

Figure 4.1   Specification to delivery, a complete cycle (from W. Stubblefield, personal communication: reproduced by courtesy of Learning Tree International).

Consequently the objects modelled at this level are very high level such as enterprises, work groups, business units, business processes, policies and rules for the business.

At the next level, analysis seeks to obtain a thorough understanding of a specific problem domain, by representing the real world as a collection of intercommunicating objects. This model should provide a basis for the design and construction of applications for that domain. The analysis model is free from design and implementation considerations. This aids clear thinking, and means the model can be used as the basis for alternative design and implementation solutions. Analysis at this level is typically restricted to the scope of a single (or set of related) application(s).

Examples of the kinds of objects typically used at this level of analysis include customer, accident, budget, owner, manager (for commercial domains) and sensor, motor, gear box, engine and oven (for engineering domains).

Traditional structured analysis normally takes the form of producing two sets of information: namely a data model and a process analysis. The data model results in a set of entity relationship diagrams (ERDs). The process analysis determines what processes are needed and results in data flow diagrams (DFDs). Appendix A illustrates a typical ERD and DFD.

Data-driven structured analysis involving entity relationship diagramming is a standard approach in the DP world. However, identifying entities is a less familiar procedure to real-time systems developers. The principle behind object-oriented analysis and design is quite similar to data entity relationship modelling. However, for data entities substitute classes and instead of simply considering data, consider also process functionality since encapsulation combines data and process. Inheritance provides an association between classes. This facility is available in structured analysis via entity relationship subtyping.

OO analysis must identify classes of objects, their attributes and the services they provide. It is possible to represent the interactions between objects in a similar way to the use of data flow diagrams in structured analysis. A better term for this technique is object interaction modelling (OIM) since it is the messages with data and their interactions with methods providing processing, which are being described. The life cycles for these dynamic objects may also be considered through some form of object state modelling (OSM) technique.

To summarize, there are four basic techniques which provide the essence of object-oriented analysis:

(1) Class relationship modelling

(2) Class inheritance modelling

(3) Object interaction modelling

(4) Object state modelling

The process of analysis is iterative and involves the following stages:

- Quantify the business objectives. This will produce a list of system requirements to achieve the business objectives.

- Identify candidate classes in the problem domain. Language analysis can be very effective: plural nouns nearly always identify classes.

- Identify the properties of classes – responsibilities and collaborations with other classes. Words and phrases meaning possession indicate properties. Verbs indicate operations. (Class relationship diagrams)

- Identify the methods of the classes. Many of these are exposed by thinking through the various interactions the system must support, that is, the dynamics of the scenario. (Object interaction diagrams)

- Develop the life-cycle stages for each identified class. (Object state tables)

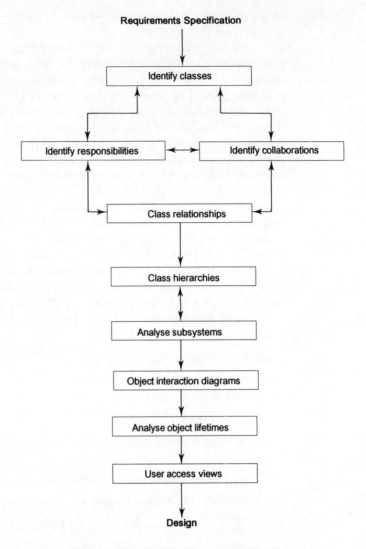

Figure 4.2   Phases of analysis and design.

- Identify the user interfaces to the system. (User access views)
- Rationalize the classes found so far. This entails factoring out the common essential characteristics among classes and promoting general classes. (Class inheritance diagrams)

The diagram types mentioned within brackets are introduced in the next section. Figure 4.2 summarizes this procedure.

The notion of a responsibility-driven approach is very important. It represents a revolutionary swing away from traditional structured techniques. To use the example of a horse (Wirfs-Brock, 1990):

> A **data-driven** approach describes a horse in terms of its parts: head, tail, body, leg(4).

> A **procedural** approach describes a horse in terms of operations it can perform: walk, run, trot, bite, eat, neigh.

> A **responsibility-driven** approach describes a horse in terms of its responsibilities: communicate, carry things, maintain its living systems.

The data-driven and procedural approaches correspond with the intrinsic capabilities while the responsibility-driven approach corresponds with the usage of an object. The responsibility-driven approach requires a slightly different discipline for the way we view and analyse the world around us. The usage characterization results from a preliminary understanding of the system while the intrinsic capabilities emerge when the individual objects are analysed in more detail.

Section 4.2.1 illustrates the process of analysis by using a generic framework developed within the Institute of Software Engineering.

4.2.1   The essence of object-oriented analysis

An object-oriented analysis (OOA) method should provide several representations of the system in order to fully specify it in a way that includes encapsulation, message passing and inheritance. This section presents one such set of diagrams which illustrates the essence of OO analysis. The resulting diagrams are:

> Class relationship diagrams

> Class inheritance diagrams

> Object interaction diagrams

> Object state tables

> User access diagrams

> Textual specification documents.

The techniques which produce these diagrams use the object-oriented concepts described in Chapter 2.

The diagrams relate to the analysis of a fictitious hospital system for patient intake. The system registers all patients when they are received and assigns them to a particular hospital ward and a particular surgeon. The surgeon arranges surgery for his or her own patients. For comparison, Appendix A shows an analysis of the same system using structured techniques.

Class relationship diagrams

The objective of class relationship diagrams is to specify the classes in the problem domain and the relationships between them in terms of aggregation and association.

For the hospital patient intake system the class relationship diagram shown in Figure 4.3 was created. The figure shows the five fundamental classes in the system:

Ward	a hospital ward
Inpatient	an inpatient in the hospital
Surgeon	the surgeon responsible for the admitted patient
Theatre	an operating theatre in the hospital
Surgery	the instance of a surgical operation

with one other class, namely a ward **Nurse**, who is assigned to look after particular beds (and their occupants) in a ward.

A Ward has many Inpatients. An Inpatient may undergo many instances of Surgery. A Surgeon may perform many instances of Surgery and a Theatre may be the site of many instances of Surgery. Often the relationship will include an indication of the cardinality. For example, an instance of Surgery can occur in one, and only one, Theatre, and there must be a Theatre before there can be any instances of Surgery. This implies a one-to-many mandatory relationship between Surgery and Theatre.

The bottom part of Figure 4.3 shows the components of a Ward class, exposing two *contained* classes, Nurse and Bed, of which a Ward is composed. In some cases a Bed may be simply an attribute of a Ward – in others, where a Bed has behaviour such as not accepting a new Inpatient until the mattress is renewed, the Bed is a class. This demonstrates the principle of aggregation (introduced in Chapter 2). Aggregation is an abstraction in which a relationship among classes is represented by a higher-level, aggregate class. In this example, a Nurse *is responsible for* a Bed. A Ward represents this concept at a higher level.

At this stage of analysis the fundamental classes have been identified. The next stages are to determine the attributes and behaviour (methods) associated with these classes. Some of the methods and attributes

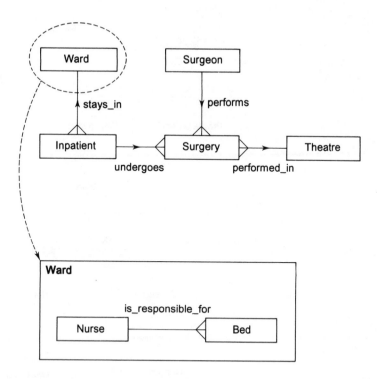

Figure 4.3   Class relationship diagram for the hospital patient intake system.

may be identified immediately. But others will not come to light until the system is analysed from different viewpoints. For example, many methods required in these classes will be identified during the dynamic modelling exercises which produce object interaction diagrams. However, for the meantime we will concentrate on the static views of the system.

Class inheritance diagrams

This view of a system enables generalizations and specializations to be established. Figure 4.4 depicts this view for part of the hospital system.

This example shows class hierarchies for only two of the five classes depicted in Figure 4.3, namely the Ward and the Inpatient classes. However, it serves to illustrate the point that an Inpatient may be a specialization of a more generic class Patient which may be used elsewhere in the overall system. Similarly a general Ward may be used to create several **specializations** such as an intensive care unit. These specializations inherit the attributes and relationships of a Ward, including any classes from which it is composed, and can also create additional attributes, methods and class relationships as the bottom part of Figure

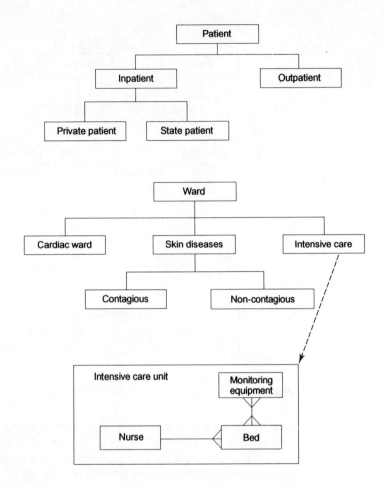

Figure 4.4   Class inheritance diagrams for part of the hospital patient
intake system.

4.4 illustrates – where an intensive care unit contains not only the Nurse
and Bed classes but also a class of specialized monitoring equipment. The
addition of inheritance creates some very powerful features for analysis.
If a relationship exists between an Inpatient and a Ward, and if a
Private_Patient is a specialization of an Inpatient, then the same
relationship holds between a Private_Patient and a Ward. This can be
overridden if a particular specialization does not exhibit the same relationships as its ancestors.

   These are the two main static views of the system being analysed.
But they show only half of the picture. Computer systems (and real life)
require analysts to consider the dynamics of the environment. Indeed,

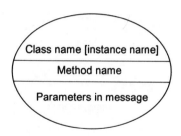

Figure 4.5   The representation of a received message in an object interaction diagram.

much of the behavioural component of the classes identified this far will not be completely exposed until the dynamic interactions between objects are considered.

Object interaction diagrams

Whereas the class inheritance and relationship diagrams consider class-level details, object interaction diagrams consider the dynamic behaviour of system components. They view the system at run-time and deal with instances of classes, that is, objects. These diagrams present a high-level representation of the message passing between objects. They show the dependencies between objects.

Object interaction diagrams are used to model the sequences of messages which pass between interoperating objects, in order to perform some aspect of the overall system operation. The diagrams show the message/operations and arguments which pass between objects (and within objects if appropriate). The message and receiving object are represented by an oval shape. Text in the top part of the oval denotes the receiving object's name and the name of the owning class. Text in the middle of the oval denotes the method to be invoked in the object and text in the bottom part of the oval denotes the parameters in the received message. Figure 4.5 shows the representation of an object.

Figure 4.6 illustrates an object interaction diagram for an In-patient being booked for surgery. In this example, the arrival of a new inpatient causes a new instance of an Inpatient to be created. The new inpatient is assigned to Cardiac_Ward *cardiac_1* by sending a message to the *cardiac_1* object. The Cardiac_Ward *cardiac_1* sends a message to a Surgeon called *Smith* to add the new patient to *Smith's* list. *Smith* books a time slot for surgery on the newly admitted patient by sending a message to one of the operating theatres – *theatre_1* in this example. Finally the operating theatre causes a instance of Surgery to be created. This object of class Surgery holds information relating to the date and time scheduled for the surgical operation, and other necessary details. It could be

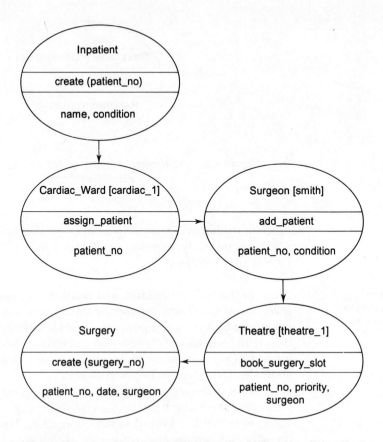

Figure 4.6   An object interaction diagram for the hospital patient intake system.

used, for example, to trigger a reminder to the Surgeon (*Smith*) or anyone else, at an appropriate time.

Another fundamental concept which should be modelled during analysis is the life history of an object, from creation to destruction. This can provide valuable information concerning the states an object can be in and some of the events (or messages) which that object will receive during its lifetime.

Object state tables

If we take the example of an Inpatient in the hospital system the partial object state table shown in Table 4.1 denotes some of the significant events that might take place in the life of an Inpatient. The table shows the list of allowable states for the object (Created, Admitted, Operation_Scheduled, Recovery, Discharged and Terminated in this case).

Table 4.1   Partial object state table for a hospital system.

State	Event	Action	New State
Created	Patient assigned to ward	—	Admitted
Admitted	Surgery booked	Set notification timer running	Operation_Scheduled
Operation_Scheduled	Operation complete	Notify ward nurse	Recovery
Recovery	Fully recovered	Notify reception	Discharged
Discharged	Delete	Remove records	Terminated
Terminated	—	—	—

For example, a new instance of Inpatient may be created at some time. When a new patient is received at the hospital reception desk, that patient is assigned to a hospital ward and an appropriate event (or messsage) is sent to the idle Inpatient object, causing its state to change from Created to Admitted.

Object interaction and state diagrams help expose more details about a class over and above the details developed through static, structural views (class relationship and class inheritance diagrams).

User access diagrams

These provide a view of the user interface to the system. They support the design of the menu structure and show the access points to the user requirements of the system. In the hospital example the Ward Access to the overall system might be depicted by Figure 4.7.

The figure shows that ward staff firstly create an object of type Ward (or of type Cardiac_Ward called *cardiac_1* in this case). They can assign nurses to that ward and they can assign a Surgeon (*Smith* in this case) to be responsible for the new inpatient. Similar user interfaces could be created for the other users of the system, namely the surgeons and the theatre administrators.

Text documents

The details of classes, objects and methods/messages sent between objects are documented using pre-defined templates. For example, a class specification document for the Surgeon class might look like this:

Class name:	Surgeon
Description:	Details of all doctors in the hospital
Superclass:	MedicalStaff
Attributes:	
Name:	Name
Description:	Surgeon's Christian, and surname
Type :	String
Cardinality :	One
Name:	Address
Description:	Surgeon's address
Type :	String
Cardinality :	One
Name:	Performs
Description:	Details of surgery performance
Type :	Surgery
Cardinality :	Many
Public methods:	
Name:	add_patient
Parameters:	patient:Inpatient
Description:	Place patient under care of surgeon
Private methods:	
Name:	book_surgery_slot
Parameters:	patient_no, priority, surgeon
Description:	Books a theatre time slot for surgery.

A key point to note from the class description is the 'Performs' attribute in the attribute list. This represents a relationship between two classes and is often referred to as a **property** of the class. From an analysis viewpoint classes can therefore be considered as having three fundamental categories of information: attributes (data), methods (functions or procedures) and properties (relationships). Later, when we discuss object-oriented design, we will see that these properties translate into attributes or other classes (design-level classes).

Through these diagrams, an analyst can construct a complete definition for any object. It is clear from this section that there is a need for good CASE tool support to amalgamate the various class and object views into a single OO model.

It is essential that the OOA method provides guidance on identifying classes from the problem domain (that is, from the real-world problem to be simulated). Identifying classes is very difficult to do well. There are different types of classes in a typical real situation: concrete classes such as People, Buildings and so on are fundamental and are unlikely to change significantly over time. But beware of roles such as Customer. A Customer may become a Vendor in another scenario. Then there are classes such as a Document_Form which are important for

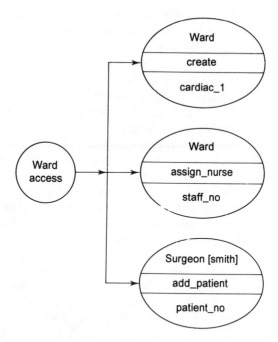

Figure 4.7 User access view for the ward in the hospital patient intake system.

what they contain, not for themselves. Therefore document classes are more likely to change than concrete classes. Any good method should provide guidance on the choice of classes and how to handle roles and other unstable classes such as events or happenings.

4.2.2 OO analysis versus structured analysis

Object-oriented analysis offers several advantages over structured analysis. Firstly, the technique provides a more consistent approach to system modelling. All six views described in the previous section relate to either classes or instances of those classes. This contrasts with structured analysis where ERDs relate to entities in the system while DFDs relate to the processing in the system. The main link between the DFDs and ERDs is through the DFD data stores which correspond to entities in the ERDs. Often the processes specified in DFDs relate to several data stores or entities. This results in DFDs specified at the logical level not translating directly into modules in the physical design, whereas the classes specified through OO analysis and design can be directly implemented using an OO programming language and/or object DBMS.

Furthermore, structured analysis (DeMarco, 1979) encourages the analyst to use names like 'open window', 'edit card', 'produce payroll', 'check invoice', 'book theatre', for processes. This spreads the classes (window, card, payroll, invoice, theatre) all over the DFD map. When you look for a class you find it everywhere. Names like 'window manager', 'payroll system' are anathema to structured analysis.

Secondly, the object-oriented view more closely reflects the 'real world' where humans are used to thinking in terms of 'things' which possess both attributes and behaviour. For example, when you think of a bank, you immediately associate it with money and perhaps a number of different types of account such as a cheque account with instant access to money, and a longer-term savings account which provides interest on money but requires, say, three months' notice for withdrawals. The money represents an attribute and the two types of account represent behaviour or services which the bank, as a object, provides.

This advantage is illustrated in the foregoing example of the hospital patients intake system. Through the OO analysis, the responsibilities of individual entities are easily identified. The surgeon is responsible for booking a time slot in an operating theatre. This is obvious from the object interaction diagram (Figure 4.6). However, from the DFD in Appendix A, it is not obvious who is responsible for booking the operating theatre – it is done through a process called Book-Theatre-Slot, but this does not necessarily map directly onto anything in the real world. The benefit is in a clearer means of communication between the analyst and the end user. When the results of this analysis stage are taken into OO design and subsequently into an OO implementation, these stages will also directly reflect the initial description of the problem. Therefore, the learning curve for a new software maintainer should be smaller than that for understanding software systems developed using a traditional structured technique.

The third, and for many the most important, advantage of an OO analysis is in the reuse possibilities from the class hierarchy views of the system. If, at a later date, there is a new requirement to support a different type of hospital ward then the generic Ward class can be reused through inheritance. The additional features of the new ward can simply be added to this generic specification.

The fourth advantage of an OO analysis approach is in its ability to model the user interface to a system. This interface is becoming more important in the world of GUI environments. GUIs are composed of 'objects' with both data and behaviour, which can be modelled easily using OO analysis. However, traditional structured analysis notation provides little help in modelling the user interface.

At the strategic or enterprise modelling stage, proponents of information engineering emphasize data modelling over process modelling.

They claim that the functions in an organization's systems change more frequently than its data. This claim becomes even more valid when an organization adopts a corporate database as a central data source to reduce redundancy and inconsistent usage of data.

Object-oriented analysis can produce an enterprise-wide model. But if the goal is to capture stable data then an object-oriented approach may at first sight appear to be less effective since it automatically joins data with the less-stable control and functional aspects. However, such arguments are not strictly correct! If the data was stable in an information engineering approach then it should be stable in an object-oriented approach. If processing is unstable using an object-oriented approach then it will also be unstable (arguably more unstable) when derived from information engineering. Changes to the less-stable process-oriented aspects can be more manageably introduced through the processing within objects than through the processing defined using a structured methodology simply because of the improved modularity and organization inherent in the object-oriented approach.

4.2.3 Shortcomings of OO analysis

OO analysis techniques are still the subject of much debate and research. Traditional analysis uses a top-down technique. Similar techniques are required for classes. For example, in analysing a banking application, an interest rate, a branch office, a teller machine, a corporate account and a monthly statement are all candidate classes to model during analysis. However, they represent different layers in the problem domain. Research continues into abstraction layering and decomposition techniques for selecting classes during analysis which facilitate such a layered approach.

Another debate is whether inheritance should be considered part of analysis or design. Coad and Yourdon (1990, 1991a) recommend that classification relationships (that is, inheritance relationships) be captured and documented at the analysis stage, whereas Mellor (1990) states that

> 'no analysis approach should incorporate concepts of a pre-chosen design approach. This applies especially to inheritance, which exists only to a limited extent in the real world'.

This mixing of the analysis and design methods is a problem with OO techniques. The problem is particularly important for the software development manager who must identify discrete stages in order to measure project progress. From a management standpoint, it may be desirable to increase artificially the differences between analysis and design to enhance the ability to control and manage OO software development projects.

Although OO analysis is still the subject of considerable research, several methods are now available. Section 4.5 summarizes a selection of these methods.

4.3 OO design

In the OO world, as in other models, there is a distinction between analysis and design. Because of the strong relationship between data and function (behaviour), the transition from analysis to design is easier using objects than in other approaches. In fact, many OO methods distinguish between analysis and design techniques, but not life-cycle stages. In a life-cycle-stage-oriented approach, analysis comes before design, whereas in a technique-oriented approach it is possible to iterate between the techniques. The distinction between OO analysis and design is therefore not always very clear. The classification relationships shown in the class inheritance diagram (Figure 4.4) are often considered a design activity. Indeed, during the design stage these class hierarchy diagrams will be developed further with new classes added where necessary.

Blurring between the traditional boundaries of analysis and design is typical in life cycles which promote a high degree of iteration as in an object-oriented life cycle (refer to Chapter 3). A similar blurring is seen between the design and implementation phases where class implementation begins before the final application design is complete (see Chapter 3).

The analysis phase models the problem domain by deriving classes, logical relationships and interactions between objects. The design phase starts when there is enough analysis information to begin considering system implementation. The design phase invents new classes which enable the analysis to be implemented in the chosen hardware and software environment. It focuses on segmenting an application into groups of objects which support the user interface, business logic and information management aspects of the application.

Design considerations include:

Hardware
- Will the system be centralized or distributed?
- In a distributed system, how are objects located to satisfy performance security, availability and extensibility criteria?
- Are more objects needed to facilitate inter-process communication?

Software

- Are separate processes required – that is, should the design involve one program or several interacting programs?
- What extra classes are required to create a user interface (iconic and dialogue objects)?
- Are additional classes required to facilitate relationship associations?
- If a database environment is being used, what extra classes will be needed to interface with the DBMS?
- Does data redundancy need to be eliminated?
- Are third party class libraries to be used?
- Will objects communicate synchronously or asynchronously (concurrency)?

and so on

Typical classes introduced at this stage include GUI classes, database classes, dialogue and persistent object types, objects to create relationships, objects to provide referential integrity, transactions and concurrency. Objects may be placed in semantic groups or collaborations thereby identifying modules of computation.

4.3.1   Problems with traditional structured design

According to Meyer (1988), traditional top-down functional decomposition has several flaws:

- 'It fails to take the evolutionary nature of software systems into account';
- 'Often the data structure aspect is neglected';
- 'Working top-down does not promote reusability'.

Top-down design imposes a strict order in which actions are executed. This impedes the process of change as system requirements evolve. However, as Meyer (1988) suggests: 'much fruitful design work can be done on individual components before their temporal relationships (that is, the sequences of function calls) are frozen.' Any design should accommodate design changes as easily as possible. Figure 4.8 shows how a change in the requirements of a system necessitates a change in the top of the functional decomposition diagram. This results in much reworking since the lower functions, having been decomposed from the uppermost function, are highly dependent on this main system function.

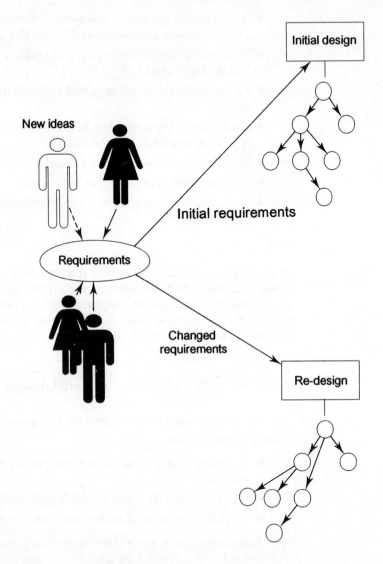

Figure 4.8   The effect of change on a top-down functional design (adapted from Henderson-Sellers, 1990: Copyright 1990, Association for Computing Machinery, Inc.).

The design of a submodule, based on the needs of the higher-level module, does not promote reusability. Reusable software implies developing systems by combining existing components – this is the essence of bottom-up design.

4.3.2   Class and application design

In object-oriented design (OOD) the designer lists the various operations (or methods) which apply to a certain kind of data, and specifies the effect of each operation, but defers specifying the sequencing of actions (or temporal relationships) for as long as possible. OOD is a pick-and-mix approach, where the final application is composed from the classes in a hierarchy, and lends itself more readily to change.

OOD has two separate components which are blended in the development of an application: class design and application design.

Class design

Class design is 'wrapped inside' application design. The design of an application leads on from analysis which identifies the kinds of entities involved. These entities may be tangible objects such as traffic lights, chairs or aeroplanes. They may equally well be abstract concepts such as roles, interactions or incidents. Once these entities are described, application design proceeds by connecting instances of the classes so they interact with each other resulting in a solution to the stated requirements. The main stages in a class design are listed below:

- Identify classes;
- Identify subclasses within each class;
- Identify abstract behaviour of each class;
- Identify common behaviour (abstraction) ;
- Identify specific types of behaviour (specialization)

Figure 4.9 illustrates the process.

The main purposes of class design are to design for reuse and to design in a highly modular way. The process of abstraction and specialization creates better reuse possibilities. Concentrating initially on

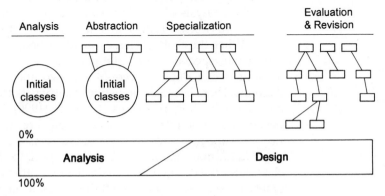

Figure 4.9   Analysis leading to the stages of class design (from Gossain, 1990: Copyright 1990, Association for Computing Machinery, Inc.).

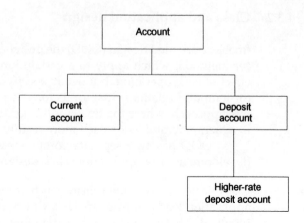

Figure 4.10   An example class hierarchy based on bank accounts.

individual classes rather than the architecture of the end application creates a more modular system.

According to Gossain (1990): 'Finding **abstract classes** is not easy. It may take several iterations before a suitable class can be determined.' No reliable method exists for determining abstract classes; as Gossain (1990) suggests, it largely depends on the experience and ability of the designer. However, as Gossain points out: 'the pre-existence of a class component environment can aid the class design process considerably, both by setting examples of design and by providing useful classes upon which to build or from which to abstract.' Furthermore, 'A truly abstract class is never instantiated. Its behaviour will be general to an extreme.' There may be very few truly abstract classes in a class hierarchy. The abstract classes provide a high-level understanding of the overall problem domain. They may be associated directly with the classes derived from the analysis phase. For example, a current account and deposit account are two forms of an abstract class called Account.

When the abstract classes are identified, the next stage is to design the various specializations of a particular class. For example, a current account and a deposit account are two specializations of a generic Account. There is usually a distinct interplay between the generalization and specialization processes. Gossain (1990) indicates that in class design: 'common pitfalls are subclassing carelessly and over-specialization. The former leads to unbalanced, wasteful designs and can also result in too many similar classes. Over-specialization causes too detailed classes, for the design of the main classes within a domain requires generality to be preserved in all but the lowest level of abstraction.' Gossain (1990) indicates that 'A further subclass of Deposit Account could be a higher-rate deposit account, requiring notice before withdrawal.' Figure

4.10 illustrates the resulting class hierarchy. Gossain (1990) indicates that 'as each layer is introduced into a solution, we are provided further possibilities of reuse, at different granularities.'

Evaluation and revision involve examining classes at each level to identify what Gossain terms **inter-class** and **intra-class** modifications.

Inter-class modifications include the following, which are summarized from Gossain (1990):

- Distribution of behaviour among classes. Classes should be examined so that their behaviour can be verified for consistency with objects of that class.
- Classes may merge. Two classes can sometimes perform very similar tasks. In such cases the classes may be merged into one, or the two classes may become specializations of a common parent providing shared functionality.
- Classes may require specialization if they are deemed to be too general.
- Classes may require generalization if they are too specific. Such a decision might be based on reuse considerations.
- Conjunct classes requiring redefinition. If a class represents behaviour characteristic of two or more classes then it must be split appropriately.

Intra-class alterations include the following, which are again summarized from Gossain (1990):

- Modifying a class interface, leading to a change in parameters.
- New private methods may be required in a class.
- It may be possible to remove superfluous class members.

The product of the class design stage should be a set of classes arranged in a number of hierarchies. The higher-level classes match the classes identified from the analysis stage and the lowest-level classes combine to form the ultimate application. During the class design stage, application design is considered. This results in additional classes for the class hierarchy in order to create an overall solution to the original requirements.

Application design

End-application design is a top-down and bottom-up process, designing the application from the existing building blocks. Additional classes are required as a result of overall architectural issues. For example, an aeroplane and a pilot are tangible objects but these two entities may be bound together by the incidence of a flight. The flight is also an object

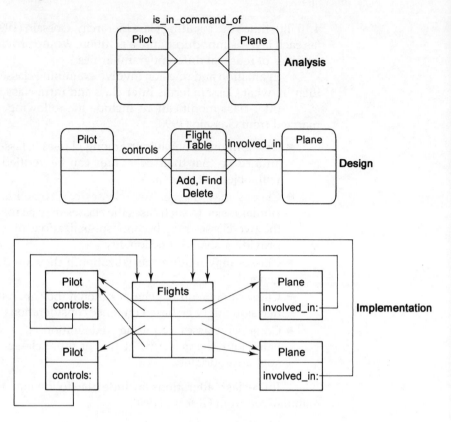

Figure 4.11   Analysis to design to implementation.

which describes the particular aeroplane and the particular pilot as well as passengers, cargo and so on. The class describing a Flight may not be identified until the application design stage. The pilot and passenger objects might be abstracted to a common class called Person. Pilot and Passenger classes would then inherit behaviour from Person. Linking two classes by inheritance means that future improvements to the super-class will become improvements to the subclass automatically.

Relationships between classes defined during analysis indicate the interactions which occur between the classes as defined in the state-ment of requirements. These relationships become part of the design of the application. For example, the pilot 'is_in_command_of' a particu-lar aeroplane would be represented at the analysis stage as shown in Figure 4.11.

From the analysis stage two classes are identified, Pilot and Plane, with a many:many relationship between them. Over time a pilot can command many planes and a plane can be commanded by many pilots. In this example, during the design process a decision is taken to create an additional class called Flight_Table to handle instances of flights. A flight connects one pilot with one plane. During implementation a decision is taken to implement the Flight_Table as a two-dimensional array of pointers to objects. Thus the many:many relationship is implemented.

The reader should refer to Chapter 3 which presents a software life cycle reflecting the two distinct design activities – class and application design.

4.3.3 Benefits from OO design

Common to all methodologies is the goal of creating a 'good' design. The term 'good' refers to a design which is clear, easy to implement and easy to maintain. There are many facets to a good design. In particular, the idea of modularity is very important. Myers (1978) and Yourdon and Constantine (1979) indicate the importance of two factors in determining the quality of a design, namely coupling and cohesion.

Coupling measures a module's dependence on others. It identifies the extent and method used in maintaining data connections with other modules. A design which exhibits complex and numerous interconnection between modules is 'tightly coupled' as opposed to a simpler 'weakly coupled' design with few connections. Tightly coupled designs are difficult to maintain because of the heavy interdependence between modules. This makes the overall system difficult to understand and blurs the ramifications on the overall system of a given change to one module.

Cohesion is a qualitative measure of how well the parts of a system 'hold together'. Functional cohesion, where all parts of a module contribute towards the same single purpose, is best. Designs exhibiting sequential cohesion, where the output from one module is used as the input to the next, are almost as good as functionally cohesive designs in terms of maintainability. At the other end of the spectrum is **coincidental cohesion** where the components of a module are combined for no good reason. This is extremely poor and tends to result from chopping up a monolithic piece of code into smaller pieces in an attempt to create a 'modular' system!

This section discusses the merits of an OO design based on these principles of good design. The main benefits from OOD result from the inherent modularity which comes with encapsulation and information hiding. The client/server relationship between objects creates a framework for weak coupling and strong cohesion.

Modularity The object-oriented paradigm provides natural support for decomposing a system into modules. In this case the modules are classes. This means that not only does the design process support modularity, but the im-

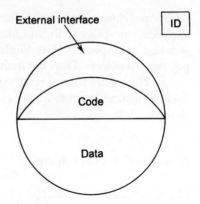

Figure 2.2 revisited   Inherent modularity through encapsulation.

plementation process also supports it through the class definition. Encapsulation binds modules tightly and creates more easily maintained systems. Referring back to Figure 2.2 from the basic concepts in object-orientation (Chapter 2), we see the idea of a tight shell which creates a modular system.

Information hiding

One objective of the design process is to hide the attributes of an object from the users of that object. The methods in the public interface represent the possible behaviours of the object. One of the responsibilities of these methods is to provide for the controlled access to the attributes of the object. The representation of these attributes and the corresponding implementation of the methods is (or should be) hidden from users of the class. Referring back to Figure 2.3 from the principles of object orientation (Chapter 2) shows how the external view of an object differs from its

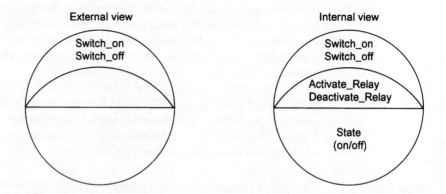

Figure 2.3 revisited   Information-hiding in object-oriented systems.

internal implementation. This enables the internal design to change without necessarily affecting either the external interface or other objects which communicate with the changed one.

Establishing 'contracts' between interacting objects through the external object interfaces produces clearly defined interfaces and leads to weak coupling between objects.

Weak coupling   Classes are designed as collections of data and the set of allowable methods to act upon that data. The class interface methods enable access to, or modification of, the internal data in that class only. This leads to fewer connections between classes.

The couplings between classes come from two sources. The 'containing' relationship between classes (where one class contains another class) results in a coupling between classes. The other class interaction is where the interface methods of a class may take instances of another class as parameters. Thus, a pointer to an object may be a parameter in a call to a method of another object type. These design characteristics tend to increase the coupling between objects and can cause knock-on effects when object specifications change.

Strong cohesion   A class is a naturally cohesive module because it is a model of an entity. However, the inheritance mechanism can weaken module cohesion, particularly if the class hierarchy is not well designed. The data and methods inherited from another class form a separate group from those data and methods defined within the new class. All the pieces should come together to represent one concept and this falls within the category of **functional cohesion** – the strongest form of cohesion.

Extensibility   Inheritance supports extending designs in several ways. First, inheritance facilitates reuse to ease the development of new definitions. Second, the polymorphic property of the typing system in OO programming languages supports extensible designs. Thus, instances of new classes can be introduced and handled using parameters in an identical manner to existing object types.

By concentrating on class design and then developing the final application design from this class design, the temporal relations between functions (which is a problem with structured design) are reduced. The emphasis in class design is on creating a reusable and extensible framework of classes whereas in structured design the emphasis is on designing an application. It is therefore unlikely that the same concentration on creating reusable generic functions will take place in a traditional structured design.

4.3.4   Shortcomings of OOD

There are four main difficulties with OOD at present. These are:

(1) Identifying classes.

(2) Blurred boundaries between design and both analysis and implementation.

(3) Variable degrees of object-oriented support in existing CASE tools.

(4) Elaborate and complex notations.

The problem of identifying classes from the problem domain is most apparent for real-time software developers. Traditional structured analysis and design supports both data- and process-oriented views of a system. The data-oriented view is the preferred view of information system developers, whereas, for real-time developers, the preferred view is the process view. In the data-oriented view, a data entity may translate into a class. But a process (or method) does not necessarily translate to a class. Hence a problem can arise!

Design concentrates on creating a solution from the stated requirements. Both real-time and information system developers experience some difficulties identifying classes within an application. Skill in OOD builds with experience. While identifying Objects may be more intuitive at the analysis stage when modelling the problem domain, it is definitely not intuitive at the internal software design stage.

The second problem relates to the blurred boundaries between design and both analysis and implementation. The boundary between analysis and design has been discussed in the analysis section of this chapter. The boundary between design and implementation is blurred because class implementation can begin during class design and before application design is complete. There only needs to be a few classes designed before a class developer begins implementing them. Application implementation proceeds by constructing groups of inter-working classes, and this can happen in parallel with both the class and application design. Therefore a project manager cannot easily determine when the design stage is complete, just as he/she cannot determine accurately when the analysis stage is complete. It may be necessary to impose a strict discipline on a development team to measure progress. At the very least, analysis should be staged such that preliminary analysis is completed before any design work begins. Similarly first-stage class design should be complete before any implementation work begins. The dynamic behaviour of the class design, particularly in the early stages, suggests that class implementation ought to be left until the class hierarchy begins to stabilize. Only experience will show how long is required for this to happen in a given development environment.

Booch (1991) suggests that productivity can be measured by a practice of continuous integration. Progress is measured by counting the number of stable classes in the logical design. Over time, as the class design stabilizes, a smaller and smaller percentage of classes in the overall library will change from one day to the next. At some appropriate stage, when the percentage reaches a lower threshold, class implementation can begin.

Since analysis and class design, or class design and class implementation are partially parallel activities, there may be a larger number of resources working on a project at a given time than there would be on a comparable traditional software development. This in itself presents greater management problems.

The third difficulty with OOD is the variation in degrees to which so-called 'object-oriented' design methods support the basic principles of object orientation. Some OOA&D methods may not be fully supported through CASE tools. This arises because some tools were initially developed to support structured techniques and are being modified to incorporate OO methods. Many of these modifications fall short of a full OO support model. Of course this is a transitory problem resulting from the immaturity of the whole area. But careful evaluation is required to ensure that a suitable design method and tool are purchased.

Lastly, the notations which accompany most object-oriented design methods are very complex (see Appendix B for example). Experience with structured analysis and design shows that the most successful notations (such as entity relationship diagrams and data flow diagrams – see Appendix A) do not involve verbose symbology. Unfortunately object orientation introduces new concepts such as polymorphism and dynamic binding which will always be more difficult to represent pictorially. This reinforces the need for good CASE tool support in object-oriented design.

4.4 A reference model for analysis and design

The purpose of this section is to define a common reference model which you can use to compare object-oriented analysis and design methods. The reference model describes the main characteristics of an OO analysis and/or design method. It is a superset of the main features to be found in any given method. The reference model described here has been developed especially for this book and should not be confused with any other reference model such as that published by the Object Management Group (OMG). The OMG reference model includes many more features than used here.

The reference model is introduced at this stage before Section 4.5 which summarizes several methods, describing their main features as well as those ideas which are special to one or other method. Section 4.7 then raises a number of questions to ask about a method if you are considering which one to choose. Section 4.7 includes tables of features for many methods. You may prefer to read through the methods first and then study this reference model. In either case, you will need to consider this reference model when reading through the tables of features in Section 4.7.

Many object-oriented methods distinguish between analysis and design techniques, but not stages in the software development life cycle. In a life-cycle-oriented approach, analysis comes before design whereas in a technique-based approach it is possible to iterate between the techniques. This degree of consistency is the product of using a single unified object model in analysis, then in design, and ultimately in the implementation.

An object model is one of the mainstays of an object-oriented analysis and/or design method, but there are other distinct components making up an overall reference model:

(1) Object model concepts

(2) Techniques

(3) Notation

(4) Process

(5) Deliverables

(6) Quality criteria

Techniques provide ways to manipulate the object model concepts and generally involve using some kind of pictorial *notation*. Techniques are strung together to form a complete *process*. Methods should provide output (typically diagrams and documents) at distinct stages in the process. The outputs should be measurable against a set of clearly defined quality criteria.

To compare different methods some common reference model is required. I have developed this reference model based on the above six aspects of a method. Many of the concepts used within an object model have been described in Chapter 2 under the heading Object concepts. Figures 4.12 and 4.13 illustrate the components of the reference model for object-oriented analysis and design. The following text explains the model and the terms used in the figures in detail.

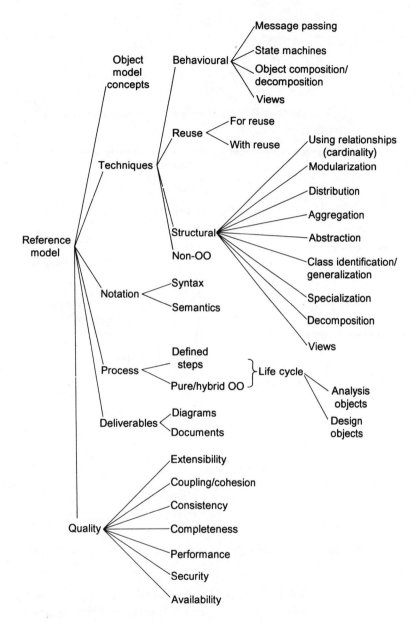

Figure 4.12   Composition of the reference model.

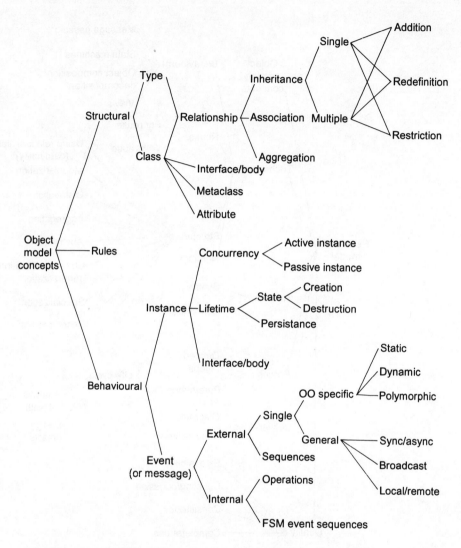

Figure 4.13   Decomposition of the object model part of the reference model.

The reader should note that these figures are intended primarily to represent component relationships. For example, in Figure 4.12, message passing, state machines, object composition/decomposition and views are all components (or elements) of behavioural techniques.

The reference model (level 1 in Figure 4.12, reading from left to right) is a generic model developed from consideration of several existing methods, which seeks to identify the general properties and characteristics of an object-oriented analysis and design method.

4.4.1   Object model concepts (level 2)

An *object model concept,* in this context, represents one of the constituents or building blocks on which the general object-oriented approach is founded. Concepts are shown in Figure 4.13.

Concepts break down into *structural, behavioural* and *rules.*

Structural concepts (level 3)

This relates to a description of aspects of a system concerned with the associations (cardinality and inheritance) and visibility amongst classes or types. These are essentially static views of a system.

Static concepts break down into *type*-related and *class*-related.

Type (level 4)

A type represents a definition of some set of *instances* with similar behaviour. The behaviour is normally expressed by the operations defined on the type, without regard for the potential implementation of the type. A type is a semantic property.

Class (level 4)

A class is a description of a group of *instances* with similar properties, common behavioural semantics and relationships. A class represents a particular implementation of a type.

Relationship (level 5)

A relationship represents some logical connection between classes or types.

Inheritance (level 6)

This is a special kind of relationship between two *classes* or *types* which normally represents generalization/specialization. Classes or types bound by this kind of relationship share attributes and operations. Inheritance can be either **single** – where a class or type can have no more than one parent, or **multiple** – where a class or type can have zero, one or more parents.

Inheritance in a type hierarchy is commonly called subtyping/supertyping. Such relationships apply the 'is_a' nature of inheritance where the parent 'is_a' supertype of the child. Typing is most commonly used at the analysis stage in a software development life cycle where the emphasis is on determining *what* a system must do rather than *how* it will accomplish it.

Inheritance in a class hierarchy can exhibit more features than that in a type hierarchy. Class inheritance may exhibit **addition** – where the subclass merely adds some extra properties (attributes or methods) over what is inherited from its superclass(es). Class inheritance can also involve **redefinition** – where some of the inherited properties are re-defined. Class inheritance may also exhibit **restriction** – where only some properties of the superclass are inherited by the subclass. These specific forms of inheritance are dependent on the capabilities of the ultimate programming language.

Association (level 6)	An **association** between two types or classes represents some logical relationship between the classes. A **using** association is a relationship denoting that an instance of one class makes use of an instance of another. **Using** associations may have a cardinality indicating that an instance of one class is associated with many instances of another class – such as a Teacher 'is_responsible' for many Pupils. **Using** relationships amongst classes indicates message-passing interactions between corresponding instances.
Aggregation (level 6)	An aggregation relationship between classes indicates components which combine to form the whole, or are part of the whole. The whole may be a high-level class (an Abstract class) that encapsulates the constituent lower-level classes. Constituent classes may have associated relationships between themselves (either Using or Whole-Part). The encapsulation may provide lexical scoping, that is, where the constituents are invisible outside the encapsulating class, and don't have access to the world outside. In this case the encapsulating class provides an interface for communication between inside and outside. Alternatively the constituents may have access to, and be accessed from, outside – in which case lexical scoping does not apply.
Interface/body (level 5)	A class is composed of two parts – namely an interface and a body. The interface defines the services which that class offers to users. The body is the detailed implementation of the class. It is an internal structure not visible outside the class itself.
Metaclass (level 5)	A **metaclass** is a higher-order class, responsible for describing other classes. Metaclasses provide a useful way to manage *instances*, viz. create and destroy.
Attribute (level 5)	An attribute is a data element associated with a class or type. It represents some information relevant to a class which must be held within the class.
Rules (level 3)	A rule is a policy or condition that must be satisfied by an object type. For example, 'account numbers must be unique for type "Account"'.
Behavioural concepts (level 3)	This relates to a description of a system in terms of concepts that are significant during the execution of the system. Behavioural concepts describe the dynamics of an environment. Dynamic concepts relate to *instances* of classes (that is, the run-time occurrences of classes) and the *events* – or *messages* – which pass between such instances.
Instances (level 4)	An **instance** is a creation of a given class. The class is the blueprint from which any number of instances may be created.

Lifetime (level 5)	An instance has a definite **lifetime** from when it is created to when it is destroyed. In between these two events, an instance may spend time in a number of interim states. For example, the Inpatient instances used in the scenario of Section 4.2.1 can assume the states: Created, Admitted, Operation_scheduled, Recovery, Discharged and Terminated.

      If the lifetime of an instance can exceed the lifetime of the application or process that created it (such as happens in database storage) then the instance is said to be **persistent**.

Interface/body (level 5)

As with a class, an instance consists of an interface and a body. The interface describes the services which that instance can offer to other instances. The body describes the internal state and behaviour of the instance through the operations controlling the instance.

Concurrency (level 5)

Instances of a class can perform part of an overall process or they can be separate processes in their own right. Instances can therefore execute either in parallel (**active**) or in serial (**passive**) with others.

Events – or messages (level 4)

Events are stimuli within instances. An external event is a message received by an instance. An internal event is an event generated internally within an instance which may cause a state change (through a finite state machine) or other action (defined by an internal operation) to be taken within that instance. Such actions may involve generating messages to be sent to other instances – whereby a sequence of events (or messages) may ensue.

      Various mechanisms may be used to deliver a message to its destination, depending on the capabilities of the implementation language. For example, a message may employ static binding – where the destination is known at application compile-time. Conversely, a message may employ dynamic binding, where the message destination cannot be resolved until application run-time. In the case of dynamically bound messages, message-sending polymorphism may result – where the same message may be sent to more than one type (class) of instance.

      Messages may be categorized as either **asynchronous** (where the message is sent from originator to receiver and the originator continues processing – as would happen between two active instances), or **synchronous** (where the thread of control passes from the originating instance to the receiving instance – as would happen where both instances were part of the one overall process). Messages may also be sent in broadcast mode where there are multiple destinations. Where an overall system is distributed amongst several processes which may execute on the same or separate hardware platforms, messages may be either **local** or **remote**.

4.4.2   Techniques (level 2)

A technique is a set of guidelines for identifying occurrences of the *concepts* and developing associations between those occurrences.

Techniques decompose into those for manipulating behavioural and structural views of a system. Techniques for developing structural views may include ways of identifying classes; abstraction; generalization and specialization; decomposition into finer and finer levels of detail; aggregation with or without lexical encapsulation; logical grouping into modules; and distribution around a local or wide area network.

Behavioural views of a system may involve techniques for developing message-passing relationships between instances; state machines within instances; object composition from lower-level instances (logical groupings); and support for different 'views' of an instance depending on the services which that instance is offering to particular client instances (via a client/server contractual notion of a relationship).

Reuse (level 3)   A method may provide techniques for designing systems for future reuse and designing systems based on reusing existing components from previous projects. The reuse could be reuse of analysis or design information.

A method may, in some cases, employ traditional structured techniques as well as object-oriented techniques. For example, some methods use traditional structured techniques for designing the processing within an object (internal object behaviour).

4.4.3   Notation (level 2)

The notation is the symbolic representation of the *concepts*. The notation is combined in a prescribed way via a *technique(s)* to develop **diagrams** showing associations and/or interactions between occurrences of the *concepts*. Methods are generally strong on notation illustrated through example. Examples are important but the notation syntax and semantics should be rigorously defined within the method.

4.4.4   Process (level 2)

The process represents the overall procedure involved in developing one or more *deliverable(s)*. A process may encompass many *techniques* and a *notation* to produce many **diagrams**, **documents** and other such deliverables. The process dictates the order in which techniques are used and determines what the (interim) deliverables are used for. It acts as a general road map, showing how to progress from origin to destination. The overall software development process is governed by a life cycle which represents an overall process from analysis to implementation (and possibly maintenance). However, within the analysis and design stages there are processes which may develop interim deliverables to be used in subsequent techniques within design or implementation.

The objects manipulated during analysis relate to the problem domain. During design, the object types manipulated include presentation objects, dialogue objects, persistent objects, transaction objects, objects supporting relationships and objects supporting the management of distributed systems. The method should show how to build increasingly detailed models of systems using such object types.

The process may support an evolutionary (or hybrid) OO life cycle involving a mixture of OO and non-OO techniques, or it may enforce the use of OO techniques in a more revolutionary (or pure) life cycle.

4.4.5   Deliverables (level 2)

A deliverable is some tangible asset derived from a technique or as the end result of a process involving several techniques. A deliverable may therefore be a design document, a diagram, a formal textual description, a complete executable program, and so on.

4.4.6   Quality criteria (level 2)

Quality criteria are designed checks, the main purpose of which is to ensure that some aspect of a technique or process has been adhered to, or to assess the effectiveness of a deliverable. Methods may provide some means of checking the following quality criteria:

- **Extensibility.** Does the method provide any suggestions for checking on the ease of modification and enhancement of a design?
- **Coupling/cohesion.** Are there any guidelines for checking the degree of coupling between classes or instances, and for assessing the degree of cohesion exhibited by an instance?
- **Consistency.** Are there guidelines for checking the consistency of a class or instance across the different views and diagrams that the particular class or instance appears in?
- **Completeness.** Is there any way of checking the completeness of a particular design?

- **Performance.** Are there any guidelines for assessing the performance of a particular part of a design?
- **Security and availability.** Are there any checks to ensure that security and availability considerations have been made?

Many of these quality criteria will only be practical to assess using a CASE tool which supports a given method.

4.5   Summary of some OO analysis and design methods

This section summarizes several OO analysis and design methods:

- OO analysis and design (Coad and Yourdon, 1991a, 1991b)
- Booch method (Booch, 1991)
- OOSE (Jacobson, 1992)
- OSMOSYS (Winter Partners)
- OO systems analysis (Shlaer and Mellor, 1988)
- OMT (Rumbaugh, 1991)
- RDD including the CRC method (Beck, 1989; Wirfs-Brock *et al.*, 1990)
- OORASS (Reenskaug, 1989, 1991)
- HOOD method (HOOD, 1989a, 1989b)
- OOSD (Wasserman *et al.*, 1990)
- Object-oriented software development (Colbert, 1989)

This selection of methods was chosen because they illustrate varying degrees of support for object orientation and clearly show the current state of the market – with pure and hybrid approaches satisfying the revolutionary and evolutionary migration paths respectively. The list is not exhaustive, some 30+ methods currently exist, including PTECH from Associative Design Technology, Fusion from Hewlett-Packard, Marketing-to-Design from ICL Ltd, Design Ways from Design Technology Support, and many others.

Each of these methods is summarized according to the defined process, notation, pragmatics and finally a brief discussion of the strong and weak points of the method. The process relates to the defined steps within the overall method which lead from problem through to a solution. The notation refers to the diagramming and other documentary techniques/outputs and associated techniques used within particular stages of the process. The pragmatics relate to the management of the process through the process and associated CASE tool support.

Where a method is widely used or offers some particularly interesting ideas, more detail is provided. Other methods are heavily summarized, picking out the salient features only.

4.5.1   OO analysis and design (Coad and Yourdon, 1991a, 1991b)

Coad and Yourdon have two books published. One covers OO analysis while the other covers OO design. Their philosophy is one of OO analysis resulting from a merger of information modelling, object-oriented programming languages and knowledge-based systems (KBS) – the concepts which have a solid basis in underlying principles for managing complexity. Information modelling provides the constructs analogous to attributes, instance connections, generalization–specialization and whole–part. OOPLs and KBS provide encapsulation of attributes and services, communication with messages and inheritance.

The analysis process

At the analysis stage Coad and Yourdon (1991a) identify five major layers:

(1) **The class-&-object layer.** An object is an abstraction of data and process, reflecting the capabilities of a system to keep information about or interact with something in the world. A class is the blueprint for objects. This layer is concerned with finding suitable classes to describe the problem domain. The method suggests ways to identify classes such as looking at structures, external systems, devices, events remembered, roles played, operational procedures, organizational units *and* physical locations. The output from this stage will be a set of classes with names but little else. These diagrams are called class-&-object diagrams.

(2) **The structure layer.** Classification structure portrays class member organization, reflecting generalization–specialization. Assembly structure shows aggregation, reflecting whole and component parts. The output from this stage is a set of inheritance and whole–part relationships between the classes/objects identified previously, with the possible addition of classes identified as a result of considering the structure. The results from this stage are (i) generalization–specialization structure diagrams and (ii) whole–part structure diagrams.

(3) **The subject layer.** A subject is a means for controlling how much of a model a reader considers at one time. It is a way of segmenting a problem, creating a boundary between groups of closely related classes. Subject diagrams are created at this stage.

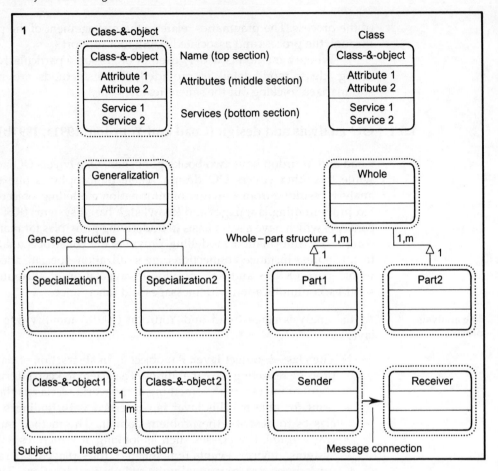

Figure 4.14   Coad/Yourdon notation.

(4) **The attribute layer.** An attribute is a data element used to describe an instance of a class. At this stage the method adds instance connections – representing associative relationships (with cardinalities) between classes or objects. This stage gives rise to (i) attribute diagrams and (ii) instance connection diagrams.

(5) **The service layer.** A service is the processing to be performed upon receipt of a message. This is the first point at which the dynamics of the environment being analysed are considered. The method introduces the object lifetime concept of state. The services an object must offer and the associated messages sent and received by an object are analysed and added to the identified objects. The output from this stage is a set of objects/classes with specified services and message connections between them. The

results from this stage are (i) service diagrams; (ii) message connection diagrams; (iii) service/state tables; and (iv) object state diagrams.

Notation

Figure 4.14 illustrates the Coad/Yourdon notation used for object-oriented analysis and design.

The design process

Coad and Yourdon (1991b) also use the above five major layers in object-oriented design. The same notation is used in both the analysis and design stages. The five layers to the method are applied to four components during design:

- **Problem domain component.** This component takes the results of the analysis phase and adds detail to the identified classes to make them implementable such as including existing classes from commercially available libraries. The method talks about ways to design reusability into the classes brought from the analysis phase.

- **Human interaction component.** This component is concerned with the design of the user interface. It introduces additional objects required to create a user interface such as presentation and dialogue objects.

- **Task management component.** This component is concerned with identifying the tasks (or processes) in the system. Architectural issues are considered at this stage. Design considerations include threads of control within an application such as concurrency and task management across several processors. How tasks get scheduled and how they intercommunicate are also part of this component.

- **Data management component.** This component is concerned with the data aspects of the system, such as how data is stored and retrieved and whether flat-file, relational or object-oriented schema should be used. The issue of normalized data (1st–5th normal form – for example Date (1986)) to remove data redundancy is considered here.

Pragmatics

The method has been embedded in a CASE tool called OOA*Tool*. It is available for the Apple Macintosh, and IBM PC under Windows 3 and OS/2. The tool organizes design information into OOA models, OOA model filters and OOA drawings. The OOA model is organized into the five layers mentioned above. OOA model filters are created to control the amount of the underlying model that will be seen by a user, for example, filtering out all unnecessary detail for review by senior management. OOA drawings are the drawings that, together with the related filters, make up a model. Changes made to one drawing in the model are automatically reflected in the remaining drawings in the same model. The tool does not generate code.

Object International Inc. has also developed a CASE tool supporting the design stage within the overall method – called OOD*Tool*. Both OOA*Tool* and OOD*Tool* are evolving products, however they are relatively inexpensive and represent a good way to gain a deeper insight into OO analysis and design without spending a lot of money. They are available from Object International Inc. (see vendor references section for address and contact numbers).

Discussion

I like the simplicity of the notation used in this method – an observation borne out by the fact that it has been adopted (albeit in a slightly modified form) by many other method developers. The documentation for the analysis phase is better than that for design at present. The design phase is somewhat sketchy and as the authors admit, it is likely to evolve and develop over time. The analysis text is into a second edition while the design is (at the time of writing) still in first edition.

While the method clearly differentiates between analysis and design, it would be helpful to have some examples showing the interplay between these two phases in more detail. Instead the method treats the two phases separately, although one good point is that the same notation is used in analysis and design so there is no need for a transformation between analysis and design.

The method does not prescribe a development life cycle. Instead the authors suggest that the various techniques be used in any combination and sequence that suit. There is some merit in this approach, but I think an overall life-cycle strategy with some defined milestones and how to measure them would help software development managers with the management of projects using the method. In particular, the method could provide guidelines on the types of staff required, the interplay between these staff and the stages of development when they are required. There is little discussion of general project management issues.

4.5.2   Booch method

Booch (1991) defines a method and graphical notation which has its roots in the Ada community. It is most applicable to the design of real-time systems. This method is very popular and several workers have developed OOD methods based on it. The Booch method supports classes, objects, inheritance, message passing and polymorphism.

The design process

Booch suggests that this is an incremental design process with continuous refinement to existing classes, unearthing more classes in the process in a spiral development model. The steps performed for each cycle in the spiral are:

- Identify classes and objects at a given level of abstraction.
- Identify the semantics of these classes and objects.
- Identify the relationships among these classes and objects.
- Implement these objects and classes.

Booch separates the logical and physical designs of a system; the logical design involves class and object structure while the physical design involves module and process architectures. The supporting notation for these views includes class and object diagrams, as well as module and process diagrams.

Booch also separates the static views from the dynamic views, indicating that class, object, module and process views primarily depict static elements while state transition diagrams and timing diagrams illustrate the more dynamic aspects of a system such as object lifetime and message-passing sequences, although message-passing sequences can also be shown on object diagrams.

Using the Booch method, the designer firstly identifies objects. The process of abstraction enables common classes to be identified. Mechanisms are then defined. A mechanism is a composite object, where the constituent objects work together to provide some behaviour that satisfies a software requirement. A mechanism may make use of several objects, and a number of mechanisms combine to specify the overall system. The next section which details the Booch notation includes an example Booch mechanism.

During the second step, the designer identifies the semantics of the classes identified previously. Here the classes and objects are viewed from the perspective of their interfaces – defining the externally observable behaviour of the objects. Booch suggests trying to describe the lifetime of an object from creation to destruction, including the characteristic behaviour.

During the third step, Booch advocates the use of class–responsibility–collaboration (CRC) cards (Beck, 1989) as a good technique for identifying the relationships among classes and objects. This technique is very popular and is described in a subsequent section describing the RDD method (Wirfs-Brock *et al.*, 1990). Booch also advocates the use of prototyping at this stage – particularly when designing the user interface. The product of this step will be a complete logical design of the system.

The final step in the Booch method involves implementation

design considerations for the classes and objects. This involves allocating classes and objects to modules, and programs to processes.

Notation

The Booch notation is rich in symbols. The reader should refer to Booch (1991) for full details. The diagrams presented here show only a subset of the full symbology.

The Booch notation is quite complicated and in order to explain the symbols properly, reference is made to the hospital scenario introduced in Section 4.2.1.

Class diagrams

Booch discusses the different types of relationship that can exist between two classes:

- Inheritance
- Using

Note that two other class relationship types are defined in Booch (1991) – namely *metaclass* and *instantiates*. For the purpose of clarity these relationship types have been omitted here.

An important feature of the Booch method is in its distinction between the parts of a class (or object) into the *interface* and the *implementation*. Booch states that the Using relationship (where one class uses another class) can take two forms: either a class's interface can *use* another class; or a class's implementation can *use* another class. In many cases these distinctions between interface and implementation are design issues which must be made quite early in the design process. Class *using* relationships imply that some form of messaging interaction will take place between instances of the connected classes.

In the case of **interface using relationships**, the used class is visible through the interface of the using class, in other words, the used class can be accessed directly via the interface to the using class. However, in the case of **implementation using relationships** the used class cannot be accessed directly through the using class's interface. Booch provides symbols for representing each of these *using* relationships.

Figure 4.15 illustrates the main symbols used in creating Booch class diagrams.

Using these symbols Figures 4.16 and 4.17 illustrate some class diagrams which could be developed from the hospital example scenario (introduced in Section 4.2.1).

Booch does not provide symbols to describe mandatory relationships, although optional relationships can be described using a cardinality of zero. Figure 4.16 is incomplete because the *using* relationships do not indicate whether the interface or implementation is to be used. Figure 4.20 develops part of this diagram further (specifically the Inpatient/

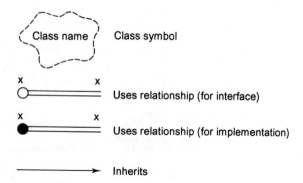

Figure 4.15   Symbols used in developing Booch class diagrams.
Notes: (i) For inheritance relationships, the arrow-head points towards the
superclass. (ii) The cardinalities of class relationships are denoted by 0,1 or m
positioned as illustrated by an 'X' in the above diagram.

Ward relationship) to show full details of interface and implementation
using relationships in class diagrams.
    Figure 4.17 illustrates a Booch inheritance diagram which should
be compared with Figure 4.4.

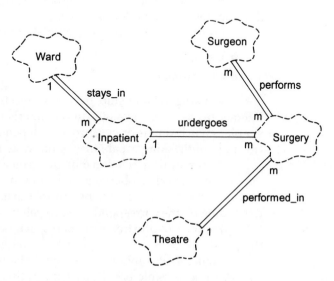

Figure 4.16   An incomplete Booch 'Using' class diagram.

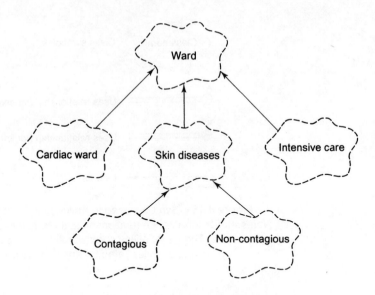

Figure 4.17   A Booch 'Inheritance' class diagram.

Object diagrams

Booch object diagrams provide a means of describing the dynamic behaviour of a system under design. Message sequences between interacting objects can be modelled and collections of interacting objects (called mechanisms) can be assembled. Object diagrams can be decomposed to show further interacting objects, thereby providing a way to develop finer and finer levels of detail.

Booch provides two types of relationship between objects:

- Using
- Containment

A **using** relationship between objects implies that the objects interact by sending messages to one another. These messages may be simple, asynchronous or synchronous depending on the threading control and multitasking capabilities of the system under design.

A **containing** relationship between objects indicates that one object contains other objects as sub-components. Such objects may or may not be directly accessible from outside the containing object, depending on the corresponding class relationships.

Figure 4.18 illustrates the Booch symbols used for creating object diagrams.

Figure 4.19 combines these symbols in an object diagram which suggests one possible Booch mechanism that could be used to describe the admission of a person into a hospital.

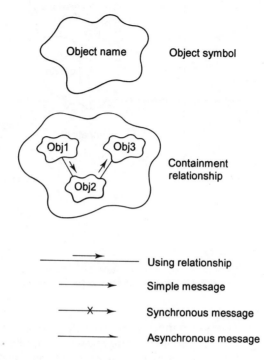

Figure 4.18   Symbols used in Booch object diagrams.

Figure 4.20 illustrates the connection between Booch class and object diagrams. It takes the hospital scenario a little further by considering a ward to contain both beds and monitoring equipment which might be modelled as classes.

In the class specification of Figure 4.20, the class Ward uses the class Inpatient in its interface. This enables objects of class Inpatient to be checked into a Ward through the Ward interface. Many Inpatients may stay_in a Ward. A Ward may house many Beds. A Ward uses Beds through its implementation. An Inpatient does not need to know anything about a Bed – the Ward handles that detail and so the Bed is hidden from the Inpatient.

Now consider the object diagram in Figure 4.20. This shows that Beds and Monitoring equipment are *contained* within a Ward – such detail is not shown explicitly in the corresponding class diagram.

Inpatients are admitted to a ward and released from the ward in this scenario – they need to know nothing else about a hospital ward.

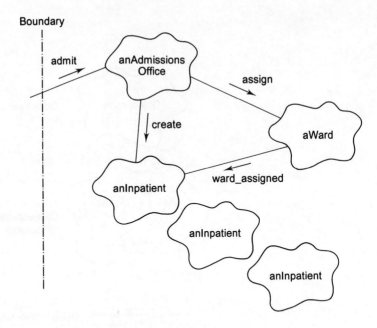

Figure 4.19   A Booch mechanism (object diagram).

Timing diagram

The Booch mechanism depicted in Figure 4.19 can be compared with the Booch timing diagram shown in Figure 4.21. This timing diagram illustrates the time ordering of events between three interacting objects.

The event Admit causes an operation new_patient to be invoked within anAdmissionsOffice. A new instance of anInpatient is created and an operation initialize is invoked within anInpatient. Control returns to anAdmissionsOffice which then sends a message Assign to aWard. This causes the object aWard to invoke an operation add_patient which in turn causes the message ward_assigned to be sent to anInpatient. The object anInpatient receives the message ward_assigned which invokes an operation change_state. After the object anInpatient has changed its state, control eventually passes back to anAdmissionsOffice.

This example illustrates the connection between the events illustrated in the object diagram of Figure 4.19 and the internal operations invoked within objects shown in Figure 4.21. Figure 4.21 also shows the creation of an instance of anInpatient.

State transition diagram

In Booch state transition diagrams, states within an object are depicted by circles enclosing the state name. Transitions between states are depicted by arrows between circles. Referring back to the states which an Inpatient can assume during its lifetime which were detailed in Section

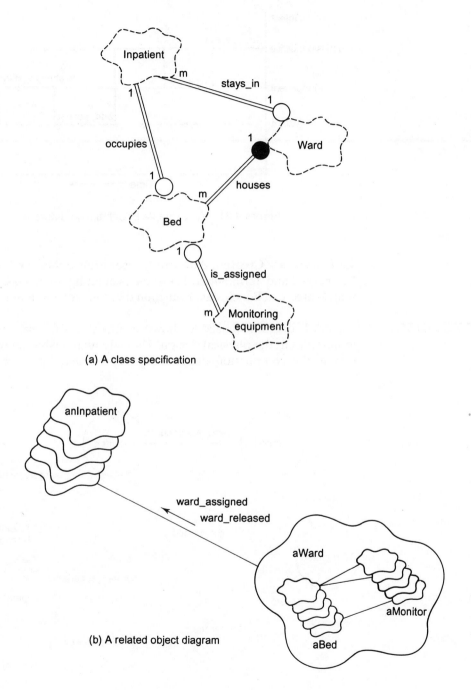

Figure 4.20   Associated Booch class and object diagrams.

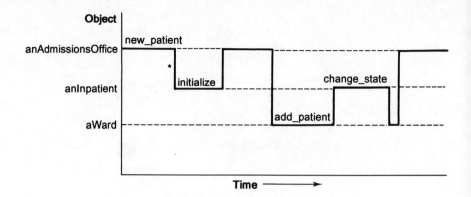

Figure 4.21   An example Booch timing diagram.

4.2.1, these are Created, Admitted, Operation_Scheduled, Recovery, Discharged and Terminated. These states of an Inpatient class would be represented in a Booch state transition diagram as shown in Figure 4.22.

Module diagram   A module diagram is used to show the allocation of classes and objects to modules in the physical design. The only relationship between modules is the compilation dependency, represented by a directed line

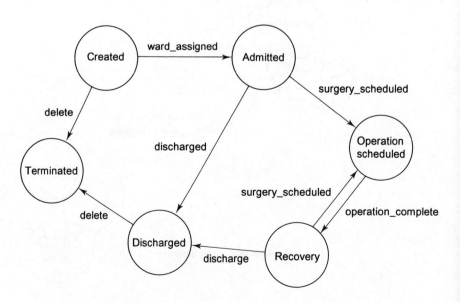

Figure 4.22   A Booch state transition diagram.

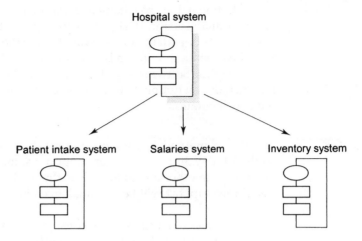

Figure 4.23 A Booch module diagram for a hospital system.

between two modules. Figure 4.23 illustrates a Booch module.

The diagram shows that the hospital patients intake system is just one module in a larger system called the hospital system.

Process diagram   Process diagrams show the allocation of processes to processors. Even for systems that execute on a single processor, process diagrams are useful for illustrating active objects. If there is a program called the Hospital System Controller which executes on one processor and the Hospital System (defined in Figure 4.23) executes on another processor, this would be represented by the Booch process diagram illustrated in Figure 4.24.

Pragmatics   Booch (1991) discusses management issues associated with object-oriented software development projects, suggesting development team skills required and the proportions of resource effort needed for each of analysis, design, coding, testing and integration in an object-oriented software development project. The method addresses the difficult issue of when to stop designing and start implementing.

Figure 4.24 Booch process diagram.

Rational Inc. has launched Rational Rose, a graphical object-oriented analysis and design tool to support the Booch method. It is language independent, and is available for the IBM RS6000 and UNIX Sun SPARCstations and can be accessed from Motif or OpenWindows.

Popkin Software's System Architect PC-based front-end CASE tool includes an optional object-oriented design module which supports the Booch notation.

Discussion   The Booch method is arguably the most commonly used OO design method today. It does however support a somewhat more complicated notation than other methods such as the method of Coad and Yourdon. CASE tool support will be essential, even just to draw the complicated symbols used.

The method addresses OO design. It does discuss object-oriented analysis but spends little time guiding the reader through the painful process of identifying objects from the problem domain. Instead it cites the techniques used by others for analysing the problem. In fact, the overall method is approached from the viewpoint of a set of techniques without a well-defined process (in common with many object-oriented methods).

One interesting point is that whereas the Coad/Yourdon method differentiates between associative relationships and message passing between two objects, in the Booch method an association between two objects *implies* a message-passing relationship between the related objects. This makes sense considering that objects can only interact through message passing.

The Booch method picks individual techniques from many other methods, including the use of CRC cards to develop object relationships. The method documentation (Booch, 1991) includes many examples which are necessary to understand many of the subtitles of the complicated notation.

4.5.3   OOSE

Objective Systems of Sweden has developed a method called object-oriented software engineering (OOSE) (Jacobson, 1992). The method encompasses analysis and design. It works with five different models:

- The requirements model – which captures functional requirements.
- The analysis model – which concentrates on developing a sound, extensible object structure.

- The design model – which refines the object structure to suit the current implementation environment.
- The implementation model – which is used in implementing the system.
- The test model – to verify the system.

Each of these models uses objects. The method provides rules for transforming between these models.

The requirements model captures functional requirements by **use case modelling**. Use case modelling is similar to data flow diagramming. It identifies scenarios in which business processes are instigated and controlled. For each process, a rough sequence of events is planned out. When a user uses the system this performs a behaviourally related sequence of transactions in a dialogue with the system. These special sequences are the use cases. The relevant objects in the system are then identified from these use cases.

When the system behaviour must change, the use cases are remodelled. The whole system architecture is therefore controlled from what the users wish to do with the system. Unlike most other methods such as Coad/Yourdon, Shlaer/Mellor and Rumbaugh, which suggest identifying candidate objects from the terminology of the problem domain, OOSE is suggesting that a better way is to look at how an object works with other objects and under what conditions.

The analysis model considers how modifications will affect the system. This enables the objects identified from requirements analysis to be made more robust and extensible. Three types of objects are used during analysis: (i) entity objects which hold information about the system which must survive a use case (behaviour associated with this information is contained within these objects), for example a person; (ii) interface objects which model behaviour and information dependent on the interface to the system, for example the user interface functionality for requesting information about a person; (iii) control objects which hold behaviour not naturally associated with entity or interface objects, for example doing some computations that operate on several entity objects.

A typical use case will have interface objects at its ends, with controller objects directly behind the interface objects and entity objects residing somewhere at the heart of the use case.

The analysis model is adapted to the actual implementation environment and further refined in the design model using the use cases to describe how the overall functionality will be created. The design model takes specific application issues into consideration, such as interfacing to a DBMS, distribution, real-time requirements, concurrent processes and hardware adaptations. In design an object is represented as a block (see notation below). One block should implement one analysis object,

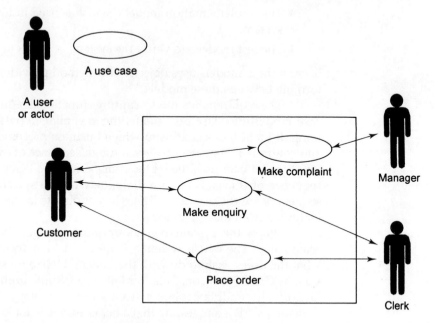

Figure 4.25   A OOSE use case diagram.

although often design considerations will necessitate the creation of two or more blocks which map logically to one analysis object. The communication between blocks is represented by stimuli and shown in interaction diagrams.

State transition graphs for describing an object's (block's) lifetime are supported in the method. These diagrams are very similar to the one presented earlier in the Booch method. The use cases are implemented by source code. The final testing is well structured because the use cases provide support when defining test sequences.

Use-case diagrams can be composed of different levels so that entities and messages identified on a particular diagram can be decomposed into another diagram showing more detail.

Objective Systems advocates an incremental life cycle where the initial stage involves a complete requirements specification with partial development of the analysis, design and implementation models. Further stages involve developing the analysis, design and implementation models iteratively until the system development is complete. Each increment should be about 5–20 use cases and take 3–6 months to complete.

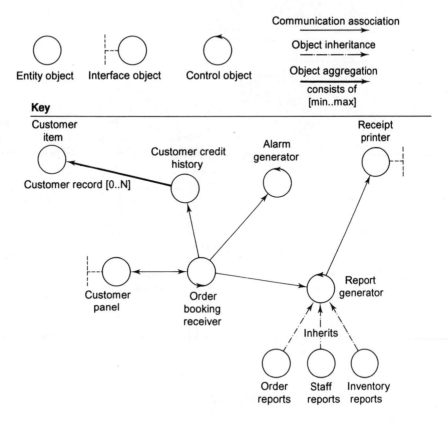

Figure 4.26   The objects supporting the use case 'Place Order'.

Diagrams and notation

Use-case modelling

The first stage is identifying use cases based on user interfaces, as illustrated in Figure 4.25. The scenario shows a customer accessing some facilities within a company.

Analysis modelling

In this stage the use cases are refined and made more detailed and robust. Figure 4.26 illustrates how OOSE represents the three types of relationship: association, inheritance and aggregation. The diagram is an expansion of the Place Order use case illustrated in Figure 4.25.

Design modelling

Environmental considerations are made and detailed interaction diagrams developed. Figure 4.27 shows how stimuli, represented by arrows, are sent between blocks and invoke activities (such as 'check customer credit' and 'create report') within these blocks.

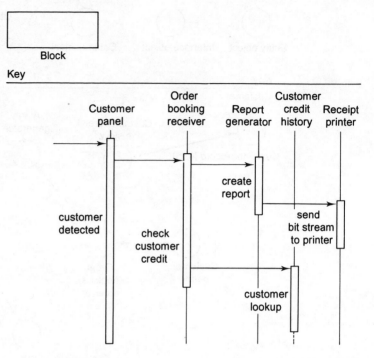

Figure 4.27   An example OOSE interaction diagram.

Pragmatics   Objective Systems has developed a CASE tool around a variation on this method. The tool, called Objectory, is available from Objective Systems. Only limited details of the method and associated CASE tool have been published, for example Jacobson (1987); this is available through a commercial course.

 The method documentation considers the complete software development life cycle including implementation and testing. It discusses project staffing issues, software quality assurance and software metrics. The OOSE method is available in a published text (Jacobson, 1992).

Discussion   The two-stage analysis procedure, involving use-case requirements modelling followed by analysis modelling, provides a different perspective on the problem domain from the perspectives obtained using many other methods including Booch and Coad and Yourdon. The OOSE method develops an analysis model which should be more robust and maintainable for future changes, rather than using the directly identified problem domain objects as a basis for design and implementation.

4.5.4 OSMOSYS

OSMOSYS is a toolset providing a method for OO analysis and design along with a suite of tools supporting library services, user interface building, modelling, validation, configuration management, documentation and code generation. It has been developed by Winter Partners (see vendor references section for address) and is a proprietary method.

The process　　The method advocates two development approaches: the functional approach and the object-oriented approach.

Using the functional approach the business operations (processes and tasks) are captured from an organization-wide perspective, using the technique of task analysis. Using object-oriented concepts the business entities and operations are integrated into a single object model.

For analysis and design the method defines these main activities:

- The essential model – which specifies the application's environment (part of the business model).
- The conceptual model – which specifies the application's functional requirements and defines its boundaries.
- The conceptual interface – which specifies and documents the interface objects of the application's conceptual model.
- The logical model – which specifies the application's logical design.
- The logical interface – which specifies the interface objects of the application's logical model.

Each of these activities is further decomposed into a number of iterative steps which cover:

(1) Object identification: entities, operations and interfaces;
(2) Data specification: including data types;
(3) Relationship specification: static – aggregation, classification; dynamic: messages;
(4) Method definition: interfaces, parameters, pre- and post-conditions;
(5) Life specification: object behaviour, states and transitions;
(6) Reuse;
(7) Method implementation: coding of method bodies;
(8) Model testing: verification, validation with end users;
(9) Model documentation.

The analyst initially identifies classes from the problem domain. Class

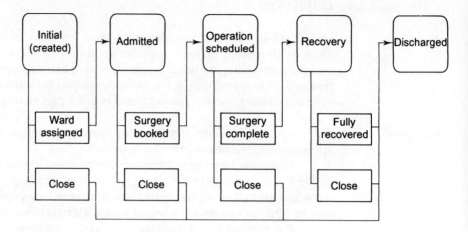

Figure 4.28   Class life history for Inpatient.

relationships are established through class relationship diagrams and class hierarchy diagrams (similar to the class relationship and hierarchy diagrams shown earlier). All classes possess a state. These class states are developed using class life diagrams.

Classes combine to form clusters. These clusters are higher-level modules in the system and are shown in correspondingly higher-level views of the design specification. The main purpose of a cluster is to hide details of a set of classes that are irrelevant outside the cluster. In addition, clusters provide a modular way to manage development projects. Like classes, clusters can have relationships defined between them. An application is composed from several clusters.

Diagrams and notation   The main diagrams developed in the OSMOSYS method are:

- Sub/application diagrams
- Cluster diagrams
- Class inheritance diagrams
- Class relationship diagrams
- Link diagrams (showing all classes linked to the selected class)
- Class life diagrams
- Method implementation diagrams
- Script diagrams

Most of these diagram types have already been discussed with regard to other methods.

The message passing between classes and clusters is shown through the class life diagrams, where an incoming command message to a class is represented as an event. The event causes an appropriate method invocation depending on the state of the class when it received the external event. Figure 4.28 shows the class life history diagram for the Inpatient used in the example in Section 4.2.1, where the states of an Inpatient are:

(1) **Initial.** Inpatient is received into hospital and awaits assignment to a Ward.

(2) **Admitted.** Inpatient has been assigned to a Ward.

(3) **Operation Scheduled.** Inpatient has been booked in for Surgery.

(4) **Recovery.** Inpatient has entered the recovery phase.

(5) **Discharge.** Inpatient has been discharged from hospital.

A Close message received in any state causes a state change to the final state – Discharged.

Pragmatics

An analyst models business requirements within the tool using the OSMOSYS OO analysis and design method. A knowledge base provides a suite of generic business specifications from which an analyst can inherit information and develop specializations as required. The toolset provides facilities for validating designs in an incremental fashion before cutting the final software. In essence, the validation tool enables designs to be executed using an interpreter. When the analysis and design stages are complete, relational database schema and application software are generated automatically. The application generator automatically handles the object-to-relational transformation.

The three class screens (namely the relationship, hierarchy and life diagrams) provide the three different views of the classes. An analyst can make changes to any one of the three diagrams and those changes are automatically reflected in the other diagrams. A fourth screen, called the dialogue generator, provides screen painting facilities.

This information is classified into three basic forms:

(1) **Classes.**

(2) **Types.** This is the vocabulary - it corresponds to the data dictionary in a traditional system, that is, the user-defined types such as date, currency and so on.

(3) **Dialogues.** These are user interface screens.

All three forms of information are implemented as classes. They can all inherit. There are three primary actions a user may wish to apply to each class of information. These are:

(1) **Browse/Edit.** To inspect and/or modify the information.
(2) **Validate.** To activate (or execute) a given class or dialogue specification, to simulate how the implemented specification will behave.
(3) **Generate.** To cut some code for a given class.

The full toolset consists of:

> **Library services.** A set of generic analysis specifications designed to increase productivity. The analyst inherits generic specifications from the library, creating specializations as required.
>
> **User interface.** The user interface tool enables the analyst/designer to develop graphical or character-based user interfaces for the application.
>
> **Modelling.** This tool enables class life specifications to be developed. It provides a fast iterative approach to developing specifications.
>
> **Validation.** This tool validates specifications by interpreting them interactively.
>
> **Configuration management.** OSMOSYS can be used in a multi-user environment. This tool controls the version management of individual components of a specification or design.
>
> **Documentation.** This facility is linked to Microsoft Word for OS/2. It enables full specification and design documentation to be produced automatically. Users can supplement the documentation with free text and graphics as required.
>
> **Generator.** This tool generates relational database schema and cuts application software.

Discussion   The strength of this method is in its well-documented process and, as expected with a proprietary method, the tool support. Unlike many methods which concentrate on the notation, this method concentrates on the techniques and overall process.

The toolset addresses the evolving area of object-oriented analysis and design while safeguarding the existing investment many organizations have in relational technology. This is achieved by ensuring that every object relationship is represented by primary and foreign keys. It serves to remind the reader that object technology and relational technology can be integrated by ensuring that data structures within objects reflect the tabular structure of data within a relational system. Chapter 6 discusses the issues surrounding objects and persistence.

4.5.5   Object-oriented systems analysis (Shlaer and Mellor, 1988)

This method (Shlaer and Mellor, 1988, 1992) is really an adaptation of traditional structured methods using entity modelling. Initially OOSA by Shlaer and Mellor (1988) was essentially information analysis. OOSA failed to capture behaviour and did not contain inheritance or classification. Therefore, contrary to the name, it was not a properly object-oriented method. However, Shlaer and Mellor have developed the method further (Shlaer and Mellor, 1992). It now deals with the behavioural properties of objects in analysis.

The analysis process

The method breaks down into three steps: the information model; the state model and the process model. The cornerstone of the method is the information model which is used to identify the entities in the problem domain. The information model formalizes knowledge about the world in terms of objects, attributes and relationships. It is a data-oriented view of the system.

The second step involves the state model. Here the analyst considers the dynamic behaviour of the entities identified in the information model. All objects and relationships have life cycles. A life cycle is composed of a finite number of states. In a given state, operating policies and rules regulate the behaviour of an instance of the entity. Instances of entities move between states in a very controlled way, based on events received from the outside world. A given event in a particular state causes a prescribed action to take place.

The third step is the construction of a process model. In this step a separate data flow diagram (DFD) is constructed for each state in each state model. The DFD graphically depicts the action processes associated with that state. Only attributes from the information model are allowed to appear on the data flows. The only data stores in the DFDs are those specified in the information model, and the data stores can be shared by all data flow diagrams in the system.

At this stage the analysis is complete and design can begin. Design is much more object-oriented in nature. It includes the distinction between classes and objects (or instances), inheritance and even more detailed concepts such as polymorphism. However, because the analysis phase is essentially based on structured techniques while the design phase concentrates on objects, there is an inevitable transition between the two phases! (Indeed a chapter in Shlaer and Mellor (1992) discusses this transition.)

Diagrams, notation and pragmatics

Shlaer and Mellor analysis creates the following outputs.

At the information modelling stage:

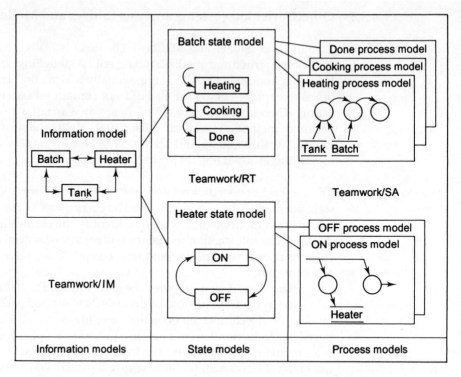

Figure 4.29   Object-oriented systems analysis by Shlaer and Mellor (1988).

- Information structure diagrams. These are essentially traditional entity relationship diagrams.
- Object and attribute descriptions. These, although called objects, are really data entities – where the attributes are merely data fields.
- Relationship descriptions. These are documented lists of the relationships in the analysed system.

At the state modelling stage:

- State transition diagrams.
- State transition tables.
- A description of each action on the state transition diagram.

At the process modelling stage:

- Data flow diagrams to represent the internal transformations associated with an action on the state transition diagrams.

This analysis methodology is supported by Cadre's Team*work* CASE tool (workbenches IM, RT and SA). Team*work*/SIM allows simulation of the state and process models. Figure 4.29 illustrates typical output from each stage in the method.

Shlaer and Mellor (1992) include an appendix on a language-independent notation for object-oriented design – OODLE. This notation is object-oriented (contrary to the analysis notation). It includes symbols representing classes distinct from instances, inheritance, and even polymorphism. The main design diagrams are:

- Class diagrams – which depict the external view of a class. These are based on notations of Booch (1991) and Buhr (1984).

- Class structure charts – which show the internal structure of the code and operations within a class. These charts are based on traditional structure charts such as Page-Jones (1980) and Yourdon and Constantine (1975).

- Dependency diagrams – which illustrate the client/server relationships between classes.

- Inheritance diagrams – which show inheritance relationships between classes.

OODLE is supported by Cadre's Team*work*/OODLE CASE tool. However the reader should note that there is, at present, no automatic way of progressing from the analysis stage using the OOSA method embodied in Cadre's Team*work*/IM/RT/SA tools to the design stage using Team*work*/OODLE.

Discussion This method is most applicable to the specification of real-time systems. It basically represents another approach to traditional structured analysis. One criticism is in the sharing of data stores, defined in the information model, between several DFDs. This dilutes the concept of encapsulation which is so important in the object-oriented paradigm. This analysis method will appeal to structured analysis practitioners as it represents a pragmatic move *towards* OO. As a report by New Science Associates (1992) comments: 'there is no use of the term class which identifies a template for objects in almost every other method. Instead, Shlaer/Mellor use the term object. This was the cause of some confusion in data modelling when *object* and *entity* were occasionally used interchangeably, and Shlaer/Mellor have perpetuated this by using the term object without qualification.'

The design method is strong on notation which supports inheritance, classes, and even polymorphism. But it lacks any real design procedure or process! OODLE is not a method, it is merely an object-oriented design notation. As such it may appeal to many organizations which prefer to develop their own techniques but may be willing to adopt a third party notation.

The analysis and design phases of this method feel as if they have evolved from totally different perspectives. They support totally different conceptual models, analysis based on structured concepts with design based on object-oriented concepts. Hence the transition when moving from analysis into design.

4.5.6   OMT

Rumbaugh *et al.* (1991) have developed the object modelling technique (OMT). OMT covers both analysis and design phases of the software life cycle. It combines object-oriented concepts (class and inheritance) with information modelling concepts (entities and associations).

The process   The method is presented as three phases; analysis, system design and object design. The input to analysis is the problem statement and the output is a formal model that identifies the objects and their relationships, the dynamic flow of control and the transformation of data through the system. The system is then organized into subsystems during system design using the formal model from analysis. During object design, the analysis models are refined and optimized.

In analysis, OMT combines three views of modelling systems. Each model describes one aspect of the system, but contains references to the other models. The **object** model captures the objects in the system. The **dynamic** model describes the reaction of objects in the system to events, and the interactions between objects. The **functional** model specifies the transformations of object values and constraints on these transformations.

The object model represents the static, structural, 'data' aspects of a system. It shows the objects in the system, relationships between the objects, and the attributes and operations that characterize each class of object. It supports generalization, aggregation, inheritance and polymorphism. The method uses enhanced entity relationship diagrams to represent this information.

The dynamic model represents the temporal, behavioural, 'control' aspects of a system. The dynamic model is represented graphically with state diagrams (Harel statecharts). Each state diagram shows the state and event sequences permitted in a system for one class of objects. State diagrams also refer to the other models, namely the object model and the functional model. Actions in the state diagrams correspond to functions from the functional model; events in a state diagram become operations on objects in the object model.

The functional model describes those aspects of a system concerned with transformations of values – functions, mappings, constraints and functional dependencies. The functional model captures what a system does, without regard for how or when this is done. The functional model is represented with data flow diagrams. These show the dependencies between values and the computation of output values from input values and functions. Scenarios are introduced. These are similar to the 'use cases' proposed in the OOSE method (Jacobson, 1992).

The data flow diagrams contain processes that transform data, data flows that move data, actor objects that produce and consume data, and data store objects that store data passively. A data store is a passive object in the OMT method. Unlike an actor, a data store does not generate any operations on its own, but merely responds to requests to store and access data. Functions are invoked as actions in the dynamic model and are shown as operations on objects in the object model. The processes in the functional model correspond to operations in the object model. Each process is implemented by a method in some object.

The object model is the most fundamental and important view in this methodology. The designer must convert the actions and activities of the dynamic model and the processes of the functional model into operations attached to classes in the object model.

The next stage, system design, involves deciding on the organization of the system into subsystems and the allocation of subsystems to hardware and software components. Finally, object design involves further refinement of the initial models to address the requirements of an execution environment. Classes are carried from analysis into design.

Diagrams and notation

The principal output from object modelling is a set of object diagrams showing named objects with attributes, associative and inheritance relationships. From dynamic modelling the analyst develops event trace diagrams describing scenarios, event flow diagrams and state diagrams for classes. Functional modelling produces data flow diagrams where the data stores correspond directly to objects identified from the object model. The main symbols in the OMT notations are shown in Figure 4.30.

Pragmatics

Martin Marietta Advanced Concepts Center has released OMTool, which supports Rumbaugh's notation of the book (Rumbaugh, 1991). OMTool is basically a graphics editor for constructing object diagrams.

Discussion

OMT breaks analysis into three components: static modelling of objects; dynamic modelling of states; and functional modelling of business processes. This is similar to the Shlaer/Mellor method discussed earlier.

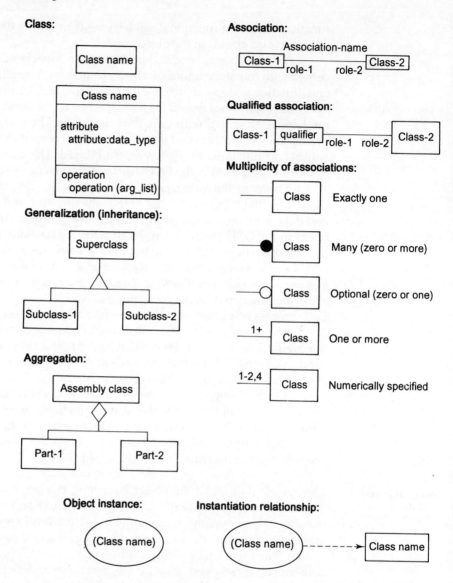

Figure 4.30   The main symbols in the OMT notation.

OMT uses many of the same tools as structured analysis and design, but the emphasis is quite different. OMT places much more emphasis on specifying what an object is rather than how it is used. This approach to objects makes OMT the most likely successor to structured analysis and design for those developers looking for an evolutionary rather than a revolutionary migration strategy to object-oriented analysis and design.

The published text is comprehensive and provides much good advice of use in general analysis.

4.5.7 Responsibility-driven design – RDD (with CRC technique)

In contrast to the OMT method described previously, RDD (Wirfs-Brock *et al.*, 1990) is a revolutionary approach to object-oriented analysis and design, requiring the user to apply an object model throughout the development life cycle. It is an anthropomorphic (humanoid) approach, requiring the analyst to think of objects as 'cooperating and collaborating agents', with responsibilities through which they become 'clients and servers'; their interactions are described by 'contracts'.

The process   The process requires that a written specification exists and concentrates on analysing these requirements. Steps 1–3 are called the exploratory phase and steps 4–6 are the analysis phase. They are summarized below (source: OMG OOA&D SIG working document, version 4.0, March 1992).

Step 1   Classes. This is the initial act of finding classes. The method suggests natural language analysis; looking at noun phrases and hidden noun phrases from the specification. A short statement of the purpose of the identified classes is written on CRC cards (see notation for a description of CRC cards).

Step 2   Responsibilities. Determine the responsibilities of the classes found from the previous step. This is achieved by using the purpose of the class and by extracting information from the specification. Actions that must be performed by the system are extracted as is information that must be maintained by the system. These actions are allocated to specific classes using various guidelines. Additional responsibilities are discovered by looking for relationships between classes. These responsibilities are written on the CRC cards.

Step 3   Collaborations. A collaborator is a 'use' relation that classes have in order to fulfil a responsibility. The method suggests asking questions like: 'Does this class need resources or information to fulfil a responsibility?', 'Which classes have these resources?', 'From which class can the required information be obtained?' The collaborators are written down on the CRC cards.

Step 4 Hierarchies. This is the first step in the analysis phase. This phase concentrates on formalizing the design information and making it as complete and consistent as possible. Although the previous steps have identified class hierarchies, this phase is intended for restructuring the hierarchies on the basis of a better understanding of the system. The analyst then tries to identify abstract and concrete classes and to draw a complete inheritance graph. Responsibilities are moved as high as possible in the hierarchy and contracts are defined by each class. The inheritance relationships are written on the CRC cards.

Step 5 Subsystems. The method suggests drawing a complete collaborative graph of the system, identifying possible subsystems in the design using various guidelines. Subsystems are classes that collaborate frequently and in a complex manner. Classes in a subsystem should be strongly cohesive and should be loosely coupled to other classes or subsystems. A CRC card should be made for each subsystem, with responsibilities and collaborators added.

Step 6 Protocols. Protocols are constructed for each class. Responsibilities are refined into sets of signatures which maximize the usefulness of classes. The CRC cards are now substituted by a more complete design specification for each class, subsystem and contract.

Diagrams and notation

One of the main problems with OOD is that the concepts are new and can be difficult to apply. Beck (1989) and Wirfs-Brock *et al.* (1990) developed a simple manual method for a novice OO designer to get to grips with developing a class hierarchy and mapping this to an application design. The method uses CRC (class, responsibility and collaboration) cards to aid in the fundamentals and subtleties of thinking with objects.

The idea is that in the early stages of a design, as the designer identifies objects and classes, he or she writes the class name of the object on a 4"×6" index card. The responsibilities of that class identify the problems which that class must solve. These responsibilities are written on the card. All objects stand in relationship to others, on which they rely for services and control. The card also details all collaborator objects which are sent messages, or from which messages are received. Design with the cards tends to progress from knowns to unknowns, as opposed to either top-down or bottom-up. This technique has received wide acclaim from the object-oriented community as a good vehicle for learning about OOD

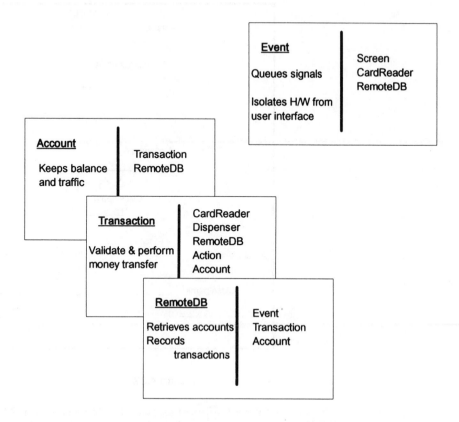

Figure 4.31   The use of CRC cards – an automated banking machine example (reproduced with the permission of Association for Computing Machinery Inc.).

and for initial design work. However, obviously it is only useful for systems with a manageable number of classes. Figure 4.31 illustrates an example of the use of CRC cards.

The full method (Wirfs-Brock *et al.*, 1990), which revolves around the use of CRC cards, also includes hierarchy graphs (to represent inheritance), collaboration graphs (to display and analyse the paths of communication between classes) and contract specifications (holding details of the client/server contracts between classes). RDD notation is shown in Figure 4.32.

Pragmatics   This method is good for organizations starting out with objects. Its proponents advocate using simple tools (index cards and blackboards) for object identification and refinement. However, the manual-based CRC card technique is obviously limited in use to about 20–30 classes. Any more than this and the physical cards become unwieldy!

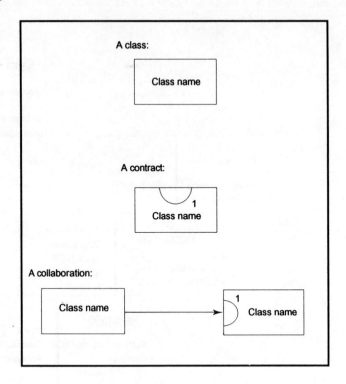

Figure 4.32   RDD notation.

CASE tool support is available for RDD from Mark V Systems' ObjectMaker.

Discussion   The CRC card technique has been widely adopted within other methods as a way of developing classes and class relationships, for example Booch advocates its use in his method. The use of collaboration graphs and contracts is similar to the technique of interaction diagrams used in the OOSE method summarized in an earlier section.

RDD is a truly object-oriented approach to analysis. It expects the user to apply object-oriented techniques throughout the development life cycle. However, as reported by New Science Associates (1992): 'traditionally analysis refers to the activity of understanding and representing essential behaviour and data requirements. Design usually refers to the allocation of the activities and data from the analysis phase to processors and adding implementation-specific data and processing. In RDD, the analysis phase is part of design. In this phase the designer analyses the exploratory products, applies a set of design heuristics and refines the resulting model. The goals of this phase are the same as those of conventional structured design.'

Here we see the differing interpretations which methods give to the terms analysis and design. From a manager's viewpoint the important thing is to be able to distinguish clearly between these two phases, regardless of where the boundary lies. In RDD the boundary is not well defined.

4.5.8 OORASS method

OORASS – object-oriented role analysis, synthesis and structuring (Reenskaug and Skaar, 1989; Reenskaug *et al.*, 1991) – is developed and supported by a Norwegian software company, Taskon A/S. The general goal of Taskon is to produce tailored personal work environments with a minimum of effort. This is obtained by maximum reuse of concepts, design and code, exploiting similarities between environments to the fullest possible extent.

OORASS supports an evolutionary systems development process. The method is based on a fully object-oriented model. It supports analysis and design phases as well as construction.

The concepts and techniques used in OORASS are quite different from those described elsewhere in this chapter. For this reason a concepts section is included.

Concepts Compared to the other methodologies in this survey OORASS introduces the concepts of roles and role models and uses these as its main modelling concept. A role model may roughly be described as a purification of concepts such as Booch's mechanisms or RDD's collaboration graphs. A role model is a model of object interaction described by means of messages between roles. Role models focus on describing patterns of interaction without connecting the interaction to particular objects; in this way OORASS may be viewed as a framework design methodology.

The activities of the method are:

- **Role modelling.** Describes patterns of interaction with respect to some area of concern. The advantage of using the role concept (in addition to objects, classes and types) is that it adds important capabilities with respect to reusability and modularity. Objects of various types may play a certain role, and a given object may play different roles in different contexts. Other methodologies describe object interaction in terms of object diagrams, OORASS combines such descriptions (diagrams) through its synthesis operation.

- **Type specification.** Describes the externally observable capabilities of some object(s). Types are organized in a type hierarchy, with single or multiple inheritance. Types are designed to play one or more roles in different role models. The concept of a class is used to denote the implementation of a type, and a type may be implemented by more than one class. Class hierarchies may be different from type hierarchies.

The major difference between OORASS and other OOA/OOD methodologies is in the use of role modelling and so the summary will concentrate on this concept. The four basic concepts connected to role modelling are role, role model, port and contract, presented below. They are presented both in terms of a metaphor of human organizations, and in terms of general object-oriented concepts.

Role

Organization metaphor

People play different roles in different contexts. At work we play the roles of employee, manager, project participant, and so on. At home we play the roles of wife, father, television watcher, among others. The key point is that in different contexts we *require* different things from our surroundings. To be a manager, we *require* certain resources (people, office, and so on), we have certain competence (experience, education, and so on) and we have certain rights (take decisions, allocate people to certain tasks, and so on). If we do not have the resources available, competence or rights, we cannot fulfil our role as a manager.

OO concepts

An object is always participating in some structure where it fulfils some purpose. Thus an object uses **different aspects** of its capabilities in different structures (that is, plays different roles). This is often reflected in the class hierarchy where a role played by several classes is generalized into a superclass. For example, a graphical object in a linked list will use different parts of its capabilities when it is playing the role as a list element, than when it is playing the role as a graphical object.

The fundamental idea of OORASS is the organization of objects into functional structures. A particular function, called **area of concern**, is described by a number of cooperating objects. The objects of a particular function are organized into a structure, and all objects having the same position in the structure are abstracted into a role, that is, the objects play the same role in the function. A role is defined as:

> 'Role is the *why* abstraction. Why is this object included in the structure of collaborating objects? What is the position in the organization, what are its responsibilities and duties? All objects having the same position in the structure of objects play the same role'.

A role only has meaning as a part of some structure. This makes the role different from objects which are entities that exist 'in their own right'. An

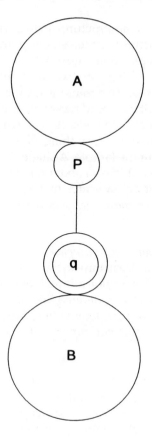

Figure 4.33   Basic role diagram in OORASS.

object has identity and is thus unique, a role may be played by any number of objects (of any type).

Role model

Organization metaphor
A set of people in an organization will perform many different functions (for example, budgeting, hire people, buy equipment, sell goods, and so on). Each function will involve a number of different people and it would be hopeless to try to understand the total picture (that is, make a conceptual model of all persons in all functions). But what we are capable of understanding is what one person is doing in a specific function (that is, the role they are playing).

OO concepts
Since objects play different roles in different structures, we must concentrate our efforts and describe one structure at a time. For each object in the structure, we model the aspect relevant to the structure (that is, its

role in the structure). In this way, we will get a model of some mechanism (function) of interest. The graphical representation of a simple role model is depicted in Figure 4.33.

There are two roles called A and B shown as large circles. A path between two roles means that a role may 'know about' the other role so that it may send messages to it. A path is always terminated by port symbols at both ends. A port symbol may be a single small circle, a double small circle or nothing. Nothing means that the near role does not know about the far role. A single circle (p) indicates that an instance of the near role (A) knows about none or one instance of the far role (B). A double circle (q) indicates that an instance of the near role knows about none, one or more instances of the far role.

Port

Organization metaphor

In an 'ideal' bureaucracy, two different people can talk to each other if the job description allows them to do so. In the 'ideal' bureaucracy, there will exist clearly defined lines of communication. If you are going to do some job, you can look at the job description and find out who you can talk to and what you can expect from them.

OO concepts

For a role to fulfil its responsibilities it may *require* capabilities from its neighbours in the structure. Two roles that know about each other are connected with a path between two ports. A port is basically a reference to an object that plays a particular role.

In Figure 4.33, p is a reference to some object playing the role B. Which object this is may change during the lifetime of A. But if some object is present, we are always assured that it is capable of playing the role B.

A role may also know about many other objects that play a certain role, implemented as a set of references to objects. The number of such objects may vary from time to time, the only thing that we can be sure of is that they are all playing the specified role.

Contract

Organization metaphor

If two people talk to each other, they may do this in different contexts (for example, in one context you are preparing a budget together with your manager, in another you are preparing a company party). The phrases you may use depend on the context; such a context is called a contract. Note that an OORASS contract differs from a contract as defined in the foregoing section on contracts.

OO concepts

To a port symbol, one can define an associated set of operations. A set of operations is called a contract. Note that these operations are the ones that the near role *requires* from the far role, not what the near role implements. The signatures *offered* must be deduced from what is required in the other end.

Synthesis: composition of role models

The basic idea of role modelling is to make small and simple role models that the designer understands completely, and then combine them together in a controlled manner in order to create larger models. OORASS is the only available methodology where an analyst is allowed to take separately defined object interaction models and combine them in a uniform way. This improves the capability to reuse analysis and design results.

The process and techniques

This part describes the process of making a role model for some area of concern.

The process is iterative and the steps described below are by no means sequential. The process of making role models is called analysis in OORASS terminology. The term analysis is used in its dictionary sense:

(1) Separation of a whole into its component parts.

(2) An examination of a complex, its elements and their relations (Webster).

The analysis is, in this sense, a top-down process, but it is not hierarchical. There are no notions of breaking a role model into other role models. The idea is that we choose an area of concern from the problem domain and try to make a role model out of it. If the chosen area of concern can be understood completely, we are at a sufficient level of detail and can make a stable role model. If we identify several mechanisms that can be separated, we redefine our area of concern, and repeat the process. The goal is to find stable and well-understood mechanisms that can be combined in different ways later.

The term synthesis is used to denote the integration of separate role models:

(1) The composition or combination of parts or elements so as to form a whole.

(2) The combination of often diverse conceptions into a coherent whole (Webster's).

The process of making a role model is a process of trial and error. An analyst often starts by choosing a set of objects in the problem domain by identifying typical scenarios of interaction. This process will lead to a separation between the various mechanisms (or functions) that are present, that is, an object behaves differently in different contexts. One such mechanism is formalized into a role model. The different steps can be described by:

(1) Area of concern. An area of concern is a function that is maintained by the system. This function must be specific enough to create a role model. An analyst may also view an area of concern as an aspect of the system seen from a specific point of view.

(2) Stimulus–response. Look for events (actions) in the area of concern (problem-specification, problem-domain, and so on) and describe the appropriate response. The events will be candidates for messages, and the responses will be candidates for responsibilities.

(3) Choose the objects. This step is concerned with questions like: What is a good object? and Where do we look for objects? This step is the same as in any other object-oriented methodology (for example, Booch, 1991 or Coad and Yourdon, 1990).

(4) Object interaction scenarios. Use the CRC cards (class–responsibility–collaboration) (Wirfs-Brock *et al.*, 1990). The index cards are suitable for simulations, reconfiguration, adding and deleting. The main purpose of this step is to delegate the responsibility to the appropriate object and to decide simple message interaction sequences. Draw message sequence diagrams. This gives a good overview of the collaborators and the sequences of messages in the system.

(5) Role diagrams. The role diagrams are the WHY structure in the method, they describe the reason for the existence of objects. A role is a well-defined and concrete job that must be done in the system (with respect to another collaborating role).

(6) Message contracts. Formalize the message interaction sequences in the system, decide on the signatures of the messages and constraints and invariants. A contract has a unique name and is composed of a description of one or several paths (a pair of ports).

To summarize, a role model describes patterns of interaction among objects, not the objects themselves. Any object that satisfies a certain contract can play the corresponding role.

The notation   The only graphical notation defined in the methodology is notation showing roles, role models, ports and contracts. The basic notation is illustrated in Figure 4.33 on page 141. A textual notation also exists. Role models and synthesis operations have well-defined semantics. Different representations of roles and role models are available (finite state machines, textual language). However, there is no notation for describing static structures (whole-part, inheritance, relationships), but any other notation can be used.

Pragmatics

There are some published articles on the methodology, but no books are available yet. The method is supported by a CASE tool from Taskon A/S (called OORAM) and courses are available from the Taskon company. The methodology is aimed at systems where message passing is the fundamental concept (cooperative work, telecommunication, distributed systems).

Discussion

OORASS is a proprietary method and as such is not widely known at present. It presents some interesting ideas on viewing the analysis of problem domains using object roles and this is why a large section has been devoted to describing it. As with many object-oriented analysis and design methods, it borrows ideas and notation from others such as Booch and Wirfs-Brock.

4.5.9 OOSD method

Interactive Development Environments Inc. (IDE) has developed an object-oriented design method (more notation than method) called Object-Oriented Structured Design (OOSD) (Wasserman *et al.*, 1990). It is a synthesis of various techniques including structure charts from structured design and some parts of the Booch notation. It claims to be able to take the results of traditional structured analysis and produce an object-oriented design.

Notation

The notation supports classes, exception handling, inheritance, genericity and dynamic binding. As with other elaborate notations (such as Booch), the graphical conventions of OOSD can result in diagrams that are too complex to be intelligible. Appendix B lists the OOSD notation. The inclusion of monitors, which model communication and control between concurrent processes, makes this notation suitable for designing distributed applications.

Pragmatics

At the time of writing, OOSD is supported by the Software Through Pictures OOSD/Ada CASE tool (from IDE). This tool supports only those parts of the method which relate to the facilities offered in the Ada programming language. For this reason, the CASE tool does not support inheritance and polymorphism.

Discussion

OOSD is only a notation for object-oriented designs. There is no method defined and developers are expected to define their own techniques.

The notation permits separation of data from behaviour, therefore violations of encapsulation are possible. The OOSD notation permits such features as stand-alone functions, or 'function-nodes' – anathema to object-oriented purists. The method is most applicable to real-time software development. OOSD is not currently associated with an analysis method. It therefore stands alone and addresses only the design aspects of a software development project.

4.5.10   The HOOD method

The European Space Agency has specified that an OOD method called HOOD (hierarchical object-oriented design) (HOOD, 1989a, 1989b), is the preferred design notation for use in-house. It is a method for the architectural and detailed design phases of the software life cycle. The process recommends using structured techniques such as SSADM for analysis although no support is given for transforming the output of analysis to HOOD.

HOOD grew out of the Ada community and an important goal of HOOD is to map its features directly to Ada concepts. From Chapter 5 the reader will appreciate that Ada is an object-based programming language and as such it does not support the concepts of a class or inheritance. HOOD supports encapsulation but not inheritance or dynamic binding. Several workbenches which support this method are now commercially available from Software Sciences, Systematica, Intecs and IPSYS. It is therefore a multi-vendor method and is managed by the Hood User Group consisting of a HOOD technical group (with responsibility for maintaining the HOOD documentation) and several HOOD Working Groups. HOOD has four levels: (i) a textual definition of the problem ; (ii) a textual first-cut solution which decomposes the system to the first level of logical objects; (iii) full identification of the objects, operations and object abstraction to classes; and (iv) specification of the design using the Booch notation mentioned in a previous section. The reader should note that although the words 'object-oriented' appear in the name HOOD, it is not properly object-oriented.

4.5.11   The object-oriented software development method

Colbert (1989) has developed a very practical approach to object-oriented analysis and design. The method concentrates on objects (or instances) initially. Classes are very much a secondary consideration to ensure that the commonality between objects is identified and duplication therefore eliminated.

It considers an object to be active if it displays independent motive power; if it does not, then it is considered passive. Passive objects act only under the motivation of active objects.

The process   The method uses a consistent object model throughout the life-cycle stages as opposed to some others (such as the Shlaer/Mellor method described earlier).

The method covers requirements analysis, preliminary design and detailed design.

Requirements analysis   Four activities are performed to create the model of the application from the problem statement:

(1) Object-interaction specification (OIS);

(2) Object-class specification (OCS);

(3) Behaviour specification (BS);

(4) Attribute specification (AS).

These activities can be performed in any order. OIS identifies objects, their interactions and the hierarchical relationship of objects. Two graphic representations are used in this activity: object interaction diagrams (IOD) and object hierarchy diagrams (OHD).

OCS identifies the classes of objects and the relationships between the classes. The class relationships primarily depict component type relationships (is_part_of). Other relationships between classes and objects may be shown.

BS identifies the dynamic behaviour of an object. Typically state transition diagrams similar to those described elsewhere in this chapter are used to depict the life states of an object.

Finally AS identifies the quantitative and qualitative measures and resources for each object in the system. An attribute specification table enables the analyst to record quality criteria such as portability, performance and reusability criteria which must be associated with an object. These represent the minimum and desired measures to be met.

Preliminary design   The objectives of design are to refine the model developed during analysis and add sufficient rigour to create an implementable solution. It creates a language-independent description of the software architecture of the system. The object interaction, object hierarchy, object class and state transition diagrams, along with the attribute specification tables, from the analysis phase are refined.

Detailed design   This stage creates an implementation-specific representation of the software architecture. Again the same model and techniques used earlier are

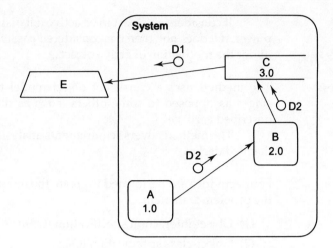

Figure 4.34   An object interaction diagram.

used. Decisions are now made on how to represent the objects, identified during analysis and preliminary design, in a programming language.

Diagrams and notation

Object interaction diagrams represent the interactions between objects. An interaction involves an operation and optional information flows. Rounded rectangles represent active objects, open rectangles represent passive objects and ordinary rectangles (or sometimes a trapezium) represent external objects which are outside the scope of the system to be implemented. Figure 4.34 illustrates the symbols used in an object interaction diagram.

Object hierarchy diagrams represent the decomposition of a system into its components. This use of the term 'hierarchy' should not be confused with an inheritance hierarchy of classes – the two are completely different. Generally there will be a top OID which describes the whole system. This will explode into a more detailed OID representing lower-level objects from which the system is composed. Each of these IODs may in turn explode into finer and finer levels of detailed objects. The object hierarchy diagram merely summarizes this decomposition of objects in a hierarchical view for the purpose of better understanding. Figure 4.35 illustrates an object hierarchy diagram for the objects shown in Figure 4.34.

Object class diagrams show relationships between classes and corresponding objects and information flows defined in object interaction diagrams. Class relationships to other classes are also shown. Figure 4.36 illustrates an object class diagram.

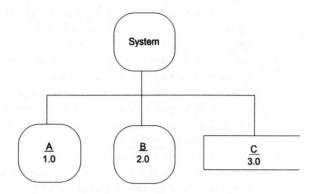

Figure 4.35   An object hierarchy diagram.

Pragmatics

The diagramming notations of Colbert's method are supported by the ObjectMaker CASE tool from Mark V Systems. This tool is actually a metaCASE tool which means that it can be reconfigured by its users to include additional rules and associations as and when they are introduced into the method.

With most object-oriented analysis and design methods currently being very immature, this approach of supporting the method in a highly extensible CASE tool makes a lot of sense!

Discussion

This method is particularly well suited to the development of real-time applications because it concentrates on developing object interactions – the most important aspect in real-time systems. Chapter 8 includes a real-life user case-study involving the method as applied to a real-time software application.

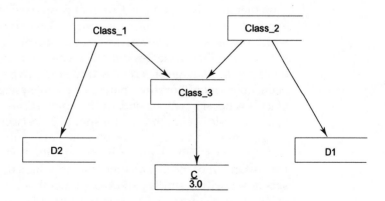

Figure 4.36   An object class diagram (cf. Figures 4.34 and 4.35).

The method is very brief and little, if any, guidance is given relating to how to identify objects and so on. The object interaction diagrams are probably the best feature of the method. The object class diagrams are not well defined – for example, in preceding sections we have identified several different types of class relationship (associative, inheritance and component). Colbert's object class diagrams do not provide any clear way to distinguish one type of relationship from another. In fact, the method does not discuss class inheritance at all!

Colbert (1989) discusses the use of the Ada programming language with the method. Ada does not support inheritance and this is consistent with the fact that inheritance is not discussed within the method, although other literature (de Champeaux, 1992) suggests that multiple inheritance is a part of the Colbert method.

4.6   Experiences with OO analysis and design

A fundamental objective in carrying out OO analysis and design is to derive a good class hierarchy. In OOD considerable time is spent extracting the commonality from the initial set of objects derived from an analysis of the system requirements. If the commonality is not extracted properly then changes to the system requirements can affect more of the overall system than is necessary. Determining the right level of abstraction can limit knock-on effects when requirements change.

Studies to date indicate that a developer's first few object-oriented designs tend to progress more slowly than corresponding traditional design for the same system. However, Booch states that a proficient OO designer will complete an OO design for about the same cost as a traditional structured design, if both start from scratch. The big benefit for the OO designers comes if they can reuse existing material!

The class hierarchy is never right first time, because deriving a class hierarchy is subjective. Different people working on the same problem will come up with different designs. There is no definitive answer to which one is best. However, the designer ought to be fairly conservative with the number of classes initially created – a smaller class library will be easier to manage. There is a trade-off between a good design and being able to configuration-manage the final system. Whilst the final size of a class library will depend on the applications being developed from it, a good rule of thumb is that it should be between 5 and 9 levels deep, with a similar fan out in terms of numbers of subclasses associated with one superclass. This depth of hierarchy allows for good reuse possibilities. A fan out of more than nine (that is, where there are more than nine subclasses with a single parent) suggests that it ought to be possible to abstract more commonality from the nine subclasses, thereby creating an intermediate class and possibly reducing the overall fan out.

Other indicators of a poor design are:

(1) If a class has no data structures and only one or two methods.

(2) If a class has no data structures but many methods (better than (1), but not good).

Many designs will include a few classes which fit into one of these two categories. This is acceptable – the problem occurs when many classes fall into one or other category!

Ideally a class should contain several data elements and a number of methods. One suggested style guideline is that for a method to be a member of a class it must either access or modify data defined within the class. Another design decision is whether an object should contain another object or simply use another object. In other words should a containing object or an external object be created. It is good practice to create containing objects initially and migrate to external objects later if this becomes appropriate. Furthermore, an object of Class A should not send a message directly to an object of Class C which is contained within an object of Class B. Instead, object A should send a message to object B, which in turn communicates internally with object C.

Four basic kinds of class can be identified during the development of an application. These are defined by virtue of the stage in the development process where they are first identified. They are as follows:

- **Foundation classes.** Foundation classes provide a top-level (or root) class and a set of subclasses that implement common behaviour. Typical foundation classes include string and array classes. Most foundation libraries also provide several abstract classes that define a common protocol for all subclasses. Foundation classes are often part of a language vendor's class libraries (for example Objective-C, see Chapter 5). These classes are well defined and are useful in many application areas across many business domains.

- **Application framework classes.** These classes build on foundation classes and aid in the development of the application's user interface. Typical classes include windows and other GUI classes such as buttons, menus, scroll bars, printers, and so on. Application framework classes are often part of a vendor's class libraries (for example Smalltalk, see Chapter 5).

- **Business classes.** These are the classes identified from an analysis of the business domain. They are identified from object-oriented analysis. For example, in a hospital system, typical business classes would include PATIENT, WARD, THEATRE, and so on. Business classes tend not to be specialized. They are unique to a business area but often common to many applications in that business area.

Booch (1991) lists several sets of guidelines from other methodologists which help the analyst identify business classes. These are quoted here (from Booch, 1991) for completeness. Shlaer and Mellor (1988) suggest that business classes derive from the following sources:

Tangible things	Wards, theatres, car
Roles	Manager, director, teacher
Events	Request, assignment, allocations
Interactions	Meeting, surgery

and from Coad and Yourdon (1990):

Structure	'Kind of' and 'part of' relationships
Organizational units	Groups to which users belong
Locations	Physical locations, sites, rooms
Devices	Devices with which applications interact
Events remembered	Historical events which must be remembered
Other systems	External systems with which the application interacts.

- **Application classes.** These are the most highly specialized. They are often unique to the application under development. There will usually be several layers of application classes, with the generic application classes towards the top of the inheritance hierarchy and more specialized application classes towards the bottom. Application classes are not always obvious – they can be difficult to find and often the successful identification and understanding of these classes is a predictor of a project's success. Typical examples include classes to support business transactions, user dialogues and relationships between other classes.

Figure 4.37 shows how business, application, foundation and application framework classes relate.

The first thing to note is that the library contains several class hierarchies. Foundation, application framework and application classes fit into implementation class hierarchies, with the more reusable classes situated towards the top of the hierarchies. Business classes don't generally fit into a class hierarchy with the other three class types. Business classes fit into an implementation class hierarchy (or hierarchies) of their own. Business classes make use of services provided by the other class types, through class associations.

Object-oriented analysis identifies the business classes needed within an application. Discovering the application classes involves the

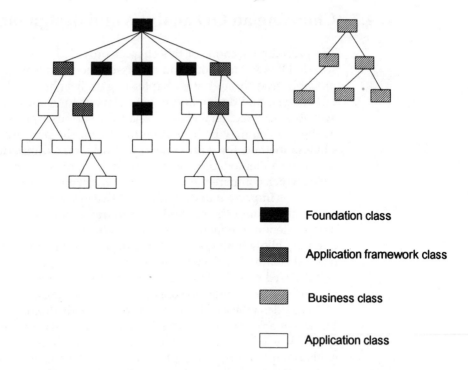

Foundation class

Application framework class

Business class

Application class

Figure 4.37   Categories of classes in a typical application class library.

design process. Event modelling can help uncover these classes. An event is something that happens in the system's environment and to which the system is responsible for sending a response. An event leads to an execution thread through software. Event modelling forces the designer to consider the execution thread in detail (see the object interaction diagram in Figure 4.6 for an example of an execution thread). Event-handling classes are the most application-specific application classes. Along with the business, foundation and application framework classes, event-handling classes are the minimum raw material to explore when considering the potential classes in a system.

Decisions regarding hardware platform, language, data management, communications protocols and environment enable identification of the foundation and application framework classes from suitable pre-existing class libraries. However, it may be necessary to build other foundation or application framework class libraries. The Applied Logic Computers user case-study described in Chapter 8 is an example of such development work.

Final application design will unearth more application classes which may be generalized and added to the class library.

4.7   Choosing an OO analysis and design method

The preceding sections of this chapter provided a brief introduction to several OOA&D methods and discussed the main features of each. You probably read through this chapter to gain insight into the workings of OO analysis and design and to get a flavour for some of the techniques available. This section will help collate the various aspects of an OOA&D method which may be important to you for the purpose of selecting a suitable method for your company. It asks many important questions regarding a method and answers many through a comprehensive set of tables which compare the methods summarized in Section 4.5.

It is important to distinguish between the notation used to represent a design and the method used to derive the design. A notation is independent of the method used to produce the design. While the notation may allow both good and bad designs to be represented, a design method is intended to yield the best possible design.

Based on the reference model proposed in Section 4.4, the following text suggests things to consider when choosing an OOA&D method and provides tables of features for the methods discussed in this book. The tables are designed so that Y(es) and N(o) answers are sufficient. If the answer is superscripted with an 'M' this indicates that only the method supports the concept. Similarly, if the answer is superscripted with an 'N' this indicates that only the notation supports the concept.

> **Disclaimer.** Some of the entries in Tables 4.2 to 4.11 may be inaccurate. Many issues are debatable. For example, the issue of a method supporting reuse. It is not sufficient for a method to simply mention reuse, or to state that reuse is addressed through the development of a generalization/specialization class hierarchy. The method MUST provide good guidelines to help the reader develop for reuse before that table entry is marked with a 'Y' for Yes. In some cases table entries are marked with '–'. This indicates that there is some mention of the issue in question but that I could not decide whether enough detail is provided to warrant a 'Y' vote.

4.7.1   Conceptual issues

- **The degree of object-oriented support.** The preceding sections illustrate that not all methods support all the object-oriented principles to the same degree. From Chapter 2 you will have decided which principles are of most use to you. To what extent are these principles supported in the various methods? Does the method support the usual meaning of the terms object (instance) and class? Can a class be described in terms of its distinct parts: an

Table 4.2   Basic object-oriented elements.

Method	Instance	Class		Metaclass
		Interface	Body	
Coad/Yourdon	Y	Y	Y	N
Booch	Y	Y	Y	Y^N
OOSE	Y	Y	Y	N
OSMOSYS	Y	Y	Y	N
Shlaer/Mellor	Y	Y	—	N
OMT	Y	Y	Y	Y
RDD	Y	Y	Y	N
OORASS	Y	Y	States only	—
HOOD	Y	N	N	N
OOSD	Y	Y	Y	N
Colbert	Y	Y	—	N

interface and a body? Does the method support metaclasses as implemented in programming languages such as Smalltalk and CLOS? See Table 4.2.

● **What class or instance relationships does the method support?** Does it support inheritance? If so, then does it support single or multiple inheritance? Does the method distinguish between subclassing (that is, implementation inheritance with restriction and redefinition as well as addition) and subtyping (with just addition)? Are associative relationships (with cardinalities) supported? What about aggregation (container) relationships? See Table 4.3.

● **Does the method enable object lifetime to be charted?** According to Arnold (1991): 'A method may be restricted to dealing with static systems of objects in which all objects have the same lifetime

Table 4.3   Object relationships.

Method	Single inherit	Multiple inherit	Subclassing	Associations	Aggregation
Coad/Yourdon	Y	Y	N	Y	Y
Booch	Y	Y	N	Y	Y
OOSE	Y	Y	N	Y	Y
OSMOSYS	Y	N	N	Y	Y
Shlaer/Mellor	Y^N – design only	Y^N – design only	Y^N – design only	Y	N
OMT	Y	Y	N	Y	Y
RDD	Y	Y	N	Y	Partial
OORASS	Y	Y	N	Y	N
HOOD	N	N	N	Y	Y
OOSD	Y	—	—	Y	Y
Colbert	Y	Y	—	—	—

Table 4.4   Object concurrency and lifetime.

Method instance	Active instance	Passive	State	Persistence	Creation	Destruction
Coad/Yourdon	N	Y	Y	N	N	N
Booch	Y – through message types	Y	Y	Y^M	Y	Y
OOSE	N	Y	Y	N	N	N
OSMOSYS	N	Y	Y	N	N	N
Shlaer/Mellor	N	Y^N – in design only	Y	N	N	N
OMT	Y	Y	Y	Y	Y	Y
RDD	N	Y	N	N	N	N
OORASS	N	Y	Y	N	N	N
HOOD	N	N	Y	—	Y	N
OOSD	Y	Y	Y	N	Y	Y
Colbert	Y	Y	Y	N	—	—

as the system. If this is not the case then the method must contain some facility for dynamically creating objects (by instantiating a class). Similarly for destroying an object.' Does the method support the notion of an object state? Can an object persist beyond a single execution of the application that created it? Can the method handle concurrently executing objects (active versus passive objects)? See Table 4.4.

● **What kinds of dynamic relations can exist between objects?** Interactions between objects concern the kinds of message passing available. Message sending can involve either static or dynamic binding and can be polymorphic. Furthermore, does the method allow for representing only single messages or can sequences of associated messages be modelled? See Table 4.5.

● **What models of communication does the method support?** According to Arnold (1991): 'Synchronous communication requires the sender to suspend execution until the receiver accepts the message, whereas asynchronous communication allows the sender to continue.' Does the notation distinguish between messages destined for local objects and messages destined for remote objects? This is pertinent in the design of distributed applications. See Table 4.6.

4.7.2   General method issues

● **Is the method oriented at real-time or information systems (IS)?** Some methods support both, but most are heavily oriented towards one type of development or the other. How much of the

Table 4.5   Message passing.

Method	Single message	Multiple message	Differentiation between static and dynamic binding	Polymorphism
Coad/Yourdon	Y	N	N	N
Booch	Y	Y	N	N
OOSE	Y	Y	N	N
OSMOSYS	Y	N	N	N
Shlaer/Mellor	Y^N – in design only	Y^N – in design only	N	Y^N – in design only
OMT	Y	Y	N	N
RDD	Y	Y	N	N
OORASS	Y	Y	N	N
HOOD	Y	N	N	N
OOSD	Y	—	—	—
Colbert	Y	Y	N	N

software life cycle does the method cover? Does it cover analysis and design? See Table 4.7.

- **Are there guidelines for separating analysis from design?** Does the methodology help with project management issues such as defining boundaries between analysis and design?

- **What resources are available to support the method?** Is the method fully supported by a CASE tool? Some methods are only partially supported. What hardware and software does the tool require? Does the environment support multi-user development? If there is CASE tool support, does it provide semantics processing

Table 4.6   Communication semantics.

Method	Differentiation between synchronous and asynchronous calls	Differentiation between local and remote calls
Coad/Yourdon	N	N
Booch	Y	Y
OOSE	N	N
OSMOSYS	N	N
Shlaer/Mellor	N	N
OMT	Y	N
RDD	N	N
OORASS	Y	N
HOOD	Y	–
OOSD	Y	Y
Colbert	Y	N

Table 4.7 Pragmatics.

Method	Real time	Information systems	Analysis	Design	CASE support
Coad/Yourdon	—	Y	Y	Y	Y
Booch	Y	—	N	Y	Y
OOSE	Y	Y	Y	Y	Y
OSMOSYS	—	Y	Y	—	Y
Shlaer/Mellor	Y	—	Y	OODLE	Partial
OMT	Y	Y	Y	Y	Partial
RDD	Y	Y	Y	Y	—
OORASS	Y	—	Y	Y	Y
HOOD	Y	—	N	Y	Y
OOSD	Y	N	N	Y	Y
Colbert	Y	N	Y	Y	Y

such as simulation and code generation? What other resources are available to support the method such as published texts and so on?

- **The ability to interwork with other CASE tools.** This is important where a tool must integrate with other tools such as a project management system, or a standard documentation system. Several standards are emerging in the area of CASE tool integration – such as the CDIF (CASE Data Interchange Standard) or the PCTE (Portable Common Tool Environment) which specify standard import/export formats to/from a repository.

- **Tool maturity.** If commercial-grade software is going to be developed then the tool must offer a degree of robustness characteristic of a mature product.

- **How scalable is the method?** According to Arnold (1991): 'Scalability is concerned with whether techniques and notation can be used effectively on large systems. Notations need a mechanism for partitioning descriptions into smaller and more manageable modules and composing the whole from those modules. It should also provide some means of controlling the visibility of names across modules.'

- **Is good training available?** This goes without saying!

- **Extent of use of the method.** Is the method supported by more than one consultancy firm or CASE vendor? The existence of user groups and conference tutorials are an indication of widespread usage.

- **External factors.** Some large customers, notably government bodies, insist on certain methodologies – for example the European Space Agency has stated a preference for the HOOD method.

Table 4.8   Process.

Method	Well-defined steps (process)	Pure or hybrid	Notation	Traceable across life cycle
Coad/Yourdon	Y	P	Y	Y
Booch	Partial	P	Y	—
OOSE	—	P	Y	Y
OSMOSYS	Y	H	Y	Through tool
Shlaer/Mellor	N	H	Y	N
OMT	Y	H	Y	Y
RDD	Y	P	Y	Y
OORASS	—	P	Limited	Y
HOOD	Y	H	Y	Y
OOSD	N	H	Y	N
Colbert	Partial	—	Y	Y

- **How well has the method been defined?** Is there a well-defined set of steps by which the various techniques are strung together? Are objects traceable across the life cycle? Does the method advocate only object-oriented techniques (pure) or does it suggest using some traditional structured techniques (hybrid)? Does the method support a defined notation? See Table 4.8.

- **Are there syntactic and semantic definitions for the notation, or do the syntax and semantics have to be deduced from examples?** According to Arnold (1991): 'The syntax of a notation is a set of rules which describe the primitive components of a notation and the legal combinations of those symbols. There are well-known techniques, such as the Backus–Naur Form, for formally defining textual syntax, but such techniques for diagrams are less well established. There should, however, be a clear definition of the icons and their legal combinations. A defined syntax is a requirement for effective use and also for automated tool support. The semantics of a notation is a set of rules which gives the meanings of the syntactic primitives and their combinations.'

4.7.3   Techniques

- **Does the process address the architectural issues of the system under design?** This is the capability of a method to split a system into subsystems. There are three facets to this: (i) decomposition into logically related parts; (ii) collection of logical parts into modules which may be separately compiled; and (iii) deciding on the physical location where different parts belong (processors, platforms, etc.). See Table 4.9.

Table 4.9   Architectural issues.

Method	Decomposition	Modularization	Distribution
Coad/Yourdon	Y	Y	—
Booch	Y	Y	Y
OOSE	Y	Y	Y
OSMOSYS	Y	Y	N
Shlaer/Mellor	Y	Y	—
OMT	Y	Y	Y
RDD	Y	Y	Y
OORASS	Y	Y	N
HOOD	Y	Y	Y
OOSD	—	Y	Y
Colbert	Y	Y	—

- **Does the method provide guidelines to help identify candidate objects?** This is a most fundamental issue. You can't start manipulating and massaging objects until you've found some. An object can play different roles through associations with different objects. Does the method provide techniques for modelling the different views of an object?

- **Are there guidelines for developing inheritance hierarchies?** Associated with this is the issue of designing for reuse. Reusable components and designs must be developed, they are not simply a by-product of using objects. A method needs to provide explicitly activities which are intended to identify reusability and support the development of reusable components and designs. See Table 4.10.

- **Does the method enable objects to be viewed in different roles?** Some methods allow objects to provide different services to different clients.

- **What guidelines does the method provide to ensure quality?** Are there guidelines on consistency, completeness, coupling and cohesion, and design extensibility? See Table 4.11.

Analysis is particularly important because it provides a means of communicating between people with dissimilar backgrounds: the end user (from the problem domain) who may be naive of the technology; and the systems analyst who will be familiar with the software development process and must bridge the gap between the problem domain and the solution domain. Therefore the analysis method must provide a clear means of communication. It should be as intuitive as possible to both the end user and the software development team, with a clear precise notation for pictorially representing the information being discussed.

Table 4.10   Techniques.

Method	Class identification	General/ special	Object views	For reuse	With reuse
Coad/Yourdon	Y	Partial	N	Partial	Partial
Booch	Y	Y	N	—	—
OOSE	Y	Y	Y	Y	—
OSMOSYS	Y	Y	Y	Y	N
Shlaer/Mellor	—	—	N	N	N
OMT	Y	Y	N	Partial	N
RDD	Y	Y	Y	Y	—
OORASS	Y	Y	Y	Y	—
HOOD	—	N	N	Y	—
OOSD	N	N	N	N	N
Colbert	N	N	Y	N	N

Check if there is any tool support for the method. Tool support is very important in OO analysis and design so that various views of a system can be easily linked. Also, the complex notations which often go hand-in-hand with OOA&D methods require CASE tools to make them at all usable! Tools can provide consistency checking, completeness checking and validation. Some tools can execute (simulate) design specifications. They can help the analyst/designer browse through the products of analysis and design in a relatively unconstrained way. While looking at a class relationship diagram, a developer might want to study the details of a particular class specification. Using tools in this manner frees developers from the tedium of keeping all the details of the analysis or design consistent, allowing them to concentrate on the com-

Table 4.11   Quality issues.

Method	Completeness	Consistency	Coupling/ cohesion	Extensibility
Coad/Yourdon	N	N	Y	N
Booch	N	N	Y	N
OOSE	N	Y	Y	Y
OSMOSYS	Y – through tool	Y – through tool	N	Y
Shlaer/Mellor	N	N	N	N
OMT	Y	Y	Y	Y
RDD	N	Y	Y	Y
OORASS	N	N	Y	Y
HOOD	Y	Y	—	—
OOSD	N	N	N	—
Colbert	Y	Y	N	N

municative aspects of the analysis process or the creative aspects of the design process. Significant benefit can be derived from tools which run on laptop PCs and can therefore easily be transported to a user site where some of the analysis work takes place.

4.8   Summary and conclusions

This chapter introduced techniques and tools to support object-oriented analysis and design. It discussed the relative merits and problems with OO compared with traditional structured techniques and suggested several questions to consider when choosing a method and CASE tool.

Although there are many methods claiming to be 'object-oriented', some of them do not support all of encapsulation, classes, inheritance and polymorphism. They are not truly object-oriented. These methods support various forms of a hybrid approach to object-oriented analysis and design where perhaps the analysis employs traditional structured techniques while the design method is a mixture of structured and object-oriented methods. Such techniques enable developers to migrate 'towards' an object-oriented approach without full commitment, but may not provide the same benefits as a truly object-oriented approach.

Some methods are strong on process and techniques but weak on notation while others are strong on notation but the process is almost non-existent. It is definitely easier to specify what you want than how you should achieve it!

Many methods are variations on a theme (not surprisingly). However there are some notable exceptions such as the OORASS method (Reenskau, 1992) and RDD (Wirfs-Brock *et al.*, 1990), both of which introduce some novel ideas for identifying and modelling objects and object relationships. In particular, the CRC technique defined in the RDD method is used in various methods including OSMOSYS and Booch.

Object-oriented analysis and design has been used successfully on large and small systems in a variety of areas from technical and real-time systems to business information systems.

Case tools   Some CASE tools amount to very little more than graphics drawing tools. Others provide a degree of consistency checking and validation across several views of a system. But many CASE tools are suffering from the 'structured development lag'. They have evolved out of tools supporting structured techniques and unfortunately still support mostly structured techniques with a smattering of objects thrown in for good measure.

But there is no doubt that the effective use of an object-oriented analysis or design method requires good CASE tool support. New Science Associates (1992) identify two common approaches taken by vendors:

(1) To automate syntactic and semantic checking of the notation but provide little overall method support, and support many notations simultaneously. This approach has been taken by ObjectMaker from Mark V Systems, for example.

(2) To automate the notation checking and implement the prescribed process/techniques, but for one method only. This approach has been taken by Rational Inc. in its tool called Rose which supports the Booch approach.

Analysis

Although there are several OO analysis methods available, OO analysis is still the subject of much research. OOA brings several benefits: (i) a consistent modelling approach; (ii) the ability to reuse specifications; (iii) a clearer, more natural means of communication between analyst and end user; and (iv) the ability to model GUIs. However the boundary between OO analysis and OO design is not well defined and this can cause problems for managing OO projects.

The migration from traditional structured analysis to OO analysis will not happen overnight. It is more of a cultural issue than a technical one. Many DP departments have too much inertia to switch. New methods are generally accepted only when the old ones fail to solve new problems with which an organization is faced.

Hybrid OO methods such as Shlaer and Mellor and OSMOSYS will be more attractive to organizations with well-established structured analysis skills. However the pure OO methods such as RDD, OOSE and OORASS may become politically acceptable in environments where structured analysis has failed on large visible projects, and also on projects where reusability and GUIs are seen as key issues from the outset.

Design

Encapsulation and data hiding create a framework for weak coupling and strong cohesion. However, inheritance tends to increase the coupling between classes and will increase the degree of difficulty associated with maintaining the software.

Class design proceeds in a bottom-up fashion to provide genericity through abstraction. The design of an object-oriented application proceeds using a mixture of top-down and bottom-up procedures. This provides a more flexible approach which accommodates change more readily than a traditional structured top-down functional decomposition can.

5 Object-oriented programming languages

The intended readership includes the technical 'gatekeeper' charged with introducing new techniques, as well as project leaders and programmers. The information is of a highly technical nature.

CONTENTS

*CHAPTER
PRE-
REQUISITES* The chapter assumes a knowledge of object-oriented principles as detailed in Chapter 2.

*CHAPTER
OVERVIEW* This chapter introduces the main object-oriented programming languages in existence today. Detailed sections present C++, Objective-C, Eiffel and Smalltalk. Each of these languages is reviewed with respect to: (i) the language syntax; (ii) the development environments, tools and libraries available; (iii) standards and future issues; and (iv) end application performance.

Each detailed section includes a worked example to illustrate the languages' characteristics and use. For comparison the same example is used for each language. The example has two classes: (A) an employee class with two data attributes, name and salary, and three methods for (a) creation, (b) increasing salary and (c) querying the salary; and (B) a manager class which inherits from the employee class and defines one additional data attribute, car_allowance, and two additional methods to: (a) increase car allowance and (b) query car allowance.

Smaller sections cover six other noteworthy languages: Simula, Trellis, Actor, Object Pascal, CLOS and Object COBOL.

The chapter includes a section to help you choose an OOPL. It suggests some questions to ask and provides many answers through comprehensive tables of features covering all the main languages.

Some summary case-studies are presented here, but Chapter 8 presents detailed user case-studies for some of the languages discussed. These will give you an appreciation of what areas OO programming is being applied to, as well as the experiences – both good and bad – which development teams have had.

5.1   Object-oriented language foreword

The history of object-oriented programming languages can be traced back to the early 1960s, and to a computer simulation language called Simula developed at the Norwegian Computing Centre (Dahl and Nygaard, 1966). Figure 5.1 shows the evolution of modern object-oriented programming languages since those early days.

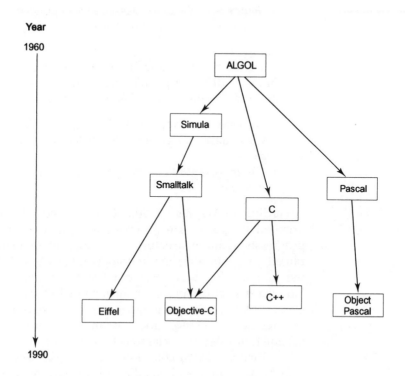

Figure 5.1   The evolution of modern OO programming languages.

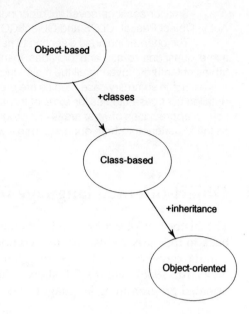

Figure 5.2   Wegner's classification of programming language object orientation.

The term 'object-oriented programming language' means different things to different people and there are varying degrees of object orientedness. Wegner (1987) classifies these degrees as follows:

> **Object-based languages:** *the set of all languages that support objects*
> **Class-based languages:** *the subset that requires all objects to belong to a class*
> **Object-oriented languages:** *the subset that requires classes to support inheritance*

According to Wegner (1990): 'Object-based, class-based and object-oriented languages are progressively smaller language subsets with progressively more structured language requirements and more disciplined programming methodology. Object-based languages support the functionality of objects but not their management. Class-based languages support object management but not the management of classes. Object-oriented languages support object functionality, object management by classes, and class management by inheritance.' Figure 5.2 illustrates Wegner's classification.

Wegner (1990) continues: 'The object-based languages include Ada, CLU, Simula and Smalltalk. They exclude languages like Fortran and Pascal which do not support objects as a language primitive. Simula,

Table 5.1 Classification of 3GLs.

Traditional structured	Object-based	Class-based	Pure object-oriented	Hybrid object-oriented
Fortran	Ada	CLU	Smalltalk	C++
C			Eiffel	Objective-C
Pascal			Simula	CLOS
COBOL			Trellis	Object Pascal
			Actor	Object COBOL

CLU and Smalltalk are also class-based languages since they require their objects to belong to classes. However Ada is not class-based because its objects (packages) do not have a type and cannot therefore be passed as parameters, be components of arrays or records, or be directly pointed to by pointers (these language characteristics are only available for typed entities). Simula and Smalltalk are also object-oriented according to the above definition, since their classes support inheritance. However, CLU is class-based but not object-oriented because its objects must belong to classes (clusters) but clusters do not support inheritance.'

Object-oriented programming languages (OOPL) further decompose into pure and hybrid. A **pure OOPL** is one which not only supports the paradigm but also enforces it, such as Smalltalk and Eiffel, whereas a **hybrid OOPL** such as C++ does not enforce the paradigm.

It is important to note that a line of code in an OOPL is similar to a line of code using a traditional third generation language. It is the underlying architecture, upon which the lines of code build, which differs between a procedural 3GL and an OOPL.

Table 5.1 classifies the main third generation languages in use today.

One way in which some languages (pure OOPLs) enforce the use of object-oriented behaviour is by requiring that all functions, procedures and variables be declared internal to some class. In such a system there are no global variables, and no free-standing functions or procedures. Objects encapsulate all states, and all code executes relative to some specific object. The main program becomes the constructor method in the class that defines a specific application.

For example, consider an executable program called *pay_roll*. Issuing a command '*pay_roll*' from the command interpreter causes a message to be sent to a class called *pay_roll* within the pay-roll application. A method within the *pay_roll* class then causes an object of class pay-roll (called Pay-roll-application in Figure 5.3) to be created. This object manages the overall application. The application runs by creating more objects and passing messages between them. Figure 5.3 illustrates the start-up of a pure object-oriented application.

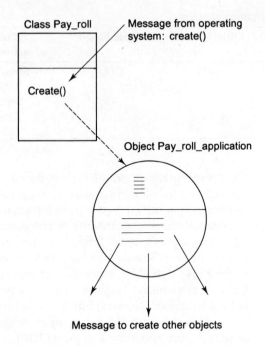

Class Pay_roll

Message from operating system: create()

Create()

Object Pay_roll_application

Message to create other objects

Figure 5.3 Starting sequence for a pure OO application.

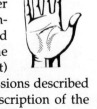

Before embarking on a fuller description of the features and facilities of a number of OOPLs there is one other concept to introduce. All OOPLs support the basic concepts of objects, classes, message passing, inheritance and polymorphism to some degree or other. However, some languages support a class being an instance (or an object) of a higher-order class called a **metaclass**. Earlier discussions described objects as instances of classes. A class contains the description of the structure and behaviour of its instances. In most OOPLs classes are *factories* that create and initialize instances. However, some languages (such as Smalltalk and Objective-C) support the idea of a class as an object. Therefore two types of objects exist in such languages:

(1) **Class objects** (belonging to a higher-order class called the metaclass) – whose instances are classes;

(2) **Terminal objects** (belonging to a given class) – objects that can only be instantiated but cannot instantiate other objects.

There are two advantages in treating classes as objects: The first is that classes can store group information. If a class is treated as an object, then information global to all instances of the class can be stored in class instance variables (class variables). Methods associated with the class (class

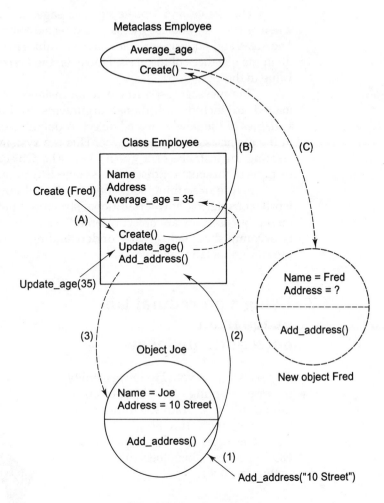

Figure 5.4 Metaclasses.

methods) can then manipulate the values of class variables. For example, for a class Employee, Average_age may be important global information used by clients of the class. This would store the average age for all instances of the class Employee. Therefore, as well as storing information for creating and manipulating individual employees, the Employee class also includes information for the collection of employees (instances of Class Employee) as a group. Aggregate information for the existing instances of a class is very convenient if the extension of the class is maintained.

The second advantage of class objects is their use in the creation and initialization of new instances of the class. Figure 5.4 illustrates the concept of a metaclass.

The Create and Update_age messages are directed to the class whereas the Add_address message is directed to an instance of the class. The Name and Address variables have no values in the class whereas they do in the instances of the class. However, the Average_age variable has a value in the class.

The message used to create an instance of a class can be overloaded to include additional arguments to initialize the instance variables of the newly created object. A default create() method appears in the metaclass for an employee. This is a system-defined method for creating an instance of a given class. The Objective-C and Smalltalk sections of this chapter discuss class objects further.

Before describing some object-oriented languages in detail it is worth considering how a traditional structured programming language might be used in an object-oriented way. Understanding how this is accomplished helps with understanding how an object-oriented programming language works.

5.2   Using a procedural language in an object-oriented way

This section is devoted to the feasibility of implementing an object-oriented design using a traditional programming language. It will give you an insight into the implementation of some OO concepts which become implicit within an OOPL.

5.2.1   Example

Although the full benefits of the OO approach can best be realized in an OOPL, Butler (1989) applies many of the concepts to simulation software written in Fortran. The following example illustrates encapsulation, classes, inheritance and dynamic binding using Fortran.

Encapsulation   A basic requirement for information hiding is a mechanism for encapsulating an object's attributes and methods together in a single module. In Fortran-77 encapsulation is achieved using a subroutine with multiple entry points. The ENTRY statement enables creation of two or more entry points in a subroutine. A side-effect of this is that different ENTRYs have access to the same local variables. A block structure is preserved by ensuring that each ENTRY leads into a block of code of the form:

ENTRY(arguments)

RETURN

Using the SAVE statement in Fortran-77, it is possible to ensure that the subroutine's local data (the attributes) is preserved and can therefore be accessed on entry to any point within the subroutine. Thus the idea of several methods bound to a set of local data, that is, encapsulation and the concept of an object, is created.

Classes

Now that it is possible to construct an object, the next stage is to produce an object template (that is, a class), so that many instances of this template can be created (that is, many objects). This is achieved, in a limited way, by defining all the local data (attributes) as arrays of data (attribute arrays). In other words, if an object of class Vehicle must have an attribute called Model, then the class definition will declare an array of models, for example Model(20). To refer to the data of Vehicle object number 3 of this class, the program refers to the index 3 in the array, that is, Model(3). In this example memory usage is preset to a maximum of 20 objects, whereas in an object-oriented system each object creation would cause memory to be dynamically allocated, however the effect is similar.

The following example illustrates the implementation of a class and an object in Fortran where the 'c' in the left margin denotes a comment line.

```
      SUBROUTINE VehicleClass
c....Maximum number of object instances
      PARAMETER (MAXOBJ=20)
      SAVE
c....Vehicle Class Attributes
      INTEGER Make(MAXOBJ), Model(MAXOBJ), EngSize(MAXOBJ)
c....create a Vehicle Object
      ENTRY VehicleCreate(VehType, VehName, Engine)
      IF(Found.NE.FindObj(VehType, VehName, Engine))THEN
        next = NextFreeObj
        Make(next) = VehType
        Model(next) = VehName
        EngSize(next) = Engine
      ENDIF
      RETURN
```

```
         c....list all Vehicle objects in existence
            ENTRY VehicleList()
            DO 10 I=1,MAXOBJ
               PRINT *, I,' ', Make(I),' ', Model(I), ' ',EngSize(I)
       10 CONTINUE
            RETURN
            END
```

The example shows the definition of a class called Vehicle (through the Fortran subroutine VehicleClass) with three class attributes: Make, Model and EngSize. The variable MAXOBJ (with a value of 20) is used to define array sizes. In this example up to 20 vehicle objects can be created of the class Vehicle. The class has two methods: VehicleCreate and VehicleList, which respectively create a new instance of a Vehicle and list all Vehicle objects currently in existence. These are the two entry points within the Fortran subroutine called VehicleClass. The method VehicleCreate employs two functions called FindObj and NextFreeObj (for the sake of clarity, implementation details are not given). FindObj is used to check that a vehicle of a given make, model and engine size does not already exist and NextFreeObj is used to return the index of the next free element in the array – that is, the next slot for storing details of a new Vehicle object.

Inheritance   A limited form of inheritance can be implemented by creating a new class with methods which refer to the parent class. Consider that a new subclass of Vehicle, called Car, is needed. A Car inherits from a Vehicle and defines some additional attributes such as Wheels – denoting the number of wheels on the car. A new subroutine called CarClass is required. Creating an instance of a Car is achieved by reference to the parent through the following ENTRY point in the subroutine CarClass:

```
         ENTRY CarCreate(Make,Model,Engine,Wheels)
            CALL VehicleCreate(Make, Model, Engine)
            ....
            ....
```

Thus creating a Car would cause the elements of a Vehicle to be created also.

Dynamic binding   The implementation of dynamic binding with resultant polymorphism boils down to a case (or switch) statement. Basically an operation is requested to be performed on an object, where the object's type is not known until run-time. At run-time a message is sent from one object to another. The receiving object determines the object type to which the operation must be applied and then issues a procedure call. This can be understood by considering the following example.

Consider two classes of object, CAR and BICYCLE, and one instance of each, called Escort and BMX. If the operation Wheels is to be invoked and will return the number of wheels on the object, then issuing the message Wheels escort will initially cause the routine Wheels to be called. This routine has the following logic:

```
wheels (name)
 BEGIN
 IF (findassoc (name, CAR))
   num = wheels_car() ;
 ELSEIF (findassoc(name, BICYCLE))
   num = wheels_bicycle() ;
 RETURN (num)
 END
```

So dynamic binding can be implemented by creating a front-end function to type-check the object on which an operation is requested via a message. Adding a new type of vehicle to the program would necessitate adding an extra limb to the wheels subroutine to cover the new case.

5.2.2   Summary

This example illustrates some of the underlying concepts required in an object-oriented programming language. Implementing these constructs in an application using a traditional language is difficult and presents complicated management problems especially when the application changes. However, the example shows why object-oriented programming languages, particularly where dynamic binding is used, tend to perform more slowly than conventional languages. Butler (1989) indicates that in their applications, the object-oriented implementation (in Fortran) was between 10–50 % slower than the same implementation using traditional structured programming principles in Fortran-77. The exact performance degradation depends on the size of the object methods. Figures of between 10–20 % overhead in OO systems compared with traditional implementations are more common.

5.3   C++

C++ (Stroustrup, 1991a) is a superset of the C language with support for object-oriented programming. It was developed by Bjarne Stroustrup at AT&T Bell Labs in the mid 1980s. Having its origins in C it provides the most comfortable migration path for C-developers and this trend is now apparent. Although programming environments, providing language-sensitive editors, class browsers and so on, are available for C++ (for example, ObjectWorks from ParcPlace Systems), it is basically a language in the traditional mould, using a standard edit–compile–test cycle.

Two forms of C++ are available – the AT&T C++ Translator (CFRONT 3.0) which converts C++ into C which can then be compiled for any target system, and straight C++ compilers which produce object code directly.

C++ is a hybrid object-oriented language. It is **strongly typed** and supports both **single and multiple inheritance**. By the use of *private*, *protected* and *public* parts in a C++ class, the inheritance tree and use of polymorphism can be controlled. **Dynamic binding** is implemented as a virtual function call, where the function to be called depends on the type of object and cannot be determined until run-time. However **static binding** is provided via normal function calls which can be determined at compile-time.

There is no background garbage collection facility in C++. Instead, the language provides storage allocation and deallocation facilities via functions called *constructors* and *destructors*. C++ does not provide any object-based persistence mechanism for disk storage.

C++ does not enforce object-oriented programming. It is possible to program in a normal structured sense without reference to object-oriented techniques. However, the strongly typed characteristics of the language combined with its compilability make C++ a suitable base for developing real-time systems.

C++ is link-compatible with C and any other language with which C code can be linked.

5.3.1   Language

A C++ program, like a C program, starts with a 'main'. The major difference is that whereas a C program is composed of functions, a C++ program should be composed of special functions belonging to classes.

A class is a generic blueprint for a type of object. It will typically contain **data members** (hitherto called attributes) and **member functions** (hitherto called methods). A class is an extension to the concept of a 'structure' in the C programming language, and is used in a similar way.

The data members are the local data and the member functions are the functions defined within that class. Objects communicate by calling the publicly available member functions of one another. In the following pages a small example of how C++ is used to (i) define a class, (ii) create an object of that class, (iii) communicate with the object and (iv) define an inheritance relationship between two classes, is presented.

Class definition

Consider a class to manipulate an employee's salary details, which is defined as follows:

```
class employee
    {
    int salary ;
    char name[20] ;
public :
        void employee (int, char *) ;
        void increase_sal(int) ;
        int query_sal() ;
    } ;
```

Data and function members are treated similarly. All items before the word public are private to the class and can only be accessed by the member functions. All items after the word public can be accessed from outside the class. This class definition would typically be placed in an 'include' file (for example employee.h) and included in all C++ code files which use the employee class type. The class implementation, that is, where the function code is defined, would be held in a separately compilable file.

Class implementation

For the above class, a possible implementation would be:

```
void employee :: employee(int sal, char* per_name)
    {
    salary = sal ;
    strcpy(name, per_name) ;
    }

void employee :: increase_sal(int increment)
    {
    salary = salary + increment ;
    }
```

```
int employee :: query_sal()
    {
    return salary ;
    }
```

Here there are three member functions – all are defined with reference to the class they apply to. The first function – employee() is special as it has the same name as the class itself. This type of member is called a **constructor** and it is used to initialize the class's data members. It would also be used to allocate memory if this was needed. The other two member functions manipulate the data members.

Using a class   This class (employee) could be used in a function or main module as follows:

```
#include <employee.h>

1     main ()
2     {
3     employee emp1(10000,"Joe Bloggs") ;
4     employee* emp2 ;
5     int max_sal ;

6     emp2 = new employee(12000,"John Green") ;

7     emp1.increase_sal(1000) ;

8     emp2->increase_sal(500) ;

9     max_sal = emp1.query_sal() ;

10    if (max_sal < emp2->query_sal)
              max_sal = emp2->query_sal() ;

11    }
```

Line 3 shows an object of type employee, called emp1, being created and initialized with a name and salary. Line 4 shows an object pointer being defined to point to an object of type employee. At line 6 an anonymous object is created using memory allocated via the operator new, and pointed to by emp2. emp2 will persist until it is either destroyed via a call to delete or the program terminates – that is, if this object had been created within a function, it could persist beyond the lifetime of the function.

Lines 7–10 show how member functions are invoked (in an analogous way to the use of structures in the C language).

Inheritance

The final part of the example demonstrates how inheritance is implemented in C++ using the case of a class called manager which inherits many characteristics from an employee – that is, it has a salary and a name, but in addition also has a car allowance.

```
class manager : public employee
        {
        int car_allow ;
public:
        void manager(int, char*, int) ;
        void increase_car_allow(int) ;
        int query_car_allow() ;
        } ;
```

---

where

```
void manager::manager(int sal,char *per_name,int car a):
                                        (sal, per_name)
        {
        car_allow = car a ;
        }
```

---

is used to initialize the manager object and its inherited employee details by passing the parameters sal and per_name to the parent's constructor.

The public members defined within class employee become public members of the manager class.

The manager class is known in C++ as a **derived** class. It has inherited characteristics from the employee class.

Dynamic and static method binding

Dynamic binding in C++ is implemented through the use of explicitly declared **virtual** functions. The programmer defines virtual functions in a base class. The definition of these functions can be deferred or they can be redefined in any derived class. The compiler and loader guarantee the correct correspondence between objects and functions applied to them. For example, consider a virtual function called print – defined in class employee and then redefined in the subclass manager:

```
class employee
      {
      int salary ;
      char name[20] ;
public :
      void employee (int, char *) ;
      int query_sal() ;
      virtual void print() ;
      }
```

where

```
void employee::print()
      {
      cout << "Employee" << name << "\n" ;
      }
```

Then in a derived class for a manager:

```
class manager : public employee
      {
      int car_allow ;
public:
      void manager(int, char *, int) ;
      void print() ;
      }
```

where:

```
void manager::print
      {
      cout << "Manager" << name ;
      cout << "Car Allowance" << car_allow << "\n" ;
      }
```

Dynamic binding can then be demonstrated from the following fragment of code:

```
employee *e ;
manager *m ;

m = new manager (12000, "bloggs", ....)
  .
  .
  .
e = m ; /* e assumes a polymorphic form */
e.print() ; /* print function via dynamic binding */
```

The appropriate print() function will be called depending on the object type at run-time.

From a logical viewpoint, when a class is created which has virtual functions, a virtual function table (VFT) is created (by the C++ preprocessor) for that class with the addresses of all its virtual functions. When an object of this class is instantiated at run-time, the object creation is accomplished through a constructor which adds the address of the virtual function table into an internal reference within the object. When a virtual function is called, a function in the called object performs a look-up on the VFT for that object. This look-up returns the address of the virtual method which is then invoked. The sequence can be understood from Figure 5.5 – route (A).

The message employee–>print requires a dynamic look-up of the virtual function table to determine the correct polymorphic form of the 'print' method to be invoked for that particular object (manager). So the actual method invocation is a two-stage process.

However, in the call to employee–>query_sal, the function query_sal is not defined as virtual – the only version that exists is the version defined in the Employee class. Therefore in this case the called function can be resolved at compile-time and static binding would be implemented leading to a direct, one-stage, method invocation at run-time as shown in Figure 5.5 – route (B). In effect, employee–>query_sal is not a message sent to an object, but a direct function call, implemented in the same way as a normal function call in C.

5.3.2   Integration of C++ and C code

Note: The following details apply equally to both the C++ compilers and C++ translators detailed in subsequent sections.

One important issue when considering a move from a C-development environment to C++ is the integration of C++ and C code because

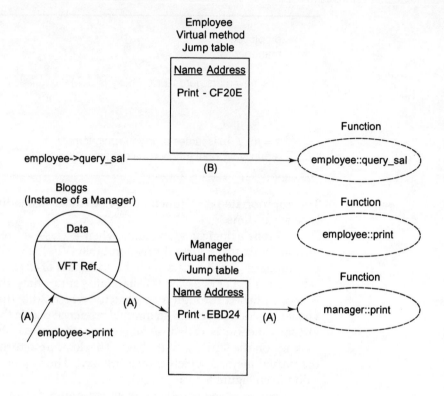

Figure 5.5   A logical view of dynamic and static binding in C++.

many project managers will hope to use C++ only in specific areas such as GUI development, with the bulk of the project being developed using standard C-code.

Type-safe linkage is employed in the C++ language. This mechanism ensures that function calls in different modules are correctly checked against the function's declaration and definition. It also provides a mechanism which allows C++ programs to be linked to files compiled through other programming languages such as C. The system is highly dependent on the disciplined inclusion of header files for library functions, which is why all functions must be declared before being used. The requirements of type-safe linkage mean that every C++ function has an internal signature appended to its name by the compiler, called **name-mangling**. The mangled name includes information on the number and type of arguments (for function overloading) and the class name – for member functions. Both C++ member functions and non-member functions have their names mangled (a non-member function is a standard C-function which is not part of a class).

Name mangling causes problems when attempting to make function calls between C++ and C. To avoid the problems, C++ provides a method of specifying to the C++ compiler not to expect this special name-mangled signature. This provides a general interface for linking procedures written in other languages to code written in C++. The linkage specifier to use for a particular function is specified by encapsulating its function prototype in a linkage directive. The syntax is (for example)

```
extern "C"
    {
    int c_funct1(void) ;
    int c_funct2(int) ;
    }
```

5.3.3 C++ compilers

The main advantage of C++ compilers over C++ translators has, in the past, been that C++ compilers directly provide C++-specific symbol table representations (therefore symbolic debugging capabilities) whereas C++ translators could not. However this situation is rapidly changing as discussed in the C++ translator section.

C++ compilers provide a shorter edit–compile–test cycle since they eliminate the translation stage of a C++ translator. Furthermore, the development environments provided with C++ compilers are generally better integrated than those available for C++ translators. The compiler manufacturers boast that C++ compilers generally provide a faster compilation cycle than translators.

There are several C++ compilers on the market today. The main ones are from Borland, Zortech and Oregon. (The Free Software Foundation provides an unsupported Gnu C++ compiler.)

5.3.4 C++ translators

AT&T developed C++ in the form of a translator which processes C++ code producing C source code, which must then be compiled in the normal way – see Figure 5.6.

The AT&T translator is an unsupported product. A source licence can be purchased directly from AT&T.

There are a number of companies developing C++ translators, including Glockenspiel, ParcPlace, Sun and Sabre. These companies have

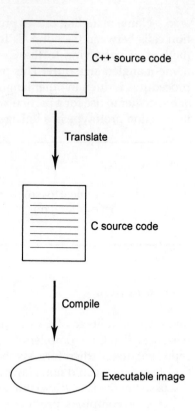

Figure 5.6   C++ to executable code via translation.

licences to port the AT&T translator – CFRONT. One of the main advantages of using a C++ translator is in protecting existing investment in C compilers and linkers. This is particularly true for companies involved in porting applications onto a wide variety of hardware platforms. Furthermore, there is an industry trend towards RISC processors to increase performance and since most RISC processors have instruction sets specifically designed to efficiently execute C, the C++ translator is able to cost-effectively take advantage of this industry trend with minimal development cost.

Initially there were no debuggers that provided C++-level debugging. However with release 2.0 of the AT&T implementation, routines are provided that understand the name-encoding algorithms used by the translator. These routines are being incorporated into existing C-debuggers, permitting the debugger to provide a more complete C++ debugging environment. Utilities also exist that can be run against a program to rebuild its symbol table, replacing the encoded C names with their C++ representations.

5.3.5 Development tools and libraries

Most C++ vendors offer a **class browser** of some description. Figure 5.7 shows the graphical class browser from ParcPlace systems for its ObjectWorks\C++ development environment.

The browser shows a class hierarchy on the left hand side, with the implementation of a highlighted class being shown on the right hand side.

C++ **interpreters** are now coming onto market. These create a highly incremental development environment, particularly useful for rapid prototyping.

There are many third party developers of C++ class hierarchies for a wide range of applications from GUIs to serial communications. Zinc Inc. (see references section for address) markets a user interface building tool for DOS graphics and Microsoft Windows. CNS Inc. markets C++/Views. This is a class hierarchy and graphical browser for MS-Windows developers. It is compatible with the Zortech and Borland C++ compilers. Vleermuis Software Research markets GUI_MASTER – a class tree for C++ development of MS-Windows or OS/2 Presentation Manager. Genesis markets Tier1 – another C++ class library for develop-

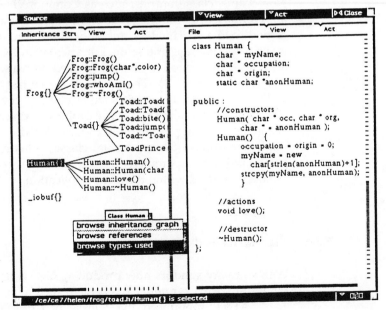

A browser shows an inheritance graph in the left subview and source code, corresponding to the selected class, in the right subview.

Figure 5.7   ObjectWorks\C++ (release 2) graphical class browser.

ing MS-Windows user interfaces. Blaise Computing markets Win++ – yet another C++ GUI class library, supporting the Borland C++ compiler.

ParcPlace markets ObjectKit\C++. This is a set of four class libraries providing support for finite state machines, error handling, list and string manipulation, and so on.

ObjectCraft Inc. has developed a PC (MS-DOS)-based object-oriented visual programming tool (also called ObjectCraft) which generates C++. It can be used to draw objects and their relationships in a graphical environment similar to a Draw or Paint program. When the developer is satisfied with the application which has been diagrammed, ObjectCraft automatically converts the application to C++.

Sequiter Software Inc. markets CodeBase++. This is a multi-user dBASE-compatible class library for C++ programmers. It provides a suite of CodeBase++ classes to access and change the data, index and memo files of dBASE IV and III. It is compatible with C++ compilers under DOS, OS/2 and Microsoft Windows.

The list of C++ products goes on … .

For purchasers of C++ class libraries, one important consideration is the exact nature of the class libraries: are they cosmic or non-cosmic? Non-cosmic class libraries, such as CommonView (from Glockenspiel), are composed of independent component hierarchies, each one concerned with a specific task: memory allocation, user interface management, object storage, and so on. Libraries such as C++/Views and Win++ are cosmic because all classes are derived from a single parent class (usually called 'OBJECT'). The OBJECT superclass provides generalized methods for everyday needs such as cloning, comparing and archiving objects of a descendant class. The problem with cosmic class hierarchies is that there are, at present, no standards. Vendors are creating their own implementations of fundamental classes. This can lead to chaos with name-clashes and parameter incompatibility when two or more cosmic libraries are used within the same application.

5.3.6   Standards and future issues

With so many vendors now producing C++ compilers and translators, the ANSI X3J16 Committee has been formed to promote a C++ standard.

AT&T announced the release of CFRONT 3.0 at the end of September 1991. This implementation of C++ includes parameterized types using class *Templates* and an exception handling mechanism via reserved words *throw* and *catch*. These features are described in Stroustrup (1991).

5.3.7   Performance

C++ allows the generation of very efficient code when invoking member functions, with none of the look-up overhead characteristic of many OOPLs. Virtual function calls are also efficiently implemented using a jump vector that exists for each class. This involves only one additional level of indirection over a normal function call. Some OOPLs delay the computations needed to determine the proper function to call until run-time. This approach does provide greater flexibility, however it slows down program execution and delays the detection of some errors until run-time (for example, if a function has not been specified, this fact would not become apparent until the program attempted to invoke the function at run-time). C++ does not have this characteristic and therefore provides good performance combined with a guarantee of the construction of complete programs.

5.3.8   Summary user case-study

IBM Ireland Information Services Limited participated in the worldwide IBM Innovative Solutions program, launched to encourage non-research IBM sites to try out new ideas and processes without business risk.

Despite the growing interest surrounding OO, IBM IISL considered there were few, if any, 'test cases' – comparisons of OO techniques with what traditional procedural techniques could have accomplished in exactly the same situation. IISL put a project together, the objective of which was to help fill this gap by making a head-to-head comparison of a procedural application and an OO version of exactly the same program. Mark Humphrys was the project leader within IBM.

IBM chose the Glockenspiel C++ translator with the Common-View GUI class library.

The project selected for re-implementation was a typical IS application – an order entry system employing a user-friendly front end to a host computer. Originally written in C for OS/2 using a standard procedural design, the data capture section was rewritten in C++, also for OS/2 PM, but using an object-oriented design.

As part of the object-oriented redesign, Humphrys found himself developing a generic library for this sort of data capture. Humphrys explains:

> 'This may surprise those coming from a procedural background, to whom writing anything generic is usually much harder than writing something application-specific. But one must understand

that this does not hold in the object-oriented world, where it is often easier to build non-working classes, expressing generic behaviour and then inherit them into application-specific, working classes'.

Findings

Humphrys found that most of the code in the old program was similar to work found in other applications within IISL. However, using the procedural methodology, it was very difficult to extract the generic properties common to many applications into a sharable library. The OO methodology was able to do this much more readily.

As a result of developing a generic class library, the new application was stripped down to less than 20 % of its original size, inheriting work from a library unrelated to the application's specification. Such a library can be shared by other applications, thus reducing the size of each one, as well as the costs involved in developing and maintaining them.

Humphrys continued:

'The language, C++, is a serious development language, losing none of the power and freedom of its procedural antecedents. The use of an object-oriented language was an essential feature in the success of the innovative design'.

Table 5.2 summarizes the statistics associated with the traditional procedural development, along with comparison statistics associated with the development of a generic class library and with the redeveloped application. Straightforward extrapolation from these figures indicates that if a site is to spend time designing its own generic objects, then it will have a sizeable initial expenditure, but it will be **cutting the cost of further applications by 50 %.**

In conclusion, Humphrys has demonstrated the power of the object-oriented technique but he does not believe it necessary to abandon completely the procedural approach. **The procedural approach can be built upon.** This is one of the benefits of a hybrid OO programming

Table 5.2   Summary of statistics from the IBM IISL experiment.

	Procedural program	Generic library	OO-specific program code
Time taken	35 days	51 days	17 days
Lines of code	5827	3919	1059
Size of executables	346K	221K	132K
Global variables	245	6	5
Average function size	39 lines	7 lines	6 lines

language such as C++ in that developers can migrate to OO in a more gradual way, building upon existing techniques without abandoning all that went before!

A full account of this project is available from Humphrys (1991).

Chapter 8 contains more comprehensive case-studies from several developers including the use of C++, Objective-C, Eiffel and Smalltalk.

5.4 Objective-C

Objective-C (Cox, 1986) is a hybrid object-oriented language which contains a superset of ANSI C and major parts of Smalltalk-80. It is a proprietary product developed by the Stepstone Corporation and marketed by Stepstone, NeXT and IBM. The system includes a compiler, browser, tracer, a foundation class library and a graphical user interface class library.

The language adds one new data type called an object and one new operation called a message, to the types and operations already available in C. The programmer develops source code with a text editor and then compiles it into binary with the Objective-C compiler. The Objective-C compiler generates C source code which is then compiled using a target C compiler for the host system. In an Objective-C program it is typical to have a number of files containing straight C-source code. Other files will make use of OO concepts and use the specific Objective-C constructs.

The developer can control binding on a compilation unit basis so that some units can be compiled with **dynamic binding** and other units with **static binding**. Objective-C supports single inheritance and provides a basic mechanism by which objects can be stored on a disk via **-storeOn:** and **-readFrom:**. Similarly there are methods available for allocating and deallocating memory, which are not automatic.

In a similar fashion to C++, Objective-C source code can be written without reference to object-oriented constructs!

5.4.1 Language

In common with C++, Objective-C uses classes and objects. An object is a new data type called an 'id'. An entity of this type is a pointer to an object's physical address in memory. A class is composed of (i) data – the information held within the class and (ii) methods – the functional logic associated with the class. The values of the data are unique for each object, whereas the methods are shared by all objects of that class.

There are two types of methods, namely class and instance methods so the language supports the notion of a class being an object (although the notion of a class variable is not supported) – refer to Section 5.1 for an overview of metaclasses. Class methods are applied to the class as a whole and are applied through factory objects. A factory object is built at compile-time and assembled into memory by the loader. Its purpose is in providing a way to create initialized instances of its class type and to provide methods that deal with all objects of a class. By convention, factory object names always begin with an upper-case character.

Instance methods act only on instances of the class or one of its subclasses. A class method must be invoked to create an instance of a class before any instance methods can be applied to that instance. By convention, instance method names always begin with a lower-case character.

All classes shipped by Stepstone are derived from a root class called 'Object' which includes, amongst others, a default class method for object creation via the command 'new'. A root class is defined as a class that has no superclass and a user may define any number of root classes.

There are two stages in defining a class. Firstly there is the definition of the class interface. This is intended for users of the class and is specified in an interface file. An example for the Employee class would be as follows:

```
#import "object.h".

@interface Employee : Object
{
        int salary ;
        char *emp_name ;
}
+create ;
-emp_name: (char *) aname ; // sets up employee's name
- (char *) emp_name ;
- salary: (int) asalary ; // sets up employee's salary
-(int) salary ;
-increase_sal: (int) sum ;
@end
```

This interface definition would be stored in a file called Employee.h.

In this example the + sign indicates a class method and a '-' sign denotes an instance method. So the above interface definition has one class method, five instance methods and two instance variables (**salary** and **emp_name**).

The implementation of a class is described in a class description file, which is the unit of modularity. Programmers create class description files, not programs or modules. An example of a class implementation for an Employee follows:

```
1    #include <objc.h>
2    #import "Employee.h"
3
4    @implementation Employee : Object
5
6    //Create new employee using the superclass 'new' method
7
8    + create
9    {
10           id newInstance ;
11           newInstance = [self new] ;// create new instance
12           [newInstance salary: 0] ;     // Initialize salary
13           [newInstance emp_name: "NoName"] //Initialize name
14           return newInstance ;          //return the new instance
15    }
16
17    - (void) emp_name: (char *) aname
18    {
19           emp_name = aname ;
20    }
21
22    - (char *) emp_name {return emp_name ; }
23
24    - (void) salary: (int) asalary
25    {
26           salary = asalary ;
27    }
28
29    - (int) salary {return salary ; }
30
31    - (void) increase_sal: (int) sum
32    {
33           salary = salary + sum ;
34    }
35    @end
```

This code resides in a file called 'Employee.m'; it would be compiled and linked into the final program.

Line 2 indicates that the class definition for Employee is imported into the class implementation. Line 4 indicates that the class Employee inherits methods and data from the root class – Object. Lines 8–15 define a class method used to create an instance of this class – this uses the selector new which is inherited from the class Object. The square brackets on line 11 are used to create a message – this will be described later. Lines 17–34 detail the implementation of the various instance methods which this class supports. The whole class is defined within the @ delimiter. The main program might look like this:

```
1       # include <objc.h>
2       # import "Employee.h"
3
4       main (argc, argv)
5       int argc ;
6       char *argv[] ;
7       {
8               id anEmployee ;
9               Employee *anEmp2 ;
10              int large_sal ;
11
12              anEmployee = [Employee create] ;
13
14              anEmp2 = [Employee create] ;
15
16              [anEmployee emp_name: "jbloggs"];//Dynamic binding
17              [anEmployee salary: 12000] ;
18
19              [anEmp2 emp_name: "gwilson"] ;// Static binding
20              [anEmp2 salary: 11000] ;
21
22              large_sal = [anEmployee salary] ;
23
24              if ([anEmp2 salary] > large_sal)
25                      {
26                              large_sal = [anEmp2 salary] ;
27                      }
28
29              [anEmployee increase_sal: 2000] ;
30
31      } // end of main program
```

Line 2 imports the definition of the Employee class. Line 8 establishes an object identifier anEmployee, but at this stage it has no value. Line 9 sets up a pointer (anEmp2) to an object of type Employee. At this stage anEmp2 points to nothing. Lines 12 and 14 create instances of the Employee class. Because of the different ways in which anEmployee and anEmp2 were declared, anEmp2 can only point to instances of an Employee whereas anEmployee could potentially point to any type of object – it is loosely typed and its type can vary during program execution.

Lines 16–29 demonstrate how message passing is implemented in Objective-C using a [followed by a receiver (that is, the instance name) followed by the selector (that is, the method to be invoked), followed by a colon followed by an argument list to be passed to the selected method, followed by a]. Message expressions are allowed anywhere function calls are allowed in the C-language – for example the if statement on line 24. The reader should compare the messages sent to instances of a class (as in lines 16–29) with messages sent to the factory object of the class (as in lines 12 and 14) where the class name is used as the selector instead of the instance name.

Messages to anEmp2 could be statically bound because the receiver type is known. However messages to anEmployee cannot be statically bound because its type is not known (an object of any type can be stored in anEmployee) until run-time.

Inheritance is illustrated by the Employee class inheriting from the generic root class 'Object'. If a new class called Manager is required, where Manager is like Employee but with one additional instance variable for a car allowance, and two additional instance methods to manipulate the car allowance, then the Manager class definition would look like this:

```
# import "Employee.h"

@interface Manager : Employee
{
        int car_allow ;
}
+create ;
- car_all: (int) aCar_allow ;
- (int) car_all ;
@end
```

An implementation of the Manager class can then be created in the same manner as for the Employee class. All instance variables and methods defined for the Employee class are now available for the Manager class as well as the additional methods associated with the car allowance.

5.4.2   Development environment, tools and libraries

Objective-C comes with a number of tools to support software development. In addition to the Objective-C compiler, there is a source browser which handles both C and Objective-C source code, and three class libraries: (i) a foundation library, ICpak 101, which includes the root class Object and extends to 20 classes with 300 methods; (ii) a graphical user interface class library, ICpak 201, with 58 classes and some 1100 methods, used in developing GUIs; and (iii) a two-dimensional graphics class library – ICpak 301.

Figure 5.8 shows the Objective-C class browser. Reading from left to right, the developer can select a class hierarchy, observe the list of classes in that hierarchy, examine the list of methods associated with a given class (either inherited or defined by the class), and determine what other methods (and classes) use a given method within a given class.

Objective-C has a run-time support environment with run-time diagnostics including a message tracing facility which causes the system to generate a record for every message sent, showing the receiver of the message, the message name and argument list as well as the sender of the message. This information can be directed to a file for subsequent analysis. Message tracing is only possible on dynamically bound messages because these messages are handled by the Objective-C central messenger. The message tracing facility can be turned on or off during execution of a program by toggling a C global variable true or false. Tracing of class object initialization is provided as a compiler option.

The Objective-C compiler is a multi-stage processor which translates Objective-C into ANSI C which is then compiled.

The basic Objective-C product contains message and allocation tracing support as already mentioned, but does not come with a debugger. Debugging is handled by the host system's C debugger such as CodeView on systems with Microsoft software and dbx on UNIX

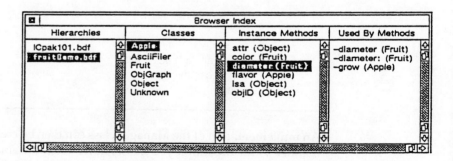

Figure 5.8   Objective-C class browser from Objective-C version 4.3.

platforms. The CodeView and dbx debuggers can be used to debug Objective-C at the source level. Literature provided with the compiler details how to achieve this.

5.4.3   Standards and future issues

Stepstone plans to implement a new set of tools for Objective-C including a new interpreter. This interpreter will provide facilities for:

- Line-by-line interpretation of source code;
- Inspection of data structures during debugging;
- Interactive definition of variables;
- Execution of statements as they are entered.

Stepstone has created some alliances, most notably with NeXT and IBM, to develop the ICpak 101 library to support a broad range of IBM hardware.

Stepstone is committed to the concept of ICpaks for the development of software systems. With this in mind it is likely that further class libraries will follow in the future.

5.4.4   Performance

In Section 5.4.1 details were given of the way in which Objective-C implements classes. Objective-C can be 'compiled' for either dynamic or static binding on a module basis. It is implemented by a compiler switch which enables the compiler to use static binding in cases where the receiver type is known. Static binding is much more efficient, requiring fewer levels of indirection.

For both static and dynamic binding, message passing is implemented through a messenger. When using dynamic binding, this messenger uses the first argument in the message (the selector) to locate the receiver's private part. There is a pointer within the private part which provides a link to the receiver's shared part (that is, the instance methods) and its dispatch table of method names and implementation addresses. This route adds a performance overhead to message passing compared with a straight C function call. Cox (1986) indicates that message passing is about 2.5 times slower than a direct function call. However, on average Objective-C applications run only 43 % more slowly than C applications because much time is spent executing normal C-code at full speed. Stepstone Corp. suggests that the figure of 43 % is because the application was so short that the initialization code (which is run once at the beginning of every Objective-C application) provided a large overhead. 'In typical commercial applications the range is 6 to 20 %'.

5.5 Eiffel

Eiffel was invented by Bertrand Meyer in the mid 1980s (Meyer, 1988) and is marketed by Interactive Software Engineering Inc. in the USA. The language is no longer a single vendor product. SIG Computer GmbH has developed a version of Eiffel (albeit only an Eiffel compiler) for the PC market running MS-DOS. This version is called EIFFEL/S. The ISE version of Eiffel comes with a programming environment but is based on the usual edit–compile–test cycle.

It is a **pure** object-oriented language with Pascal-like control structures.

The Eiffel system consists of a compiler and a set of development tools. These include facilities for automatic configuration management, debugging, documentation tools, an optimizing postprocessor and a library of about 50 basic classes for common data structures such as lists, trees, and so on. There is also a library to interface with the X11 window system. The language is implemented by compilation through C. The postprocessor can generate C which can then be used for delivery on systems which do not support Eiffel. However the language itself is an original design and has no relation to C.

Eiffel is a **strongly typed** language and includes a number of features:

- Assertions to express the formal properties of classes including **preconditions, postconditions** and **invariants**.
- Generic parameters to represent types in class declarations.
- A *rename* feature to support multiple inheritance by resolving name conflicts when a class has more than one parent.
- Feature redefinition in descendant classes to permit dynamic binding despite static type checking.

The language forces very **strict type checking** at compile-time. **Multiple and repeated inheritance** and **polymorphism** are supported. Storage allocation and deallocation is handled by a run-time system which includes an incremental garbage collector, although the garbage collector can be switched off.

5.5.1 Language

In common with normal OO nomenclature, Eiffel uses classes. A class is characterized by its **features**. There are two kinds of features, namely **attributes** (the data held within the class definition) and **routines** (the functional logic associated with the class which enables the class to provide services – hitherto called methods). In common with C++ and Objective-C, a class is a compile-time concept and an object is a run-time concept.

Consider the class to manipulate an employee's salary details; this would be defined as follows:

```
1      class EMPLOYEE export
2              create, increase_sal, query_sal
3      feature
4              salary: INTEGER ;
5              name: STRING ;
6              min_inc : INTEGER is 200 ;
7              max_inc : INTEGER is 2000 ;
8              max_sal : INTEGER is 25000 ;
9
10             create(who: STRING, val: INTEGER) is
11             -- Assign EMPLOYEE to name and set salary
12             do
13                     name := who ;
14                     salary := val
15             end ;
16
17             increase_sal(sum: INTEGER) is
18             require
19                     sum >= min_inc, sum <= max_inc
20             do
21                     salary := salary + sum
22             ensure
23                     salary <= max_sal
24             rescue
25                     -- Log an error message
26             end ;
27
28             query_sal() : INTEGER is
29             do
30                     Result := salary
31             end ;
32     invariant
33             salary >= 0
34     end ; -- End of Class definition
```

The EMPLOYEE class has three publicly accessible features – two procedures (create and increase_sal) and one function (query_sal). It has five other features, not accessible from outside the class – namely two variables (salary and name) and three constants (min_inc, max_inc and max_sal). The syntax is Pascal-like. Eiffel allows a number of assertions to be specified. Three examples of assertions have been used here.

On line 18 the require assertion has been included within the routine increase_sal. This asserts the valid range of salary increment with which the routine can be called. Line 22 shows the ensure assertion which ensures that the employee's salary does not exceed a set maximum. There is a rescue block on line 24 which will be called if a run-time exception occurs as a result of an assertion being false. When the rescue block has been executed an exception will be triggered in the calling routine (that is, within the object which called this routine). The third example of an assertion is found on line 32 – the invariant assertion applies to the whole class to ensure that a property of all objects is satisfied at all observable instants of their lives. Note that the use of assertions is optional and even if they are included within the software, they can be conditionally compiled in or out (see later section on the Eiffel environment for more details). The use of pre and postconditions combined with the exception handling facilities in Eiffel make the language particularly elegant when compared to Objective-C.

Creating an object of the class type EMPLOYEE is accomplished at run-time. In an Eiffel program, the system is made to execute in the normal way by running an executable file. This has the effect of issuing a message to the root class of the Eiffel program. Eiffel systems have no distinct 'TOP' – that is, there is no main program (and no global data) to which execution always returns when function or procedure processing has completed – all code is imbedded within classes so the language enforces the use of OO concepts. Every Eiffel program must have a root class, from which all other classes are directly or indirectly called. A Create message is sent to the root class and this causes a direct instance of the root class to be created and calls the root's Create procedure on this instance. Execution of other procedures and the creation of other objects then follows. The arguments provided on the command line when running the system are passed to the root's Create procedure. Subsequent instances of a given class are created in the following manner.

First define an entity of the class type:

```
person : EMPLOYEE ;
```

– this defines 'person' to be a reference to an object of type EMPLOYEE; then

```
person.create(jbloggs, 14000) ;
```

where the create feature is defined starting at line 10 in the above example. This creates an instance of the EMPLOYEE class type. The create feature is special. The Eiffel system provides a default create feature which allocates memory for the entire object. Any user class-defined create feature merely adds extra functionality such as initializing local data to non-zero values, for example. Once the object has been created, the public features can be accessed via messages such as:

```
person.increase_sal(2000) ;
```

or

```
get_sal := person.query_sal
```

This person object exists until

```
person.forget
```

is invoked. However, a local scope object can be created via the syntax:

```
person : Expanded EMPLOYEE ;
```

This creates an object of type EMPLOYEE. The EMPLOYEE object only persists until the object within which it was created is destroyed. So the object would be internal to some other object from which it was defined.

The way in which inheritance has been achieved in Eiffel can be understood by reference to the following example where a specific type of the Employee class is required – namely a Manager. The Manager class naturally inherits properties from the Employee class such as salary and name, but also defines a car-allowance feature in this example:

```
class MANAGER export
        increase_car_allow, query_car_allow
inherit
        EMPLOYEE
feature
        car_allow: INTEGER ;

        increase_car_allow() is
        do
                -- function
        end ;
```

```
query_car_allow() is
do
            - - function
end
end - - class MANAGER
```

Inherited features can be used directly in a child class and children can redefine inherited features as necessary.

5.5.2   Integration of Eiffel with C-source code

The Eiffel V2.3 compiler is a multi-pass translator of Eiffel source into C source, which then relies on a C compiler for further compilation. This use of C as an intermediate language has given Eiffel a good degree of portability across different UNIX platforms, and has made external interfacing with C relatively straightforward. Eiffel can call routines written in other languages such as C or Fortran.

Eiffel-to-C function calls

An Eiffel routine may rely for its execution on 'external' routines written in C. In this case the body of the routine must include an external declaration, thus:

```
increase_sal(sum: INTEGER) is
external
        check_inc(amount: INTEGER): INTEGER
        name "check_inc" language "C"
        do
            if check_inc(sum) then
                    salary := salary + sum
        end ;
```

The first feature name of the external declaration introduces the Eiffel name and the name in quotes is the C-language function name. It should be noted that operations on Eiffel objects by non-Eiffel routines may endanger the consistency of objects – for example it is easy to destroy the validity of an invariant.

C-to-Eiffel calls

For a C function to call a feature within an Eiffel object, it is necessary that the C function knows the address of the feature as well as precise details relating to the particular object involved. The Eiffel object must pass details of the feature address and the object address to the C function. The C function will then store these for use in future calls as appropriate. When a call has to be made, the address of the feature is called, passing an appropriate argument list with one additional argument at the beginning of the list. The additional argument is the address of the object to which the feature call relates and is necessary because of the absence of a notion of 'current instance' in the C-language. So, for example, an Eiffel call of the form:

```
target.feature (argument_1, argument_2)
```

will have a C counterpart of the form:

```
c_feature(c_target, c_argument_1, c_argument_2)
```

where c_target is a pointer to the actual instance of a class.

5.5.3 Development environment, tools and libraries

The ISE version of Eiffel comes with a programming environment. This environment includes a compiler, postprocessor, documentation tool and class browsing tool. A number of libraries (for example, for X-windows, character windows, data structures, parsing and lexical analysis) are also included.

SIG Computer GmbH has developed an Eiffel compiler for the PC market running MS-DOS. This version is called EIFFEL/S.

Eiffel compiler Eiffel is a compiled language. However, a run-time environment must be built with the application code. This environment is produced as object code along with the application so the developer ends up with one executable image. There are no run-time licensing arrangements for the environment. The environment and application are compiled through a system description file (SDF) called 'eiffel'. This SDF enables the user to switch various compilation options on or off: assertion monitoring, preconditions only, debug, trace, optimization, garbage collection and c-package production. The size of the environment depends on which options are selected, but generally ranges from 30K to 100K bytes in addition to the application code.

Assertion monitoring has already been discussed within the language-specific section. The 'debug' option is used to enable conditional compilation of debug instructions within the code. The 'trace' option enables all calls to routines within classes to be monitored. The use of debugging tools such as dbx is discouraged. However, Eiffel includes an interactive debugger called 'viewer' which can be used to observe the states of objects at run-time.

The garbage collector is used to remove objects automatically when all references to them within the software are gone. The memory used by the object is deallocated and released back to the system.

The Eiffel compiler performs all necessary version control, recompiling only source files which have changed since the last compilation. Each Eiffel class is contained in a separate file. The SDF is given a list of directories where needed classes are to be found (via the UNIVERSE statement). A list of all precompiled external files is given via the EXTERNAL statement. To produce an executable package, a set of classes is assembled, choosing one of the classes as the 'root'. A class called employee, for example, must be stored in a file called employee.e. In this way, the Eiffel compiler can build a complete system, starting from the root class and determining each class to be included by the references made to it from within the currently compiling file. So there is no need to keep track of dependencies through manual 'makefiles'.

C-package generation

The 'c-package production' option in the SDF is used to cause the postprocessor to generate stand-alone C-source code. It generates the following elements:

- A main program (corresponding to the create procedure of the root class in the system).
- A set of C functions which can be called from other C programs.
- A full copy of the Eiffel run-time system, including memory management and garbage collector.
- A makefile allowing recompilation of the C package on any target platform.

Documentation tool

Problems caused by documentation and software inconsistency can be reduced using Eiffel because the development environment can automatically document the source code. In the *short* form, all exported features as well as the class assertions can be documented. In the *ancestors* form, a class hierarchy can automatically be documented. The *flat* form will show the properties of a class without reference to its ancestors.

Class browsers

Two forms of class browser are available with the Eiffel development environment: (i) a character-based browser and (ii) a graphical class browser requiring an X-windowing system. These enable the developer to explore the available classes and their features as specified in the UNIVERSE entry in the SDF.

Libraries

Some 50 basic classes accompany the product. These classes have been developed by Interactive Software Engineering. Third party libraries for Eiffel systems are now starting to appear. One such library, developed by an Italian company Unirel, provides Motif and Open Look toolkits.

5.5.4   Standards and future issues

Interactive Software Engineering has placed the specification of the Eiffel language in the public domain. However the source code for the ISE compiler is not in the public domain. An industrial consortium called the Nonprofit International Consortium for Eiffel (NICE) was established in October 1990. NICE has been formed to advance the Eiffel method, language and libraries through industry consensus. NICE membership is open to any company or individual. One of the main tasks facing this consortium will be the development of a validation suite, to ensure that third party Eiffel products are legitimate.

Interactive Software Engineering will release Eiffel V3.0 in early 1993. This will include significant improvements to the development/debugging environment along with improved compiler performance and faster end-application performance. Eiffel 3 (Meyer, 1991) will support a highly incremental development cycle using a new compiling technology – the so-called 'melting ice technology'. When a small change is made to an Eiffel application, the Eiffel environment enables inter-preted code (corresponding to the parts of an application that have been modified since the last full compilation) to be mixed with compiled code so that no linking is necessary when a change has to be tested quickly.

Eiffel 3 introduces EiffelVision, a repository of Eiffel graphics classes, together with EiffelBuild, a graphical application builder enabling the interactive development of user interfaces. EiffelStore provides class libraries to interface with DBMSs such as Oracle and Ingres. There are plans to provide interfaces to both Versant and O_2 object-DBMSs.

Changes to the Eiffel 3 syntax from version 2.3 necessitate a translation of old code into the new syntax. Part of this translation must be performed manually!

5.5.5   Performance

Several attempts have been made at benchmarking the run-time performance of Eiffel applications. Attempts at comparing Eiffel with C++ typically use the standard Eiffel libraries which have some built-in inefficiencies in striving for maximal reusability. All

assertion checking and garbage collection must be turned off to see Eiffel in a comparable mode. Generally Eiffel is quoted as being between 1.2 and 2.0 times slower than C++ (source: *Journal of Object-oriented Programming*, September/October 1990, p. 86).

Cognos Inc. ran into serious performance problems with Eiffel applications which ultimately resulted in the project being shelved. Details of this project are presented in the summary user case-study in the following section.

The performance on the V2.2 compiler was better, but still not good enough according to Cognos. The V2.3 compiler is now available, however Cognos has not yet evaluated it. It is expected that Eiffel V3.0 will resolve many of the Cognos issues.

5.5.6   Summary user case-study

The dangers of expecting too much benefit from an OOPL without enough effort were highlighted in a well-publicized example by Cognos Inc. Cognos is a CASE tool vendor based in Ottawa, Canada. The company originally developed software using C. It decided to embrace object-oriented techniques and technology for the development of its Powerhouse CASE tool.

The company originally evaluated C++, Objective-C, Eiffel and Smalltalk, based on object-oriented capabilities, performance and portability. Only limited performance testing was done and the results were ambiguous. Cognos finally decided on Eiffel V2.1.

Eiffel V2.1 turned out to have serious performance problems. However, Cognos admit that many of the errors on the project were failures of management and other problems unrelated to the decision to use an OOPL. To quote from Leathers (1990):

> '... the fact that we were using an OOPL was important because it contributed to an attitude which would not otherwise have existed... The very real benefits of using OOP are presented in a very one-sided fashion which too often leads to the view that OOP is a panacea. This better-than-life outlook induced a euphoria in management which caused suspension of the normal procedures and judgement criteria. As a result, the product was inadequately defined, schedules were unrealistic and the design process was wholly inadequate'.

After many millions of dollars had been spent the project was eventually terminated. However Cognos learnt a lot from the experience. The research and development team numbered 200 staff at one stage – indeed Cognos could boast one of the biggest labs devoted to object-oriented research in the world. The experience has not soured either the technical staff or management on OOP. There is a desire to resume use of OOP when it is practical to do so. When compared with C++, Objective-C and Smalltalk, Cognos still states that 'Eiffel is the best of an ugly bunch'.

Chapter 8 presents a detailed user case-study using Eiffel.

5.6 Smalltalk

Smalltalk is an example of a pure object-oriented programming language. It was developed by Xerox from 1972 and released to the world in 1983. The development has been taken over by ParcPlace Systems – a business unit of Xerox started in 1986 to commercialize object-oriented technology. The product is now called ObjectWorks\Smalltalk. Smalltalk was previously marketed by ParcPlace systems as Smalltalk-80 (Goldberg, 1984; Goldberg and Robson, 1989). ObjectWorks\Smalltalk comprises some 350 classes with over 7400 methods. It is available for UNIX workstations under X-windows and also on 80386 and 80486-based PCs under MS-DOS with Windows.

Smalltalk is a multi-vendor language, the other main vendor being Digitalk. Formed in 1983, Digitalk has developed its own version (albeit cut down) called Smalltalk-V which runs on PCs under MS-DOS, Smalltalk-V Windows for MS-Windows, Smalltalk-V/PM running on PCs under OS/2 and Smalltalk-V/Mac for the Apple Macintosh environment. Smalltalk-V comprises some 100 classes with about 2000 methods. ObjectWorks\Smalltalk and Smalltalk-V are derived from completely different class libraries, and code which uses the user interface is not portable from ObjectWorks\Smalltalk to Smalltalk-V.

Smalltalk is not simply a programming language, it is a complete programming environment which includes a graphical user interface and a run-time environment with various housekeeping facilities such as garbage collection. The Smalltalk environment also includes a class browser for examining and manipulating class and method information. The Smalltalk system uses the same set of classes which is available, and built upon, for user applications.

Both versions of Smalltalk are interpreted or, to be more exact, programs are stored in an intermediate code format (byte codes) when added into the Smalltalk environment. Then each method is compiled into native machine code when it is called. The ParcPlace implementation uses a memory cache for storing recently invoked methods. This cache stores the compiled method, and thereafter the method is executed at full compiled speed. However, if the application is stopped for any reason, only the intermediate code is stored so the compilation process must be performed again. The philosophy behind an intermediate code format is that it potentially increases the portability. In theory, applications can be run across platforms without even having to recompile code. In practice, porting is rarely that simple especially where specific calls are made to the operating system or directly to hardware components.

Only limited separation between the development system and the delivery system can be achieved, because the user application runs within an environment. The developer can use a 'stripper' to remove unused classes and much of the actual development environment, that is, the editor, browser, and so on. However, much of the environment must remain to support the application at run-time, providing facilities such as the dynamic compilation and garbage collection. This can lead to performance problems caused by the overheads of the housekeeping facilities and, combined with the need to compile code at run-time, renders the language poor in the area of real-time systems.

The environment encourages highly interactive, incremental development methods and the dynamic typing of the language makes it an excellent vehicle for rapid prototyping and building user interfaces. The language provides single inheritance, dynamic binding and unconstrained polymorphism, strict encapsulation and the entire current execution state can be saved to disk.

However, on the minus side, individual objects cannot be saved to an external file through the facilities of the basic system and in general it is difficult to get Smalltalk programs to interwork with other systems although a primitive means of interworking with other languages is provided in the implementations from both vendors.

5.6.1   Language

Smalltalk is basically a language composed from a large number of classes, although there are only two predefined control structures, namely message sending and blocks. Unlike traditional languages which are implemented around a number of reserved words, in Smalltalk everything is constructed from a library of interacting classes and objects. A significant part of learning the language is in mastering this class library and for many developers this is its main weakness. Furthermore, the user is free to change the language as all the system class libraries are provided in source code form and readily accessible to the developer. The developer's application is composed of a set of classes which merge with the Smalltalk system classes. All classes are derived from a root class called Object.

Smalltalk is a pure OOPL and as such enforces encapsulation of both data and functionality in objects. To run a Smalltalk application, the user sends a message to one of the application's methods from the Smalltalk command interpreter. This causes a 'chain reaction' by which objects are created and messages are sent from one object to another, and thus the application executes.

The language supports the concept of a metaclass with both class variables and class methods, as well as class instances (objects) with instance variables and instance methods (refer to Section 5.1 for a general description of metaclasses). There are also global variables which can be accessed by all objects and pool variables which are shared among a group of objects. When a class is created, a new metaclass is automatically created. All metaclasses are instances of the same class called **Metaclass**. All run-time entities are objects, so even integers are instances of an integer class. This causes storage and performance overheads because every integer must have a pointer to its class descriptor.

Through the dynamic typing in Smalltalk, **unconstrained polymorphism** is allowed. This form of polymorphism does not require the inheritance subtyping relationship described in Chapter 2. In unconstrained polymorphism, any method can be called. At run-time, the dynamic type checking in the Smalltalk environment verifies that the required method is a part of the called object. If not, then a run-time exception results.

Consider the example of an Employee class to hold employee details on salary and name. This class would be created by:

(1) Opening a class browser;

(2) Selecting a class;

(3) Selecting the add subclass menu option.

A dialogue asks for a class name, and a superclass name on which the new class will build. The Smalltalk development environment then provides a new class template for class and instance variable name declarations. The environment also provides menu choices to create new methods for classes and instances. The class information that can be specified is as follows:

- The class name;
- The names of the named instance variables for objects of the class;
- The names of the class variables available to all objects of the class;
- The names of the pool dictionaries which define shared variables available to objects of the class and possibly other classes.

There are some differences in the Smalltalk syntax between Object-Works\Smalltalk and Smalltalk-V, notably the assignment operator is '<–' in ObjectWorks\Smalltalk and ':=' in Smalltalk-V. The following example uses the ObjectWorks\Smalltalk notation.

```
1     class              Employee
2     superclass         Object
3     instance variables name salary
4     comment            Holds employee details
5     class variables    MaxSalary
6     class methods

7     create: aName with: aSalary
8         "Create a new instance of the Employee class."
9         | tempStore |
10        tempStore <- Employee new.
11        tempStore initialize: aName with: aSalary.
12        ^tempStore

13    setMaxSalary: aSalary
14        "Set the maximum base salary for all Employees"
15        MaxSalary <- aSalary.

16    instance methods

17    initialize: aName with aSalary
18        "Establishing the initial employee details"
19        name <- aName.
20        salary <- aSalary.

21    increaseSalary: aSum
22        "Increasing employee's salary"
23        | tempSalary |
24        tempSalary <- salary + aSum.
25        (tempSalary < MaxSalary)
                  ifTrue: [salary <- tempSalary]
26                ifFalse: [salary <- MaxSalary]

27    querySalary
28        ^salary
```

The class Employee has two instance variables (name and salary) and one class variable (MaxSalary). It also contains two class methods (create and setMaxSalary) and three instance methods (initialize, increaseSalary and querySalary).

An instance of the Employee class would be created like so:

Employee create: 'jbloggs' with: 12000

This causes a message with selector create to be passed to the class object

Employee (that is, the receiver) with the name of jbloggs and a salary of 12000 (that is, the message arguments). Note that the argument list is split by extensions to the selector. The Smalltalk system stores the associated class method name as:

CREATE:WITH:

The class method create causes a new instance of Employee to be created (line 10) and initialized with the name jbloggs and a salary of 12000 (line 11) via a call to the instance method initialize, associated with the new instance tempStore. A reference to the newly created object is returned to the caller at line 12. The create message can equally well be sent to the class Employee from the Smalltalk command interpreter or programmatically from another object. This ability lends itself well to an incremental style of development and, combined with the dynamically typed nature of the language, makes it a good vehicle for rapid proto-typing.

If the above create message is sent programmatically then the object which sends it may subsequently want to send other messages, so an object emp1 could be used to store the returned reference to the newly created Employee – jbloggs:

emp1 <– Employee create: 'jbloggs' with: 12000

then the message:

emp1 increaseSalary: 2000

increases the employee's salary by 2000. Similarly to query the employee's salary:

pay <– emp1 querySalary

The use of the class variable MaxSalary can be demonstrated by the following scenario. Using the class method setMaxSalary, the maximum salary for an employee can be altered thus:

Employee setMaxSalary: 25000

This new value will immediately be accessible by all employee objects and descendants. This provides a means of redefining boundaries as time passes. Lines 25 and 26 illustrate the use of the class variable and also the use of the 'ifTrue, ifFalse' control structure predefined in one of the Smalltalk classes.

If there is a 'Manager' class which inherits from the Employee class and adds one additional instance variable (carAllow), one class method (create), two additional instance methods (increaseCarAllow and queryCarAllow) and redefines two instance methods (initialize and increaseSalary), then this class would again be defined through the Smalltalk class browser and would contain the following details:

```
1    class              Manager
2    superclass         Employee
3    instance variables  carAllow
4    comment            Holds Manager Details
5    class methods

6    create: aName with: aSalary and: aCarAllow
7            "Create a new instance of a Manager"
8            | tempObj |
9            tempObj <- Manager new.
10           tempObj initialize:aName with: aSalary and:
                                            aCarAllow.
11           ^tempObj

12   instance methods

13   initialize: aName with: aSalary and: aCarAllow
14           name = aName.
15           salary = aSalary.
16           carAllow = aCarAllow

17   increaseSalary: aSum
18           "Increasing employee's salary"
19           | tempSalary |
20           tempSalary <- salary + aSum.
21           ( tempSalary < (MaxSalary * 1.1))
22                          ifTrue: [salary <- tempSalary]
23                          ifFalse: [salary <- MaxSalary]

24   increaseCarAllow: aSum
25           carAllow<- carAllow + aSum

26   queryCarAllow
27           ^carAllow
```

Line 21 shows how the maximum salary for a manager is defined to be 10 % more than that for a base employee. Therefore upon increasing a manager's salary, the class variable defined in the Employee class is loaded by 10 % and used to check that the salary limit is not exceeded. The inheritance mechanism enables all instance and class variables to be inherited. Variable names defined in new classes must be different from those defined in superclasses. New methods can be added, or methods already defined (for example increaseSalary in the above case) can be redefined.

5.6.2   Development environment, tools and libraries

**ObjectWorks\
Smalltalk**

This graphical development environment uses X-windows or MS-Windows and includes a number of browsers for inspecting and modifying the class hierarchies from the following perspectives: (i) the system; (ii) through inheritance; (iii) via the method dispatch, that is, client/server relationship. There is also a symbolic debugger to examine and modify the code. A change list manager handles class changes in a group programming environment. There is also an application delivery optimizer to assist in the creation of run-time applications by stripping out unnecessary classes such as those relating to the development environment.

The system is supplied with a class library of about 350 types with 7400 methods. These include the classes used to create the development environment and useful classes for developing graphical user interfaces such as widgets and menus, along with the usual classes for manipulating strings, arrays, sets, and so on. Third party classes are available from various vendors including Knowledge Systems Corp.

The development environment provides a means of interworking with other languages, such as C, via so-called user-defined primitives.

Smalltalk-V

This version provides a graphical development environment for PCs and the Apple Macintosh. A version of Smalltalk-V for MS-Windows is available. There is a class browser, an inspector and a debugger. Again the developer has access to all the Smalltalk source code and so there is the potential for not only messing up the application under development but also the development environment itself. Smalltalk-V provides a means of interworking with other programming languages via assembly language primitives.

Various extension kits are available through Digitalk – an EGA/VGA extension kit which enhances the system's bit-mapped graphics capabilities; a communications applications pack for communicating with remote computers or electronic bulletin boards; and several 'goodies' application packs providing facilities such as a spelling checker for Smalltalk methods and environmental extensions which reduce the number of keyboard or mouse operations needed to use Smalltalk-V.

Third party class libraries are available from several vendors including Artefact.

One particularly useful add-on product from Coopers & Lybrand – called AM/ST – enables the integration of work from several developers in a LAN environment. This addresses one of the major drawbacks of Smalltalk-V – that it is essentially a single user development environment.

Both environments favour an incremental style of development best suited to rapid prototyping and computer modelling/simulation applications.

5.6.3   Standards and future issues

Smalltalk is basically a two-vendor language, with several other minor vendors. A number of suppliers have united to form the Smalltalk Consortium in order to promote the use of the language and environment and to guide its technical evolution. There is also an IEEE Microprocessor Standards Committee (P1152) involved in establishing standards in the Smalltalk world. But basically every Smalltalk product from every vendor is a unique system that is different and incompatible with every other Smalltalk product.

5.6.4   Performance

Smalltalk is an interpreted language and this limits the ultimate performance of Smalltalk applications. However, in the ParcPlace implementation, when each method has been executed once, object code for that procedure resides in memory enabling the application to run more efficiently. Performance is then limited by the various housekeeping functions, such as the garbage collector and the dynamic binding facility, performed by the run-time environment which accompanies all applications. All run-time entities are objects and therefore require pointers to class descriptors. This also limits application run-time performance. These features restrict the usefulness of Smalltalk for time-critical applications.

5.6.5   Summary case-study

In 1990, Electronic Data Systems (EDS) in Troy, Michigan benchmarked an object-oriented project against an already developed preventive maintenance system in several General Motors plants.

Using traditional development techniques with PL/1 and an Ingres DBMS, Polilli (1991) reports that the application required 265 000 lines of code. The project took 152 work-months to complete. The object-oriented benchmark, using OS/2 and Smalltalk, produced 22 000 lines of code in about 11 months. There was a 5:1 reduction in elapsed development time and a 12:1 reduction in code size, with all screens and procedures identical to the traditional development project.

It was noted that the performance of the object-oriented application was slower, particularly on complex screens.

Chapter 8 includes a more comprehensive Smalltalk user case-study.

5.7 Other noteworthy OOPLs

There are many other object-oriented languages currently available. The following short sections sketch out the main features of several other OOPLs.

5.7.1 Simula

The origins of all object-oriented programming languages can be traced back to Simula. Simula was developed at the Norwegian Computing Centre in the early 1960s by Dahl and Nygaard (1966). They took the block-structured concept of ALGOL one step further with the notion of an object, a class and inheritance and produced Simula-67. Although the roots of Simula-67 are in ALGOL, it was mainly intended as a simulation language. Thus Simula objects had an independent existence and could communicate with each other during a simulation – providing quasi-parallel processing.

The current version, Simula-86, is a multi-vendor product. Simula does not enforce strict encapsulation. The language is strongly typed. There is a run-time environment which provides facilities such as garbage collection. The developer can choose between static and dynamic binding. Application portability is achieved through the portable Simula system (S-Port) which consists of an independent package composed of a compiler which generates an intermediate language called S-code, a run-time support system and a symbolic debugger. There is also a target-dependent system which consists of a compiler to translate S-code into the target-executable code and a collection of interface routines.

Simula-86 is developed and marketed by Simula a.s., a Norwegian company set up in 1984. There have been several other implementations including one by the Lund Software House AB in Sweden.

5.7.2   Trellis

This language has been developed by the Digital Equipment Corporation (Schaffert *et al.*, 1986). The language is of an original design rather than adding extensions to base languages such as was done in C++. The design of Trellis was influenced by Smalltalk-80 although it is a strongly typed language with a Pascal-like syntax. The language supports multiple inheritance, with all classes (called types in Trellis) inheriting from a root class called Object. In common with other strongly typed languages such as Eiffel, Trellis supports dynamic binding through the subtyping (inheritance) mechanism, although where the call destination can be resolved at compile-time, the message-passing mechanism is replaced by a direct procedure call. The language also supports the use of parameterized types and function overloading (called type union in Trellis).

Trellis comes with a number of class libraries including types for window-based tools, graphics, text i/o and collections. The language also provides two mechanisms for interworking with other languages such as C, Pascal and Fortran, via the Call-out Library and a corresponding Call-in Library.

The language comes with a programming environment which consists of a number of tools that share a consistent user interface and a common programming environment database.

The tools include:

- An editor;
- An incremental compiler so that a minimum set of definitions is recompiled when changes are made;
- Browsers to display lists of categories (semantic groupings of classes), classes and class definitions;
- A cross-reference tool. This can list the definitions which invoke a particular operation;
- A type (or class) hierarchy tool to display hierarchy information.

The programming environment database contains objects that represent the definitions which make up an application program. Each definition contains source and object code, as well as other information produced by the compiler.

Trellis requires a run-time environment which supports the message-passing mechanism and provides a garbage collection facility.

5.7.3   Actor

Actor (Whitewater Group, 1989) is a pure OOPL, based on Pascal and specifically designed for developing Microsoft Windows applications. It provides a library containing classes to perform a variety of functions, mostly dealing with Windows objects – menus, icons, graphics and so on. Everything in Actor is an object – even classes themselves are objects with variables and methods. The language supports single inheritance and includes a linked-in run-time environment which provides a garbage collector. Both dynamic and static binding are supported, however static type checking is employed at all times.

In addition to the language, Actor comes with a development environment which includes (i) an inspector to enable the user to examine and change the contents of an object; (ii) a class browser; and (iii) a debugger – implemented as a combination of the inspector and browser. Actor also has the capability to 'seal off' a program to create a stand-alone application, and requires no royalty on the resulting product.

Because of its purpose, that is, for developing MS-Windows applications, Actor is only available for the PC (MS-DOS + MS-Windows) environment.

5.7.4   CLOS

The Common LISP Object System was formed by a committee (Bobrow *et al.*, 1988) based on an earlier language called LOOPS. It is a **hybrid** object-oriented language with a LISP-like syntax. CLOS provides a similar incremental style to Smalltalk and is likewise an interpreted language with weak typing making it useful for performing rapid prototyping. CLOS is included here because of its wide use in the AI community and its significance, since there is an ANSI X3J13 committee which is standardizing the language. Xerox and Symbolics are involved in its development.

5.7.5   Object Pascal

The Joint Pascal Committee, a standards-development body for ANSI that comprises compiler vendors and other industry experts, is seeking to develop a standard OO Pascal. However at present there are several popular object-oriented extensions to Pascal. The main ones are Object

Pascal for the Macintosh from Apple Computer, QuickPascal from Microsoft and Turbo Pascal from Borland, both for IBM PCs. As a consequence of the lack of standards in this area, the offerings from the various vendors are not necessarily compatible.

Object Pascal (Schmucker, 1986) was designed by Niklaus Wirth and a group of Apple engineers. It has since been placed in the public domain. It extends the Pascal language to support the notions of abstract data types, methods and inheritance. It extends the Pascal RECORD structure to support the notion of class definitions, so a RECORD can contain both data and method fields. Methods are defined as Pascal procedures or functions, qualified by the name of the class. Messages are sent using the normal Pascal construct for field qualification.

Object Pascal adds extensions to the Pascal language in a similar way to the development of C++ from C. However in the Pascal arena, all vendors are offering compilers whereas in C++ there are both compilers and preprocessors available.

Borland's Turbo Pascal adds four new constructs to procedural Pascal, namely object, virtual, constructor and destructor. It provides dynamic binding through a virtual method table in a similar way to C++. Turbo Pascal for Windows also includes The Whitewater Group's Whitewater Resource Toolkit, a set of tools for building Windows menus, dialogue boxes and other resources, as well as a Turbo Debugger for Windows which runs full-screen under DOS.

Rather than approving any of the current OO Pascal derivations as a standard, the ANSI standard is likely to combine parts of the current OO Pascal extensions with new extensions, while maintaining compatibility with the most recent standards for procedural Pascal. New features likely to be added include multiple inheritance and data hiding.

5.7.6   Object COBOL

One potentially massive area for migration to an object-oriented approach is COBOL. There is an estimated 70–80 billion lines of COBOL source code in the world today. COBOL has a trillion dollar market and there are still programmers to be tapped that want long-lived maintainable code which fourth generation languages cannot provide.

With its roots in the conservative mainframe world, the COBOL community has traditionally been slow to adopt new programming principles. This time, however, the object-oriented promise of allowing developers to reuse code more easily and of reducing maintenance effort has prompted leading vendors of COBOL compilers to keep pace with the rest of the programming community.

In November 1989, a significant meeting was held in Scottsdale, Arizona. It was a symposium sponsored by the Codasyl COBOL Committee to explore the relevance of the object-oriented methodology to the COBOL language. The meeting resulted in the formation of an object-oriented COBOL Task Group charged with creating standards for a COBOL object-oriented language. According to a report by Garfunkel (1990), the goals of the task group include the following:

- 'Compatibility with existing COBOL language syntax. That is, no new syntax will be added to make older COBOL programs obsolete.'
- 'Simplicity of language features – simple and direct syntax.'
- 'Consistency with current COBOL syntax and semantics; that is, the behaviour of any well-defined COBOL features will not change.'
- 'Minimum changes to run-time operations.'
- 'Encapsulation of old code in an "object wrapper" thereby allowing the current huge inventory of COBOL programs potentially to work with the newly created and designed object-oriented COBOL programs.'
- 'Transformability, or the ability of an object to adapt to various different uses in different environments with a minimum of effort.'

The key issue is to get object-oriented COBOL out of standards committees (including the American National Standards Institute (ANSI) [X3J4] and the International Standards Organization (ISO) [WG4] COBOL committees) and into practice. When the proposed Object COBOL syntax is accepted by the Codasyl COBOL Committee, Garfunkel (1990) believes 'some COBOL vendors may go ahead and add this syntax to their COBOL compilers as vendor extensions. They won't wait for it to become an official ANSI and ISO standard.'

Extensions can be added through either a preprocessor or a compiler. Each has advantages: a preprocessor could allow any computer system which has COBOL to use the new product. However, the method places a greater distance between the programmer and what is being run. In contrast, the compiler method would require the development of a new compiler for each hardware platform covered. Essentially the issues are the same as those presented in an earlier section on C++, where both C++ translators and compilers are being developed.

Leading the migration to OOP are Hewlett-Packard, Micro Focus Inc. and Realia Inc., each of which submitted working papers with proposed OOP extensions at the Codasyl meeting. The OO extensions will become an addendum to the current ANSI COBOL 85 standard.

Micro Focus plans to release an object-oriented preprocessor for COBOL/2 as well as a Smalltalk-based front-end development environment through an agreement with Digitalk that will allow Smalltalk-V PM to be integrated into the COBOL/2 workbench. The workbench will provide a messaging interface between Smalltalk objects and COBOL applications. This partnership illustrates the trend towards more sophisticated user interfaces connected to traditional back-end COBOL-based DP systems in the first instance, with possibly Object COBOL back-ends at some future date.

5.8 General object-oriented programming issues

The various user case-studies presented in Chapter 8 will give the reader details of users' experience with specific programming languages. However, there are several issues which relate to more than one language and are included in this section.

Having read through Chapter 2 you will appreciate that OO principles lead to a more flexible approach to software development. However, this flexibility is introduced at the expense of simplicity. So what effects does an OO approach have on software development and debugging?

5.8.1 The effects of inheritance on the development process

Inheritance provides advantages and disadvantages in the development of software. On the plus side, inheritance – particularly multiple inheritance – tends to result in less code redundancy. However, multiple inheritance is difficult to manage and requires good developer environment support to resolve problems such as name clashes.

It is common in many OO languages that changes in the class hierarchy force a full recompilation of every class in the hierarchy. Every client of every class may also have to be recompiled. This is a violation of the principle of encapsulation because the effect of minor changes in the relationship between two classes could propagate throughout the entire class hierarchy in an unrestricted manner. Experience with C++ and Eiffel shows that system recompilation following a change in the inheritance hierarchy can be a serious problem for users.

One possible solution involves link-time binding. Instead of full recompilation, a relink of the class hierarchy would be sufficient.

5.8.2 The effects of OO constructs on the debugging process

Purchase (1991) provides a good text on debugging tools for object oriented programming. In this paper they discuss the various principles to consider for their affects on the debugging process, including:

(1) Data abstraction through the object's interface
(2) Inheritance
(3) Dynamic binding.

Observations from Purchase (1990) are summarized in the following three sections.

The effect of data abstraction

The encapsulation of an object's data and method implementations, through the use of a clearly defined interface and message passing, prevents the formation of hidden dependencies between objects. All dependencies are explicit and so bugs are easier to isolate.

'Careless bug correction often introduces more bugs to a software system. Data abstraction helps reduce this because it localizes changes made to an object's data or methods.' This localization on an per-object basis also helps prevent the introduction of bugs during incremental development and prototyping.

The notion of an object as an independent software component also supports unit testing. 'Clearly defined objects constitute ideal subjects for unit tests: they are self-contained and are specified in advance of implementation' so that test cases can be generated early.

The effect of inheritance

'The major flaw of inheritance is that it violates data abstraction to some degree. Inheritance allows classes to use directly the data representations and methods defined in superclasses.' Consequently bugs can propagate through a class hierarchy and some localization is lost.

Inheritance 'decreases the ease of program modification'. Complex dependencies can be created in subclass/superclass relationships. This can cause problems when a method or data representation has to be changed.

'Multiple inheritance raises the possibilities of method run-time clashes. An incoming message may match two or more methods inherited from different classes. Such clashes are solved automatically in some systems by linearization of the class hierarchy such as in C++, or by manual arbitration.'

Developers may create generic classes to achieve high degrees of reusability. However these generic classes are merely templates from which specific classes are created. But generic classes have no instances and a behaviour that is so free of context as to be non-executable.

'Undisciplined or multi-disciplined use of inheritance can lead to complex, overly deep structures that are confusing. These class hierarchies may, at first glance, appear to be well formed, but are flawed.'

The effect of dynamic binding
'The scope for subtle errors in polymorphism is enormous. A tester who is unaware of how a given method is overloaded may have false confidence in a bugged variant after other variants pass prescribed tests.'

The complexity of polymorphism and dynamic binding can confuse developers and testers by, for example, obscuring the origin of a bug.

The lack of compile-time consistency checking which is found in unconstrained polymorphism (such as Smalltalk) removes the static level of bug finding which is normally covered by a compiler.

Purchase (1991) reports that it is debatable whether 'the tendency of dynamic binding to conceal subtle bugs and thereby lengthen their location time is compensated adequately by the flexibility it offers.'

5.8.3   Languages without class libraries

Languages commonly provided without a foundation library and an application framework introduce several problems for developers trying to save time by using multiple third-party libraries. Without a common foundation library, all application framework and add-on library vendors are forced to provide their own classes for commonly used data types such as arrays and strings. This was discussed in the C++ section, where it is particularly pertinent. It is the problem of the cosmic versus the non-cosmic class libraries. Combining several third party class libraries then results in overlapping class libraries. This causes naming conflicts in class names and problems with parameter incompatibilities where, for example, each class hierarchy will only accept instances of its own string class as parameters into member functions.

C++ vendors will soon bundle proprietary foundation libraries and application frameworks with their C++ compilers. This will reduce the number of library clashes, but it will introduce a new set of problems. First, an application design and implementation will be dependent on the class library, and that leads to a dependency on a particular C++ vendor.

Second, developers of add-on class libraries will often have to redesign their products for each foundation library and application framework. This will prevent some class library vendors from providing versions of their product for more than one environment. Smalltalk class library vendors are facing this problem today: only a minority of the commercial class libraries work with both ParcPlace Systems' ObjectWorks\Smalltalk and Digitalk's Smalltalk-V.

When industry standards for foundation class libraries emerge, the concept of pluggable application classes will become a reality.

5.8.4   Issues for large development projects

Praxis (1989) identifies two problems that can arise with large class libraries (Rosamund Rawlings, personal communications).

Class explosion
On a large system, numerous, possibly unrelated classes can proliferate. The implementation of a set of classes generally results in one object containing or referencing other objects. Both the containing and the contained objects may be represented by classes, each with their own characteristic behaviour. The structure is clear at the design stage, but in the implementation what results is a set of apparently unrelated classes. The result can be a daunting proliferation of classes, which may be hard for maintainers or new developers to understand.

It is therefore important to impose some higher-level structure on the implementation. This can be done by identifying groups of classes representing some component of the design, such as a subsystem. In a large system, several levels of structure could be used, such as a system, subsystem, sub-subsystem and so on. Such structure should be present in the design, if any sort of hierarchical analysis has been used. The entity modelling method of Jacobson (1987) can be used in this way to give a hierarchy of data items, the lowest level of which corresponds to a class. Many OOA&D methods summarized in Chapter 4 include techniques for decomposing systems into subsystems.

Message explosion
The other problem with large object-oriented developments is the message explosion. Here, the problem lies in the fact that the class structure can be understood without reference to its run-time behaviour. The dependencies between classes can escalate because each class contains messages sent to instances of many other classes. The maintainers may have to understand the interfaces between a given class and all other classes before they modify the given class. Such code can become very difficult to understand. Message explosions are typical of wrongly chosen class structure. In a well-structured system, messages should typically be sent only between classes in a closely-related group.

This condition is easier to detect in a statically typed language such as C++, where the inter-class dependencies are made visible. In a dynamically typed language, such as Smalltalk, where the inter-class dependencies are not obvious, a more disciplined design and coding regime is required. For example, all dependencies must be well documented in the code.

5.9 Choosing an object-oriented programming language

The foregoing sections of this chapter introduced a number of OOPLs and discussed the features of each. Some outstanding issues related to the software coding and debugging process were also discussed. You may have read through this chapter for a first stage, paper-based, evaluation of the current language offerings. This section will help collate the various aspects which may be important to you in choosing a language.

The things to consider when choosing a programming language include:

- **The degree of object-oriented support.** The preceding sections illustrate that not all languages support all the object-oriented principles to the same degree. From Chapter 2 you will have decided which principles are of most use to you. To what extent are these principles supported in the various languages?

- **The associated development environment.** Are there browsers and debugging facilities available? Does the environment support multi-user development?

- **Type of inheritance.** Does the language support single or multiple inheritance? How can the inheritance be managed? Are there facilities to help with the resolution of naming conflicts and so on?

- **Characteristics of the final application.** How fast will the final binary image execute? How large is the binary image? Does it include a large proportion of code devoted to housekeeping facilities such as garbage collection and assertion checking?

- **The typing system.** Is the language statically or dynamically typed? The answer to this question has important implications for the type of software being developed. Dynamically typed languages are better for rapid prototyping whereas statically typed languages create a more rigid framework suitable for developing commercial-grade software.

- **The ability to interwork with other languages.** This is important where investments in existing software necessitate its reuse through interworking with a new language. Or where interfaces are needed to lower-level languages to perform systems type functions.

- **Are there standards for the language.** If the decision on a language is strategic for your organization then standards will be important.

- **Language maturity.** If commercial-grade software is going to be developed then the language must offer a degree of robustness characteristic of a mature product.

- **Language support by vendor and through third party products.** Introducing any new technology has teething problems and vendor support will be necessary. Third party products may enhance your development capabilities.

- **Commercial factors.** Another consideration is the degree to which the various products have penetrated the market. Market success does not necessarily indicate technical excellence, however it indicates which products are most likely to become long term standards. The current market for traditional languages supports two major players, namely COBOL and C. It is likely that one, or perhaps two OOPLs will dominate. Other OOPLs will find niche markets and some will inevitably not survive for one reason or another. Obviously no one wants to choose a language from this last category!

The answers to many of these questions can be found in the relevant sections of this chapter. For the sake of comparison, the following text discusses some of these issues. Tables 5.3 and 5.4 then provide a summary set of answers to the above questions.

5.9.1 Degree of object-oriented support

This section relates to the main object-oriented languages C++, Objective-C, Eiffel and Smalltalk.

C++ is a hybrid language employing a C-like style of syntax. Static type checking is used at all times. The language provides the syntax and semantics for encapsulation. It supports multiple inheritance, however, there is no predefined root class or class hierarchy. The language requires a main program and the developer is free to define non-member functions which are equivalent to normal C-functions. This makes the language a suitable replacement for existing C development work. The default policy in C++ is static binding, dynamic binding is applied to routines declared as 'virtual', so dynamic binding is dictated by the programmer.

Eiffel is a pure OO language organized into autonomous software units (classes). There is no main program and no global data, and the language enforces an object-oriented discipline. It provides a means of semi-formally specifying the contracts between objects by using assertions. The language has an inbuilt mechanism for handling exceptions. Eiffel provides generic classes, that is, parameterized by types, so for example, a class LIST[T] can use any type (class) as an actual generic parameter. In Eiffel, the compiler is responsible for exploiting the performance of static binding over dynamic binding. Static (strong) typing ensures that operator–operand mismatches are discovered at compile-time. The language supports multiple inheritance. Eiffel is suitable for higher-level applications development. It can interface to C and other 3GLs.

Objective-C is another extension to the C-language. It requires the use of a main program and code can be developed in a traditional manner without reference to objects and classes! The language partially supports the notion of a class object through the use of class methods, although class variables are not supported and there is no concept of a metaclass. The language also provides a root class (Object) from which all user-defined classes can inherit methods. Every class (except Object) has exactly one parent so only single inheritance is supported. Both static and dynamic typing are supported which favours a quicker change-to-execution cycle at the expense of security. Both static and dynamic binding are supported. The syntax and semantics for encapsulation are also provided. Again Objective-C is suitable for use in areas traditionally developed using C.

Smalltalk is a pure OO language organized into classes. There is no main program but the concept of global data exists. The language supports only dynamic binding and single inheritance through a root class called Object. The language also supports the notion of a class object, with both class variables and methods. Objects are instances of classes and can include both instance variables and instance methods. There are no formal types in the language so identifier names for objects must be carefully chosen to indicate the class to which the object belongs. There is a run-time environment which provides facilities such as garbage collection. Both variables and methods are inherited and inherited methods can be redefined. The syntax and semantics for encapsulation are also provided in the language. It is an interpreted language. Smalltalk is the most mature of all OO languages, being first released as a product in 1983. The dynamic typing and interpreted nature of the language make it particularly useful for rapid prototyping of applications.

To classify the four languages in terms of their degree of object-oriented support, they could be ranked as follows:

Smalltalk > Eiffel > Objective-C > C++

Based purely on OO technical merit, Smalltalk is the best choice with Eiffel a close second.

5.9.2   Development/run-time environments

C++ is currently the only truly multi-vendor OOPL. Most of these vendors also supply a development environment including an editor, class browser, and so on (for example, ParcPlace and Sabre). There is no standard set of classes supplied with the language – the amount of supporting class library material varies from one supplier to another. The language does not require a special run-time environment. There is consequently no background garbage-collection facility and when using static binding the language produces code which is as efficient as C. C++ is probably the most efficient code of any object-oriented language.

Objective-C is supplied by one vendor. There is a standard development environment supplied with the language which includes a class browser. The language implements message passing through a central messenger, and this provides a means of message tracing. Message tracing is provided through a compiler switch which adds the facility to the run-time environment. Objective-C applications are quoted as being about 20 % slower in execution than comparable C applications.

Eiffel is supplied by two vendors. The language comes with a full development environment and graphical class browser as well as a number of class libraries. The development environment provides a powerful means of resolving name clashes caused by inheritance. The language requires a fairly extensive run-time environment which provides facilities such as a background garbage collector and assertion checking. The performance of Eiffel applications is likely to be slower than for Objective-C or C++.

Smalltalk is supplied by basically two vendors. The language comes with a complete development and run-time environment including browsers and a substantial class library which is also used by the Smalltalk system. The run-time environment includes a garbage collector. The development environment is supplied in source-code form so that developers can add-to/enhance the existing classes – this requires the application developer to be very careful. The language is interpreted and this renders it less useful for developing real-time applications. A given application is likely to perform most slowly when implemented in Smalltalk as compared to C++, Objective-C or Eiffel.

For all OO programming languages, inherited methods provide more generality and this tends to result in small applications developed using procedural languages being smaller than similar applications written using an OOPL. This observation may be offset in larger applications by the fact that inherited code is loaded only once and shared in many places.

5.9.3   Commercial factors

Another way to compare the various offerings is by examining their uptake by customers.

To date about 3000–4000 copies of Eiffel have been sold worldwide. Some 3500 copies of the Objective-C compiler have been sold worldwide, with about 25 % of these sold in Europe. It is estimated that the installed base of C++ in 1990 was 137 000 and for Smalltalk in 1990 the figure was 168 000 units. In 1991 the installed base of C++ was estimated at 400 000 units (source: Stroustrup, 1991b).

C++ is the only truly multi-vendor OOPL at present. There are third party training courses run by a number of organizations and C++ libraries are appearing from independent companies such as Zinc, Vleermuis, Genesis, Sequiter, and others. Eiffel is available from two sources, however Interactive Software Engineering is still the dominant source. Objective-C is a proprietary language. Neither Eiffel nor Objective-C has received the same widespread acceptance as C++. Third party developments for these languages (such as libraries) are certainly not significant as yet. All support for Objective-C is provided through the parent company in the USA.

The product costs vary depending on functionality and hardware platform so a direct comparison based on cost would not be very meaningful. What is more important is the market penetration and supporting products. On these considerations, C++ has the brightest future.

A report by Ovum Ltd (Ovum, 1989) predicts that the market for the C++ language and tools worldwide will rise from US$ 64 million in 1990 (US$ 19 million in Europe) to US$ 398 million by 1994 (US$ 159 million in Europe). For Smalltalk the corresponding figures are US$ 19 million in 1990 (US$ 4 million in Europe) to US$ 227 million in 1994 (US$ 61 million in Europe). Figures were not available for other OO languages, but based on revenue forecasts for object-oriented systems it is likely that the market for all other OO languages mentioned in this book (excluding CLOS) will be about 20 % of the figures given for C++ in 1990 and 1994 respectively.

5.9.4   Standards

For any language to be fully accepted there must be non-proprietary public standards that define the language. A standard defines the syntax and semantics of a language that all vendors and all versions of the

Table 5.3   Table of features for the main OO languages presented in this book.

	C++	Objective-C	Eiffel	Smalltalk
Inheritance	Multiple	Single	Multiple	Single
Message/ method binding	Default-static Optn-dynamic	Default-dynamic Optn-static	Dynamic	Dynamic
Type checking	Static	Dynamic and static	Static	Dynamic
Run-time environment	Minimal	YES – linked-in	YES – linked-in	YES – separate
Library support	3rd party (not standard)	YES	YES	YES
Ability to interwork with other languages	YES	YES	YES	Difficult
Standards bodies	ANSI X3J16	NO	NICE	IEEE (P1152)
Storage management	Manual	Manual	Automatic (optional)	Automatic
Encapsulation	Weak	Weak	Strict	Strict
Classes as objects	NO	YES (limited)	NO	YES
Support for polymorphism	YES	YES	YES	YES
Tools support	3rd party (not standard)	YES	YES	YES

language must support. Today there are no proper Smalltalk standards (although the IEEE P1152 body has been mentioned in the preceding Smalltalk section). The same is true of Objective-C. Eiffel has been placed in the public domain, but currently C++ is the only one of the four major object-oriented programming languages for which there is a recognized standards body in place.

Tables 5.3 and 5.4 summarize the answers to a number of pertinent questions related to choosing an OOPL.

Table 5.5 summarizes the most appropriate areas of software development for each of the languages presented in this book.

Table 5.4   Table of features for other OO languages presented in this book.

	Simula	Trellis	Actor	Object Pascal	CLOS
Inheritance	Multiple	Multiple	Multiple	Single	Multiple
Message/ method binding	Dynamic or static	Dynamic or static	Dynamic or static	Dynamic or static	Dynamic
Type checking	Static	Static	Static	Static	Dynamic or static
Run-time environment	YES – linked-in	YES – separate	YES – linked-in	NO	YES
Library support	YES	YES	YES	YES	YES
Ability to interwork with other languages	YES	YES	YES	YES	Difficult
Standards bodies	Simula Standards Group	NO	NO	ANSI Pascal Committee	ANSI X3J13
Storage management	Automatic	Automatic	Automatic	Manual	Automatic
Encapsulation	Weak	Strict	Weak	Weak	Weak
Classes as objects	NO	YES	YES	NO	YES
Support for polymorphism	YES	YES	YES	YES	YES
Tools support	YES	YES	YES	YES	YES

5.10   Summary and conclusions

This chapter presented details on four of the main OOPLs in use today, with brief details on five other languages. These languages illustrate some of the many different interpretations of the basic principles of object orientation (encapsulation, classes, inheritance, polymorphism), from the extensions to traditional languages as seen in C++, through the strict statically typed nature of compiled languages such as C++ and Eiffel, to the dynamically typed, interpreted languages such as CLOS and Smalltalk.

Table 5.5 OOPL primary areas of applicability.

Low-level systems work	High-level application prog.	Graphical user interfaces	Info. systems*	Prototypes	Knowledge-based systems
Objective-C	Objective-C	Objective-C			
C++	C++	C++	C++		
	Eiffel	Eiffel			
	Actor	Actor			
	Trellis	Trellis			
	Object Pascal	Object Pascal			
	Simula	Simula		Simula	
	Smalltalk	Smalltalk	Smalltalk	Smalltalk	
	CLOS	CLOS		CLOS	CLOS
	Object COBOL				

* Denotes information systems development using an object-oriented DBMS.

Based on the myriad of features available, the languages have been categorized and information has been given to help the reader decide which languages are most suitable for their development environment.

Early experiences with the use of these languages have been mixed. But most users have observed poorer end-application performance compared with traditional language implementations, although each new release brings with it faster end-application performance. The principle of data abstraction through encapsulation leads to clearly defined interfaces between objects and improves the structure of software compared with traditional (structured) practices. The properties of inheritance and dynamic binding introduce new opportunities for the creation of bugs. But, as with all software development, experience, care and good management will help reduce the potential for problems.

The real advantages of pure object-oriented languages are in eliminating pointer problems, storage management problems and providing environments that support change. Weighted against this argument is the fact that the hybrid OOPLs, and in particular C++, generally provide the best end-application performance because they don't incur the penalties associated with run-time environments.

Class browsers are essentially first generation design tools providing a means of seeing the design separate from the source code. The whole object-oriented software development process revolves around the class hierarchy. It is therefore important to choose a development environment which supports navigating through a class hierarchy from several views.

New technology can be introduced in one of two ways: either in a revolutionary fashion, by making the change completely and instantly, or in an evolutionary way, making the change incrementally and gradually in time. The OO programming approach allows both ways of introduction. Selecting the revolutionary approach, Smalltalk provides a suitable conceptually consistent object-oriented programming language. As Ramackers (1989) suggests, 'Programmers concentrate on learning the new paradigm consistently because Smalltalk only allows OO programming.'

Using a traditional language with OO support such as Objective-C or C++ enables the introduction of OO in an evolutionary manner. According to Ramackers (1989): 'Programmers may still use procedural code next to OO code. The percentage of OO code grows gradually as programmers get used to the new approach to programming.' However, to have any hope of successfully using the hybrid OOPLs like C++ and Objective-C requires a good OO design. This should result in the programmers finding the easiest solution through the use of the OO constructs in the language. Training in OO programming is very important! As LaLonde *et al.* (1989) observed, it is difficult to take experienced C programmers and have them program the majority of their code in an object-oriented style because they have the natural tendency and the language support in C++ to resist.

Ramackers (1989) suggests that the hybrid OOPLs 'offer more compatibility with existing hardware and software environments because they are based on existing technologies. These languages could be used in a revolutionary manner but such a method would require a very disciplined approach.'

'The more integrated type-checking systems such as Eiffel and Actor form an intermediate choice between a conceptually consistent approach as in Smalltalk, and a production-oriented approach as in Objective-C.'

The reader should refer to Chapter 8 which includes several user case-studies using the main programming languages described here. The summary and conclusions section of Chapter 8 augments this section.

6 Developing information systems using OO techniques

INTENDED READERSHIP

Managers and project leaders involved in developing any kind of information systems should read this chapter. Particular sections will be of interest to MIS managers and software developers from traditional data processing backgrounds.

CHAPTER PRE-REQUISITES

Chapter 2   Concepts
Chapter 4   Analysis and design
Chapter 5   Object-oriented programming languages

Readers should be familiar with the object-oriented principles presented in Chapter 2. The reader should also be familiar with the techniques of data modelling. Chapter 4 introduces data modelling through a generic OO analysis approach. Most object-oriented database management systems (OODBMSs) are provided as an extension to an object-oriented programming language. The reader is therefore advised to read selected parts of Chapter 5 – principally the sections on C++ and Smalltalk.

This chapter also assumes a familiarity with the broad concepts of a database management system involving a schema, data definition and data manipulation languages.

CHAPTER OVERVIEW

Traditionally, software engineering and database management have existed as separate disciplines. Database technology has concentrated on the static aspects of information storage, while software engineering has modelled the dynamic aspects of software. With the arrival of object-oriented database management systems (OODBMSs), the two disciplines are combining to allow the concurrent modelling of both process and data.

This chapter presents a brief history of database management systems leading up to the third generation of databases. The data management requirements of both engineering and traditional environments are considered. It is suggested that relational technology has some inadequacies with respect to traditional as well as specialized environments.

Two approaches to the development of a third generation DBMS – (i) the revolutionary approach using pure OODBMS and (ii) the evolutionary approach, adding object-oriented extensions to relational DBMSs – are presented. Both approaches are discussed in detail, with examples showing what is involved in each. Several commercially available OODBMSs are presented in summary, and a number of points to consider when choosing an OODBMS are discussed.

A third approach to introducing object orientation into database applications, via the use of object-oriented applications employing relational DBMSs, is described. Several object-oriented 4GLs and application generators are presented.

The chapter concludes with a discussion of the likely impact of OODBMSs over the next few years.

6.1   A brief history of database management systems

Some 30 years ago programs interacted directly with storage devices, each program having its own file model and manipulation operators. The advent of general file access methods such as the indexed sequential access method (ISAM) replaced the program-specific models with standardized access methods.

DBMSs represented the next stage in evolution. These systems sat on top of the access method software, interfacing with programs in a hardware-independent manner, although the program still had to navigate the underlying files. These first generation DBMSs, such as the CODASYL system, provided a **data definition language** (DDL) and **data manipulation language** (DML). The DDL enables users to define records and their contents, while a DML allows instances of records to be accessed. Network and hierarchical DBMSs are examples of first generation DBMSs.

Relational DBMSs presented a higher level of abstraction by virtually eliminating the need for navigation. These systems are referred to as second generation DBMSs. They are the dominant type of DBMS on the market today. In a relational system, data is organized in tables with a row–column structure.

One of the strengths of the relational approach is that data can be accessed in a very flexible way, which is not the case with the older network and hierarchical models. Another strength is that they enable almost complete separation of data access and manipulation operators from program code. Using a high-level query language such as

Structured Query Language (SQL), it is possible to specify which data is required without specifying how the data should be accessed. The DBMS works out the optimum means of retrieving the requested data. This makes the application programmer's job somewhat simpler.

The original ISO standard for SQL, established in 1987, was followed in 1989 by an extended version (ISO 9075). SQL2 is now standard and work on SQL3 is under way, so clearly some form of SQL is set to continue for many years to come.

Work is underway to develop the next generation of DBMS (the third generation). This generation addresses several problems inherent in relational

technology. The next section discusses these problems and the section after that discusses the approaches to developing a third generation DBMS. One important approach to a third generation DBMS is the object-oriented DBMS. This DBMS replaces the data/procedure segregation found in a relational DBMS, by the segregation of one object from another, while at the same time, an object's data and methods information is encapsulated. This concept of encapsulating an object's data and methods (procedures) is the key conceptual difference between a relational database and an object-oriented database. Figure 6.1 depicts the evolution of databases over the past 30 years, and puts the OODBMS into perspective.

6.2 Limitations of relational technology

Performance

Relational DBMSs suffer from performance problems which are especially noticeable when manipulating complex data requiring many tables of information, such as found in the area of computer-aided design (CAD), or when performing high-volume on-line transaction processing. This results from the excessive use of keys and the overhead of set processing.

Support for relationship semantics

The relational model cannot capture and control the semantics of complex applications. For example, although the relational model enforces referential integrity, it has no mechanism for distinguishing between

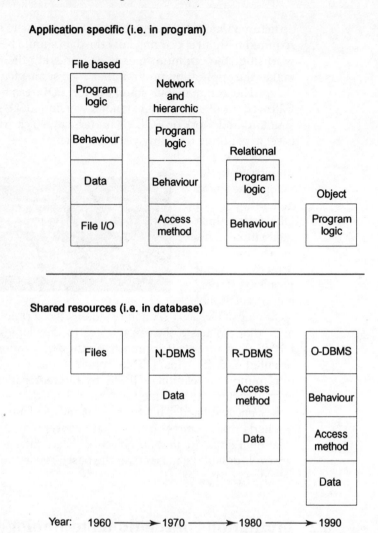

Figure 6.1   Data management generations (Lyngbaek, 1991, reproduced with kind permission of Hewlett-Packard Laboratories).

the different kinds of relationship which may exist between entities Many different kinds of relationship exist. These include: one-to-one, one-to-many and many-to-many. To be more specific, a relationship might be 'uses', 'is owned by', 'is part of', and so on. If such distinctions are made then the semantics of operations to create, update and delete instances of relationships can be defined differently for each case.

The operator 'delete entity' when applied to an entity representing a project may first have to determine if the project is involved in any 'assignment' relationships with company employees before deciding on the actions implied by deleting that entity. By distinguishing the many kinds of entity and relationship types that can exist, there is scope to be more expressive in representing the semantics of the application domain.

Support for complex types

Relational DBMSs implement a limited number of data types, typically integer, real, character, money and date. However, many applications (such as computer-aided design) require more complex object types. In turn, these types require new operations to be defined. Conventional RDBMSs tend to allow only insert, update, delete and retrieve. SQL is unable to define new data types and operators which might be needed in specialized applications such as a geographic information system (GIS). For example, instead of simply doing an SQL query based on attributes such as the following:

```
select * from area where owner = "Smith"
```

a programmer might like to restrict the search to a specific geographic area along the following lines:

```
select * from area where owner = "Smith"
           and location intersects work_area_1
```

The precise syntax of this particular example is not significant – it is intended to illustrate the principle of a spatial query in SQL where the operator intersects would cause some kind of (perhaps) complex comparison between location and work_area_1. In this example the operator intersects might be associated with the owner class, that is, intersects could be a method within the owner class.

Relational DBMSs do not even support some business IS needs all that well. For example, consider a real-estate agent application that stores information about houses for sale, such as owner's name, address, and so on. It may also have to store an image of each house. Such data elements are difficult to store and manipulate in a second generation DBMS. Pictures can be stored as BLOBs (binary large objects) in some relational databases. However, BLOBs only work for scanned images with no internal structure. The in-memory data structure has to be flattened into a linear representation so that it can be stored on disk between executions of the application. This means that such images can only be stored and displayed – it is not possible to manipulate the internal details of the images. It would not be possible to recall or manipulate only specified parts of a picture. For example, a real estate agent might want to enhance or modify the features of a house in a stored image to show a prospective customer the potential of the house. Different window frames or a different door could drastically change the overall appearance. Such modifications cannot be made to a scanned image devoid of any internal structure. The house must be stored as a complex object with internal structure if such modifications are to be accommodated.

Type hierarchies   Type hierarchies are recognized as an important modelling concept. Many commercial systems do not provide a mechanism for implementing this feature. Consequently, in a relational system it is difficult to record the fact that while a manager has a number of attributes in addition to those possessed by an employee, manager tuples should be included in the result of a query that retrieves all employees.

Impedance mismatch   Application software for relational systems comes in two basic forms: either using a third generation (3GL) or a fourth generation language (4GL). Fourth generation languages provide more productive development environments. However, they are often proprietary solutions for a relational DBMS and do not offer the same level of programmer flexibility as a 3GL. Third generation languages such as C and COBOL are still widespread and offer good portability across different hardware and software platforms. Such 3GLs use embedded SQL (the data manipulation language – DML) to access relational database systems. The programming language provides a more complete processing capability which is missing from SQL.

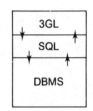

There are several drawbacks to this two-language approach. Firstly, the programming and database languages use different models to represent data (for example, SQL allows Date and Money which are not available in a traditional programming language). This makes the integration of the programming language with the database language artificial and forced. A loss of information occurs at the interface, if the programming language is unable to represent database structures, such as relations, directly. Part of the application program is devoted to converting between the two models; for example, from program variables in the programming language's type system to fields in the relational tuples in the database. Furthermore, since there are two type systems, there is no automatic way to type-check the application as a whole.

Secondly, SQL is set oriented, that is, for a given query, it returns a set of records which satisfy that query. However, 3GLs are one-record-at-a-time oriented, that is, they can process only one record at a time and therefore the programmer must provide sufficiently large buffers to hold the information returned from an SQL query. These two problems highlight the so-called **impedance mismatch** that exists between programming languages and the SQL database language.

The performance problems and a demand for increased support for complex objects and operations are forcing another stage in the evolutionary process for DBMSs – the third generation DBMS. At the very least, a third generation DBMS must provide a more sophisticated DML. At the very most, the next-generation DBMSs may employ a completely different way of storing, as well as manipulating, information.

6.3 Third generation database management systems

Opinions regarding the next generation of DBMSs are split. On the one side there are those vendors who are extending the relational model (the evolutionary

You need a completely new approach . . . Ah, Rubbish!

approach). To this end the Third Generation Database System Manifesto (1990) (see Appendix F) has been published by the Committee for Advanced DBMS function. The other camp which includes heavy representation from Academia proposes the Object-oriented Database System Manifesto (1989) (see Appendix E), which suggests a new approach to DBMSs, relying on the inherent modularity of the object-oriented paradigm (the revolutionary approach). The following sections discuss each approach.

6.3.1 A pure OO approach

The definition of an object-oriented database is by no means fixed. The Object-oriented Database System Manifesto (1989) (Appendix E) puts forward a set of features which all OODBMSs should include. The criteria are the most complete attempt so far to define the rules for an OODBMS.

OODBMSs are intended to address the shortcomings with first and second generation DBMSs which Section 6.2 discusses. They provide an object-oriented storage mechanism combined with a direct interface to an OOPL. They are, in their simplest form, OOPLs with support for persistent objects. However OODBMSs support all the normal database concepts, that is, persistence, disk management, sharing, reliability, *ad hoc* querying and security. In addition, OODBMSs support complex objects; encapsulation; types and classes; inheritance; late binding and extensibility – as proposed in the Object-oriented Database System Manifesto (1989) (OODBSM – Appendix E).

Overview

Object-oriented DBMSs support a generalized form of the concept of semantic data modelling. Abstract data types (ADTs or classes) are used to logically encapsulate data and procedural code. These ADTs are stored in the database. The OODBMS supports various kinds of relationships between these ADTs including information on inheritance – related to a type hierarchy. Class methods provide complex data manipulation operations, thereby creating a mechanism for progressing from a purely structural model of data towards a **behavioural model**, combining facilities for both the representation and manipulation of data within the same model.

The idea of dealing with a database that is made up of encapsulated objects such as a department object which 'knows what it means' to add an employee or change the manager, instead of having to understand relations, tuple updates, foreign keys, and so on, is naturally attractive from a user's point of view.

Data representation for storage

Using an OODBMS simplifies the programmer's task by allowing an object-oriented program to be written as though there was access to a large object address space in which both **transient** and **persistent** objects are uniformly addressable. Transient data is only valid inside a program or transaction and is lost when the program or transaction terminates. Persistent data is stored outside the program and survives program termination. The object programmer does not have to write special code to read persistent objects from a disk file and construct an in-memory version of the data structures that represent the objects; the objects are simply referenced. Nor does the programmer have to write special code to translate the in-memory representation of an object into something that can be stored on disk. He or she merely commits the transaction within which the object was created or modified. The OODBMS takes care of storage allocation and deallocation and mapping objects up and down the storage hierarchy from disk to memory. Figure 6.2 depicts the situation.

Figure 6.2 illustrates that the object structure represented in the executing application (the transient part of the figure) exactly mirrors that of the stored objects in the database (the persistent part of the figure). There is consequently no translation required between the transient and persistent object structures.

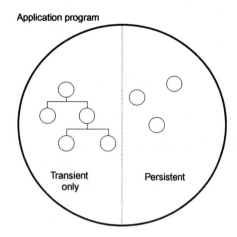

Application program

Transient
only

Persistent

Figure 6.2   An object database application (adapted from Versant Object Technology, 1990).

Architecture of an OODBMS

'Most OODBMSs are implemented as logical database shells requesting data from underlying storage managers. The storage manager, or *Object Server* (the Object Manager) is responsible for the allocation of disk space to objects etc. The higher-level system interprets user operations within the constraints of a particular data model, converting them to requests for particular objects, which it issues to the object server' (the Object Manager), (Brown, 1991). Figure 6.3 illustrates the basic architecture of an OODBMS.

All OODBMSs, like relational systems, use a data definition language (DDL) to define the classes of object which will be stored in the database, and the relationships between those classes – both their direct relationships and their supertype/subtype relationships via a type hierarchy. This structure of information is termed the database **schema**. Many OODBMSs use C++ as the basic standard DDL with some extensions to support the data modelling concepts needed by schema designers such as associations (relationships) and database triggers. The other part of the interface to an OODBMS is the data manipulation language (DML – shown in Figure 6.3 as the database access shell), used to create, retrieve, modify and destroy data within the database. Different vendors employ various ways to provide a DML. The next section discusses these in some detail.

The allocation of services (that is, operations to be performed on an object's data) between the higher-level shell (linked to the application) and the object manager varies from one OODBMS to another. In some OODBMSs, the object manager maintains minimal semantics about the objects it stores (such as relationships). In this case, the database shell holds the methods which act on the stored data. This database shell is

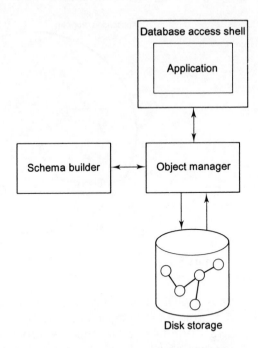

Figure 6.3   Basic architecture of an OODBMS.

linked into the application program. A programmer makes calls to instance methods held in the database shell. These methods manipulate the associated attributes (data – stored in the database) via the object manager.

Other object managers (for example GemStone) can record information about the behaviour of the objects they manage. In this case the objects stored in the database are often called **active**. Active objects have both their data and access methods stored in the database. The methods provide the behaviour for the data and dictate how the data is accessed and manipulated. This scheme enables the object manager to make use of the extra information it has to perform disk storage allocation, object retrieval, and so on.

Data manipulation in an OODBMS   There are several approaches to providing a DML in an OODBMS. In fact, Khoshafian (1990) identifies at least six ways. In this section four of the main approaches are summarized from the text of Khoshafian (1990):

(1) '**Extending an existing object-oriented programming language with database capabilities.**' This approach introduces database capabilities to an existing object-oriented programming language. The extensions incorporate database features (querying, transaction support, security, concurrency, persistence, and so on),

while the programming language already provides the basic object-oriented constructs for managing classes, inheritance, message passing, and so on. An example of this approach is seen in the Gemstone product from Servio which uses a proprietary language called OPAL – an extension of Smalltalk.

(2) **'Providing extendible object-oriented DBMS libraries.'** This approach also introduces database capabilities into existing object-oriented programming languages through the addition of class libraries which support aggregation, types and mechanisms for start/commit/abort transactions, exception handling, concurrency, security, and so on. The libraries must be included in the application and generally all application objects, for which persistence is required, must inherit methods and data from these DBMS class libraries. An example of this approach can be seen in the offering from Ontos Inc. This company's OODBMS – Ontos – provides a library of classes for C++. This is the approach favoured by most OODBMS vendors.

(3) **'Embedding OODB language constructs in a conventional host language.'** Database languages can be embedded in host programming languages. For example, SQL has been embedded in C and Fortran. Some object-oriented databases take this approach with a host language and an object-oriented database language. An example of this approach is the O_2 DBMS from O_2 Technology (see Appendix G).

(4) **'Extending an existing database language with object-oriented capabilities.'** SQL is a standard in the relational world and some companies are extending it to provide object-oriented constructs, reflecting the underlying capabilities of the database management system. This new form of SQL is called Object SQL or OSQL. There is currently no standard for OSQL but a number of companies – both relational vendors and object-oriented vendors – have developed their own flavours of OSQL and include it as part of their portfolio of products. Examples of this approach are detailed in a subsequent section of this chapter (see the Postgres and IRIS database systems).

The tighter coupling between the programming language and the database through the use of extensions to existing programming languages and OODBMS libraries removes the impedance mismatch between the DML and the programming language and eliminates many of the inefficiencies which occur in translating from one language to another.

The first three alternatives involve the development and/or use of an OOPL with its inherent ability to manage classes, inheritance, dynamic binding, and so on. The OOPL becomes the DML and therefore the DML is computationally complete for these systems. OOPLs support complex objects through the abstract data typing facilities of the languages. The first eight points from the Object-oriented Database Systems Manifesto (Appendix E) are therefore automatically met. Points 9 to 13 are satisfied through the services offered by the language extensions or libraries to interface to the OODBMSs, and the OODBMSs themselves.

The fourth alternative way to provide a DML involves using a high-level query language such as SQL with extensions to handle inheritance, user-defined types and user-defined operations on those types. Object SQL is discussed later in this chapter.

Handling complex data

Providing a set of generic database manipulation operators for complex objects increases the ease with which the database can be used. The 'insert', 'delete' and 'update' operators are rarely the level required, but these simple operators can be used in developing more complex operators. Recognizing the need for a specific set of operators to be defined for each complex object type, OODBMS systems allow the class developer to define both the data and the set of operations with which the user can access and manipulate such objects. The operators are *encapsulated* with the structural (data) definition of the object. Ensuring that the operators for an object provide the only way to access that object means that an interface can be defined for each class of object. The implementation of the object is hidden from users of that object.

A software engineer therefore develops an OO database application by programming classes. The private methods within a class can provide system **triggers** when an object is modified. They enable referential integrity, security and the other housekeeping functions normally associated with a DBMS. These private methods are known as daemons and they can support bi-directional relationships automatically, thus guaranteeing referential integrity. The public methods contain the application logic, the logic which supports a user business requirement. They are invoked when a message is received from another object. The data component in an object can only be accessed through the public methods of that object. Figure 6.4 and the associated text (in the section below entitled 'Capturing semantics in an OODBMS') outlines an example to illustrate the concepts discussed here.

Although OODBMSs support the notion of encapsulation at a logical level, most do not actually store the methods along with the data in the database. Most OODBMSs store only the data part of an object. The method part resides in the database libraries linked into the application. The exception to this is GemStone from Servio which allows data access methods to be stored along with the data in the database. A profile of GemStone is presented in Appendix G.

Unique object identification

A special feature of object systems is that every object has its own unique **identity** (UID). This identity never changes and does not depend on the object's name, key or location. The identity is normally implemented through some kind of object identifier attribute which is dispensed by the system at object creation. Relationships (or *properties*) can be expressed directly using this object identity and can be directly traversed. This is in contrast to relational DBMSs where properties that reference other portions of the database are usually keys such as, for example, employee numbers.

The difference between key references and object references is that keys must be resolved through a query and may be ambiguous, while object references can be resolved directly and are unique. Furthermore, sometimes keys have to be changed and this causes problems in relational DBMSs. Resolving object references is typically performed faster than resolving key references because it avoids the need to do indexed look-ups or time-consuming joins to reassemble high-level information structures.

Capturing semantics in an OODBMS

Semantic data models such as Chen (1976) and Codd (1979) require the storing of 'meaning' as well as data. This involves recording the meaning of relationships between data entities in a generic way. However it has proven to be very difficult and attempts to provide generically useful constructs at a higher level of abstraction than the basic relational model have enjoyed very limited success.

So relational DBMSs cannot store this 'meaning', although OODBMSs can. A data definition language (DDL) is used to describe the structure of, and relationships between, objects stored in a database. Specifically, the schema of an OODBMS is the collection of object types and corresponds to a type hierarchy. The supertype/subtype relationship between types is maintained as part of the schema, along with the direct relationships between objects (such as 'is_part_of').

In fact many OODBMSs have a number of built-in relationships such as 'super class of' and 'uses'. In addition, the software engineer can define characteristics. For example, if a *department* object 'knows what it means to add a *manager*' then at some stage a software engineer must have developed some software to perform the operation 'add a manager', and included this operation in the definition of the *department* object. The DBMS does not intrinsically know what it means to add a manager.

A database class therefore contains data (attributes), functions (methods) and properties (relationships). As a more explicit example,

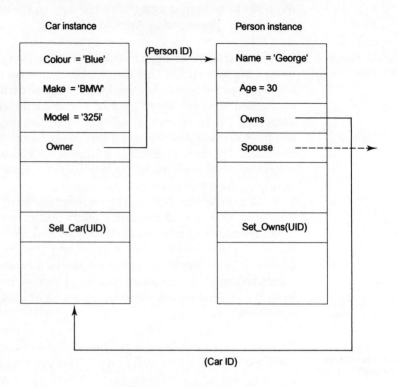

Figure 6.4   Object references.

consider a Car which has an *owner* property, of type Person. A particular instance of a Car, a blue BMW 325i is owned by a Person called George. In an object system the relationship between the BMW and George can be maintained by a reference which may be the unique ID of that object. Figure 6.4 illustrates this example.

In addition, an object may refer back to an object that refers to it – such as the property *owns* in Figure 6.4. Some OODBMSs allow bi-directional relationships so that referential integrity is supported automatically. Relationships can be one-to-one, one-to-many or many-to-many. The ability of an OODBMS to represent many-to-many relationships directly is something that relational systems cannot provide – for example, George and Caroline own a BMW 325i and a Ford Escort.

The method Sell_Car(UID), in Figure 6.4, might be used to transfer ownership of the BMW 325i to someone else. This method may have the following outline implementation:

```
Sell_Car(UID)
    {
    /* Remove reference to the BMW 325i from George */

    remove_owner()

    /* Establish Links with the new owner */

    Owner = UID ;

    establish_new_link ;
    }
```

This pseudocode illustrates implementing referential integrity through the private methods in the CAR class. The private methods are remove_owner and establish_new_link. remove_owner sends a message (Set_Owns(NULL)) to George, causing the owns property in George to be set to null. In effect, remove_owner is a trigger used to ensure referential integrity. (A trigger is a monitor placed on a data item that initiates an action on access to the item.) establish_new_link would set up the owns property in the new owner's data area.

In effect, the method Sell_Car represents semantic information associated with a Car.

Since methods are the only way to access data, the method compiler or interpreter (part of the schema builder) can detect expressions that access monitored data, and can insert additional code to accomplish the trigger action.

Organizing objects to remove data redundancy

For typical commercial application, classes may be used to store data in a similar form to the use of relational tables within a relational system. In such cases, the rules used for removing data redundancy in relational systems – called normalization of data (Codd, 1974) – can be equally applied to the data held within object database systems.

Consider the following table of information associated with ordering products:

Product order table

Order #	Cust name	Address	Part #	Description	Quantity	Date ordered
A175	Esso Stn.	120 Main St	4	Petrol cap	5	6/10
A175	Esso Stn.	120 Main St	2	Filter	11	6/10
A200	Joe's Garage	65 Oak St.	4	Petrol cap	16	4/5
4756	George W.	52 Front Rd.	31	Ham sandwich	1	N/A

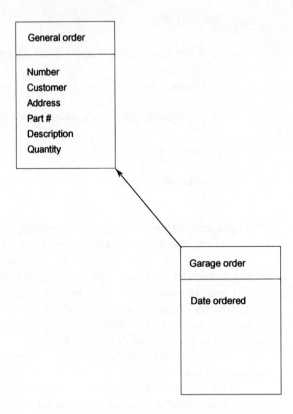

Figure 6.5   Using inheritance to support 1st normal form. The arrow denotes an inheritance relationship.

- **First normal form:** *Each attribute can take only atomic values.* Order # is non-atomic at present: it represents both parts-orders from garages to some warehouse, and sandwich orders from a bakery. One side effect of this is that the Date ordered field is unnecessary for sandwich orders (and the Part# field is not well named for sandwich orders!). In an object-oriented system this table would be converted into first normal form using inheritance – creating a general order form which could be used to handle sandwich orders and a specialization which would be used to handle garage parts (Figure 6.5).

- **Second normal form:** *Every non-key attribute must fully depend on the primary key* (that is, each value of the key must uniquely identify a row in the table). The primary key is Order#. Based on this rule for second normal form we can say that:

- Address depends on Customer and not on the key. Therefore it should be moved into a separate table.
- Customer and Date ordered depend only on the key.
- Description depends only on Part#.
- Quantity depends on the combination of Order# and Part#.

Based on these observations the table decomposes into the following separate tables:

Order table

Order #	Cust name	Date ordered
A175	Esso Stn.	6/10
A200	Joe's Garage	4/5

Customer table

Cust name	Address
Esso Stn.	120 Main St
Joe's Garage	65 Oak St

Parts table

Order #	Part #	Description	Quantity
A175	4	Petrol cap	5
A175	2	Filter	11
A200	4	Petrol cap	16

- **Third normal form:** *Remove any remaining dependencies between non-key attributes.* The three tables, Customer, Order and Parts, are also in third normal form.

In object-oriented terms second and third normal forms translate into: *Every attribute in an object depends on the object ID only.* Figure 6.6 illustrates the classes and class relationships this produces. It represents some of an object database schema for a parts ordering system.

There are three classes: Customer, Order and Part. Customer has two attributes – Name and Address, along with a relationship 'places' to the class called Order. The relationship 'places' is a reference to an object ID which corresponds to an instance of the Order class within an object DBMS. In other words, the object database replaces the notion of a key (Order#) by a direct reference to another object.

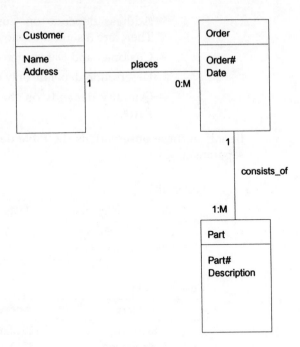

Figure 6.6   Using class/object relationships to support 2nd and
3rd normal form. The solid connecting lines denote associative relationships
(refer to Chapter 4 for details).

Similarly, the class Order has a relationship 'consists_of' with the class Part. Again this relationship maps into reference pointers to object IDs in an object database.

The field named Quantity in the Parts Table is not shown by an attribute Quantity within either the Part or Order classes. This is because the class called Part is contained within the Order class as shown in Figure 6.6. Therefore, the corresponding object diagram would show 5 instances of Part #4 and 11 instances of part #2 contained within Order #A175 – in other words, the quantity required is implied by the number of contained parts.

Of course this example has concentrated on the data aspects of several classes. In reality, the behavioural aspects would also be considered. However, the example illustrates how data redundancy can be reduced in an object database using a similar approach to the traditional techniques used in relational systems.

Transactions and concurrency   Transactions and concurrency involving complex objects may require different considerations from the normal transactions involved in typical business applications. Many OODBMSs handle concurrency using a 'check-in/check-out' approach, where objects are checked-in to the database, and checked-out to the user's private workspace as required. Complex objects often involve the following types of transaction:

- Conversational – where perhaps a CAD system is used to design some component for a car engine. The designer may work on parts of the design in an interactive way.

- Long lasting – where perhaps the engine part is held on an 'update' for several days while the design proceeds.

- Involve many records – complex objects may involve many records.

- Non-atomic – updating one design diagram may involve updates to many other diagrams.

Therefore OODBMSs must employ sophisticated contention resolution mechanisms.

The most conservative way to ensure data consistency is to allow a user to lock all records or objects as soon as they are accessed and release the locks only after a transaction commits. This solution is traditionally known as a conservative or pessimistic policy. However by distinguishing between reading the data and acquiring it to modify (write) it, greater concurrency can be provided. Under an optimistic policy, two conflicting transactions are compared in their entirety and then their serial ordering is determined. As long as the database is able to serialize them so that all the data viewed by each transaction is from a consistent state of the database, both can continue even though they have read and write locks on common data. Thus a process can be allowed to obtain a read-lock on data already write-locked if its entire transaction can be serialized as if it occurred either entirely before or entirely after the conflicting transaction.

Distributed computing

Object-oriented DBMSs must expect to function in a distributed computer environment. Appendix G summarizes the main features of several commercially available OODBMSs. All these systems are designed to work in a distributed environment. Work is under way to establish standards for transparent access to multiple OODBMSs from different vendors in a distributed environment. This work by the Object Management Group is described in Appendix D.

The ability to store data access methods as well as data on a database server (as opposed to having all the access methods within the application, on a client site) has important implications for distributed systems. If the DBMS uses these data access methods associated with specific objects, then the resulting network traffic is significantly reduced because much of the data processing is achieved locally (that is, where the data is stored) rather than remotely – within the application. Of course, this also means that the database server (where the local processing is accomplished) could become a bottleneck if the demand for that server is sufficient.

Versioning

OODBMSs have the potential to provide intrinsic versioning. This is the automatic generation and control of historical versions of objects. Version management consists of a number of tools and constructs to automate or simplify the construction and organization of versions or configurations. This has many potential uses, such as those cited by Bloor (1990):

(1) 'where an audit trail of all changes to data is required, such as a clinical trials system in a pharmaceuticals company.'

(2) 'Record versioning allows queries to run simultaneously with updates without the update interfering with the query.'

(3) 'In a similar way database backups can be done without denying users access to the database. Thus, when a transaction is aborted recovery is relatively simple.'

6.3.2   Commercially available OODBMSs

A number of OODBMSs are now commercially available. These include:

(1) GemStone from Servio Corp. – based on Smalltalk ;

(2) Ontos from Ontos Inc. – based on C++ ;

(3) O_2 from O_2 Technology – based on O_2C ;

(4) ObjectStore from Object Design – based on C++ ;

(5) Versant from Versant Object Technology – based on C++ ;

(6) Objectivity/DB from Objectivity Inc. – based on C++.

These systems provide the usual DBMS functions such as concurrency control, consistency and security in common with standard relational technology. In addition they provide tools to support software development, viz. graphical class browsers, schema constructors, user interface libraries and so on. Appendix G includes a short description of each of these OODBMSs.

6.3.3   Advantages and disadvantages of OODBMSs

The benefits to be gained from an OODBMS are:

(1) Potentially better performance than relational technology through the use of object IDs.

(2) Improved maintenance through the use of OO techniques – conventional DBMSs tend to offer very limited facilities for the expansion or modification of existing data structures because of the loose coupling between the database schema and the application programs. The tight coupling between applications and data in the OO model offers considerably more scope for schema evolution through the extension and refinement of existing data structures and the effective reuse of application code through inheritance.

(3) More powerful modelling capabilities through the use of inheritance, and user-defined types. The ability to store more semantic information within the database using abstract data types and unique identifiers. Also the ability to represent many-to-many relationships.

(4) A single language interface removes the problems of impedance mismatch associated with embedding SQL in a 3GL with a relational DBMS. This eliminates many of the inefficiencies which occur in translating from one language to another.

(5) Applicability to environments in which relational technology is not suitable, such as computer-aided design (CAD), computer-aided software engineering (CASE), geographical information systems (GIS) and office information systems (OIS).

Relational maturity

Pitted against these advantages are the advantages of relational technology. To quote from Batty (1991), the advantages of relational technology include: 'wide acceptance in the industry, established international standards, and a large base of existing skills. The OO approach lacks all of these which is understandable since it is an emerging technology. However, the existing investment in relational databases is something which cannot be dismissed lightly. If there are ways of achieving some of the good ideas of the OO approach within the basic framework of the relational model, there is a very strong argument for pursuing these.'

Storing methods – good and bad?

Batty (1991) further suggests that in many commercial areas, one of the main reasons for using a DBMS is to make the data somewhat independent of the applications that run against it. Different applications can be given different views of the data, and the behaviour of a given item of data may be different in different applications. Therefore, whilst storing a lot of semantic information within the database may enable objects to solve some problems more easily, it may make other problems much harder to solve.'

Navigational querying or set operations

According to Brown (1991): 'Navigation from one object to the next is by far the most common mode of data access in an OODBMS. This is in contrast to the set-based operations which are the cornerstone of relational DBMSs.' Brown (1991) cites some examples where navigation is useful, for example, 'in browsing a parts explosion in a hardware design application, or in exploring a hierarchy of documents in an office information system.' However, there are limitations. If the physical data is reorganized, there is no way for the navigational interface to automatically take advantage of such changes. The programmer must modify his program.

The seamless approach of a programming and data manipulation language precludes the possibility of a single standard OODB query language; in general, the typing systems of different programming languages are incompatible. While SQL itself has a number of known limitations, there is no doubt that there are many advantages from having a commonly understood query language. Indeed, if a standard OO query language could be defined as some form of (upwardly compatible) extension to SQL, then further advantages of controlled system evolution and compatibility with existing (relational) applications might also accrue. This would encourage the uptake of object-oriented DBMSs into the industry at large rather than the present situation where they have been adopted in mainly technical database areas where they are acting as an enabling technology – that is, enabling solutions hitherto not technically feasible.

Performance

Since OODBMSs directly address the problem of managing and manipulating complex data types, they must inherently provide much better performance than their relational counterparts. Direct comparisons of speed between relational and object-oriented technology have to be treated with a healthy suspicion because certain kinds of information management may be better suited to one type of DBMS than another. However, vendor-supplied figures indicating a 100-fold improvement in speed for OO over relational DBMSs are common (Versant, 1991).

The US Navy conducted tests on an OODBMS and a relational DBMS. The test consisted of processing part information contained in either an object form or within relational tables. The test involved both reading and writing to the databases. The results for 2500 objects indicated that the object-oriented DBMS processed 100 times faster than the relational system. The argument that OODBMSs can provide such a level of performance is also supported in Maier (1986).

6.3.4 Choosing an OODBMS

At present deciding on an OODBMS goes hand-in-hand with deciding on which OOPL to use as the two are inextricably linked. Key issues to consider are:

- **Does the product support standards?**
  Invest only in products supporting open standards such as UNIX, X-Windows and C++. Make sure your vendor is positioned to support standards for DMLs and DDLs that will evolve over time. Vendors should be tracking or participating in OO standards efforts such as the Object Management Group and the ANSI X3J16 C++ committee.

- **Is a full object model supported?** Look for a database that supports a full object-oriented data model that can be implemented across multiple languages. ODI (Object Design Incorporated, 1990) points out that 'some so-called OODBMSs compromise on true object orientation by offering minor enhancements to second and third generation products. By adding the ability to store binary large objects (BLOBs) such as pictures, some relational database companies claim support for objects.' Others provide an object-oriented user interface, but store data in tables at the cost of performance. Neither approach should be confused with true support for object-oriented principles!

- **Graphical aids can enhance productivity.** Graphical aids for designing the database schemas, and class library browsers are important tools for aiding the understanding of data semantics. What support do the tools offer for modelling relationships – 1:1, 1:N, N:M, 'super class of' and 'uses'. Can relationships be bi-directional? Some schema designers support only inheritance whereas others enable the developer to include the semantics of associations or relationships between objects.

- **What facilities are you used to?** Make sure the OODBMS provides all the facilities you are used to from relational systems including security, recovery and integrity.

- **General tool support.** Does the product offer an Object SQL? Or at least a form of high-level query language?

- **Facilities.** Does the product support versioning, distribution over heterogeneous environments, long transactions? Check how the OODBMS provides recovery. Be careful of claims about transaction recovery across distributed systems. This problem is very complex and few systems have really cracked it fully.

- **Evaluate performance.** ODI (1990) suggests that: 'For interactive engineering and multi-media-based applications, high performance in handling complex "non-record oriented" data such as video is the single biggest factor in the success or failure of an OODBMS. OODBMSs must attain performance which is orders of magnitude faster than their relational predecessors in order to manage this type of data.' Various benchmarks are available, such as the Sun Cattell standard (available from Sun Microsystems). Another possibility suggested by ODI (1990) is to take a typical part of your code and have your OODBMS vendor help benchmark that code using their product on your data. Getting involved with OODBMS vendors is a good idea – see the Ontos user case-study in Chapter 8.

- **Migration.** Most companies considering the move to OO technology have a large investment in code for older technologies. Evaluate the migration path by taking a representative subset of an existing application and convert this to work with an OODBMS. At the end of this process ask the following questions:

  - 'Which OODBMS required the fewest changes and was easiest to develop for?' (ODI, 1990)
  - 'Which OODBMS offered the easiest conversion of the existing data?' (ODI, 1990)
  - Which OODBMS performed fastest, provided the richest functionality and security features, and so on?
  - How good was the vendor support during the whole process?

Table 6.1 summarizes the facilities provided by the six OODBMSs mentioned in this chapter and described further in Appendix G.

> **Disclaimer:** The information contained within Table 6.1 will date. It is provided merely to illustrate the essential features available within a range of popular OODBMSs.

6.3.5   OO extensions to relational technology

So far this chapter has concentrated on pure object-oriented DBMSs – the revolutionary approach to a third generation DBMS, with reference to several commercially available products. These products were all developed from scratch or from research prototypes. They use new techniques for storage along with manipulating data in a more flexible way. The other approach to the next generation of DBMSs involves a more

Table 6.1 Table of features for OODBMSs.

	GemStone	Ontos	O₂	ObjectStore	Versant	Objectivity
Language interfaces	Smalltalk C C++	C++	O₂C C C++	C C++	Smalltalk C C++	C C++
DDL	OPAL	C++	O₂C	C++	C++	C++ with extensions
High-level query language	No	Ontos-SQL	O₂QUERY	Yes – via a DML	Versant Object SQL	No
4GL	FACETS	Shorthand	O₂C	Yes – DML preprocessed through C++	Versant Object 4GL	No
Versioning	No	No	No	Yes	Yes	Yes
Inbuilt support for relationships	Inheritance 1:1 1:N N:M Uni-directional	Inheritance only	Inheritance only	Inheritance 1:1 1:N N:M Uni- and bi-directional	Inheritance 1:1 1:N N:M Uni- and bi-directional	Inheritance 1:1 1:N N:M Uni- and bi-directional
Methods executed on the database server	YES – OPAL methods	No	No	No	No	No

evolutionary path, building on existing relational technology. These object-oriented extensions to relational DBMSs are commonly called extended relational DBMSs. To this end, the Third Generation Database System Manifesto (1990) (TGDBSM) has been published by the Committee for Advanced DBMS function. The manifesto is the relational DB vendors' response to the OO Database System Manifesto (Appendix E). It sets out a number of tenets as follows:

(1) Besides traditional data management services, third generation DBMSs will provide support for richer object structures and rules. Richer object structures characterize the capabilities required to store and manipulate non-traditional data elements such as text and spatial data. In addition, application designers should be given the capability of specifying a set of rules about data elements, records and collections. Referential integrity in a relational context is one simple example of such a rule; however, there are many more complex ones.

(2) Third generation DBMSs must subsume second generation DBMSs. Second generation DBMSs made a major contribution in two areas:

non-procedural access
data independence

and these advances must not be compromised by third generation systems.

(3) Third generation DBMSs must be open to other subsystems. Any DBMS which expects broad applicability must have a 4GL, various decision support tools, friendly access from many programming languages and to many popular subsystems such as Lotus 1-2-3, interfaces to business graphics packages, the ability to run the application on a different machine from the database (a client/server architecture) and a distributed DBMS.

These three tenets result in thirteen propositions from the Third Generation Database System Manifesto which are described in Appendix F.

The conclusions of this manifesto have much in common with the previous OODB Systems Manifesto. In particular they agree on the need for a richer type system, inheritance properties and encapsulation. However the TGDBSM addresses the area of integration of the DBMS and its query language in a multilingual environment, whereas the OODBSM does not discourage single-language systems with vendor-specific access methods. In practice, many of the OODBMS vendors have included a form of Object SQL in their offerings (even though there are, as yet, no standards for an Object SQL).

The main difference between the two manifestos is that they approach third generation DBMSs from different angles. The TGDBSM supports a natural evolution from current relational DBMSs to ones with the aforementioned capabilities, whereas the OODBSM emphasizes the requirements of an object-oriented DBMS.

6.3.6   Example extended relational DBMSs

Besides traditional data management services, object-oriented extensions to relational DBMSs will provide support for richer object structures and rules, that is, inheritance, functions, database procedures and methods as discussed in the Third Generation Database System Manifesto. These features implement the concept of encapsulation where the database update routines are associated with the data they manipu-

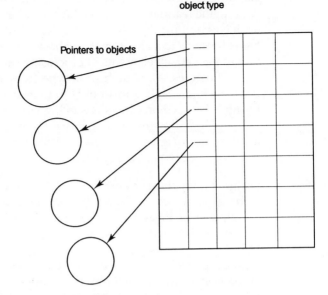

Figure 6.7   Objects in tables (adapted from New Science Associates (1989) with permission).

late, thus abstracting the process of data manipulation from the application developer. Encapsulation of data and functional logic within the DBMS can provide performance advantages in a distributed system since a retrieved function to be executed by a Data Manager involves only one round trip message between the application and the DBMS whereas if the function runs in the user application then one round trip message will be needed for each access.

The Third Generation Database Manifesto (1990) states that encapsulation does not require a new kind of DBMS but can be a natural extension of the relational database. Inherent in this approach are the concepts of consistency checking, security and distributability which are the cornerstones of traditional databases. This, together with the myriad of support and debugging tools already available, could provide the easiest migration path for applications to the next generation of DBMSs.

Several ways have been suggested as to how objects can be represented in a relational environment. The basic idea is to have objects in tables. A relational table would contain fields which are pointers to objects as depicted in Figure 6.7. These objects contain the procedural information (the methods) to be applied to the encapsulated data attributes.

Vendor support for the extension principle from relational database developers is strong, with nearly all the mainstream companies claiming an object-oriented extension already available or on the way. Among the leading relational DBMS vendors, Oracle, Ingres and Sybase are incorporating object-oriented features in their products. Ingres already has extensions to its relational database that are arguably object-oriented, in that they attach elements of processing directly to stored data.

Postgres, a research prototype from Berkeley University, incorporates Object SQL, a form of SQL to enable manipulation of 'objects'. Postgres is based on extensions to Ingres Quel.

The following two sections describe the main 'object-oriented' features of Postgres and Hewlett Packard's implementation of Object SQL for its IRIS database system.

Postgres

Postgres (Stonebraker and Rowe, 1986) is a database system designed to be a successor to Ingres (Stonebraker *et al.*, 1976). The following description of Postgres is reproduced, and adapted from a paper by Jackson (1991), with the kind permission of Butterworth–Heinemann Ltd. Although Postgres is a completely new system, it has benefited from the experiences gained with Ingres. Indeed one of the design goals of the system was to make as few changes as possible to the relational model. This is in the spirit of Codd (1982) who believed that the relational model would form the 'assembly language' of future database systems. Postgres can be considered as a relational database with object-oriented extensions.

The important additions Postgres makes to the relational model are inheritance, abstract data types (ADTs) and data of type 'procedure'.

Inheritance in Postgres

Inheritance in Postgres is implemented in the following way. To create an entity called PERSON:

    create PERSON (idno=int4, Name=char[30], Dat_of_Birth = date)

If an entity, say EMPLOYEE, is also a PERSON it is defined in the following way:

    create EMPLOYEE(Work_no=int4, Salary=int4, Manager=int4)
    inherits(PERSON)

The INHERIT clause indicates that EMPLOYEE will have the attributes declared explicitly as well as those declared in PERSON.

Postgres has a query language called Postquel – an enhanced version of Quel (the Ingres query language). To retrieve the names of all entries in the PERSON table, the programmer would use:

    retrieve(PERSON.Name)

To retrieve the names of all PERSONs, including all subtypes of PERSON, a tuple variable is used:

```
retrieve(P.Name)
from P in PERSON*
```

where PERSON* is the relation formed by the union of PERSON and all the relations that inherit attributes from it.

Abstract data types
in Postgres
All data types in Postgres, including the pre-defined atomic types, are defined as ADTs. An ADT definition specifies the type name, its length in bytes, input and output procedures, and a default value. For example, the atomic type int4 is declared as:

```
define type int4 is (InternalLength =4, InputProc=CharToInt4,
                                OutputProc=Int4ToChar, Default="0")
```

Input and output procedures are written in a conventional programming language such as C. Associated with each ADT is a set of operations. For example, the plus operator for two long integers is defined as:

```
define operator "+" (int4,int4) returns int4
      is(Proc=Plus)
```

The procedure Plus is written in C and defines the semantics of the operation.

The pre-defined types can be extended by the Postgres database designer using the same syntax. For example, a hexagon might be defined by two digits that specify the position of its centre and a third digit specifying the length of its sides. The definition of hexagon is therefore:

```
define type hexagon is (InternalLength = 12, InputProc=
                                          CharToHex,
                    OutputProc=HexToChar, Default=" ")
```

Operators such as Area could then be defined in items of type hexagon. Although Postgres does provide an ADT mechanism, this is limited in comparison with the mechanisms found in most OOPLs. ADT procedures in Postgres cannot be defined in Postquel, but instead must be written in C (or some other 3GL). There is also no inheritance mechanism associated with Postgres ADTs. This illustrates a fundamental difference between Postgres and an OODBMS where all objects are treated as ADTs whereas in Postgres objects are composed from ADTs. Postgres does not fully satisfy the criteria of encapsulation defined in the Object Database System Manifesto.

An important feature of Postgres is its ability to store attributes of type procedure. When a procedure is executed, an entity is returned. Procedure types permit a different Postquel command to be inserted in each row of an entity. Consider the two entities SUPPLIER and ITEM.

```
create SUPPLIER(Sname=char[20], QRating=int4, City=char[15])
create ITEM(Iname=char[30], PossibleSuppliers=postquel)
```

PossibleSuppliers is defined as type postquel. This indicates that it will be a Postquel query. In this example the query will retrieve the names of potential suppliers of a given item. If there are two items, Coffee which may be supplied by any local supplier in London and Resistor which must be supplied by a supplier with a QRating > 30 (quality rating), then they will be added to the database with the statements:

```
append ITEM(Iname="Coffee",
            PossibleSuppliers =
                    "retrieve (S.all) from S in SUPPLIER
                    where S.City = "London" ")
```

```
append ITEM(Iname="Resistor",
            PossibleSuppliers =
                    "retrieve (S.all) from S in SUPPLIER
                    where S.QRating > 30")
```

This illustrates the use of a form of polymorphism in Postgres where the function PossibleSuppliers executes differently for different *instances* of a given type ITEM (compare with polymorphism in object-oriented terms which enables the same function name to execute differently for different types of instance).

Details of all items with the names of possible suppliers can be retrieved by the command:

```
retrieve(I.Iname, I.PossibleSuppliers.Sname)
        from I in ITEM
```

To summarize, Postgres clearly exhibits object-oriented features, but to a lesser extent than a true OODBMS. In particular it does not fully support encapsulation and types or classes. It also does not have a computationally complete language. It supports ADTs and complex objects but these two are in no way combined.

IRIS

In the relational model, the components of a tuple must be atomic, that is, they cannot contain sub-components. This is a severe limitation when considering applications which deal with complex data struc-

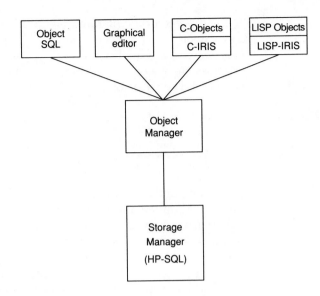

Figure 6.8   The IRIS architecture (reproduced from Brown (1991) with permission of McGraw-Hill).

tures. By contrast, third generation databases support aggregate types such as sets and bags, which are used to contain many objects of the same or differing types. Groups of objects can then be manipulated using these aggregate types. For example, Hewlett Packard has been working on its own form of Object SQL (OSQL) for its prototype IRIS OO database (Fishman, 1989).

According to Brown (1991), 'The IRIS database represents the evolutionary approach. The system consists of an Object Manager which is built on top of a relational database system (Allbase), which acts as the storage manager'. The object manager supports HP's form of OSQL. For computational completeness, functions may also be implemented in a programming language such as C or LISP. Figure 6.8 illustrates the IRIS system.

The HP form of OSQL is based on three constructs: object, type and function. Brown (1991) indicates that it extends SQL in three main ways:

(1) 'Object identity.' Every object has a system-generated unique identity.
(2) 'User-defined functions.' End users can define their own functions on data and then use those functions within queries.
(3) 'Syntactic changes. Some syntactic changes are introduced to force a new way of thinking about the language. For example, create table is replaced by create type.'

OSQL supports a type hierarchy with inheritance. This is also used to resolve overloaded function names. OSQL supports four aggregate types, namely set, bag, list and tuple (Lyngbaek, 1991). Aggregate types and aggregate objects can be composed of other types and objects using a set of object constructors:

```
Set    – { }
Bag    – [ ]
List   – [|  |]
Tuple  – <  >
```

Sets are unbounded, unordered and contain no duplicate objects. Bags are also unbounded and unordered but may contain duplicate objects. The contents of both sets and bags must all be of the same type, so that a bag of type [Person] can contain only persons. Lists are ordered collections of objects that may contain duplicates. A tuple is an ordered, fixed-sized collection of objects that are not necessarily all of the same type.

For the purpose of example, consider there is a class Person (with a number of attributes including Name, Address, Spouse and Children – these attributes may be data or methods). Then an example of an OSQL statement (all following examples come from Lyngbaek, 1991) would be:

Name: Person –> char

that is, the char would be the name of the person, and

Children:Person –> {Person}

would result in a set of person objects which are the children of the person to whom the message Children was sent. If there is an instance of the class Person called Mary then to find out the name of Mary's spouse the following statement could be used:

Name(Spouse(:mary))

in which Spouse(:mary) would return a Person object – that is, Mary's spouse. The Name message would then be sent to Mary's spouse. Querying the database is exemplified by the following use of the SELECT statement:

SELECT Name(p)
FOR EACH Person p
WHERE Address(p) = 'London'

The SELECT statement returns an object of type bag which can be assigned to an object and subsequently manipulated. The result of this statement could have been assigned to an object (called result) program-matically via:

> :result := SELECT Name (p) FOR EACH Person (p) WHERE Address (p)
> = 'London'

The SELECT statement works on both data attributes such as Name and functional attributes such as Children.

Both the data and functional components of a type are defined by the data definition part of OSQL. In a geographical information system, an object of type Contour might have a function called 'draw' associated with it, which is used to plot the contour. The following use of the SELECT statement would cause all contours above 300 metres to be plotted:

> SELECT draw(c)
> FOR EACH Contour c
> WHERE height (c) > 300

The use of polymorphism and dynamic binding, where the run-time version of a selected function is invoked, provides a powerful facility. Dynamic binding means that applications can manipulate a variety of object types without having to explicitly name the operations on each type, thereby realizing some of the flexibility associated with a truly object-oriented mechanism. This can be understood by considering an Employee class with a method Salary and the following SELECT state-ment:

> SELECT Salary (e)
> FOR EACH Employee e

where an Employee can also be a teacher, or a researcher, or a director and so on. In this case, if each of these subclasses redefines the Salary method then the individual Salary methods will be invoked at run-time, to satisfy the query.

6.4   Object-oriented applications and relational technology

It is not necessary to have a third generation DBMS to provide data stor-age for an object-oriented application. It is feasible to use a language like C++ or Smalltalk with an ordinary relational database.

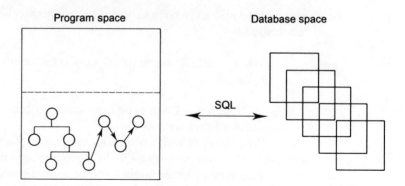

Figure 6.9   OOPL application using a relational database (reproduced with kind permission of Versant Object Technology, 1990).

In future most information systems will possess a GUI. At the moment an IS department must drop out of its structured methodology – and probably its CASE tool – as it designs its user interfaces. This poses interesting problems as many IS staff don't yet implicitly understand GUIs and object-oriented technology, while many GUI developers understand little of the mainframe life-cycle view of the world.

One possible approach is to substitute an OOPL for a 3GL and continue using a relational DBMS. The OOPL brings the ability to easily develop GUIs, combined with better reuse possibilities and greater extensibility, leading to more maintainable software (Chapter 5 discusses the issues relating to OOPLs). In this approach, the object is created and populated with data taken from the relational database as the application runs. Figure 6.9 illustrates this situation.

This approach is appealing because many OOPLs are becoming mature, and relational DBMSs are also mature. However, it presents several problems. There is an impedance mismatch again (as discussed in a previous section of this chapter), between the data manipulation language (DML) such as SQL and the programming language such as C++. There are two aspects to this mismatch. One is the mismatch of the type systems as already discussed. The other is the difference in programming paradigms, because now the programming language manipulates objects whereas the relational DBMS manipulates tables of information. A translation must take place between the programming language and the relational database.

An alternative is to use an object-oriented 4GL. These provide a higher-level view of programming and makes the translation of data representations automatically.

Ingres/Windows 4GL supports the development of objects in the form of a type and associated attributes which can include 4GL code. Objects can have graphical representations (for example, pictures, graphs, mouse buttons and pull-down menus). Developers define a window by combining a number of such objects which can reference other objects in other windows. In this way applications with complex user interfaces can be built.

Enfin/2 (from the ENFIN Software Corporation) is a 4GL and programming environment written for the OS/2 operating system. This 4GL supports a wide range of general-purpose programming classes and several sets of special-purpose classes, supporting SQL databases, APPC and the OS/2 Presentation Manager GUI. Enfin/2 uses an object-oriented language that derives many of its features from Smalltalk. Enfin/2 contains a screen editor, a model editor – to create financial or mathematical models, an SQL editor to develop SQL queries, a report generator and a class definition editor.

Dataflex (from the Data Access Corporation) is another 4GL which includes many object-oriented features to support software reuse and GUI development. The environment supports the concept of a class and enables the developer to inherit (single inheritance) from classes as well as defining new classes. The system is supplied with a user interface building toolkit which is basically a class library.

Two object-oriented CASE tools supporting database application development for the mainframe environment are SAPIENS and OSMOSYS.

SAPIENS

SAPIENS (from Sapiens Inc.) is a complete application development and maintenance platform for IBM environments. It consists of an Object Modeller (a graphical analysis tool), SAPIENS-WS (a co-processing front end for workstations) and an IBM 370 application generator.

In a SAPIENS application there are no programs. Developers define WHAT the application should do by presenting the logic of the application as a set of rules. SAPIENS then encapsulates each item of business data with all its associated rules, creating objects. SAPIENS provides an object management library from which developers can reuse objects or add their own.

A developer defines the data using a mixture of an entity relationship model, to capture relationships between data, and the subtypes of that data (where data types are objects with the usual object-oriented capability of inheritance). A front-end tool, the Object Modeller, allows a developer to represent this information graphically. Constraints are associated with the data, for example, the balance in a savings account should be >= 0.

From this data model and the specified constraints, SAPIENS generates default screens and transactions (for example creation, update and deletion of data). These defaults are instances of system-defined objects which define the properties of standard screens and transactions.

It is possible to customize these defaults. The final application consists of a collection of objects. A developer can also define menus for the application, use a screen painter to override the default screens and transactions, and define queries using QUIX.

A run-time component interprets the generated code and on-line documentation is also generated. SAPIENS supports DB2, IMS/DB, DL/1 and VSAM. SQL can be embedded in SAPIENS code to access existing databases.

A Swiss insurance company, Elvia, has been using SAPIENS for several years. It has estimated productivity gains of 300–500 % as a result of using SAPIENS, and maintenance has been reduced to 1–2 % compared with its original development environment which consisted of COBOL, Fortran, the PACBASE code generator and Cincom's Total database. Elvia has also been able to integrate code from SAPIENS with existing code developed partly using PACBASE and partly in COBOL.

OSMOSYS

OSMOSYS is a development environment providing a method for OO analysis and design along with a suite of tools supporting library services, user interface building, modelling, validation, configuration management, documentation and code generation. It is developed by Winter Partners (see vendor references section for address). OSMOSYS runs on PS/2 machines under OS/2. All tools result in information being stored back in a repository (via OS/2 DB Manager).

An analyst models business requirements within the environment using the OSMOSYS OO analysis and design method. A knowledge base provides a suite of generic business specifications from which an analyst can inherit information and develop specializations as required. The toolset provides facilities for validating designs in an incremental fashion before cutting the final software. In essence, the validation tool enables designs to be executed using an interpreter. When the analysis and design stages are complete, relational database schema and application software are generated automatically.

This product addresses the evolving area of object-oriented analysis and design while safeguarding the existing investment many organizations have in relational technology. The Application Generator automatically handles the object-to-relational transformation.

Final software generation is presently available for two application areas. These two areas represent the two ends of a spectrum and illustrate the capabilities of the system. At one end of the spectrum, the OO design can be transformed into a traditional structured design and exported to IBM's Cross Systems Product (CSP) to produce CICS applications in COBOL. These applications support traditional 3270

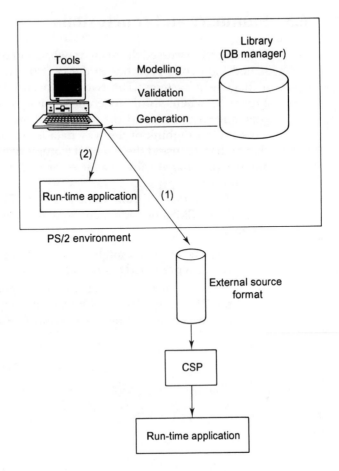

Figure 6.10   Using OSMOSYS.

block mode, character-based terminals for the user interface (see route (1) in Figure 6.10).

Figure 6.11 illustrates route (1).

At the other end of the spectrum, the Application Generator can cut code for an OS/2 environment utilizing the OS/2 DB Manager. The generated code is Smalltalk and the user interface conforms to OS/2 Presentation Manager (see route (2) in Figure 6.10). The Smalltalk software interacts with a relational DBMS. OSMOSYS integrates Smalltalk application code with relational database storage by mapping tables in a traditional database onto the data parts of classes in an object-oriented application.

Figure 6.12 illustrates route (2):

6.5 Summary and conclusions

This chapter discussed the main drawbacks of relational DBMSs and pre-sented the two approaches to the next (third) generation of database management systems. The two approaches are: (i) the evolutionary approach, where third generation databases will subsume second generation systems; and (ii) the revolutionary approach, involving a more radical re-think of the way data is stored and manipulated. The chapter has discussed the essential features of each approach and cited a number of commercially available (or in development) DBMSs using each approach.

To summarize from Cattell (1991): 'The data models of next-generation DBMSs provide many new features not present in previous systems:

> *Objects.* Data that might span many tuples in a relational DBMS can be represented as one data object.

> *Object identifiers.* Objects can be assigned unique identifiers by the DBMS. In relational DBMSs, primary keys such as employee numbers or department names must be used.

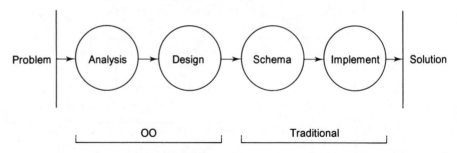

Figure 6.11   Problem to solution using OSMOSYS.

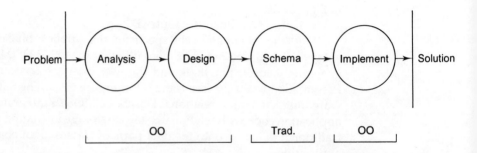

Figure 6.12   Problem to solution using OSMOSYS.

Procedural encapsulation. Procedures as well as data attributes can be stored with objects in the database, and these procedures can be used as *methods* to encapsulate object semantics.

Composite objects. Containment relationships may be defined between objects, and the transitive closure of a containment relationship may be treated as a single composite object.

Links. Relationships between objects can be represented more efficiently than in traditional relational DBMS systems, using a more convenient syntax than relational joins.

Multimedia data. Objects can contain very large values, such as audio, video or text. Many new DBMSs provide efficient operations to retrieve and edit these data values.

Type Inheritance. Object types, or classes can be organized as a hierarchy with inheritance of properties, simplifying the description of complex data schemas.

Versions. Most of the new DBMSs provide capabilities to track multiple versions of database objects.

The next-generation DBMSs provide these new features while retaining most of the important features of traditional systems, such as the ability to deal with large amounts of data, using transactions for concurrency control and recovery.' It is difficult to assess the benefits to be gained by insisting on a revolutionary approach to data storage and manipulation. According to Jackson (1991): 'Users of systems would perceive that there is a huge difference between the products. Clearly a user who already stores data on a relational database would find Postgres much more attractive than Gemstone, as existing applications could migrate without much difficulty. Postgres could be used as though it was a relational database with some powerful extensions. Gemstone, on the other hand, might appeal to users who currently use object-oriented programming languages.'

Various forms of object-oriented 4GLs are appearing in the market place. Few, if any of these, implement a full object-oriented model (see Chapter 2 for details of the full OO model). However, they do implement some specific elements, notably inheritance and encapsulation. Several object-oriented application generators are also emerging. These products enable object-oriented applications to co-exist with relational database systems.

Pure OODBMSs represent an enabling technology. They have successfully been applied in a number of areas where relational technology is not practical (mainly for performance reasons). Such areas include CAD, CASE and office information systems. Many MIS departments are currently trying to take advantage of connecting work groups in local area networks so users can work together. The data management implicit in such a workgroup model requires functionality beyond the capabilities of a relational DBMS. For example, text, graphics and voice make up some 95% of all data in an office. The databases of the future will have to handle a proportion of this information and relational systems are unlikely to play a major part. It is beyond doubt that OODBMSs will expand the database concept into application areas that have not previously been associated with database systems.

The most profitable areas for application of OODBMSs have still to emerge as it is currently a pioneering environment and few of the commercially available products are sufficiently mature and robust to become 'standard packages' within any organization.

Several outstanding issues must be resolved before the OODBMS can properly mature. These include:

(1) 'Rationalization of the object query languages.' OODBMSs exhibit significant variation in this area. There are no standards. Standardization of SQL helped promote relational databases and the possibility of open database systems (Jackson, 1991).

(2) The 'large body of theory behind the relational model' has helped develop techniques for query optimization and normalization. 'There is as yet no comparable body of theory for OODBMSs.' (Jackson, 1991).

(3) Few currently available OODBMS products are sufficiently mature for companies to invest significant commercial venture on them.

One benefit of OODBMSs is their ability to capture the semantics of data. This will be a key consideration in future, where developers wish to follow analysis and design stages with a software implementation which directly reflects the semantics of the real-world problems being modelled.

Some OODBMS vendors have locked onto the CAD/CASE and hypermedia areas whilst others are seeking to create new, hitherto untapped markets for their product. When a new generation of software products emerge it normally takes a long time before they gain market acceptance. Bloor (1991) comments that: 'Relational databases established themselves first in the niche market that they satisfied best, which was management information systems. The progress of the new generation of DBMSs will probably follow a similar pattern. They are likely to become dominant in scientific and engineering areas first. **Eventually it will become obvious to a growing number of users that these products have general application.** '

I believe this last statement is very important. It is only when end users (in many cases naive of state-of-the-art technological advances) demand sophisticated capabilities that object database systems will grow in market demand. OODBMS vendors (in common with introducing any new technology) have a strong educational role to play in demonstrating the tremendous potential impact that such systems could (and will) have on our everyday lives.

7 Migrating to an OO regime – technology transfer

INTENDED READERSHIP

Managers, project leaders and the technology 'gatekeeper' should read this chapter. It is directed at those involved in the technology adoption process.

CONTENTS

CHAPTER PRE-REQUISITES

There are no specific prerequisites for this chapter. Readers should be familiar with the broad philosophy behind object-oriented software development. Chapter 3 covers this through the software development life cycle.

CHAPTER OVERVIEW

The combined experiences of many people who have successfully or unsuccessfully attempted to introduce object orientation into their organizations is presented. This information was compiled from conference attendance, various texts and discussions with many people who have already been down this road.

The chapter presents a list of questions to ask yourself concerning the suitability of your organization for OO techniques. A nine-point plan for adopting object-oriented tools and techniques is then presented.

For completeness, the chapter contains sections on choosing an object-oriented: (i) analysis and design method, (ii) a programming language and (iii) database management system. These sections are taken from the respective chapters within this book.

7.1   Introducing new technology – foreword

Many of the stages involved in introducing object-oriented technology are common to introducing any new technology into an organization. I can recommend two books which have helped me in this area in the past: Barbara Bouldin's book *Agents of Change – Managing the Introduction of Automated Tools* (1989) and Roger Pressman's *Making Software Engineering Happen – A Guide for Instituting the Technology* (1988).

These texts cover the general issues associated with introducing new technology. They identify the main steps in the process:

- **Assessing the need.** Assessing the problems and strengths in the current software development practices.
- **Selling the ideas.** Educating both management and technical staff.
- **Selecting the technology.** Selecting and evaluating methods and tools.

We shall return to these issues later in this chapter.

7.2   Experiences introducing OO techniques

There are no quick and easy benefits to be had from adopting OO techniques. The first two or three projects will probably take longer than they would using a conventional approach, simply because the development team must build up experience in the new methods. To contemplate using the first OO project as the basis for a decision on whether to adopt OO is unlikely to convince management of the benefits to be gained.

To successfully introduce change, you must firstly understand the OO concepts and believe that this approach can yield benefits in your environment. It is then very important to establish a realistic migration strategy and identify a starter project.

A number of companies in the USA, UK and Europe have gone down the migration route to object orientation. Some have been successful and some have failed. Many of the lessons learned have been discussed at conference panel sessions such as deNatale (1990), details from which are included in the following text.

Obtain some case-studies. Case-studies, such as the ones presented in Chapter 8, highlight several issues: what application areas particular tools are being applied to; experiences with the tools; how to approach OO software development; problems to anticipate and plan for. This information is invaluable to someone embarking on a first OO project or considering OO development techniques as a replacement for existing methods.

Evaluate tools before you commit, don't just do paper studies. This book will help you complete a first-stage evaluation of the tools and techniques available. Individual chapters cover tools and techniques appropriate to: analysis and design; programming languages; and database management systems. Hopefully after reading this book you will be able to identify the tools and techniques most applicable to your development environment. The next stage is to negotiate the loan or purchase of some tools for further evaluation. Preferably try before you buy!

Don't be afraid to get help. Good consultancy can save you money. The advantage of using consultants is that they constantly move between organizations, picking up valuable insight and experience *en route*, whereas software development staff tend to be more blinkered – tight time-scales and deadlines force this. Software developers don't generally have the opportunity to talk to many people from other organizations. Even the 'technology gatekeeper' in a company may not have the same opportunity for cross-fertilization since may organizations are guarded about their plans and activities.

Use stable tools. Although the concept of object orientation has been around for ten years or more, many tools are only coming to market now. The first two or three versions of many tools can be quite poor. Unstable tools will jeopardize not only the current OO development projects but also the future of object-oriented software development within the organization.

Master the use of the tools BEFORE the schedule clock starts ticking. This goes almost without saying. Any new tool or technique will take time to master. If the schedule clock is ticking there is a natural tendency to explore only the essential features of a tool in order to get the job done. However, perhaps there are other features which, in the long run, would increase productivity or in some way improve the overall performance on the project. A first-cut set of standards should be in place for the use of any tool. These can only be established when there is enough knowledge gained from 'playing' with the tool. Of course these standards will evolve and mature as experience deepens but nevertheless an initial set of standards or style guidelines should be in place from the start.

Training is very important. Timely training helps to establish a consistent approach across all staff. Training should involve background reading, attending courses and some practical hands-on experience. All this should be completed before the schedule clock starts ticking.

Build up design and coding expertise using small to medium sized projects. Large projects may cloud may important issues because of the added complexity. On the other hand, if the project is too simple it may not enable you to properly evaluate techniques.

Don't use a bigger team than you need to. Large teams bring additional management complications. When you are trying to build experience and evaluate techniques in a controlled manner, small teams are best. Try to use no more then 2-4 people.

Ensure that version/configuration management issues are worked out before implementation begins. Any professional software development organization will realise the necessity of well organized configuration management. In OO developments this is particularly important because of the inherent component-oriented nature of the process. Final applications are made from 'building blocks' stored in class libraries. The class hierarchy reflects the need for variations on a theme. These variations must be strictly managed or the hierarchies can get out of control very quickly!

Don't make assumptions about C expertise transferring to C++ !!! C is a subset of C++. A C-programmer can quite happily continue developing C-code using C++. Eventually C++ will replace C – will you still be developing C-code? Chapter 5 presents several object-oriented programming languages and discusses the degree to which each language supports object-oriented concepts.

Class hierarchies change. Chapter 4 on OO analysis and design covers the issues of managing dynamically changing class hierarchies.

Dynamic binding is necessary to accommodate change. Chapter 2 discusses the concept of dynamic binding and how it supports extensibility.

Developing reusable software is:

- **Hard! (Buy before build).** According to deNatale (1990): 'In general the goal of reuse is to enable unforeseen changes to require altering as little as possible of what is already available. This does not only apply to future application developments; change is inherent in the process of developing and maintaining all applications.'

    It is difficult to assess exactly when the right level of generality has been achieved in a class library. It may take between six months and a year before you can say that a given class library is truly reusable. There are many class libraries now available commercially.

- **Possible.** Several of the case-studies presented in Chapter 8 detail strategies for software development which centre on developing reusable class libraries.

- **Very worthwhile.** The benefits from reuse result in lower development effort. Reusable software will have been tested for other projects and this should reduce the amount of testing required in subsequent projects.

The critical factors in adopting this technology are similar to those for any new techniques, and include:

- **Asset management mentality (reusable components are assets, that is, object administration supersedes data administration).** Many of the benefits of an OO approach derive from the reusability of classes. In a fully object-oriented approach, discrete applications give way to the notion of 'enterprise modelling' where a repository (or library) of classes is built to cover all aspects of that organization's operation. The idea is that once an organization has built a comprehensive library of classes, it should be able to build most new applications from existing classes. Thus, once a class library has been established, OO can dramatically reduce both the cost and time-scales of new systems development.

- **Business model for guidance.** The business model identifies the higher-level strategic objectives of the organization. This includes the applications areas for exploitation, target hardware and software platforms, as well as quality objectives and constraints.

- **Implementation plan.** Successful adoption of any new technology requires an implementation plan. This should describe how the evaluation and/or adoption process will take place, including discrete phases with time-scales and allocated staff.

- **Organization structure.** The structure of project teams, departments, divisions and the overall hierarchy of staff in the organization play an important role in determining if and how OO can be successfully introduced. For example, if every project team works in a totally different application area, such as telecommunications to business accounting to mathematical modelling and simulation systems, then common class libraries may only be relevant within project teams (although all these application areas may employ common user interface technology). However, if a department comprises several project teams who all work in the same application area then common class libraries may be applicable across whole departments.

- **Leadership and teamwork.** Teamwork is important in all areas of software development. It is particularly important in OO developments because of the component-oriented nature of the development process. A whole team or department may be involved in contributing components to and using components from a common class library. This requires well coordinated teamwork, good organization and leadership.

- **Skills.** Object orientation is quite different from traditional structured development. It requires a shift in mind-set for all involved from programmers to analysts, project leaders and managers. Training is very important in order to re-educate people and clarify the many issues. Skills are acquired over time. The evaluation and adoption process can provide a very useful period for acquiring skills and convincing staff of the benefits of the new approach.

- **Attitude/motivation.** People issues in reuse should not be under-estimated. Organize an appropriate rewards system – **throw away those 'lines-of-code' metrics!**

The tension between the need for innovation and the need for mature and standardized systems has always been challenging for managers of high technology. This is particularly true in that object orientation promises early adopters a competitive advantage through lower development costs and faster time-to-market. The following plan suggests a possible route to adopting object-oriented tools and techniques within an organization.

7.3 A nine-point plan for introducing object orientation

Point 1: ~~~~~~~~~
Point 2: ~~~~~~~~~
Point 3:
.....
.....
.....

Stage 1

Study the techniques carefully, gaining a thorough understanding of the concepts, tools, benefits and detriments. Attend training courses. Get involved in user groups and/or other companies that also have an interest in object orientation. All major studies of success and failure in innovation emphasize the importance of both intra-company and extra-company linkages – innovation is a process of communication. Obtain case-studies where possible.

Stage 2

Identify if, how and where your company can benefit from object orientation. Consider the following:

- Does your company develop graphical user interfaces, or make extensive use of this area in your software applications? (If YES then OO may prove useful.)
- Do you develop a product range consisting of similar sorts of systems with a common theme such as communications systems? (If YES then the reusable class library concept is likely to be very important to you.)

- Do you develop a limited range of applications but concentrate on covering a wide range of hardware platforms or operating systems? (If YES then the need to purchase development environments for each platform may prove expensive.)

- Do you develop applications which are heavily dependent on interfacing to hardware? (If YES then be careful, some OO languages such as Smalltalk provide limited capabilities for this kind of work.)

- Are the developed applications mainly real-time or information systems? (If real-time then be careful, some OO languages may not provide the required performance – see Chapter 5. If developing information systems is important consider the types of information to be stored – normal 'name, address, telephone number' type record structures are adequately handled by existing relational technology. Think of the future, what types of information would you like to be able to store? Complex data such as images may require a database with object-oriented extensions – see Chapter 6.)

- Does the company develop very large applications involving a large development team? (If YES then the inherent modularity provided by OO may produce benefits, but be careful because the development of good class libraries using a large team of people requires a lot of management and good tool support.)

- Conversely, is the company involved in developing small applications with one or two person teams? (If YES then OO may provide some benefits, particularly where manpower resources are limited but applications need to support complex concepts such as GUIs – see Eiffel user case-study in Chapter 8.)

- What programming languages are currently used? (Migration from C to C++ seems natural – but beware, OO requires significant changes to the programmer's mind-set.) Hybrid OO programming languages represent a pragmatic way to migrate from a traditional to an OO approach, but pure OOPLs will enforce OO and ensure that all developers make use of the concepts.

- What about an interim strategy towards an object-oriented DBMS via extended relational systems? Remember that object orientation can be introduced in either an evolutionary or a revolutionary way. There are methods and tools to support both approaches.

Stage 3

Determine the maturity of the in-house software development process. Object-oriented software development requires a well-organized and structured framework. Not all existing organizations are ready to move to OO. If your software developers are not used to well-organized working practices then adopting object-oriented techniques will require more effort and may have to be introduced more gradually. Ideally you should already be using a well-defined software development life cycle and be used to procedures for configuration management, change control, design, coding, testing and so on. Interview various staff at all levels to determine how any quality procedures are working in reality.

The Software Engineering Institute (at the Carnegie-Mellon University) has produced a Software Development Process Maturity Model (Humphrey, 1989) to help developers determine how mature their software development procedures are. It is particularly useful for identifying areas of concern. Appendix C presents details of the Process Maturity Model. This Process Maturity Model was originally formulated for large US defence organizations. It has been modified by the Institute of Software Engineering to suit smaller development organizations and is presented in detail in Thompson *et al.* (1992). The Software Development Process Maturity Model measures the degree of control and monitoring currently present in an organization.

Stage 4

From stages 1, 2 and 3 you should have a good feel for where and how the company could benefit (or indeed IF it could benefit) from object orientation. Draw up a list of the requirements and identify suitable tools, languages and/or OODBMSs to be evaluated. The time, resource and budget available will dictate how many tools can be short-listed for proper evaluation. The economic feasibility of all short-listed tools should be determined at this stage.

Stage 5

Produce a report on your findings to date, including where and what deficiencies exist in current practices and how object orientation could provide benefits. Include the short-list of tools in the report. This report should be directed at the decision takers (be it middle or senior management).

At this stage start disseminating information to a select few developers – the guru figures in the organization. Introducing new techniques is difficult but can be spurred on by winning approval from a few respected technical staff – the rest will follow their lead. The key thing at this stage is to generate interest in what you are trying to do.

deNatale (1990) notes that: 'Upper management needs a business perspective framed in a way that makes sense for their organization, and expressed in plain language. They are not interested in polymorphism and paradigm shifts, but in getting products developed and out to market.'

Stage 6   **Assuming you have approval to progress, buy or even better, borrow a full evaluation copy of the product for a restricted period of time – say six months.** This will give you and your team time to try the tools out in a real environment.

Build a small team so the leader can know everyone well, and can ensure that everyone is switching to the right way of working. Opinions on the mix of personnel for the team differ. On the one hand, choosing above-average developers will help ensure the success of the evaluation project. On the other hand, if the ultimate goal is to introduce OO throughout the entire organization then choosing a good mixture of abilities will enable you to judge the likely time involved in getting everyone in the organization up to speed. Ensure that the whole team receives adequate training so it can make the best use of the evaluation period.

Determine a suitable small project to test the tools and techniques – preferably an application similar to the mainstream applications developed in-house. Opinions on the type of project to use also differ. Some believe that the only valid assessment is one carried out under normal conditions with a paying project. Others suggest that the evaluation project should be viewed as a throwaway system. Perhaps a better solution is a compromise, something which will be of use to the company internally, such as a tool to support some business function, without being critical to the company's future! In any event, the OO development will require the production of a class library. This library should be viewed as an asset which can be reused in future developments. This marks the beginning of a larger undertaking to develop component (class) libraries for use throughout the organization.

LaLonde (in deNatale, 1990) suggests: 'Emphasize the iterative nature of projects. Make management aware that a "product cycle" doesn't stop, but needs constant effort in massaging the product and arriving at a powerful framework for future releases and applications. Within a project there should be incremental construction, demonstration to customers and incorporation of feedback'. Decide on a suitable life cycle but expect it to change in the face of reality. (Chapter 3 discusses an object-oriented software life cycle).

Create a class library manager post. As LaLonde (in deNatale, 1990) suggests: 'An essential part of an OO development is a person or small group with the job of thinking about the libraries, and overseeing the organization of class hierarchies.'

Stage 7   **Analyse the results of the project and choose the appropriate tool(s). Determine a first 'real' project for development and start.**

Establish conventions for working practices based on the experience gained from the evaluation project. Use the people who were involved in the evaluation and introduce one or two new personnel, so that you don't end up with an elitist OO team.

Identify the first real project carefully. Choose a project which will put the development team under some pressure but remember that your schedule estimates will be inaccurate so expect to replan frequently. Choose a project which has many elements in common with other projects in the company. In this way you can start building common class libraries for use across many projects in the future. Keep accurate statistics regarding time and effort for each stage in the project; these will be invaluable for future project estimates.

Stage 8   **Build up expertise and experience gradually.** The key is to start small and grow the organization into the new methodology. Remember it is only after two or three years that the full potential from object orientation will be realized. But don't be afraid to buy in some help to get the operation running smoothly as soon as possible.

Stage 9   **Rollout.** If the evaluation, proposal and pilot project stages are successful then plan the widespread rollout of the technology. It is important to watch carefully that the procedures 'scale-up' accordingly – is multi-user access working? Are developers with average ability taking the new ideas and techniques on board? and so on.

7.4   Choosing an OO analysis and design method

All too often managers are forced into a methodology because it is the one supported by the tool which runs on their development machines. When selecting a methodology it is best to evaluate it on paper, try it out on a small project, that is, the evaluation project suggested in Stage 6 above. If the method works then look for a tool which supports it. At the very least you will have a better idea of what you are looking for in a method.

Most of the current OO methods are immature and new methods fall like confetti from the literature. The key to a useful method (as with everything useful) is simplicity. If the method is overburdened with notation then it may be awkward to use. However be warned that object orientation introduces new concepts which require more complicated representations.

The things to consider when choosing an OOA&D method include:

- **The degree of object-oriented support.** The preceding sections illustrate that not all methods support all the object-oriented principles to the same degree. From Chapter 2 you will have decided which principles are of most use to you. To what extent are these principles supported in the various methods? Does the method support the usual meaning of the terms object (instance) and class? Can a class be described in terms of its distinct parts: an interface and a body? Does the method support metaclasses as implemented in programming languages such as Smalltalk and CLOS?

- **What class or instance relationships does the method support?** Does it support inheritance? If so, then does it support single or multiple inheritance? Does the method distinguish between sub-classing (that is, implementation inheritance with restriction and redefinition as well as addition) and subtyping (with just addition)? Are associative relationships (with cardinalities) supported? What about aggregation (container) relationships?

- **Does the method enable object lifetime to be charted?** According to Arnold (1991): 'A method may be restricted to dealing with static systems of objects in which all objects have the same lifetime as the system. If this is not the case then the method must contain some facility for dynamically creating objects (by instantiating a class). Similarly for destroying an object.' Does the method support the notion of an object state? Can an object persist beyond a single execution of the application that created it? Can the method handle concurrently executing objects (active versus passive objects)?

- **What kinds of dynamic relations can exist between objects?** Interactions between objects concern the kinds of message passing. Message sending can involve either static or dynamic binding and can be polymorphic. Furthermore, does the method allow for representing only single messages or can sequences of associated messages be modelled?

- **What models of communication does the method support?** According to Arnold (1991): 'Synchronous communication requires the sender to suspend execution until the receiver accepts the message, whereas asynchronous communication allows the sender to continue.' Does the notation distinguish between messages destined for local objects and messages destined for remote objects? This is pertinent in the design of distributed applications.

- **Is the method oriented at real-time or information systems (IS).** Some methods support both, but most are heavily oriented towards one type of development or the other. How much of the software life cycle does the method cover? – Does it cover analysis and design?

- **Are there guidelines for separating analysis from design?** Does the methodology help with project management issues such as defining boundaries between analysis and design?

- **What resources are available to support the method?** Is the method fully supported by a CASE tool? Some methods are only partially supported. What hardware and software does the tool require? Does the environment support multi-user development? If there is CASE tool support, does it provide semantics processing such as simulation and code generation? – What other resources are available to support the method such as published texts and so on?

- **The ability to interwork with other CASE tools.** This is important where a tool must integrate with other tools such as a project management system, or a standard documentation system. Several standards are emerging in the area of CASE tool integration – such as the CDIF (CASE Data Interchange Standard) or the PCTE (Portable Common Tool Environment) which specify standard import/export formats to/from a repository.

- **Tool maturity.** If commercial-grade software is going to be developed then the tool must offer a degree of robustness characteristic of a mature product.

- **How scalable is the method?** Scalability is concerned with whether techniques and notation can be used effectively on large systems. Notations need a mechanism for partitioning descriptions into smaller and more manageable modules and composing the whole from those modules. It should also provide some means of controlling the visibility of names across modules.

- **Is good training available?** This goes without saying!

- **Extent of use of the method.** Is the method supported by more than one consultancy firm or CASE vendor? The existence of user groups and conference tutorials are an indication of widespread usage.

- **External factors.** Some large customers, notably government bodies, insist on certain methodologies – for example, the European Space Agency has stated a preference for the HOOD method.

- **How well has the method been defined?** Is there a well-defined set of steps by which the various techniques are strung together? Are objects traceable across the life cycle? Does the method advocate only object-oriented techniques (pure) or does it suggest using some traditional structured techniques (hybrid)? Does the method support a defined notation?

- **Are there syntactic and semantic definitions for the notation, or do the syntax and semantics have to be deduced from examples?** According to Arnold (1991): 'The syntax of a notation is a set of rules which describe the primitive components of a notation and the legal combinations of those symbols. There are well-known techniques, such as the Backus–Naur Form, for formally defining textual syntax, but such techniques for diagrams are less well established. There should, however, be a clear definition of the icons and their legal combinations. A defined syntax is a requirement for effective use and also for automated tool support. The semantics of a notation is a set of rules which gives the meanings of the syntactic primitives and their combinations.'

- **Does the process address the architectural issues of the system under design?** This is the capability of a method to split a system into subsystems. There are three facets to this: (i) decomposition into logically related parts, (ii) collection of logical parts into modules which may be separately compiled, and (iii) deciding on the physical location where different parts belong (processors, platforms, and so on).

- **Does the method provide guidelines to help identify candidate objects?** This is a most fundamental issue. You can't start manipulating and massaging objects until you've found some. An object can play different roles through associations with different objects. Does the method provide techniques for modelling the different views of an object?

- **Are there guidelines for developing inheritance hierarchies?** Associated with this is the issue of designing for reuse. Reusable components and designs must be developed, they are not simply a by-product of using objects. A method needs to explicitly provide activities which are intended to identify reusability and support the development of reusable components and designs.

- **Does the method enable objects to be viewed in different roles?** Some methods allow objects to provide different services to different clients.

- **What guidelines does the method provide to ensure quality?** Are there guidelines on consistency, completeness, coupling and cohesion, and design extensibility?

Analysis is particularly important because it provides a means of communicating between people with dissimilar backgrounds: the end user (from the problem domain) who may be naive of the technology; and the systems analyst who will be familiar with the software development process and must bridge the gap between the problem domain and the solution domain. Therefore the analysis method must provide a clear means of communication. It should be as intuitive as possible to both the end user and the software development team, with a clear precise notation for pictorially representing the information being discussed.

Check if there is any tool support for the method. Tool support is very important in OO analysis and design so that various views of a system can be easily linked. Also, the complex notations which often go hand-in-hand with OOA&D methods require CASE tools to make them at all usable! Tools can provide consistency checking, completeness checking and validation. Some tools can execute (simulate) design specifications. They can help the analyst/designer browse through the products of analysis and design in a relatively unconstrained way. While looking at a class relationship diagram, a developer might want to study the details of a particular class specification. Using tools in this manner frees developers from the tedium of keeping all the details of the analysis or design consistent, allowing them to concentrate on the communicative aspects of the analysis process or the creative aspects of the design process. Significant benefit can be derived from tools which run on laptop PCs and can therefore easily be transported to a user site where some of the analysis work takes place.

Chapter 4 discusses many of these issues and provides a tabulated comparison of several object-oriented analysis and design methods.

7.5   Choosing an object-oriented programming language

There is a wide range of object-oriented programming languages on the market today. Many will not last the pace for a variety of reasons, not the least of which is that the market will eventually standardize on one or two, with perhaps six or so languages used in small niche markets. A number of representative languages are presented in Chapter 5. They fall into two broad categories: those which support rapid prototyping and those which are suitable for full-scale application development.

The things to consider when choosing a programming language include:

- **The degree of object-oriented support.** Chapter 5 illustrates that not all languages support all the object-oriented principles to the same degree. From Chapter 2 you will have decided which principles are of most use to you. To what extent are these principles supported in the various languages? (For example, Smalltalk enforces object-oriented principles whereas C++ does not.)

- **The associated development environment.** Are there browsers and debugging facilities available? Does the environment support multi-user development? (For example, Eiffel supports multi-user development more readily than Smalltalk-V does.)

- **Type of inheritance.** Does the language support single or multiple inheritance? How can the inheritance be managed? Are there facilities to help with the resolution of naming conflicts and so on? (For example, Smalltalk supports single inheritance whereas C++ supports multiple inheritance.)

- **Characteristics of the final application.** How fast will the final binary image execute? How large is the binary image? Does it include a large proportion of code devoted to housekeeping facilities such as garbage collection and assertion checking? (For example, Smalltalk and Eiffel have garbage collectors whereas C++ does not.)

- **The typing system.** Is the language statically or dynamically typed? The answer to this question has important implications for the type of software being developed. Dynamically typed languages are better for rapid prototyping whereas statically typed languages create a more rigid framework suitable for developing commercial-grade software. (C++ is statically typed whereas Smalltalk is dynamically typed.)

- **The ability to interwork with other languages.** This is important where investments in existing software necessitate its reuse through interworking with a new language, or where interfaces are needed to lower-level languages to perform systems-type functions. (C++ will interwork easily with C whereas Smalltalk does not interwork easily.)

- **Are there standards for the language.** If the decision on a language is strategic for your organization then standards will be important. (C++ is an internationally recognized standard whereas Objective-C is not.)

- **Language maturity.** If commercial-grade software is going to be developed then the language must offer a degree of robustness characteristic of a mature product. (Smalltalk and C++ are mature products whereas Eiffel is less mature.)

- **Language support by vendor and through third party products.** Introducing any new technology has teething problems and vendor support will be necessary. Third party products may enhance your development capabilities.

- **Commercial factors.** Another consideration is the degree to which the various products have penetrated the market. Market success does not necessarily indicate technical excellence, however it indicates which products are most likely to become long term standards. The current market for traditional languages supports two major players, namely COBOL and C. It is likely that one or perhaps two OOPLs will dominate. Other OOPLs will find niche markets and some will inevitably not survive for one reason or another. Obviously no one wants to choose a language from this last category!

Chapter 5 discusses many of these issues and compares the main object-oriented programming languages currently available.

7.6   Choosing an OO database management system

The first stage is to decide whether to go for a full object-oriented DBMS or a relational system with OO extensions. It is difficult to assess the benefits to be gained by insisting on pure object orientation. Users of systems will perceive a huge difference between the products. Clearly a user who already stores data on a relational system will find Postgres (a relational DBMS with OO extensions) much more attractive than Ontos (a pure OODBMS). Existing applications could migrate without much difficulty. Postgres could be used as though it were a relational database with some powerful extensions.

Pure OODBMSs such as Ontos, on the other hand, will appeal to those who currently use object-oriented programming languages.

At present, deciding on a pure OODBMS goes hand-in-hand with deciding on which OOPL to use as the two are inextricably linked. Key issues to consider are:

- **Does the product support standards?** Invest only in products supporting open standards such as UNIX, X-Windows and C++. Make sure your vendor is positioned to support standards for OODBMS DMLs and DDLs that will evolve over time. They should be tracking or participating in OO standards efforts from the Object Management Group and the ANSI X3J16 C++ committee (for example, ObjectStore)

- **Is a full object model supported?** Look for a database that supports a full object-oriented data model that can be implemented across multiple languages. ODI (1990) points out that 'some so-called OODBMSs compromise on true object orientation by offering minor enhancements to second- and third-generation products. By adding the ability to store binary large objects (BLOBs) such as pictures, some relational database companies claim support for objects.' Others provide an object-oriented user interface, but store data in tables at the cost of performance. Neither approach should be confused with true support for object-oriented principles!

- **Graphical aids can enhance productivity.** Graphical aids for designing the database schemas, and class library browsers are important tools for aiding the understanding of data semantics.

What support do the database tools offer for modelling relationships – 1:1, 1:N, N:M, 'superclass of'. Can relationships be bi-
directional? (For example, ObjectStore includes a graphical
schema builder.)

- **What facilities are you used to?** Make sure the OODBMS provides all the facilities you are used to from relational systems
including security, recovery and integrity.

- **General tool support.** Does the product offer an Object SQL? Or
at least a form of high-level query language? (For example,
Versant offers a form of Object SQL whereas Objectivity does not.)

- **Facilities.** Does the product support versioning, distribution over
heterogeneous environments, long transactions? Check how the
OODBMS provides recovery. Be careful of claims about transaction recovery across distributed systems. This problem is very
complex and few (if any) systems have really cracked it fully.

- **Evaluate performance.** ODI (1990) suggests that 'For interactive
engineering and multi-media-based applications, high performance in handling complex 'non-record oriented' data such as
video is the single biggest factor in the success or failure of an
OODBMS. OODBMSs must attain performance which is orders of
magnitude faster than their relational predecessors in order to
manage this type of data.' Various benchmarks are available, such
as the Sun Cattell standard (available from Sun Microsystems
Inc.). Another possibility is to take a typical part of your code and
have your OODBMS vendor help benchmark that code using their
product on your data. Getting involved with OODBMS vendors is
a good idea – see the Ontos user case-study in Chapter 8.

- **Migration.** Most companies considering the move to OO technology have a large investment in code for older technologies.
Evaluate the migration path by taking a representative subset of
an existing application and convert this to work with an
OODBMS. At the end of this process ask the following questions:

  - 'Which OODBMS required the fewest changes and was easiest
  to develop for?' (ODI, 1990)

  - 'Which OODBMS offered the easiest conversion of the existing
  data?'(ODI, 1990)

  - Which OODBMS performed fastest, provided the richest
  functionality and security features, and so on?

  - How good was the vendor support during the whole process?

Chapter 6 discusses many of these issues and compares a selection of
currently available OODBMSs through a table of features.

7.7 Summary and conclusions

This chapter raises many issues concerning the whole area of technology adoption. There are five key stages to the adoption process. Figure 7.1 illustrates the road to technology adoption.

(1) **Understand techniques.** You must thoroughly understand the techniques before you can progress towards adopting them.

(2) **Assess suitability for organization.** Determine if the techniques will fit into the organization. Do they fit with the business objectives and can the organizational structure accommodate them.

(3) **Motivate interest.** Motivate interest in both management and developers. Reports to management should match the business objectives of the company. Information for developers should match their aspirations, viz. novel techniques which are technically interesting and challenging.

(4) **Evaluate.** Conduct a pilot project in-house to evaluate tools and techniques. Report to management with results, conclusions and recommendations.

(5) **Adopt.** Create an implementation plan detailing how OO will be adopted. This should include identifying suitable projects and personnel, tools and techniques.

The key to successful adoption is to plan the strategy carefully, motivate interest, satisfy the needs of management and developers, learn from a pilot project and choose a first real project carefully.

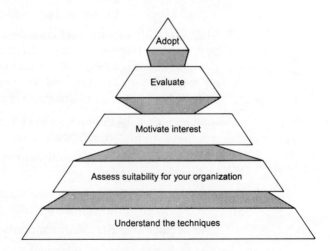

Figure 7.1   Road to adoption of OO techniques.

8 User case-studies

INTENDED READERSHIP
Project managers, the technology 'gatekeeper' and project leaders should read this chapter. It contains information on the experiences of developers using object technology and is of a descriptive, relatively non-technical, nature.

CHAPTER PRE-REQUISITES
The reader should be familiar with the object-oriented principles as detailed in Chapter 2. Some of the case-studies relate to OO programming languages, one relates to an OO database management system and one to the adoption of an object-oriented analysis and design method. The reader might wish to study the appropriate sections in Chapters 4, 5 and 6 before reading the corresponding case-studies, although these chapters are not essential reading.

CHAPTER OVERVIEW
The chapter presents several user case-studies showing how other organizations are using object technology. Four studies involve OO programming languages, one concerns an OODBMS and one illustrates a use of an object-oriented analysis and design method. The language studies cover the four major languages detailed in Chapter 5, that is, C++, Eiffel, Smalltalk and Objective-C. The database study is of Ontos. The object-oriented analysis and design study involves the use of the Colbert method (Colbert, 1989) as described in Chapter 4.

The studies cover both large and small development organizations from a wide variety of backgrounds including both technical and business environments. Each study discusses the decisions taken, the strategies adopted, an overview of the products being developed and the experiences gained from OO development.

Some of the experiences relate directly to the products used, but perhaps the most important experiences relate to the techniques in general.

Readers should NOT assume that a particular case-study is of no interest to them simply because it involves a language or database which they would not use. ALL case-studies are relevant to all OO developers.

The purpose of the studies is to:

- Demonstrate that OO does work and can be used to build commercial products.

- Give you a feel for the wide variety of application areas in which OO is being used.

- Help you make key decisions in the selection of object technology.

- Show how others have gone about adopting OO.

- Expose the benefits and problems associated with object technology.

8.1 The Applied Logic Group – a case-study using Eiffel

This case-study presents the use of the latest version of Eiffel – V2.3. The reader should note that Eiffel V3.0 is due to be released in early 1993. The Eiffel language is described in Chapter 5.

Nick Parsons, Technical Director at The Applied Logic Group, collaborated with The Institute of Software Engineering during compilation of this user case-study. His help is gratefully acknowledged.

8.1.1   Company and product background

Company: The Applied Logic Group, London, England (comprising Applied Logic Computers, Applied Logic Developments and Applied Logic Research).

Size: 15 staff.

Nature of business: Software and hardware systems house.

Hardware and operating systems: MIPS 3230, SONY NEWS, AST 386 running UNIX.

Programming languages: Informix 4GL.

Products: Various bespoke business applications such as a product rentals systems and telesales systems. Also some hardware systems including the development of a range of BABT approved modems, communication servers and facsimile transmission systems.

Involvement in EC ESPRIT II & III projects (*Business Class* and *Recycle* respectively).

8.1.2   Background

In the past Applied Logic Computers developed software applications using Informix 4GL. Applications are developed primarily for UNIX workstations.

Nick Parsons explained:

'We are a small software house, developing business applications such as product rentals systems and telesales systems. Our market is the small bespoke applications requiring no more than about one man-year of effort'.

8.1.3   Reasons for considering object-oriented techniques

Applied Logic Computers used Informix but as Nick Parsons says:

'Informix lacked the conceptual integrity we needed. That is, it lacked the ability to implement language-independent designs. Informix was not really flexible enough for our needs. We wanted a programming language that would be capable of implementing designs without having to consider significant limitations in what the language would allow us to do'.

They considered the object-oriented methodology for the following additional reasons:

High degree of commonality. Most of their business applications have many of the same components. Nick Parsons explained:

'Most business applications have a user interface and a database, with very little in between. There is consequently a large degree of commonality between applications. With traditional development techniques we were limited to a cut-and-paste approach to software reuse. This is fairly basic and we felt that the inheritance and polymorphic capabilities of an object-oriented approach would provide a much richer and more powerful means of reusing software'.

Greater modularity. Parsons continued:

'A typical bespoke development is split between two or three people. The client/server contractual view of interacting objects encourages cleanly defined boundaries between software written by different members of a development team'.

Need to develop more sophisticated applications

'Increasingly, we are being requested to develop more sophisticated applications. In a small operation with tight deadlines, traditional techniques do not readily lend themselves to sophisticated applications. We needed a better and faster way to develop software. Object orientation seemed to provide this. In particular most OO programming languages provide powerful libraries which aid the developer'.

Applied Logic considered moving to more sophisticated 4GLs. But the run-time licence fees associated with such products are prohibitive for small developments.

Parsons continued:

'The vision was to develop class libraries which would provide both the graphical users interfaces and the database component for typical business applications. These class libraries would become the programmer's tool kits for developing applications such as stock control, payroll, telesales and so on which can all use the same fundamental structure and services. The tool kits provide this fundamental structure and services'.

To summarize, the decision to use an object-oriented programming language was based on:

- The need to build more sophisticated software applications with GUIs;
- The objective of increasing the modularity within an application with the benefit of more cleanly defined boundaries between components in a multi-developer project;
- Increased application programmer productivity through the inheritance capabilities and reuse, and at the same time reduce code duplication;
- The desire for a more general-purpose programming language which would not impose severe restrictions on what could be implemented.

8.1.4   Choosing an OO programming language

The criteria for choosing an OOPL were:

- Must provide good support for software reuse.
- Must provide good support for application development, such as string and number manipulation.

- Must provide good support for GUI development.
- Must interface with C software since UNIX products provide C interfaces.
- Must incur no run-time licence fees.
- Some staff had previous experience with formal methods of specifying software. This led to a desire for a language which provided some means of formally, or at least semi-formally, specifying the software.
- An exception handling mechanism was considered useful, particularly in the event that any transaction processing would be needed. Exception handling provides a handy way to manage aborting a transaction in the event of a failure.

Parsons explained:

> 'We did paper-based evaluations of Smalltalk, C++ and Eiffel. All three languages provide good support for developing GUIs'.

Chapter 5 discusses the various class libraries available to support GUI development.

Eiffel and C++ interface to C-code quite readily (Chapter 5 discusses the issues of interworking between both Eiffel and C++ with C-code). Smalltalk does not provide the same ease of interworking with C (although recent versions do support interworking to some extent).

Nick Parsons considers:

> 'C++ seemed attractive, particularly since many of the development team had used C in previous jobs. However, C++ requires a very disciplined use if you are to develop a truly object-oriented application. I believe in the benefits from an object-oriented approach and don't want my developers to dilute, or cancel, those benefits by not adhering to an OO regime. I wanted to enforce the use of object orientation'.

At the time (late 1990) C++ did not provide any inbuilt exception handling mechanism whereas both Smalltalk and Eiffel did. (This situation has now changed – the latest version of Stroustrup (1991) includes exception handling. The C++ section in Chapter 5 discusses exception handling.)

On the basis of the preceding text C++ was therefore ruled out. Nick Parsons continued:

> 'Most product development involves a team of people. The chosen language and associated development system had to be capable of supporting a multi-developer environment. We felt that with Eiffel we could achieve this multi-developer

environment, but with Smalltalk it would be much more difficult.

Furthermore, most Smalltalk implementations carry heavy run-time penalties and result in large run-time systems – both of these ruled Smalltalk out for us'.

By developing on a computer network, Eiffel allows class libraries to be shared from a central file server. Any developer can modify or use any existing class. Concurrent use in this environment is the responsibility of the network operating system. However, in Smalltalk all classes are added into the local Smalltalk image, and become part of the local Smalltalk system. Developing in a multi-programmer environment would therefore require the periodic copying of classes from one machine to another. This is a distinct disadvantage. Smalltalk was therefore ruled out. (ObjectWorks\Smalltalk now includes a list change manager which handles class changes in a group programming environment.)

Based on the preceding arguments Applied Logic Computers concluded that Eiffel was the most suitable OOPL for its environment.

8.1.5   An object-oriented software development project

The overall development strategy hinges on an application developer's tool kit (an application framework of classes called LogicAL). LogicAL provides three libraries of generic Eiffel classes to reduce the develop-

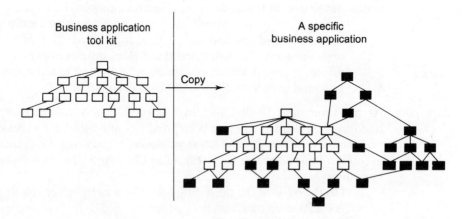

Business application
tool kit

A specific
business application

Copy

☐ Business class
■ Mixture of application classes and Eiffel-supplied classes

Figure 8.1   Developing a business application from a reusable, generic library.

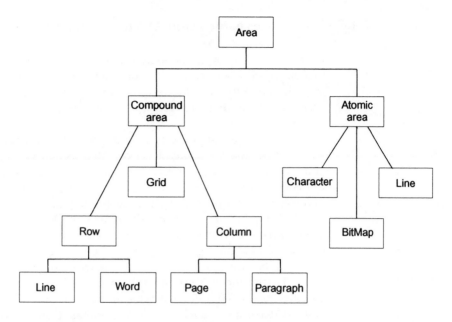

Figure 8.2   A section from the Application Developers Toolkit (© ALC 1992).

ment time in constructing new bespoke business applications. LogicAL can be used in an application in two ways: (i) statically through sub-classing as depicted in Figure 8.1, and (ii) dynamically, through message passing to objects instantiated from LogicAL at run-time.

The three libraries are for (i) a user interface, (ii) database access and (iii) business-specific classes.

LogicAL has been under development by a team of three software engineers. It has taken four man-years to develop and contains some 250 classes. Each class has an average of 150 lines of code. The library exhibits strong use of multiple inheritance and polymorphism to aid in the reuse process.

Figure 8.2 illustrates a section from the user interface library. Large parts of a business application are concerned with displaying data. This class library provides the tools for describing the projection of data onto areas of a display device. The class AREA contains a number of abstract properties and behaviour including Size, Stretch/Shrink, Position, Move, Navigate and Edit. These features are inherited into all descendant classes which can either use them directly or redefine them as necessary.

Some prototype business applications have been developed in order to refine and perfect the class library structure.

8.1.6   Experiences gained from OO development

**General
observations**

Nick Parsons believes that software development organizations should evaluate their use of software components at a corporate level, identifying commonality across a range of applications and even application areas. He feels that the resultant class libraries can aid reuse across application areas.

Designing for reuse is very important. You cannot assume that just because you are using object-oriented techniques, reuse will follow automatically. Inheritance and dynamic binding will support reuse only if it is built into the design. (Chapter 2 on OO concepts discusses issues in reuse and illustrates how dynamic binding aids software reuse.)

While one of the main advantages of OO is in the clarity of the design process, often it is difficult to decide exactly where an element of functionality should go. There might be two or three classes which all appear to be appropriate sites for a given method (feature).

Furthermore, sometimes it is difficult to identify application-specific classes. High-level classes are more easily identified. Deciding how to decompose such classes into detailed, implementable classes proved difficult on occasions. (Chapter 4 on OO analysis and design raises this issue and discusses some techniques to help expose classes.)

**Eiffel
observations**

Nick Parsons found the Eiffel assertion capabilities very useful.

> 'You can write the assertions for several associated classes first, then add the code later. This helps you think at the higher level first. The assertions form the last stage of detailed design and provide a framework for the final coding stage'.

Parsons added:

> 'Although it is still possible for programming errors to occur, the use of assertions results in errors being detected at an early stage. With Eiffel, you just don't get the kind of subtle and pernicious bugs a C programmer has to contend with'.

For The Applied Logic Group, one consideration is the portability across UNIX platforms. Applied Logic normally develops bespoke applications but may have to port the end products. They develop on one platform and may port software to several others. Using the C-Package generator facility in the Eiffel development environment Parsons produced full C-source code for a product. This was transferred to other UNIX platforms, recompiled locally and run without problem. The C-Package generator strips out unused functions and performs in-line optimizations. The resultant C-source code is 'readable' but not very pretty! The run-time performance of the application code is very dependent on the compiler options chosen, but was generally found to be satisfactory.

Nick Parsons observed:

> 'The Eiffel built-in class dependencies were excellent, especially in a multi-user development environment. If anyone changed a class, all subclasses were automatically recompiled on the next build. However, the time required to link final applications was quite long. This results from Eiffel's use of a separate file for each class, thereby creating a multitude of object-code files to be linked'.

The debugging capabilities in version 2.3 of Eiffel were never used! Parsons explained:

> 'Instead of debugging, we rely heavily on assertions and getting things right from the beginning. The whole point of assertions is that they define the system – they mean that a class is not just a collection of functions and data, but actually becomes an abstract data type. This is the way to use Eiffel'.

The Eiffel documentation tool (see Chapter 5) was used to document the assertions. This complemented the use of assertions to sketch out the logic of a number of classes before they were actually implemented.

8.1.7 Learning curve

Initially one member of staff at The Applied Logic Group was sent on an Eiffel training course. The other team members learned the Eiffel language and development environment from hands-on experience and reading Meyer's book (Meyer, 1988). All team members were fluent in Eiffel and the object-oriented methodology within three months. Figures quoted (Booch, 1991) for typical development staff indicate periods of six months before staff are fully competent class designers.

8.1.8 Life cycle used

Development of LogicAL is being accomplished under trial conditions. Applied Logic has developed its own business class analysis and design method (developed under an EC ESPRIT II project called Business Class which includes CASE tool support through an analyst workbench developed by one of the partners in the consortium).

The LogicAL designers went for a high-level decomposition into abstract classes. They tried to make the life cycle as incremental as possible, however the compile–link cycle does not support incremental development particularly well. (The Eiffel V3.0 environment includes the addition of support for incremental development through the so-called melting ice technology – see Chapter 5 for details.)

The development strategy for future business applications involves the use of LogicAL. This illustrates the essence of an object-oriented development cycle, where an abstract class library design proceeds via a mixture of top-down and bottom-up techniques. The final application design and construction revolves around this component library and involves a bottom-up style. (Chapter 3 discusses suitable object-oriented software life cycles.)

8.1.9   Summary and conclusions

Overall Nick Parsons is happy with the way object orientation has been adopted in the company so far. While Eiffel is still not a mature product, the next release (version 3.0) promises many improvements. Eiffel does provide good portability across hardware platforms and supports programming at a higher level than C, removing the need to think in terms of pointers and providing a means of semi-formally specifying software through pre and postconditions.

The use of inheritance and a generic class library reduces the amount of duplicated code and specific business applications can be developed much faster using Eiffel than was possible using traditional techniques and Informix 4GL. Furthermore, the polymorphic capabilities of Eiffel, combined with dynamic binding, have enabled much more powerful features to be programmed into Applied Logic's business applications than could have been achieved using traditional techniques in a similar time-scale.

8.2   Winter Partners Ltd – a case-study using Smalltalk

A summary user case-study involving Electronic Data Systems with Smalltalk is presented in the Smalltalk section of Chapter 5. The case study presented here uses version 1.2 of Digitalk-V/PM.

Several staff in Winter Partners helped with the production of this user case-study, including Sandy Scott (Marketing Manager), Brian Shearing (Consultant) and Yasmin Husain (Business Analyst). Their help is gratefully acknowledged.

8.2.1 Company and product background

Company: Winter Partners Ltd, London and Zürich.

Size: Over 200 staff.

Nature of business: Software house for standard global banking software.

Hardware and operating systems: Unisys A-series, DEC VAX (VMS) PC compatibles running OS/2.

Programming languages: Basic, C, COBOL, Smalltalk.

Products: Software for the banking community, BANCOS, IBS, RIBS – packages covering all aspects of retail, wholesale and private banking, including loans, deposits, money-market trading and multi-currency investment management.

8.2.2 Background

Computer Integrated Banking (CIB) is Winter Partners' strategic project. Initiated in 1985, it has evolved through many stages. It aims to provide large financial institutions with an advanced development environment for global banking applications. CIB comprises a standard knowledge base, in which Winter Partners' banking expertise is stored electronically.

The short-term goal of CIB is to create a specialized end-to-end tool for developing and customizing complex banking information systems that run in several hardware and software environments. The development of this tool (called OSMOSYS) is the subject of this case-study.

A team of eight staff are currently involved in the CIB project. OSMOSYS will be used in-house to enhance and increase the flexibility and productivity on future banking software development projects. The commercial exploitation of OSMOSYS will place Winter Partner's knowledge base at the client's disposal.

8.2.3 Reasons for considering object-oriented techniques

For the end product
The primary goal of the OSMOSYS tool is to provide a modern method for the analysis and design of banking information systems. Winter Partners wanted the tool to embody its experience in the development of such systems. The object-oriented paradigm provides a suitable technique since inheritance enables the reuse of past knowledge. An

object-oriented approach enables generic system specifications to be stored in a modular and reusable knowledge base.

The fundamentals of banking systems are very stable. A bank account will always provide the same basic facilities such as an interest-bearing repository for money with one or more named owners. Over time, modifications may be made to the account, such as linking it to credit card accounts and so on. These are essentially specializations of the basic bank account concept. Through object orientation the specification of a generic bank account becomes a reusable module in a knowledge base. Specific forms of bank account are then derived from the generic form using inheritance.

The second reason for using object-oriented techniques is associated with the flexibility that such techniques offer. Winter Partners observed that continually changing user requirements were causing severe problems for their software developers. By viewing requirements in a more modular way (through the client/server architecture inherent in object-oriented techniques) they felt that the effects of changing requirements could be minimized, and development effort would become more productive.

The final reason for considering object-oriented methods for analysis and design is connected with the clarity of representation. Winter Partners found that applications were overly complicated because software developers think like computers rather than like business people. Object-oriented methods enable developers to think more directly in terms of the product's end use. This leads to clearer software specifications which in turn lead to a more easily understood software application.

For the product development

A primary motivation for employing an object-oriented approach to the development of this CASE toolset was the need to understand object-oriented methods fully. The end product was to support object-oriented analysis and design so the insight gained through a full object-oriented development provided valuable information for the OOA&D method.

8.2.4   Choosing an OO programming language

C++ and Smalltalk were the only two languages considered because of their wide acceptance and maturity.

Sandy Scott explained:

> 'The object-oriented method embedded in OSMOSYS was developed in parallel with the actual toolkit. The problem was fairly open ended, with a specification that evolved as the

system was being developed. A highly iterative development cycle was required to enable rapid feedback. Smalltalk provided the short edit–compile–run cycle which was needed for rapid development of ideas in a very dynamically changing environment. C++ could not provide support for such a highly iterative development cycle and was therefore discounted'.

The product required a graphical user interface. Initial development was targeted at PCs running DOS, with an MS-Windows GUI. However, there was a requirement to operate on the PS/2 running OS/2 with Presentation Manger as the GUI. It was therefore necessary to choose a portable language between these two environments. Initially, both Smalltalk-V/PM and Smalltalk-V Windows from Digitalk were used by different developers, but were found not to be fully compatible.

There was no requirement to interface with other software or applications except with OS/2 for storage in its DB Manager and communication via its LAN Manager. Smalltalk-V/PM was adopted universally.

8.2.5   An object-oriented software development project

The product, called OSMOSYS, is a software development environment consisting of a method for object-oriented systems analysis and design along with a CASE tool suite supporting library services, user interface building, modelling, validation, configuration management, documentation and code generation. OSMOSYS runs on PS/2 machines under OS/2. All tools result in information being stored in a repository (via OS/2 DB Manager).

An analyst models business requirements with the OSMOSYS library using an object-oriented analysis and design method (Chapter 4 gives more details on the method). OSMOSYS provides a suite of generic business specifications from which an analyst can develop specializations as required. The toolset then provides facilities for validating designs in an incremental fashion before cutting the final software. In essence, the validation tool enables designs to be executed using an interpreter. When the analysis and design stages are complete, relational database schema and application software are generated automatically. OSMOSYS is summarized in Figure 8.3.

OSMOSYS addresses the evolving area of object-oriented analysis and design while safeguarding the existing investment many organizations have in relational technology. The Application Generator automatically handles the object-oriented-to-relational transformation.

There are four main screens through which OSMOSYS can receive and manipulate information. These are:

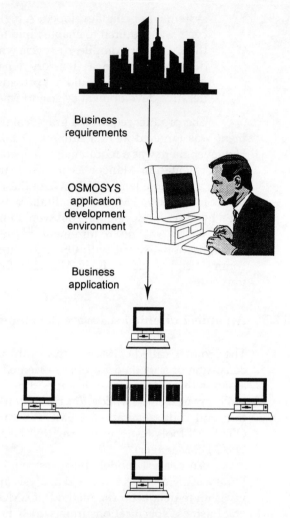

Figure 8.3   The OSMOSYS product.

(1) Class relationship diagram (similar to entity relationship diagrams)

(2) Class hierarchy diagrams

(3) Class life diagrams (finite state machines)

(4) Dialogue generator (screen painter)

This information is classified into three basic forms:

(1) **Classes.**

(2) **Types.** This is the vocabulary – it corresponds to the data diction-

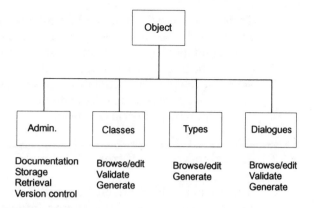

Figure 8.4   Top level of the OSMOSYS class hierarchy.

ary in a traditional system, that is, the user-defined types such as Amount, Currency, Date and so on;

(3) **Dialogues.** These are user interface screens.

All three forms of information are implemented as classes. They can all inherit. There are three primary actions a user may wish to apply to each class of information. These are:

(1) **Browse/edit.** To inspect and/or modify the information.

(2) **Validate.** To activate (or execute) a given class or dialogue specification, to simulate how the implemented specification will behave.

(3) **Generate.** To cut some code for a given class.

The Browse/edit, Validate and Generate operations are invoked from a menu in the user interface. Browse/edit operations can apply to all three forms of information, that is, classes, types and dialogues. Validate and Generate apply to classes and dialogues. Polymorphism and dynamic binding made the job of coding the Browse/edit, Validate and Generate operations easier to manage. The user interface is more succinct because there is just one menu, and the operation of each menu option depends upon the class of information to which it is applied. That is, the context-sensitive feature of the Browse/edit, Validate and Generate options was implemented through the polymorphic and dynamic binding properties of the Smalltalk language.

The top-level OSMOSYS classes inherit directly from the OBJECT superclass in the Smalltalk class library. Figure 8.4 shows the top-level class hierarchy used in OSMOSYS. The Admin class includes a full sub-tree of classes to provide documentation, storage and retrieval from the repository, as well as version control and other administrative facilities.

Each of the Classes, Types and Dialogues classes contains a full subclass hierarchy. These hierarchies provide polymorphic forms of the Browse/ edit, Validate and Generate methods discussed previously.

The project has required about 10 work-years of effort so far, using seven developers, and contains some 500 Smalltalk classes. This represents an average productivity of about one Smalltalk class per week. The class hierarchy is five classes deep.

8.2.6   Experiences gained from OO development

General observations

The use of an object-oriented approach where the overall system design and construction revolved around interacting classes greatly accommodated the constantly changing requirements. Brian Shearing explains:

> 'By having a set of autonomous objects which provide services to anyone, changes to the specification were easily accommodated by changing the specific objects concerned'.

Smalltalk observations

Language

Converting from Digitalk Smalltalk-V Windows to Smalltalk-V/PM required copying the Smalltalk classes to the new environment and recompiling them. It was necessary to rework some of the user interface classes because the Presentation Manager and Windows versions of Smalltalk used different points of origin for mapping the user interface.

Most of the benefits from polymorphism were derived from the user interface development. The same use of polymorphism was not achieved in the more abstract parts of the system such as the compiler/code generator. However, when the compiler development was complete, an interpreter for the 'validate' option in the user interface was easily implemented. The interpreter inherited the classes associated with the compiler and added extra methods where appropriate. Inheritance therefore aided code reuse.

One piece of advice Brian Shearing has for any developer about to start using the Digitalk version of Smalltalk is:

> 'Be careful if you subclass from the Smalltalk class libraries! It can be preferable to make use of the libraries via message calls. Digitalk have made significant changes to their libraries from one version to the next. If you have developed an application around classes through subclassing off the Smalltalk class library, and the Smalltalk class library changes, then you may have a lot of rework to do to make your application compatible with subsequent releases of Smalltalk'.

Note: this issue is undoubtedly due to the use of early versions of Smalltalk, and may no longer be relevant.

In Figure 8.4, all the main branches inherit directly from OBJECT – the top-level class in the Smalltalk class library. Lower classes used in OSMOSYS use Smalltalk classes via message calls, but not via inheritance. This partly defeats the benefits from inheritance and is only necessary where class hierarchies are out of your control.

The only exception to Shearing's rule concerns the use of the Smalltalk Presentation Manager classes. The Presentation Manager Smalltalk classes aided productivity on the user interface component of OSMOSYS to such an extent that it was worth embedding the OSMOSYS user interface classes within the Smalltalk Presentation Manager class library via subclassing.

Interacting with the Smalltalk class library by sending messages rather than connecting to the library via subclassing can bring problems as well as the benefits Shearing described above. One particular problem which could occur is that of a messaging explosion where a form of uncontrolled message sending happens. This is a particular problem in dynamically typed languages such as Smalltalk because the inter-class dependencies are not so visible. The issue of message explosion is discussed in Chapter 5.

All members of the Winter Partners team agree that to use Smalltalk properly, you need to fully utilize the Smalltalk library software. Knowing the extent and capabilities of the large Smalltalk class library can save a lot of development time and reinventing the wheel – but the learning curve is large!

Run-time environment

The Smalltalk garbage collector is often cited as a source of performance limitation on the grounds that it runs periodically, competing with the application for processor time. With Smalltalk-V/PM Brian Shearing explains:

> 'The garbage collector is not the limiting factor in application performance, provided there is enough memory to allow the garbage collector to operate infrequently. In practice this necessitated 16Mb of memory on the PS/2'.

Development environment

The highly incremental development cycle and dynamically typed programming language aided rapid software development. The problem was open ended, with a specification that evolved as the system was being developed.

Sandy Scott explained:

> 'Using Smalltalk, we could build it object by object, and as the actual requirements evolved, we could alter the computer model. The result was substantially more software developed

and debugged more quickly than could have been achieved using a traditional language such as C or Pascal'.

But there are problems! Without care, the highly incremental development style reduces the amount of preplanned design work. This is not a problem for throwaway prototypes but has serious implications for incremental prototypes leading to fully implemented systems.

These problems were minimized by ensuring that objects performed discrete functions and communicated with only a few other objects. Inheritance was useful for imposing fundamental changes on a group of classes by modifying the upper-level class and consequently all lower classes inheriting from this modified class automatically exhibited the new behaviour.

In situations where significant features need to change, there are times when you must go back and rework some fundamental parts of the design, rather than continually modifying bits of it. For this reason it is important to have **design reappraisals** at various stages in an evolutionary, incremental prototyping development. Performing the design reappraisal does not detract from the usefulness of prototyping. It is still a good way of getting rapid user feedback early on in the project. But reviewing the design after this process is complete ensures that the use of prototyping does not compromise the final quality of the system.

With a multi-developer team, as in this case-study, Smalltalk has some limitations. Brian Shearing explained:

> 'All new application classes automatically become a part of the Smalltalk environment. There is no means of storing classes centrally for sharing between developers. This inhibited the multi-developer environment. Class sharing necessitated physical copying of class source code from one developer's environment to another. We developed a Change Manager application in Smalltalk to perform this function'.

(Author's note: There are now products available for Smalltalk-V which support development in a LAN environment with integrated working between several users.)

The development team made extensive use of the Smalltalk debugging capabilities and found them adequate for the task.

8.2.7   Learning curve

Before starting the OSMOSYS development, the team spent several months evaluating the merits of an object-oriented approach to software development. By the start of the development they were familiar with the concepts. None of the team members experienced any significant difficulties with learning Smalltalk. However, the team represents the R&D arm of Winter Partners and is likely to include above-average software professionals.

The main learning curve was the massive library of classes which make up the Smalltalk environment. Initially developers often found themselves reinventing the wheel because of unfamiliarity with the Smalltalk library and its capabilities. As competence with Smalltalk grew, developers made much more use of the Smalltalk library classes.

8.2.8   Life cycle used

OSMOSYS development employed a very iterative life cycle. The only formal documentation which passed between team members related to the overall architectural metamodel of the tool. This proved sufficient. Most other communication between members relied on informal discussions and team briefings. The incremental nature of the development environment enabled ideas to be implemented and consequently evaluated quickly.

8.2.9   Summary and conclusions

The main benefits perceived from using Smalltalk are:

- Increased productivity through a fast edit–compile–run cycle;
- Greater flexibility from a module-oriented approach to systems development, particularly in an environment of constantly changing requirements;
- The Smalltalk Presentation Manager classes were helpful when developing the user interface.

The main disadvantage of Smalltalk was:

- The highly incremental nature encouraged by the Smalltalk environment requires careful supervision to ensure that initial designs do not evolve into an unstructured form through the use of an uncontrolled build–review cycle.

The main problems with the Digitalk Smalltalk were:

- Subclassing from the supplied class library can cause problems if the vendor releases a completely new library with the next version of Smalltalk.

- The Smalltalk garbage collector requires a lot of memory to run efficiently – typically 16 Mb of RAM were required.

- The Smalltalk development environment does not encourage multi-user effort.

This substantial software development illustrates that it is possible to undertake multi-developer software projects using Smalltalk. The prototyping nature of the life cycle which Smalltalk encourages is good for developing ideas, particularly in areas where the problem domain is not initially well understood.

8.3   British Airways plc – a case-study using C++

The case-study presented here uses Glockenspiel's C++ translator and CommonView 2 for Presentation Manager.

Graham Tigg (Development Environment Manager) and Jim Arlow (Software Engineer) of British Airways Distributed Systems Infrastructure department collaborated with The Institute of Software Engineering during compilation of this user case-study. Their help is gratefully acknowledged.

8.3.1   Company and product background

Company: British Airways plc, Heathrow Airport, England.

Size: 1000 software development staff.

Nature of business: Airline industry.

Hardware and operating systems: A wide range of hardware including IBM PS/2 – OS/2 and IBM mainframe – VM.

Programming languages: C and C++ development on PS/2 and VM, PL/1 and proprietary 4GL development on mainframes.

Products: —

8.3.2   Background

British Airways moved into the realm of object-oriented technology in late 1989, but the roots of the decision are to be found a year earlier with the publication of the findings of BA's Architectural Task Force.

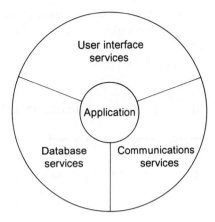

Figure 8.5   BA's architectural view of future systems.

The task force was a group set up to examine BA's IT needs and abilities and to present a vision to which the company could adhere. It produced a vision of a large organization, where most of the data resides in mainframe repositories. Users would interface with the data via intelligent workstations. Graham Tigg explains:

> 'Intelligent workstations, in essence, have three components providing services for user interfaces, databases and communications'.

Figure 8.5 shows BA's view of future systems.

Three subgroups were formed to evaluate emerging technologies in each of these areas. This vision of a client/server architecture led BA to invest in IBM PS/2s connected to IBM mainframes via IBM's SNA LU6.2 (APPC) communications protocol. The user interface subgroup identified Presentation Manager, MS-Windows and OSF/Motif as the most likely desktop graphical user interface standards of the future.

For user interface construction, BA started developing Presentation Manager applications using C. Tigg explains:

> 'We found programming Presentation Manager unproductive. It involved long training courses and the programming was very complex and at a very low level. We wanted to simplify the development of user interfaces by removing the need to program at the Application Programming Interface level of Presentation Manager'.

BA also desired portability across several platforms including Presentation Manager, MS-Windows and OSF/Motif. They recently looked at various 4GL GUI tools such as Applications Manager, IS/2 and Easel. The main problem with these tools was in the performance of the generated code. There was also concern with the instability and immaturity of some of these tools.

8.3.3   Reasons for considering object-oriented techniques and C++

The need for a simpler (but still flexible) method of developing graphical user interfaces, and the desire for portability across several user interface standards, led BA to consider object-oriented techniques. In August 1989 BA embarked on pilot projects using Glockenspiel's CommonView class libraries and associated C++ translator. C++ was chosen partly as a result of the strength of the C programming community inside BA. There were already around 100 people programming in C. Migrating to C++ was seen as the logical step. BA's decision was shaped by market forces, C++ had sufficient industry clout behind it. This gave the company confidence that it would survive. (Chapter 5 discusses the maturity and commercial factors associated with C++ and other object-oriented programming languages. It is quite clear from the discussions in Chapter 5 that C++ is emerging as the industry standard object-oriented programming language.)

By February 1990, the task force recommended the adoption of Glockenspiel's CommonView class libraries and associated C++ translator for graphical user interface development.

8.3.4   An object-oriented software development project

British Airways currently has several ongoing C++/CommonView GUI developments for IBM PS/2 machines running OS/2. One such project is called Arcadia. This project initially involved three analyst/designers and another three programmers. It has since grown to a team size in excess of 30 staff.

Twice each year BA and all other airlines meet at conferences to renegotiate landing slots for their aircraft at airports across the globe. The BA planners go to these conferences with optimum schedules based on a predetermined set of aircraft landing slots. The conferences consist of bartering sessions lasting several days and inevitably result in some give and take by all parties. The planners therefore need to know the effects of different landing slots on their schedules and resource utilization for ground staff such as maintenance, cleaners, baggage handlers, check-in desks, and so on. They work on an aircraft landing schedule and plot a histogram for this, looking at one particular ground activity such as

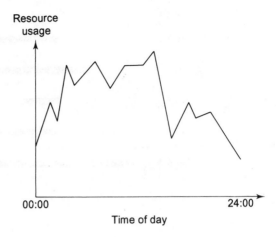

Resource usage

00:00   24:00

Time of day

Figure 8.6   Workload profile histogram for ground staff, based on a predefined aircraft landing schedule.

check-in or baggage handling. The planners plot a workload profile histogram for a 24 hour period, the idea being to utilize resources as efficiently as possible. Figure 8.6 illustrates a typical workload profile.

Another view is a Gantt chart which shows the workload for all ground staff associated with a particular aircraft stand. Figure 8.7 illustrates a typical Gantt chart. A bar represents the amount of time an aircraft spends at a particular stand. Other bars show the utilization of staff involved in maintenance, cleaning, baggage handling and check-in, for that aircraft. Figure 8.7 illustrates the Gantt chart for ten aircraft stands, showing what flights are at what stands and for how long.

The bars on the Gantt can be moved around at will, allowing the planner to observe the effects of changes in aircraft landing schedules. The system works in a similar manner to many commercially available project management packages. When bars on the Gantt chart are moved, the planner can display the corresponding workload profile histogram for a particular ground activity such as baggage handling, and determine the effective utilization of these ground staff.

Figure 8.8 shows the Arcadia architecture. It is based on a client/server relationship. The user initially enters raw scheduling information through a forms interface (via Oracle Forms). They select some particular action to perform on the database. When the action is complete, the user informs the aggregation data-processing application (AGGI) that they have changed the database and requests either a histogram or Gantt display of the resulting information. AGGI reads information from the database, massages it, and sends it to either the histogram application (to be plotted as a histogram as shown in Figure

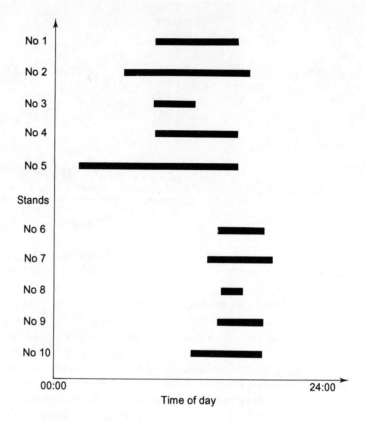

Figure 8.7   Gantt chart for ground staff and aircraft.

8.6) or the Gantt application (to be plotted as a Gantt chart as shown in Figure 8.7). Histogram and Gantt are standalone programs providing user interface and communications with AGGI. The only inbuilt processing is for determining screen positions of objects. Jim Arlow explained:

> 'All the main processing is achieved in the AGGI application. The graphical layers are thereby kept completely separate. When data is sent to them, they display it. If a user moves a bar on the Gantt chart, the rearranged data goes back to AGGI, the database is updated and the histogram application gets updated dynamically'.

The graphical presentation enables the effects of aircraft scheduling changes to be understood more easily than would be possible using numerical statistics.

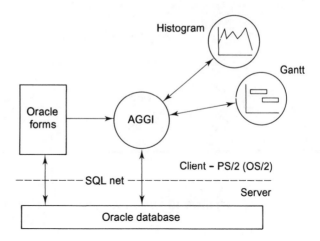

Figure 8.8   Architecture of the Arcadia system.

Both the histogram and Gantt applications were developed using C++ and CommonView. British Airways developed its own generic C++ class library called Pictures, based on the CommonView class library supplied by Glockenspiel. Figure 8.9 illustrates the final architecture of the Pictures generic C++ class library.

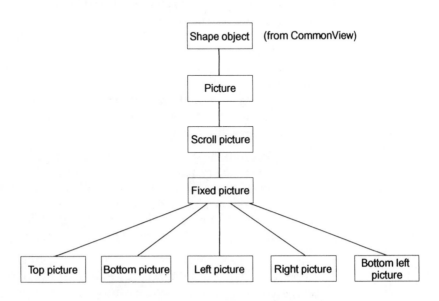

Figure 8.9   The British Airways GUI class library.

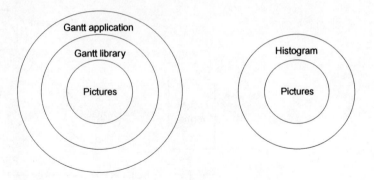

Figure 8.10   C++ class libraries used in building the histogram and
Gantt applications.

The Pictures library contains nine classes. These classes provide generic GUI handling routines combined with a capability to communicate with any application that supports Dynamic Data Exchange (DDE) via OS/2.

The histogram application was designed and constructed using class extensions to the Pictures library. Histogram consists of some 30 C++ classes, each containing about 50–100 lines of code.

The Gantt application was developed in a slightly different manner. Recognizing that various forms of Gantt presentation would be used throughout the company, a generic Gantt C++ class library was developed on top of the Pictures library. This Gantt library is used in several projects within British Airways. Figure 8.10 illustrates the composition of C++ class libraries used for building the histogram and Gantt applications.

The Pictures and Gantt libraries are managed by a Class Manager. They are shipped to other parts of the organization for use in software developments. Jim Arlow explained:

'We ship the generic class libraries and guarantee their functionality. However, the guarantee only holds provided the development teams do not actually change ANY features of the shipped classes. In effect, developers can add new classes, inheriting properties from any class in the library, but must not make any modifications to the generic class library itself'.

The AGGI application was developed using fully traditional C-code. British Airways has embraced C++ for user interface development but still needs to make more progress developing the so-called 'middle-ware' using OO techniques.

Arlow explained:

'We are redeveloping some parts of the AGGI application using C++, such as linked-list and hash-table classes. We can take an Oracle table definition and turn it into a class'.

The key to the BA philosophy has been to introduce OO into the user interface, keeping the interface components separate from the design and functionality of the body of the system.

8.3.5 Experiences gained from OO development

General observations

The first-cut Pictures class library took about four months to develop. This included the learning curve for Jim Arlow who is an experienced C programmer. He had difficulty identifying the Picture class in the class library of Figure 8.9. Jim Arlow admitted:

'It took nearly two months to identify properly the top-level Picture class in the Picture's library. Once that was done, the rest of the class hierarchy fell out quite naturally'.

The Pictures library evolved over the next six months. There were a lot of changes while the histogram and Gantt applications were being developed. Now, the Pictures library is stable and has been shipped to other parts of the company for use in their user interface developments. Jim Arlow suggests:

'You must explore the problem domain and then generalize. Play around with many class configurations – the first one will not be the final configuration'.

Once the basic class library was produced, application development proceeded quickly. Jim Arlow explained:

'We had a prototype histogram application built in one week, using the Pictures library ... At one stage, we had an analyst drawing features of the Histogram application and the application programmer developing these features at the same time!'.

But there were some problems:

'The analysts found it hard to cope with the development cycle because it didn't fit into the traditional cascade approach of analyse-design-program. The development was much more analyse-a-bit, design-a-bit, program-a-bit, then go back to the analysis again'.

This kind of problem is quite common. Because object-oriented programming languages are more mature and well understood than other object-oriented aspects of a full software development life cycle, there is a tendency to mix traditional analysis, and in some cases even design, with an object-oriented implementation. Chapter 3 discusses the problems of mixing traditional and object-oriented methods and the various 'hybrid' life cycles which result. Chapter 4 discusses the management issues associated with the blurring between analysis and design which object orientation introduces.

Testing individual classes was relatively straightforward. Generally a test harness was built to exercise each of the classes used in an application. Classes were designed to be independent of one another. There was no notion of a state machine within each class, as this was perceived as conveying some idea of a sequence between different classes which would ultimately lead to increased couplings between classes, thereby reducing the potential for reuse of those classes. Problems during integration testing, where classes are brought together in an orderly, incremental fashion, were therefore minimized.

Complexity was always introduced through inheritance. Arlow explained:

> 'Under no circumstances should any classes be modified in a well understood, reusable class library'.

Multiple inheritance was not used in the Arcadia project, nor is it used in most of British Airways C++ developments to date. Jim Arlow feels that multiple inheritance is not well understood and can cause increased coupling between classes. Multiple inheritance may be of use in specific circumstances where a developer is trying to mix classes – such as introducing a utility class (for example a linked-list class) into some other class. Multiple inheritance with such simple classes is acceptable.

BA had developed a Gantt application previously in C-code. By comparing the amount of code in the user interfaces of these two products, they discovered that the Gantt application developed using C++ and CommonView required approximately one-quarter the lines of programmer code of the C application. They attribute this reduction partly to the CommonView libraries and partly to polymorphism in C++, which they made much use of.

Graham Tigg believes the developments so far have been successful because small teams have been used. He says:

> 'You've got to break the problem down into small teams of three or four developers who all work on some small part of the problem. Prototyping is essential and in many ways what you need are analyst/programmers rather than purely analysts.

These people can talk to the customers and produce the required user interfaces. A separate team of designers can then go about extracting the generic properties and designing the overall application'.

C++ /Common- View observations There were some problems with the class library because of the immaturity of the C++ development environment. The Glockenspiel system did not contain a graphical class browser or any configuration management mechanism. However Glockenspiel has announced C++ version 3.0 with an integrated development environment which should rectify these shortcomings.

A problem with migrating from C to C++ has always been the similarities between the two languages. C++ can be used to develop software in a traditional way – C++ does not enforce the OO paradigm. Chapter 5 discusses this in more detail. However, part of the problem stems from the fact that C++ programs contain a main program. So there is a tendency to write a main program and hang a few objects off it here and there as convenient. This is not object oriented. In Glockenspiel's CommonView the class library contains the main program. The programmer does not construct it. This encourages a notion of developing classes and sewing them together – the essence of object-oriented software development.

8.3.6 Learning curve

The team of C++ developers were ex-C developers so they were all familiar with the constructs of the C programming language. The learning curve was quite long and not always obvious, explained Jim Arlow:

'There were times when we believed we had mastered thinking in an object-oriented way – but we had not really! It took a good 3-4 months to really get to grips with solving problems in an object-oriented way'.

The C++ team found the book by Bertrand Meyer (1988) particularly useful for background on object-oriented concepts.

8.3.7 Summary and conclusions

British Airways started considering object-oriented software development as a result of a corporate strategy to move towards distributed client/server computing and graphical user interfaces. (Chapter 7 discusses the whole issue of migrating to an OO regime and suggests that OO must only be considered within the overall business objectives of the organization, as BA has done. OO should not be considered as an end in itself – it is not necessarily appropriate for all software developments.)

British Airways has taken the corporate decision to recommend C++ strongly for development of GUIs in all future distributed systems. They have been using C++ for the past two years and are now beginning to see definite advantages from a corporate viewpoint in having company-wide reusable class libraries. They have concentrated on the reasonably well-defined area of GUIs, building experience gradually, before attempting any full object-oriented software developments involving not only the user interface but also the core business software making up the application.

For user interface development, BA has successfully introduced the technology and is deriving benefit from software reuse. C++ is now the *de facto* standard object-oriented programming language. The use of C++ and the Glockenspiel CommonView graphical user interface class libraries is viewed as a significant improvement over the traditional techniques of writing C source code for the application programming interfaces of Presentation Manager.

The Pictures class library is just one example of highly reusable code within the company. Graham Tigg explained:

> 'Ultimately what we would like to do is poll the various departments which are using C++, trying to identify potentially reusable components. We would then take control of these components, improve their genericity and place them under the control of a central Class Manager, who would ensure that everyone is aware of their existence. The Class Manager's job will also involve creating and maintaining good documentation for these class libraries'.

8.4   Praxis Systems plc – a case-study using Objective-C

The case-study presented here uses the Stepstone Objective-C language along with the ICpak101 foundation class library and the ICpak201 graphics library.

Rosamund Rawlings (Project Manager) of Praxis supplied the information for this case-study. Her help is gratefully acknowledged.

8.4.1 Company and product background

> **Company:** Praxis Systems plc, Bath, England.
>
> **Size:** 100 software development staff.
>
> **Nature of business:** Software house.
>
> **Hardware and operating systems:** A wide range of hardware including ICL (VME and DRS/UNIX), IBM System/88, PS/2 (OS/2), Sun 3 (Sun OS), VAX, Pyramid.
>
> **Programming languages:** C, ALGOL 68, Pascal, and others.
>
> **Products:** Mainly bespoke software, including relational database systems for several clients, computer-aided software development tools, air traffic control systems and secure systems for government departments.

8.4.2 Background

Praxis started using object-oriented techniques in 1987. They have developed several systems using object orientation mainly for tools to aid the software development process such as CASE and IPSE tools. They have used Objective-C, Smalltalk and C++.

The project described in this section used Objective-C and ran from 1987 to 1989.

8.4.3 Reasons for considering OO and Objective-C

Praxis wanted to improve product quality (reliability and maintainability) through the use of methods which encouraged a more modular approach to software construction. Rosamund Rawlings explained:

> 'The key strategy for improving maintainability is modularity. This means producing the software in manageable chunks, each of which performs a clear, well-defined function. The modules should have simple interfaces, minimizing the amount of data that needs to be passed between them. Module coupling should be minimized, so that each module communicates with as few others as possible. The impact of such factors on reusability is clear. By making the module a clear, self-contained unit of function, there is more chance that it can be used in several places in the system, rather than having several similar, but

slightly different functions. Since the functions are loosely coupled, there is a good chance that any change or extension will be localized, and will not need extensive redesign work'.

The issues of coupling and cohesion in object-oriented design are discussed in Chapter 4. The conclusions from Chapter 4 are that an object-oriented design and implementation leads to stronger cohesion and weaker coupling – the essence of a good design.

The product development required a graphical user interface. Objective-C provided a graphical class library (ICpak201) which was considered to be sufficiently mature in 1987 when the project started.

For these main reasons, the decision was taken to use object-oriented techniques and Objective-C on the project.

8.4.4   Learning curve

Most of the knowledge was self-taught through a book on Objective-C by Brad Cox (1986). Prior to project implementation, all staff were given a one-week Objective-C training course. Most staff had previously developed software in C and were completely familiar with the notion of pointers in C.

8.4.5   An object-oriented software development project

The aim of the project was to develop a multi-user distributed system to provide an integrated set of computer-aided software engineering (CASE) tools (about 60 tools in total) for use in structured systems analysis and design of information systems. The CASE tools run on Sun-3 workstations. The overall development was split between Praxis and one other partner. The system architecture comprised three main parts: (i) facilities management – to support configuration management, access to data and storage of information; (ii) a tool-writers' class library – a generic, reusable, class library to be used in each of a number of CASE tools comprising the final product; and (iii) the CASE tools (or method tools), providing graphical user interfaces and supporting different aspects of structured analysis and design such as data flow – and entity relationship diagramming. The full system would have about 60 tools – but only five were implemented by Praxis in the first phase of development.

The CASE toolset employs a multi-client/single-server architecture, enabling several tools to communicate with one server which manages access to the required data and services. Figure 8.11 illustrates the overall product architecture.

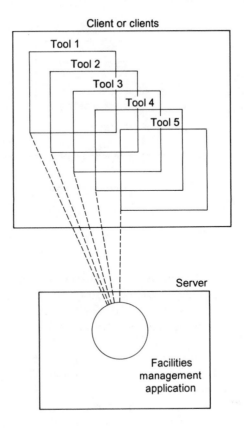

Figure 8.11   Overall architecture for the CASE tool product.

Each of the CASE tools required a similar graphical user interface. A design decision dictated that all tools would manipulate information using the same basic set of methods. For example, there was a method to create an entity. The create had to be context sensitive so that a create method in Tool 1 would execute differently from the create method in Tool 2. This structure enabled a generic class library to be constructed for building the CASE tools. The development of each tool could then be based on the generic class library (called the Tool-writers' Class Library), with specific classes added to provide its unique functionality. Figure 8.12 depicts the internal architecture of the client and server applications.

One development team in Praxis built the facilities management application (server) and the generic class libraries for use by the toolset developers. The five CASE tools were developed by another team in Praxis (the tool-writers) and the external partner also developed tools, using the generic class libraries. All parts of the system were developed using object-oriented techniques.

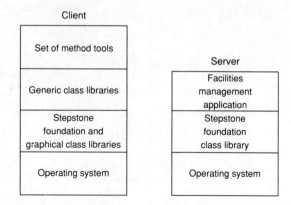

Figure 8.12   Internal architecture of the CASE tool applications and facilities manager.

The system was specified in the formal specification language Z (Spivey, 1989) and then implemented in Objective-C. No specific object-oriented analysis or design method was used. The development of the facilities management application and the class library took two years from requirements to system test, with a team size reaching eight people. The specific CASE tools developed by Praxis took eight months with a team size reaching four people. The overall effort amounted to about ten work-years.

The facilities management application (server) was developed from an application-specific class library. Rosamund Rawlings explains:

> 'Because there was only one server, it was felt unnecessary to spend excess time developing a truly reusable class library. Many parts of this library were obviously very specific to that application'.

However, the main objective of the tool-writers' class library was to develop highly reusable classes, applicable to the development of all the CASE tools.

> 'There was a lot of discussion between the team building the tool-writers' class library and the tool-writers themselves. The final set of class libraries changed by no more than 20 % from the first-cut libraries delivered to the tool-writers'.

The final tool-writers' class library had 99 classes in a hierarchy three levels deep. Each class had an average of 135 lines of code. The facilities management application comprised 153 classes. The facilities management and tool-writers' class libraries took 2235 days to complete (including requirements capture and specification, implementation and system

Table 8.1 Size of the system.

Subsystem	No. of classes
Management facilities	153
Tool-writers' class library	99
Five CASE tools	81
Total	333

testing). The five tools required 483 days to complete and comprised some 81 additional classes, again with a class hierarchy depth of three classes. Table 8.1 summarizes the size of each system component:

These figures give an average of 16.5 lines of code per work-day, or 8 work-days per class. The division of effort between the phases of the life cycle was as follows: requirements 7 %; specification (in Z) 29 %; development (including unit testing) 50 %; testing and delivery 14 %.

The tool-writers' class library was based on the Objective-C foundation and graphical class libraries marketed by the Stepstone Corporation, as shown in Figure 8.12. As each layer was added, less code was written than in the previous layer, resulting in only 1600 lines of code and 16 application-specific classes being needed for a typical CASE tool. Considering that the full system would require 60 tools, any reduction in the amount of code that had to be written specifically for one tool had a significant effect on the effort to implement the full system.

8.4.6 Life cycle used

Rosamund Rawlings explained that the software development life cycle still contained the same basic ingredients of a traditional cycle, that is, analysis, design, implementation and testing. However, where reuse was being designed into the class library, there were two design and implementation stages: namely class design/implementation followed by application design/implementation. These stages were overlapped to allow feedback into the design of the class library. This is clearly seen in the tool-writers' class library, where the class library was designed and implemented before the CASE tool applications were completely designed and implemented. Obviously some elements of the CASE tools had to be abstracted and embodied in the tool-writers' class library, but the specific application design features were left until later when the tool-writers' class library was available. The final CASE tools required 81 classes specific to those applications, in addition to the 99 classes in the generic tool-writers' class library. This life cycle agrees with the one described in Chapter 3, which suggests that designing for reuse involves a two-stage process of class design followed by application design. Chapter 4 discusses the issues related to class and application design in more detail.

The design and implementation of the facilities management server application involved a much more traditional application design cycle. The classes identified in the application design were then implemented and the application built incrementally as more and more classes become available. The distinction between class and application design was not so definite in this example, principally because the same emphasis was not given to generic design for reuse. The application design proceeded partly top-down and partly bottom-up.

There were few object-oriented design methodologies available when the project started in 1987. Praxis used a Z specification followed by a more *ad hoc* method for arranging the classes into a suitable class hierarchy. In any case, the output from the process was a set of classes with a clear idea of the interfaces each one provided, and the dynamics of the environment showing the ways in which the objects related to each other.

Unit testing of individual classes was achieved by writing a test-class for each class. Each test-class had one test method corresponding to each method in the real class. This arrangement gave a very clear structure to the tests, and identified where the tests for a particular method would be. This meant that if a method interface changed, the corresponding changes to the test-class were quickly identified. It was also possible to define the test-classes in a hierarchy mirroring the real class hierarchy, with test methods being redefined in the same cases where their real counterpart methods were redefined. The testing arrangement was therefore quite complex but provided a very thorough testing procedure.

8.4.7   Experiences gained from OO development

General observations

From this project Praxis believe that object-oriented design is well suited to being used together with formal specification methods such as Z (Spivey, 1989). In Z, systems are specified by a set of schemas, each containing a part of the system's specification. Generally a schema introduces some variables and gives some equations in terms of those variables. Schemas may be defined for the various possible operations on the system. The schema can refer to the state of the system before and after an operation. Schemas can be defined for particular objects of the system, thus giving an object-oriented style of specification.

On the issue of object-oriented design, Rosamund Rawlings had this to say:

'Discussions of modelling real-world objects make it sound as though the objects leap out of the problem domain straight into your object-oriented design. Unfortunately it is not always that simple. When building systems software, you may be dealing with concepts far removed from the real world, such as elements of an editor.

There are no magical rules for what to do in this situation. However, if you start with a clear system specification, and follow some sort of logical design process, a reasonable class structure should emerge. The classes may not correspond to real-world objects in the everyday sense, but they should represent some understandable unit of data and function. It may take several iterations to achieve the best structure, so be prepared to do some redesign if the class and message structure looks clumsy'.

Classes as containers

Rosamund Rawlings continued:

'A common problem is whether to create a class as a container for a group of loosely coupled items. Suppose we are implementing a mail order system, and find that the customer address and the order value are often passed around together, as parameters to various methods. It might be convenient to pass only a single object to these methods, so we could create a class named AddressAndValue, containing these two items. The class would then have no methods except to set and extract the two components.

Is this a good use of class definition? In general, no. Unless the new entity has some conceptual significance beyond being just a container for things, it should probably not be a class. Using a class in this way can clutter up your design with unimportant classes, and obscure the meaning of method parameters. Such classes are also likely to be used inconsistently in different parts of the system'.

Rosamund Rawlings also suggested that it is useful to make clear, by comments in the class definition, whether or not its users may specialize particular methods in a subclass. There are several possible cases to distinguish:

- Critical behaviour – must not be redefined;
- Correct behaviour – unlikely to need to be redefined;
- Default behaviour – may be redefined if required;
- Subclass responsibility – MUST be redefined.

Function and data – class composition

Sometimes the Praxis team found that they needed functions with no associated data. One reason was that a function might operate on a number of classes, but did not appear to belong to any of them. An example is a function to perform linked-list manipulation, or a similar utility-type function. In this case they tried to associate the method with one object or another. If this seemed too difficult, it may be an indication that the class breakdown was not quite right. In other cases, it may be possible to make this method available in some top-level class. Any class inheriting from this top-level class can then make use of the function. However, this practice should be discouraged since, over time, the higher-level classes become repositories for odd functions. The availability of *class methods* in Objective-C (and Smalltalk – see Chapter 5) enables this problem to be overcome. You can create a class which will have no instances, but which will respond to the required methods when called from any class. Praxis used this technique in several places. In a language which does not support class methods (such as C++ and Eiffel – see Chapter 5), an equivalent approach is to create a single instance of such a class, and make it available under a global name.

In languages which support multiple inheritance (see Chapter 5) a new class can be defined to provide the required routines, and then made available to all the necessary classes through multiple inheritance. The British Airways case-study suggested that this was perhaps the most controllable way of using multiple inheritance.

Designing for reuse

Praxis used two techniques when designing for reuse. Firstly, they created more abstract superclasses, leaving subclasses to add specific details such as the extent or alignment of a window. In Objective-C this technique is supported by the *subclass responsibility* method (or in C++ through the *virtual* method – see Chapter 5). The second technique was to keep all methods small, using subsidiary methods to carry out specific actions.

The architectural view of the overall system enabled a highly reusable class library to be developed for this project. However, Praxis does not expect to reuse any appreciable amount of the facilities management application. Rosamund Rawlings believes that for inter-application reuse:

> 'Application-specific classes like the ones in the facilities manager will almost always be so specific to a particular project that, even if well written and documented, the chances of them being useful again are negligible. Attempting to massage the classes into some more general form, perhaps parameterized for our own particular application, would almost certainly obscure the design and be counter-productive'.

However, for intra-application reuse:

> 'A less ambitious form of reuse is reuse within the same project.
> The most obvious means of reusing a class is through
> inheritance. Classes sharing much commonality, differing in a
> few details, can inherit general properties. Dynamic binding is
> also an important aid to reuse. This means that classes can send
> messages to objects without knowing their exact type'.

Objective-C
observations

Praxis has used Objective-C and C++ extensively. Whereas C++ provides the syntax of C with extensions to accommodate object orientation, Objective-C provides a higher-level feel, derived from its hybrid
origins in Smalltalk and C. Rosamund Rawlings believes that Objective-
C removes much of the lower-level systems-type programming style
from the C syntax and makes it a good language for developing
business applications.

Rawlings found the Objective-C V3.0 interpreter particularly
useful:

> 'It was a real asset. It helped make the so-called paradigm shift
> because developers were able to experiment with objects and
> message passing in a much more iterative way'.

Rawlings continued:

> 'The ICpak class libraries, supplied by Stepstone, become an
> extension of the language. They were central to the overall
> development, and were used extensively'.

This point cannot be over-stressed! An object-oriented programming
language becomes a very powerful tool with the right class libraries.
While software maintenance is reduced using object-oriented constructs,
initial software development productivity is influenced most by the
availability, and ease of use, of commercial class libraries.

8.4.8   Summary and conclusions

The team at Praxis thoroughly enjoyed the experience of object-oriented
software development. Rosamund Rawlings said:

> 'If I was given a choice, I would use object-oriented techniques
> every time. However, in a commercial software house, the
> customer often dictates the programming techniques and
> languages we use. At present C is still the language of most
> preference'.

In conclusion, Praxis successfully developed the CASE tools using object-oriented techniques and Objective-C. The development of a generic class library for use in producing each of the CASE tools increased the speed at which each CASE tool was constructed. The staff were well motivated and enjoyed using object-oriented techniques. Praxis found that, compared with conventional methods, they spent more time in design, less on coding and much less in getting the product to work.

8.5   British Aerospace plc – a case-study using Ontos

Colin Birtwistle of British Aerospace and Sean Kempton and Matthew Griffin of Valbecc Ltd collaborated with The Institute of Software Engineering during this case-study. Their help is gratefully acknowledged.

8.5.1   Company and product background

> **Company:**   British Aerospace plc, Manchester, England.
>
> **Size:**   —
>
> **Nature of business:**   Aircraft manufacture.
>
> **Hardware and operating systems:**   —
>
> **Programming languages:**   C, Pascal, and others.
>
> **Products:**   Mainly bespoke software for use internally, including relational database applications, communications and safety-critical software for aircraft computer systems.

8.5.2   Background

British Aerospace (BAe) databases are a reflection of the company: large, varied and complex. Colin Birtwistle, development engineer for this worldwide supplier of commercial and military aircraft and components, has the job of developing systems including databases to support the design and manufacture of aircraft electronics.

BAe needed some means of integrating many disparate databases. Birtwistle described the situation this way:

'We found one part of the aircraft's wire harness, a connector, was stored in over ten different systems. If we wanted to replace this connector with a different part, we had to update the data in all of those systems. Or if the lead time for a connector from the manufacturer changed from six to nine months, it would take a great deal of time to ensure this change was reflected everywhere'.

Clearly BAe needed some means of minimizing the effect of delay on a small, inexpensive part that, in the worst case, could hold up delivery of a $30 million aircraft.

The wiring harness for an aircraft typically contains more than 200 wires and each wire is identified by its properties such as signal, type and length. Design and production of this wiring harness proceeds through a sequence of steps: a high-level diagram of the wiring system; electronic design and detailed schematic wire diagram; mock-up of the physical layout of the wires; production engineering; manufacturing of materials (including the bill of materials); and functional testing. Each of these steps currently utilizes a tool such as a CAD system, a database or a file system. As a result, the data sets are in varying, loosely interfaced formats and separately managed. Furthermore, a significant amount of the data that drives these tools is updated by hand, introducing errors and delays.

If a design engineer makes a change to a schematic using a CAD system, it is difficult to ensure those changes are reflected through the bill of materials to the material purchaser. Each system was designed to do a particular job. Subsequent work is required to enable all the tools to work together.

8.5.3   Reasons for considering object-oriented techniques and Ontos

BAe's interest in OO stems from the work done by the Object Interest Group (see Appendix D). BAe was an active member of this group and was heavily involved in the evaluation of the commercially available OODBMSs. The final report from the Object Interest Group identified Ontos, Gemstone and Versant as the main commercial OODBMSs.

The capability of an object-oriented database to accommodate different data types lead BAe to consider an OODBMS for the job of integrating the disparate tools involved in the production of a wiring harness.

After some evaluation BAe chose Ontos for its fast and efficient access times.

8.5.4   An object-oriented software development project

With the help of the Ontos UK distributor, Valbecc Software, Birtwistle
and his team began building a prototype Ontos application to interface
to each of the tools involved in the production of a wiring harness. The
objective was to store all the necessary information, required by any of
the existing database systems or tools, in Ontos. Each of the computer
tools or databases could then access its view of a given component from
Ontos.

For example, a machine which uses a laser to mark numbers onto
wires (an Excismer) can access Ontos for information on the wire type,
length, identity number, spacing and size. The wiring harness designers
can access the electrical CAD data and schematic wiring diagrams to use
with their CAD systems via Ontos. The production engineers can access
Ontos to produce the bill of materials wiring data lists and locate manufacturing instruction sheets which include standards information. Figure
8.13 illustrates the overall architecture.

> 'With Ontos, we've created one database, and around that
> database we've added tools or functions,'

said Birtwistle.

> 'We can now take information out of the database, process it, use
> it, and put it back into the database. It doesn't matter that the
> data can be simple or complex, all one format or completely
> different formats. With this plug and play approach, we've
> brought all the information, from design to production, together
> to support business decisions'.

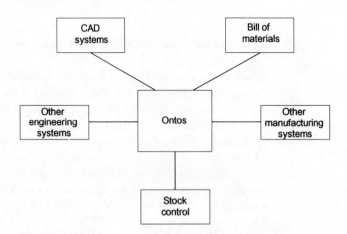

Figure 8.13   Ontos integrating data from disparate sources.

The project ran for three elapsed months. During this time five people were involved in the analysis phase. This included one end user who had no previous experience with analysis of any kind. Three people were involved in the software development and four people were involved in testing and user interface design. By Birtwistle's estimates, this prototype would have taken many more months with other technology.

8.5.5   Experiences gained from OO development

The core of the project centred around an object-oriented model of the problem domain. Matthew Griffin, a software engineer at Valbecc, had little experience programming in C++ and Ontos when the project began. He explained:

> 'You can think about the problem in terms of the problem itself – rather than about the representation of the problem in a database or programming language. Ultimately, that means you can communicate more easily and get the job done more quickly'.

The purpose of the object modelling exercise was to integrate data from design, planning and manufacture. The main problem was in finding a framework for the class hierarchy in which all of these activities could be accommodated. Different team members pushed different aspects of the information as the unifying key from which everything else could hang.

Inheritance gives objects the ability to acquire the attributes and behaviours of other objects, allowing the database application developer to model common attributes and behaviours only once, without duplicating software code. However, Sean Kempton explained:

> 'The inheritance hierarchy evolves from being almost random, to being the single most important aspect of your model. The random nature of the first-stab inheritance hierarchy normally comes from trying to model data too much, and not modelling behaviour. Identifying a meaningful inheritance hierarchy is the most difficult thing to do'.

According to Matthew Griffin:

> 'There were many complex interactions – wiring looms contain wires, wires are related through inter-connections, each wire has a wire-type, and so on. These are complicated links and we needed a database that can handle these complexities. With relational databases you would need may joins to do some of the queries that we can do instantly'.

The end result was a prototype model with 50 C++ classes. Each class required approximately one work-week to complete. Each class contained, on average, 300 lines of C++ code.

8.5.6   Software development life cycle

The general approach described in a book called *Object-Oriented Modeling and Design* (Rumbaugh *et al.*, 1991) was used (Chapter 4 includes a summary of this analysis and design technique). Owing to the scope of the problem it was recognized that an integrated model could not be produced straight off. An iterative approach proved to be the best way of understanding the problem domain. Some aspects of the problem were modelled. Classes were created to reflect a part of the problem, and a subsystem was built. The subsystem was experimented with and modifications made as necessary. The overall system was therefore designed and constructed incrementally as more and more of the problem became understood.

8.5.7   Conclusions

Birtwistle views object technology as an enabling technology for British Aerospace. The object database will allow them to evaluate the merits of particular configurations throughout design, manufacturing and support phases.

Birtwistle concludes:

> 'OO appears to be the best solution for integrating several different databases'.

This pilot project has been successful in demonstrating the capabilities of object-oriented DBMSs at handling complex information from an array of vastly different database systems. Information is entered into the database only once, and therefore subsequent changes are made only once. Furthermore, by removing the data duplication between disparate systems, Birtwistle reports that he can reduce the overall storage size of the data in the wiring harness systems by up to 90%.

This pilot project was a collaborative effort between British Aerospace and Valbecc Software Ltd. (Valbecc was a distributor of Ontos at the time). Readers should note that, particularly in the field of object-oriented database management systems, it is common for OODBMS vendors and distributors to get involved in 'first projects' with customers. This reflects the newness of the technology and is a recommended way for companies to gain some experience with OODBMSs and further evaluate the technology in their particular environment.

8.5.8   Future strategy

Birtwistle plans to use Ontos to manage the resources needed for manufacturing the wire harness. The database will help him determine available resources and the best allocation of them. He will be able to store and manipulate not only information on the type of a particular cable, but also how many workers and what skill levels it will take to build it, where to purchase it, the supplier's address and so on. Each 'cable' object will have a behaviour such as where it can and cannot be used in an aircraft, its conductivity and its weight.

According to Birtwistle:

'We want just-in-time ordering, and we don't want to keep more than one month's inventory in stock'.

While Ontos currently serves an important integration role, British Aerospace hopes to model the entire process associated with the wire harness production, from design to field support, in Ontos. Ontos will act as the hub in this system – a repository to store every piece of information as an object, from the wire type to the bill of materials. With this model, the product life cycle is modelled in, and based on, an object database. All the systems – design, engineering, manufacturing and management – will be able to access and use the database.

8.6   Satellites International Ltd – a case-study in analysis and design

This case-study illustrates how one company is using object-oriented analysis and design methods to good affect. It discusses the company's use of a method called Object-Oriented Software Development by Edward Colbert (1989), which is summarized in Chapter 4. The study involves the application of this method to the design of real-time software systems.

Guy Cooper (Software Engineer) and Andrew Aftelak (Project Manager) of Satellites International collaborated with The Institute of Software Engineering during this case-study. Their help is gratefully acknowledged.

8.6.1   Company and product background

Company:	Satellites International Ltd, Newbury, England.
Nature of business:	Development and manufacture of on-board and ground system hardware and software for satellite applications.
Products:	Diverse instrument, communications and navigation systems incorporating both hardware and software including intelligent interfaces to databases and satellite data acquisition and telemetering.

8.6.2   Background

Some years ago Satellite International used Yourdon structured design in the production of its software systems. The requirements-gathering stage was fairly informal with no recognized method used during analysis.
Guy Cooper explained:

> 'In the early days the company concentrated on developing the hardware for satellite communications systems. Software was a secondary consideration and a very much smaller part of the company than it is today'.

In common with the increasing trend away from hardware and towards software, Satellites International has evolved into a much more software-oriented company. As Guy elaborated:

> 'The company now has three engineering departments: Space Engineering which looks after developing hardware systems; another department is concerned with developing communications systems; and the third department is responsible for the software engineering activities. This last department also provides services to the other two'.

8.6.3   Reasons for considering object-oriented analysis and design

As the company's dependence on software grew, so also did the realization that they needed to coordinate effort across the various on-going projects. The company had a strong background in hardware design, which they had refined to the point where different projects could use components from a repository of tried and tested circuitry. Cooper explained:

> 'Our hardware people were already using CAD systems and reusing modules wherever possible. Our strategy for software

development was born out of the method of working on the hardware side of the business'.

Cooper continued:

'First and foremost we wanted a high degree of software modularity – just as we have on the hardware side. Secondly we wanted to be able to reuse software where possible, using tried and tested components with well-defined interfaces. We wanted to be able to test modules in isolation from one another and to validate the designs by a walk-through procedure before any software was written!

Using an object-oriented approach, software modules map directly from design objects. This enables us to verify systems at the design stage – much earlier than typically possible using structured design methods. If there is nothing missing from the design, then we are confident that the ultimate code will be complete'.

In addition, Satellites International wanted to be able to represent both hardware and software components on the same diagram. Any given project has a mix of hardware and software professionals. They need to communicate ideas between each other, and as Cooper said:

'Our systems have hardware and software. The boundaries between these are often blurred. For example, signal demodulation may be accomplished by hardware with the resulting signal being passed into the software components of the system. But we can do much of the demodulation in software now. Initially what we want to represent in a system is the discrete activities that are involved. Whether they take place in hardware or software is not always an issue at the analysis stage. Modelling system components as objects gives us this capability to describe elements of both hardware and software, that is, a complete system'.

All these reasons, born out of their method of developing hardware systems, seemed to fit with the object-oriented approach to software development and so Satellites International adopted this method of working on the software side of the business.

8.6.4   Choosing an analysis and design method

There was no rigorous procedure applied to choosing a method. Guy and his team decided what they required from a method. Firstly, most projects in the company involve real-time applications. They felt it was important to be able to specify individual messages between objects so that at a later stage, benchmark timings could be added to evaluate overall system performance on critical components.

Chapter 4 summarizes many of the main OOA&D methods currently available. Some methods provide stronger support than others for representing individual messages passing between interacting objects. In particular, some methods support multiple message views where sequences of messages between cooperating objects are modelled.

Guy and his team viewed software objects basically as finite state machines so the method had to provide ways of representing the internal mechanics of an object via the life states it can assume. As Chapter 4 illustrates, most OOA&D methods support object life modelling using state machines.

In addition, there had to be CASE tool support for the method.

Initially they looked at the Coad/Yourdon method (Coad and Yourdon, 1991, 1991a). Cooper admitted:

> 'We have successfully applied the Coad/Yourdon method to a
> few projects in the company. But there is nothing in the method
> that particularly addresses the needs of real-time software
> developers – such as timing diagrams or detailed object
> interaction diagrams'.

Satellites International then considered the Shlaer/Mellor method (Shlaer and Mellor, 1988) and (Shlaer, 1990). A key element to their software strategy was traceability through the life cycle. They wanted to be able to trace the existence and development of objects from analysis, through design and into implementation. This was important if they were going to be able to validate completeness of a specification at an early stage in the development life cycle. They felt that the Shlaer/Mellor method lacked traceability from analysis to design and so it was rejected.

Chapter 4 discusses the Shlaer/Mellor method.

At this stage Cooper discovered a method called Object-Oriented Software Development by Edward Colbert (1989). This method satisfied the needs of real-time applications development. It provided object interaction diagrams which would allow designers to model the dynamics of an application (of prime importance in assessing critical timings). It was supported by a CASE tool called ObjectMaker from Mark V Systems.

8.6.5 A software development project

The Colbert method of analysis and design has been used to develop a ground-based digital demodulator for a satellite communications Data Relay System (DRS). This system demodulates signals from low Earth orbiting satellites, transmitted via geostationary relay satellites.

The processing engine comprises a Transputer and digital signal processing network distributed through a modular high-speed digital subsystem.

The requirements analysis for the system involved identifying the attributes, responsibilities and interactions of instances (or objects) within the system. In this context attributes could be things like size or power consumption. Interactions demonstrate how the system communicates with its environment. A requirements analysis for the DRS modem may produce the system object specification shown in Figure 8.14. This shows the DRS system object interacting with several external objects.

· The DRS modem is initially modelled as a single active object, interfacing with five external objects which provide services for the DRS system. The external services provided by an object are shown as labelled arrows, and the information flows between them by arrowed circles. So, for example, the RF down converter provides a Receive service which is requested by the DRS system.

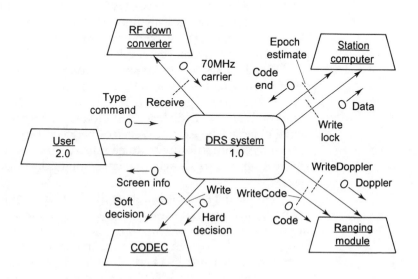

Figure 8.14 DRS modem object interaction diagram.

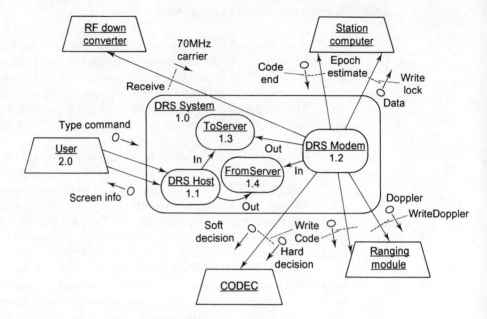

Figure 8.15   DRS system preliminary decomposition.

This specification of the system shows only object instances in a requirements analysis and not any associated object classes. On the DRS system design, no object classes were specified until the system design was considered stable. This allowed the system to be modelled and checked for consistency before any decision was taken on whether particular components were implemented in hardware or software.

Preliminary design involved decomposing the DRS system into a set of interacting objects which provide services and generate information, as shown in Figure 8.15. The figure shows the DRS system to be composed of the DRSHost, DRSModem, ToServer and FromServer active objects. The external services between the DRS system and external objects are still shown (to be consistent with the previous model – Figure 8.14), but are shown to be emanating from objects within the DRS system.

At the detailed design stage the development team made most of the implementation decisions. The objects produced at this level start to indicate the division of hardware and software. There may be several levels of detailed design culminating in hardware objects that are represented as hardware block diagrams and software objects that are specified using Colbert's C/C++ structure charts (depicting attributes along with external and internal methods).

8.6.6   Experiences gained from OO analysis and design

The main diagrams used by Satellite International are:

(1) Object interaction diagrams.

(2) Object state diagrams.

Guy Cooper explained:

> 'We concentrate on developing the object interactions. Only when we feel these are right do we start looking to see what classes already exist which might satisfy our needs. It's very much objects-first-classes-second. Choosing classes (from a library) as a priority can result in slow systems'.

This is the result of placing a higher importance on the processing than on the data within a system. Companies developing information systems will probably concentrate on classes first – treating the data aspect as a higher priority.

The ObjectMaker CASE tool supports a repository of objects, not classes. This results from the heavy emphasis which the tool puts on object modelling (modelling the dynamics of an application). Everything in the repository relates to objects and their interactions with other objects. This has meant that Satellites International has had to manage a class library separately from the CASE tool.

The method is essentially being used in an object-based way rather than an object-oriented way in this study.

Cooper admitted to having a few minor problems with the CASE tool support. However, these problems were largely a result of the immaturity of the tool. As Cooper explained:

> 'The method is still evolving to some extent. However, because the CASE tool (ObjectMaker) is actually a metaCASE tool, it has been easy to refine the method and add extra features to the tool which we felt were useful in our context. As the method has evolved, our CASE tool has evolved in step'.

On the plus side, Cooper found that being able to model object interactions enabled the effects of changes (or late delivery) to some components on other components within the system to be assessed more easily, compared with a structured technique.

All software development teams in Satellites International now use object-oriented techniques and the Colbert method.

They found reusability most feasible for common elements between projects such as user interfaces and foundation classes, plus utility classes such as objects which manage message passing in parallel systems.

Guy explained:

'We can now specify the interfaces between hardware and software using object interaction diagrams where both hardware and software components are modelled as objects having state and behaviour. This means that we have a common frame of reference to talk about both hardware and software concepts – which makes it easier for hardware and software engineers to communicate and understand each other'.

Guy gives the following advice to anyone considering object-oriented analysis and design in the development of real-time systems:

(1) Concentrate on objects initially – get the performance issues worked out. Then sort out what classes can be used/reused from previous projects. Reuse is secondary to getting an efficient design.

(2) OOP is not synonymous with OOD. Although Colbert's method supports implementation object design which is tailored to a specific programming language, Satellites International has developed final systems using non-OOPLs and still realized benefits from developing an OOD. (Colbert's method supports Ada at the implementation design stage. Chapter 5 discusses the categories of object-oriented programming language and concludes that Ada is an object-based language rather than an object-oriented language. Object-based languages do not support classes or inheritance. The Colbert method concentrates on object interactions and is weakest on classification and inheritance relationships.)

8.6.7 Life cycle used

No formal object-oriented development life cycle was used. Guy explained:

'If I had a choice, I would prefer to complete all OOA&D work before doing any OOP. However, in the real world this is rarely possible – but at least using OOA&D, if an OOPL is used, the objects identified at the analysis and design stages can be implemented largely independently of one another. Therefore much OOP can begin before the OOA&D work is necessarily complete'.

8.6.8 Summary and conclusions

This study illustrates the object-based use of an object-oriented analysis and design method. Such an approach is particularly useful in situations where the final implementation programming language is not object oriented.

The ability to model both hardware and software using the one notation (and object model) has provided significant benefits for Satellites International. This was particularly useful when they were evaluating performance criteria for certain parts of the system.

During the preliminary and detailed design stages objects were identified from the higher-level objects specified during analysis. As part of the specification of a particular object, any timing constraints on its behaviour must be uncovered. With a software-only view of an object it is not possible to characterize its behaviour in any meaningful way because it is divorced from its executing environment. Using an object approach, hardware and software objects were modelled together, producing a complete specification of a system. It was then possible to verify this specification at the design stage rather than being forced to wait until the implementation stage.

8.7 Summary and conclusions

These studies show how widely different types of companies with different needs and motivations have successfully applied object technology to the development of software applications.

The adoption process in most of these case-studies involved a small number of people working on a pilot project. Typically this team was the research and development part of the organization. Most of the studies indicate that semi-formal methods were used for object-oriented analysis and design – most organizations followed guidelines given in various text books, only one of the studies involved the use of a CASE tool to support an OO analysis or design method. This is fairly typical – the programming languages represent the most mature facet of object technology and many companies prefer to understand the capabilities of a programming language and develop their own techniques for object design based on these language capabilities.

All the projects were successfully established and in some cases are now complete. In most cases the use of polymorphism and inheritance greatly facilitated the reuse of software. However, this reuse was predominantly within a project rather than between projects. Designing for reuse was very important in all cases – without a proper design, reuse would not have been possible even within a project. The greatest potential for reuse across projects is in the graphical user interface components of a system. Other inter-project reuse is possible between projects in a similar area, but most organizations felt that reuse across dissimilar projects would be confined to general-purpose utility software such as GUIs, linked-lists and string manipulation routines, and so on. Some organizations are considering the use of a permanent Class Library Manager to identify and manage commonly used class libraries across a range of projects and project teams.

There is some concern over the ability to correctly identify classes of objects at the design stage, particularly for abstract parts, internal to a system. This has led some organizations to restrict the object-oriented component to the graphical user interface of a system. In all cases, finding the right design appears to take longer than in a traditional approach. However, once the most natural design is identified, the other parts of the development proceed more quickly. Object-oriented software developments therefore emphasize the analysis and design stages, with the resultant implementation and testing stages typically completed more quickly than in a traditional life cycle.

Languages such as Objective-C and particularly Smalltalk, which exhibit dynamic typing, support rapid prototyping. The development environment associated with Smalltalk also actively encourages prototyping and is good for developing ideas, particularly in areas where the problem domain is not initially well understood.

The OODBMS case-study involving British Aerospace illustrates a common use for OODBMSs to integrate data taken from disparate sources. The OODBMS is employed for its powerful data modelling capabilities whilst the legacy DBMSs are retained for data storage.

The analysis and design case-study illustrates something of an evolutionary migration to an object-oriented regime. In fact the Colbert method is used in an object-based rather than a fully object-oriented way (inheritance not being considered). Nevertheless, the developers involved still derived benefits from this approach compared to a traditional structured method.

Of particular note is the fact that all software teams enjoyed the experience of object-oriented development. They were enthusiastic and are keen to apply their experiences to future projects. This is a key issue as the adoption of any new technology requires the people using it to be well motivated.

9 Summary, conclusions and future trends

This book presents the broad concepts behind object-oriented software engineering. It is clear from the text that object orientation can be applied to the analysis, design and implementation stages of the software life cycle. The concepts are significantly different from traditional structured techniques and this is causing problems with development staff being required to alter their mind-set to the new paradigm (or pattern). This is one of the major barriers to successful widespread adoption of the techniques and technology.

The nature of applications being demanded by end users is changing. People are demanding more and more complicated systems. They want open systems with the capability of distributed computing and graphical user interfaces. The economics of downsizing (where applications are being redeveloped so they can be taken off central mainframe systems and distributed amongst a network of desktop systems) is already leading to an increasing use of client/server architectures. Object orientation provides a powerful means by which to model and build such complex systems.

The end user Although object technology is primarily for the application developer, there are some benefits which end users will derive as a result (Soley, 1992):

- 'An object-oriented user interface has many advantages over more traditional styles of user interfaces. In such a user interface, application objects (computer-simulated representations of real-world objects) are presented to end users as objects that can be manipulated in a way that is similar to the manipulation of the real-world objects. Examples of such object-oriented user interfaces are realized in systems such as Apple Macintosh and HP NewWave as well as in CAD systems where components of a design can be manipulated in a similar way to the manipulation of real components.'

341

- 'Common functionality in different applications (such as storage and retrieval of objects, mailing, printing, creation and deletion of objects) is realized by common shared objects leading to a uniform and consistent user interface.'

The application developer

Object-oriented software development methods are now recognized as providing significant benefits in the area of graphical user interface construction. Software developers are discovering that the object-oriented approach is a natural way to model distributed computing architectures. For example, Chapter 8 presents several case-studies showing how distributed systems are being designed using object-oriented techniques. These successes illustrate how object orientation meets the needs of modern software systems and such demonstrations will fuel the uptake of the techniques throughout the industry.

The uptake of object-oriented techniques will also be fuelled by the sheer enthusiasm of software developers. In each of the user case-studies presented in Chapter 8, the software development teams were very enthusiastic and enjoyed the experiences of the new techniques. This high level of motivation makes the job of introducing object orientation somewhat easier. However, application developers must temper their enthusiasm because there are still some outstanding issues and problems with the technology such as reports of poor end-application performance from some object-oriented programming languages; a lack of good CASE tool support at the analysis and design stages; and a lack of robust commercial-grade object-oriented database management systems at present. Chapters 4, 5 and 6 discuss the problems with the technology as it stands at present.

These current problems do not prevent the successful completion of most object-oriented development projects. However, general unawareness of the state of maturity of object orientation coupled with being unaware of the differing techniques required has led to some notable disasters (see the Cognos experience in Chapter 5). While object orientation can provide improvements over a traditional structured approach, it is not a panacea for software development. Considerable effort is still required to develop software successfully.

9.1   The software development life cycle

Software life cycles, such as the ones presented in Chapter 3, illustrate how object-oriented and traditional techniques can be mixed. These 'compromise' solutions might be considered by project managers in an attempt to offset the cost of starting with a completely new set of methods and tools. The hybrid approaches may be more pragmatic, but there is more effort required to complete a project using a hybrid life-cycle. This results from the need to translate between OO and traditional representations.

The pure object-oriented software life cycle is recommended. This life cycle encourages an iterative approach to software development. A mixture of top-down and bottom-up design for classes with bottom-up implementation for applications encourages interactions leading to more robust and flexible designs. The resulting classes can be more generic and exhibit more potential for reuse both in a given project and in future development projects. Implementation of classes can take place in parallel with much of the design work. This means that coding will start much earlier than in a traditional life cycle. More personnel are required earlier in the project. The final application construction phase should be completed much faster than in a traditional development since the investment in time and effort occurs earlier rather than later.

Some programming language development environments support highly incremental prototyping life cycles. These are particularly good in areas where requirements are ill-defined and evolve with the systems under development. However, such life cycles require careful management to avoid poorly designed systems.

Unlike today's arrangement, where a systems analyst passes requirements to another specialist for systems design, in the OO world, they will build the system. The concept of encapsulation makes it easier to 'grow' software. Prototypes can consist of discrete units of completed code, with other elements of code either missing or acting as simple 'pass through' message switches.

The use of a consistent object model from analysis through design and into application construction provides significant benefits for the maintenance phase of a development project. It reduces the learning curve for new staff being moved onto maintenance projects. It makes for more comprehensible systems exhibiting more extensible architectures. All of these features play an important part in reducing maintenance overheads.

9.2 Analysis and design

Information engineering uses techniques that 'factor out' data from the processes that manipulate it. This is based on the concept that, whilst process changes frequently to reflect changing business requirements, data remains relatively stable over time. Information engineering treats the data and process elements relatively separately all the way down the development life cycle, to the point where data is implemented in databases, and process is implemented as programs that manipulate this data. Entity relationship diagrams and data flow diagrams are the two main views of a system. Because these views consider the data and process separately, there are very loose links between the two. Such representations do not necessarily lead to a well-modularized system. Individual processes may be interconnected with many pieces of data, giving rise to difficulties when trying to identify discrete modules in the system.

By contrast, the OO view sees data and process combined. When an OO program wants to manipulate another piece of data, it sends a message to the object containing that data, requesting a method in the object to carry out the necessary manipulation. Object-oriented analysis provides a unified model in which all views consider the same fundamental elements, namely classes of objects. This results in a more modular specification which is easier to implement.

Object-oriented design leads on naturally from OO analysis. Experiences with OO design suggest that some developers have difficulty identifying abstract classes. This has led many developers to concentrate on object orientation for the user interface component of a system, where the classes of objects are more easily identified, with the remaining parts of such systems being developed using traditional structured techniques.

Formalized methods for analysis and design are now in abundance. These are, in many cases, immature or incomplete. The rich suite of facilities provided by the paradigm leads inevitably to complicated notations for representing design information. Some methods have already been transferred into CASE tools (for example OSMOSYS). However some OO methods have been bolted onto existing traditional tools which do not implement the full object method. There are also methods such as hierarchical object-oriented design (HOOD), which are not fully object-oriented (according to the concepts description detailed in Chapter 2), contrary to the name.

9.3 Programming

The programming languages represent the most mature facet of the paradigm with many languages now sufficiently robust to be used commercially. The first languages appeared in 1983-85. The constructs within the paradigm have the potential to provide reuse through inheritance and polymorphism; more robust implementations through the contractual obligations between interacting objects; ease of change through the polymorphic and dynamic binding capabilities; and easier management of complexity through the use of the encapsulating properties of the languages. Performance is still a problem issue for many of the current object-oriented programming languages.

Some companies are already deriving benefit from the reusability aspects of object-oriented software development (Chapter 8 details several user case-studies). However such companies seem to be in the minority at present. Reuse is a goal many have been working towards for many years, yet it is still not widely available. The major problem with reuse is primarily clerical and organizational rather than technical. Most users of object orientation claim good reuse of software within a project.

Inter-project reuse has been most successful in the user interfaces (user case-studies in Chapter 8 confirm this). Beyond user interfaces, inter-project reuse may only be possible within groups of very similar projects such as library information systems, stock control systems, or banking systems where the basic concepts apply over and over again. Reuse is not restricted to software. CASE tools will enable reuse of analysis and design specifications (for example the OSMOSYS product for banking applications).

Although inheritance, polymorphism and dynamic binding create a good framework for software reuse, there are some undesirable side-effects. Inheritance increases the coupling between classes which can, in badly managed projects, inhibit reuse. Polymorphism and dynamic binding introduce a new dimension of complexity to software systems which makes such systems more difficult to verify for correctness through testing.

The significant dependence on a class library introduces a new job category to an object-oriented software development team - namely the Class Library Manager. The Class Library Manager's job is to keep the class library up to date and ensure that all classes submitted to the library are adequately tested beforehand. The Class Library Manager ensures that all changes to the class library are communicated to all members of the development team. The Class Library Manager should be responsible for ensuring that future software designers make good use of the available classes in their designs. The Class Library Manager should therefore be a job description for a permanent employee rather than simply a role within a team for the duration of one project. Some organizations, such as British Airways (see user case-study in Chapter 8) are considering the use of such a Class Library Manager to rationalize the class libraries used throughout the company.

9.4   Database management systems

Object-oriented database management systems are still in their infancy. The first serious commercial product was released in 1987. The current lack of standards in this area is a major barrier to their widespread adoption, particularly the lack of a standard Object SQL.

Object-oriented DBMSs can handle many application areas for which previous technology was unsuitable such as CASE, CAD and GIS. Many object-oriented DBMSs enable semantic information to be stored along with the data. This is seen as a benefit since it allows much more of the application design to be captured in the database schema.

9.5 Overall

Development organizations that adopt object technology will undergo certain changes over time. Certainly there will be the need for a Class Library Manager. However making use of reusable code will require changes to the system by which developers are rewarded. Productivity cannot (and never should be) based on lines of code produced. In an object-oriented development project, the most productive programmers spend most of their time reading code, not writing it. In Japan most major software houses include a reuse component in performance appraisals. Developers must either use the class library or contribute to it; if they don't, their appraisals suffer.

Object orientation is one of the most powerful technologies ever to become available to the IT industry, but it is not a panacea. To derive maximum benefit requires excellent technical management with a clear understanding of its capabilities. The technology is unique in offering the degree of flexibility to changing requirements needed in modern software development projects.

Table 9.1 summarises the essential differences between the traditional procedural approach and the object-oriented approach to software engineering.

9.6 Future trends

Standards are needed in all areas of object orientation from analysis and design notations, through programming languages to database management system object query languages, before widespread adoption will take place. One area which is already receiving some attention is for the use of object-oriented applications in distributed systems (Soley, 1992). The concept of an object lends itself quite naturally to parallel and distributed systems. Indeed, the user case-studies in Chapter 8 illustrate that developers are now using OO to produce client/server applications. The Object Management Group is involved in bringing vendors together to produce standards for a distributed application architecture. Appendix D gives more information on the work of the Object Management Group.

Table 9.1 A comparison of the traditional procedural and object-oriented software development cultures (Applied Logic Group, private communication).

	Procedural culture	**Object-oriented culture**
Strategy	Top-down Some form of functional decomposition is the most prevalent technique. The data and functional aspects are considered separately.	Bottom-up Applications are constructed by picking classes of object from a class library, with minimal additional coding.
Modules	Functions and procedures	Classes
Goals	Application-oriented Concentrates on the specific application under development.	Business-oriented Concentrates on the wider issue of identifying classes of general applicability to the types of software developed by that organization.
Time	Short-term	Long-term
Economics	Profit-based – concentrate on the application-specific issues to get the current application released on time.	Investment-based – identify and develop generic classes which are submitted to libraries. The classes are then available for use in application developments within that organization.
Outcome	Results	Tools and class libraries of use in subsequent applications

CASE tools are required for all aspects of the software life cycle. The area of OO analysis and design is still relatively new, although some tools are now emerging here. Good tools for supporting object-oriented analysis and design will enable reuse of specifications. These reusable components will be assets of the enterprise, in the same way that product designs are in the manufacturing industry. Inheritance will enable software component specifications to be reused and modified on subsequent developments. The OSMOSYS product discussed in Chapters 4 and 6 illustrates this idea.

Class libraries will be of paramount importance in future. Choosing a programming language is a very important decision. The syntax and facilities of the language must be considered. However, the class libraries available for that language are becoming an even more important consideration. With object-oriented programming, the class libraries become an extension of the programming language and can provide important gains in software development productivity. All of the object-oriented programming language vendors realize this fact and are actively promoting their class libraries. Glockenspiel has CommonView-2 and -3 class libraries for developing GUIs and CommonBase for developing database applications. The Stepstone Corporation has always promoted its ICpak libraries with the Objective-C language. The Smalltalk environment is one big class library and Eiffel is supplied with various libraries for GUIs and utility functions such as array and string manipulations.

Better ways of handling class libraries to achieve reuse will evolve. Fundamental to reuse is the question of how to manage modules in an effective way so that a designer can see what modules can be reused in their application. One possibility is to have a database repository for storing different levels of class information. It should be possible to use such a repository in several ways. At the highest levels the repository would store system and subsystem specifications, such as a stock control system. The user would navigate through this specification, and could select a particular subsystem - causing the subsystem's specification to be displayed. Further decompositions would be possible until the user ends up inspecting specific, implemented classes in a given programming language.

Another way to use the repository would be to inspect only classes at a given level. For example, C++ implemented classes. At present, graphical class browsers represent the main way of inspecting class hierarchies. To make better use of available classes, a database storage medium is required. Within the database, a user could execute *ad hoc* queries, looking for specific types of class. Each class would have several pieces of information tagged to it, such as (i) a textual description of its functionality, interfaces and inheritance associations; (ii) a graphical description of the class; and (iii) a formal, or semi-formal, specification of the class. This information would help a developer to identify useful classes. The formal, or semi-formal, specification would provide a degree of confidence that the class will perform as it was designed to.

Such tools are not available as yet. They will come in time and will support object orientation in its quest to promote the software development process to an engineering discipline!

A Structured analysis
Popular Structured Analysis Diagrams and Techniques

A.1 Introduction

Any system can be viewed from three perspectives – **data, function** and **time**. All systems will exhibit each of the three perspectives but usually one will dominate. In information systems (transaction processing oriented) data tends to dominate, whilst in real-time systems it has been function and time. The main techniques for each perspective are shown below with examples based around a fictitious specification for an information system for processing hospital inpatients. The system handles the assignment of a patient to a ward, and booking a surgeon and an operating theatre for a surgical operation (surgery).

A.2 (ERD) Entity relationship diagrams

This is a very popular technique used in analysis to show the data required by a system (**entities**) and how each item of data is related to others (**entity relationships**). Each entity may then be further decomposed into its components (**data attributes**). It should be noted that there are numerous variations of ERDs, the main differences being: (1) how

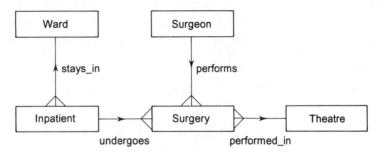

Figure A.1

relationships are represented, (2) the maximum number of entities which can participate in a relationship and (3) whether relationships can have attributes. ERDs are the most popular means of showing the **data perspective** of a system. An ERD is shown in Figure A.1.

A.3   (DFD) Data flow diagram

This is a very popular technique used in analysis to show how the data in a proposed system will flow between functions (**processes**) which

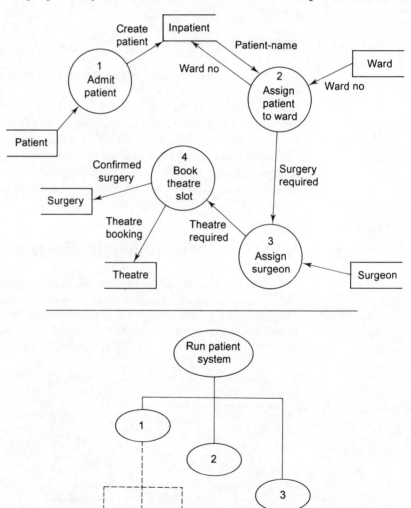

Figure A.2

transform input data into output data (refer to top portion of Figure A.2). Data may also flow to and from things external to the system (**external agents**) and may be stored in permanent or temporary computer or non-computer file storage (**data stores**). Each process can then be progressively decomposed in a separate diagram into smaller processes and these decompose and so on, in an operation known as levelling. DFDs are the most popular means of showing the **functional perspective** of a system. A subset of the levelled DFD shown in a different diagrammatic form is the **process decomposition diagram** which only shows the processes and sub-processes (refer to bottom portion of Figure A.2).

A.4 (STD) State transition diagram

This is a technique used in analysis to represent the different **states** a system can assume with time. Each state represents a period of time during which the system exhibits some observable behaviour. In the course of time state changes (**transitions**) occur from one state to another. These transitions are caused by various **conditions** and may initiate various **actions**. STDs are the most popular way of showing the time-dependent perspective of a system. A variation on the STD, more popular in data processing (IS) specifications, is the **entity life history diagram** (ELHD). A state transition diagram is shown in Figure A.3.

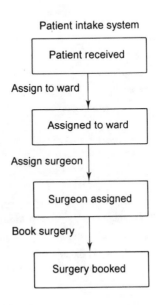

Figure A.3

B OOSD notation
OOSD Notation (IDE Inc. 1990)

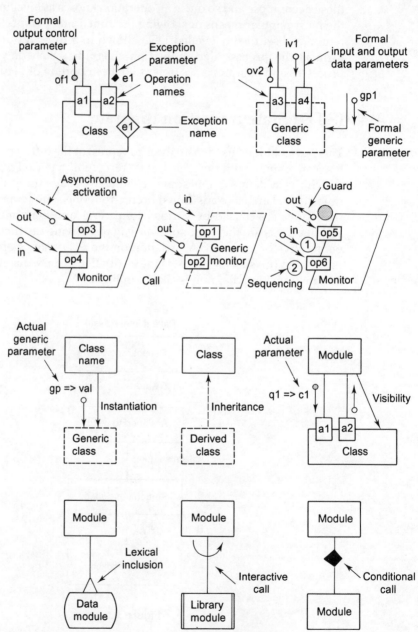

C Software development maturity
The SEI Software Development Process Maturity Model

C.1 Background

In early 1987 The Software Engineering Institute (SEI) at Carnegie-Mellon University launched a programme dedicated to helping software organizations improve their software development process. This programme grew out of work done earlier at the request of the US Air Force to enable them to assess the software development capability of potential software contractors bidding for Department of Defense (DoD) software contracts and came to be known as the Software Process Maturity Model (SPMM).

The typical profile of such a contractor would be a significant software development organization with several hundred staff working on large (100 work-year +) real-time projects using languages like Ada and attempting to comply with the requirements of US DoD Standard 2167. Watts Humphrey, the director of the SEI Software Process Program, has indicated that SPMM has been used with smaller organizations but none with less than about one hundred staff.

C.2 The SPMM model

The SPMM approach (Humphrey, 1989) is based on two premises:

(1) The process of developing and maintaining software can be defined, managed, measured and progressively improved.

(2) The quality of the software products produced is largely determined by the quality of the process which produces them.

This emphasis on process or life cycle is then developed further through a five-level model which classifies the software process maturity of a given software developer. The five levels which seem to have been heavily influenced by the five stages in the non-software-specific TQM approach (Crosby, 1979) are defined below.

C.3   The five process maturity levels

The five levels are characterized as follows.

Level 1 – every project is handled differently. The lowest level – Level 1 – is known as the **initial** level but is also described as *ad hoc* or even chaotic. A Level 1 software development organization operates without formal project plans and lacks 'defendable' effort, cost and time-scale estimates. Neither will there be any consistent mechanisms and responsibilities for tracking the progress and quality of projects undertaken. No mechanism will exist to enable changes to requirements, specifications, designs and code to be controlled. Those CASE tools which are used will be used inconsistently depending on who is managing or doing the project. Management will not really appreciate the key issues and problems in controlling software development projects.

Level 2 – every similar project is handled similarly. The first level of advancement after Level 1 is known as the **repeatable** level – this is the first level according to the model where any improvement is sustainable. From Level 2 upwards the software development process is relatively stable and is referred to as under 'statistical control'. Level 2 organizations will have achieved consistent performance with respect to project estimates and schedules *as long as the application domain is reasonably familiar.* They will have a formal project management system, a mechanism for ensuring consistent management review of projects, a clear independent organizational responsibility for quality assurance (SQA) and a change and version control system covering at least source code. There will also be formal organizational responsibility for staff training covering at least the basic project management and change control disciplines. Also the organization will attempt to retain records of past project estimates, actuals and testing error distributions.

Level 3 – a standard process is now well defined for all projects. A Level 3 organization is at the **defined** stage where all projects are based on customizations of a standard process. A software engineering process group (SEPG) will have been established with the brief of leading programmes to improve the quality and efficiency of the standard process. Organization-wide standards for project management, quality management, analysis, design, coding and test will now have been established. All new projects will undergo risk assessments. Inspection and walk-through techniques will be being used throughout the life cycle. Configuration management will now also be established throughout the life cycle and mechanisms will exist to enable requirements to be traced through to code and vice versa. An overall initial CASE framework will have been defined and installed with compatible tools available across most stages of the life cycle.

Level 4 – a measurable basis for all improvements to the process. A Level 4 organization is at the **managed** stage when it has a minimum set of quality and cost metrics defined throughout the organization and under configuration control. Enough data should exist in a centrally controlled database for these metrics to provide quantitative evidence of the effectiveness of any proposed changes to the process. Quality will have become a major preoccupation with written quality plans produced and tracked for each project. This will be backed up with appropriate training courses and a centralized quality reporting system.

Level 5 – emphasis on defect prevention. A Level 5 organization, described as **optimized**, will have become acutely aware that error correction late in the testing/trial phases of the software life cycle is a very inefficient way of eliminating errors. This type of organization will have clear guidelines, metrics and training on the types of defect which can best be eliminated by inspection and walkthrough techniques. Component reuse will also be a major emphasis of the Level 5 organization and written guidelines will exist on designing for reuse along with a set of available reuse components under configuration control. The Level 4 emphasis on metrics data gathering will also continue with the objective of improving the quality of such data by, where possible, automating the collection process. The CASE framework initially defined, installed and populated with tools in Level 3 will now have been considerably enhanced and will be backed up with clear guidelines (based on quantitative evidence in a number of places) as to which tools and techniques are most useful to which activities and project types.

D OO groups

D.1 The Object Management Group

The US-based Object Management Group (OMG) is an international software industry consortium with two primary aims:

- Promotion of the object-oriented approach to software engineering in general.
- Development of command models and a common interface for the production and use of large-scale distributed applications (open distributed processing) using object-oriented methodology.

Although the OMG is not a recognized standards group (like ISO or national bodies such as ANSI and IEEE), OMG is developing 'standards' in the form of wholesale consensus agreements between member companies leading to a single architecture and interface specification for application and enterprise integration on both the small and large scales.

The OMG was founded in April 1989, and continues to have a small, vendor-neutral core staff of seven people. Now comprising about 270 companies, the OMG membership is composed of large and small hardware and software vendors (IBM, Canon, DEC, Philips, Olivetti, AT&T, Sun Microsystems, Informix, ICL, Enfin Systems, Architecture Projects Management, Apple Computer, O_2 Technology, and others) as well as end-user companies (Citicorp, American Airlines, Royal Bank of Canada, John Deere, and so on) with a common goal: the promotion of open standards for interoperability of applications using an object-oriented framework.

A key differentiation of the OMG standards approach is that such standards are and will be based, as far as possible, on existing, commercially available products.

In late 1990 the OMG published its Object Management Architecture (OMA) Guide document. This document outlines a single terminology for object-oriented languages, systems, databases and application frameworks; an abstract framework for object-oriented systems; a set of both technical and architectural goals; and an architecture (reference model) for distributed applications using object-oriented techniques. To fill out this reference model, four areas of standardization have been identified:

(1) The **Object Request Broker**, or key communications element, for handling distribution of messages between application objects in a highly interoperable manner.

(2) The **Object Model**, or single design-portability abstract model, for communicating with OMG-conforming object-oriented systems.

(3) The **Object Services**, which will provide the main functions for realizing basic object functionality using the Object Request Broker – the logical modelling and physical storage of objects.

(4) The **Common Facilities** will comprise facilities which are useful in many application domains and which will be made available through OMA-compliant class interfaces.

The OMG adoption cycle includes *Requests for Information* and *Proposals*, requesting detailed technical and commercially available information from OMG members about existing products to fill particular parts of the reference model architecture. After passage by technical and business committees to review these responses, the OMG Board of Directors makes a final determination for technology adoption. Adopted specifications are available on a fee-free basis to members and non-members alike.

Unlike other organizations, the OMG itself does not and will not develop or sell software of any kind. Instead, it selects and promulgates software interfaces; products which offer these interfaces continue to be developed and offered by commercial companies.

In order to serve OMG membership interested in other object-oriented systems arenas besides the distributed system problem, the Group supports Special Interest Groups for discussion of possible standards in other areas. These groups at present are:

(1) Object-oriented databases.

(2) OO languages.

(3) End-user requirements.

(4) Parallel processing.

(5) Analysis and design methods.

(6) Smalltalk.

Any company, university/research institution or individual, whether end user or vendor, can become a member of this body. For further details contact:

President: Mr Christopher Stone
Technical Director: Dr Richard Soley

Framingham Corporate Center
492 Old Connecticut Path
Framingham
Massachusetts 01701
USA

D.2   The Object Interest Group

The Object Interest Group consists of 16 major UK companies – Barclays Bank, British Airways, ICI, Rolls Royce, British Petroleum, Lloyds Bank, Royal Insurance, National Westminister Bank, Prudential Insurance, TSB Bank, British Steel, Ford Motor Company, British Aerospace, British Telecom and two government departments (CCTA and DTI) – who joined forces to weigh up the credibility of the claims made for object technology.

Their study represents a user perspective and is primarily interested in the development of information systems. During 1990 and early 1991, the group's members researched the current state of the technology. The result was a detailed report which has now been circulated to all OIG members. The report concludes that object orientation could indeed achieve one of the long-sought-after goals of software engineering: to help software development become more like production line manufacturing.

The report explains that the evolution towards mass manufacturing has been based on the principle of modularity – in other words, that people work on sub-components rather than complex machines.

Depending on the interest generated in the findings of the report, the group may be expanded to include other members in the future.

For further details contact:

Chairman: Mr Norman Plant

Registered Office: 'Kinver House'
                       Guildford Road
                       Frimley Green
                       Camberley
                       Surrey GU16 6PA
                       United Kingdom

E The OO database system manifesto

This manifesto proposes the following rules for an object-oriented DBMS:

(1) **Complex objects must be supported.** The ability must exist to build objects by applying constructors to basic objects. The minimum set of constructors are SET, LIST and TUPLE.

(2) **Object identity must be supported.** This is the same as in conventional object-oriented systems where an object has an existence which is independent of its value. All objects must have a unique identifier (UID).

(3) **Encapsulation must be supported.** In an OOPL this is achieved through the use of abstract data types. In an OODBMS it is achieved by ensuring that programmers only have access to a set of operations. Both the data and the implementation of the operations on the data must be hidden.

(4) **Types or classes must be supported.** A type, in an object-oriented system, summarizes the common features of a set of objects with the same characteristics. In OO programming languages types can be used at compile-time to check the correctness of programs. A type and a class can be used interchangeably, but when the two are used in the same system, class refers to the extension (that is, all current instances) of the corresponding type.

(5) **Types or classes must be able to inherit from their ancestors.** Any subclass or subtype will inherit attributes and methods from its superclass or supertype.

(6) **Method dispatches should be bound dynamically.** Operations should apply to objects of different types (overloading). The implementation of the operation will depend on the type of the object it is applied to (overriding). This implies that implementation code cannot be referenced until run-time (late- or dynamic-binding).

(7) **Any computable function must be expressible in the language.** The data manipulation language (DML) of the database should allow a user to express any computational function. The DML must be computationally complete. This is in contrast to SQL.

(8) **There should be no distinction between system-defined and user-defined types.** In addition to providing types, the system should provide facilities to define new types. It should be possible to manipulate the new types in exactly the same manner as the basic-system-provided types.

(9) **Data persistence must be provided.** As in a conventional database, data must remain after the process that created it has terminated.

(10) **It must be possible to manage very large databases.** Traditional databases employ techniques that manage secondary storage to improve the performance of the system. These are usually invisible to the user of the system. Object-oriented systems should possess similar features that make the management of large volumes of data possible.

(11) **The DBMS must support concurrent users.** The systems should provide concurrency mechanisms similar to those in conventional databases.

(12) **The DBMS must be capable of recovery from hardware and software failures.** The systems should provide recovery mechanisms similar to those in conventional databases.

(13) **It must be possible to state database queries in a high-level, concise form.** This is an *ad hoc* query facility. The database should provide a high-level, efficient, application-independent query facility. This need not necessarily be a query language, but could instead be some type of graphical interface.

F Third generation database manifesto

The thirteen propositions from the Third Generation Database System Manifesto are:

(1) **A 3rd generation DBMS must have a rich type system.** These should include:

(a) an abstract data type system to construct new base types;

(b) array, sequence, record and set type constructors.

(2) **Inheritance is a good idea.** In particular multiple inheritance is essential to model all possible situations.

(3) **Functions, including database procedures and methods, and encapsulation are a good idea.** Encapsulation has administrative advantages by encouraging modularity and by registering functions along with the data they encapsulate. If an Employee collection changes in such a way that its previous contents cannot be defined as a view, then all the code which must be changed is localized in one place and will therefore be easier to change.

Encapsulation of data and functional logic inside the DBMS often provides performance advantages in a distributed system. If a specific function is executed internally by a data manager then only one round trip message between the application and the DBMS is executed. Whereas, if the function runs in the user program then one round trip message will be executed for each access.

Such encapsulated functions can be inherited and possibly overridden down the inheritance hierarchy.

The Third Generation Database Manifesto suggests that the functions should run queries using a high-level non-procedural access language and not perform their own navigation using calls to some lower-level DBMS data access interfaces. Or at least, such calls should be discouraged.

(4) **Unique identifiers (UIDs) for records should be assigned by the DBMS only if a user-defined primary key is not available.** If a primary key exists for a collection that is known never to change then no additional system-assigned UID is required. A primary key has the advantage of having human-readable meaning.

(5) **Rules (triggers, constraints) will become a major feature in future systems. They should not be associated with a specific function or collection.** Rules must be enforced by the DBMS but not bound to any function or collection. Associating rules with functions means that when a new function is added the rule must be hard-coded into the function. There is no way to guarantee this. Moreover, this requires duplicating the rule in all necessary functions.

(6) **Essentially all programmatic access to a database should be through a non-procedural, high-level access language.** Second generation systems have demonstrated that dramatically lower program maintenance costs result from this approach relative to first generation systems. Third generation DBMSs must not compromise this advance. In the longer term this service can be provided by adding query language constructs to persistent programming languages. In the short term, this service can be provided by embedding a query language in conventional programming languages.

(7) **There should be at least two ways to specify collections, one using enumeration of members and one using the query language to specify membership.**

(8) **Updateable views are essential.** Encapsulation of functions with a collection of data helps in this respect. When views must change, the functions to be changed are easily identified. However if a change is made to the schema it may take weeks to rewrite the affected functions. A better approach is to support **virtual collections** of data (views). Third generation systems will then support updateable views.

(9) **Performance indicators have almost nothing to do with data models and must not appear in them.** Performance is determined by:

> The amount of performance tuning done on the DBMS
> The usage of compilation techniques by the DBMS
> The location of the buffer pool (in the client or DBMS address space)
> The kind of indexing available
> The performance of the client—DBMS interface
> The clustering that is performed.

Such issues have nothing to do with the data model or with the usage of a higher-level language like SQL versus a lower-level navigational interface.

(10) **Third generation DBMSs must be accessible from multiple high-level languages.**

(11) **Persistent forms of a high-level language, for a variety of high-level languages, is a good idea. They will all be supported on top of a single DBMS by compiler extensions and a complex run-time system.** There must be a close match between the DBMS language and the application programming language. This is a problem with current SQL embeddings. In addition it is desirable to allow any variable in a user's program to be optionally **persistent**. In this case, the value of any persistent variable is remembered even after the program terminates. Each persistent language requires compiler modifications unique to the language and a run-time system particular to the high-level query language.

(12) **For better or worse, SQL is intergalactic dataspeak.** Any database must support SQL if it is to receive acceptance in the marketplace.

(13) **Queries and their resulting answers should be the lowest level of communication between a client and a server.** Expressions in the query language should be the lowest-level unit of communication between a client and its server. If a collection of queries can be packaged into a function, then the user can use a remote procedure call to cause function execution on the server. This feature is desirable because it results in less than one message per query. (Compare this with the concept of methods stored in an OODBMS and retrieved and executed in a server process.) Remote procedure calls and SQL queries provide an appropriate level of interface technology.

APPENDIX

G Some commercial OODBMSs

G.1 GemStone

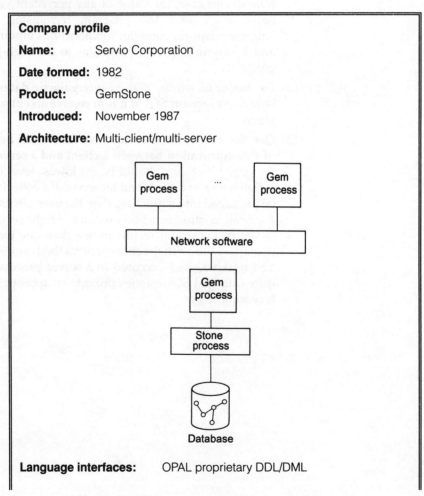

Company profile

Name: Servio Corporation

Date formed: 1982

Product: GemStone

Introduced: November 1987

Architecture: Multi-client/multi-server

Gem process … Gem process

Network software

Gem process

Stone process

Database

Language interfaces: OPAL proprietary DDL/DML

Other language interfaces: Smalltalk
C++
C

DDL: OPAL

Hardware/software platforms : DEC VAX (VMS), DECstations (Ultrix)
Sun-3 and Sun-4, IBM RS6000 (UNIX).
Clients available for Apple Macintosh
and IBM PC (MS-DOS)

Tool support : FACETS – a 4GL based on X-Windows, running
OSF/MOTIF:
The Schema Designer
The Forms Designer
The Report Writer
The Menu Builder
The Help Author – to build context-sensitive help screens

Description:
GemStone was one of the earliest OODBMSs. It uses a proprietary DDL
and DML called OPAL which is based on Smalltalk.

The two main components to the architecture are:

(1) Stone provides persistent object management, concurrency
control, authorization, transaction and recovery services.

(2) Gem provides a compilation mechanism for OPAL programs and
the pre-defined set of OPAL classes and methods. Gems access
and execute objects. The Gem process also provides a
communications server plus a means of interfacing with other
languages such as Smalltalk, C or C++.

OPAL does not have any pre-defined algebra of operations. However, the
pre-defined OPAL classes have a number of methods available which are
inherited by any subclasses that a user defines. Specific operators must
be defined for each different class by defining the appropriate methods.
These methods can optionally be stored along with data in the database.
Interacting with the GemStone database involves sending messages to
objects within the database via the Gem process. The Gem process
extracts the appropriate data and access methods associated with the
object and executes them. If the methods are stored in the database,
method execution can be performed on the DBMS server thereby reducing
network traffic.

Both the C and C++ interfaces to GemStone are offered through a directly
linked C-function library or C++ class library. Alternatively, GemStone
offers connection via remote procedure calls (RPCs). RPCs offer a slower
means of accessing GemStone than calling linked procedures. However,
RPCs remove the possibility of corrupting the database with a bad pointer.

G.2   Ontos

Company profile

Name: Ontos Inc.

Date formed: 1985

Number of employees: 45

Product: Ontos

Introduced: 1987

Architecture: Multi-client/multi-server

Each server must register with a special server called the registry. This registry holds routing information for all the servers on the network. The client gains access to a given server through the registry.

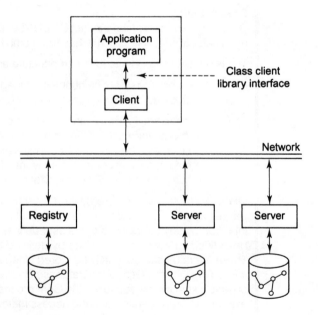

Language interfaces: C++

DDL: C++

Hardware/software platforms: Sun-3, Sun-4, Sun SPARCstation
HP/Apollo 3000, HP/Apollo 4000
DECstation 3100
PS/2 under OS/2

Tool support: Shorthand – ONTOS 4GL

ONTOS Studio – GUI Designer running under X-Windows

ONTOS SQL – SQL with object extensions

DBDesigner – interactive graphical tool for database design

DBATool – Database Administration tool

Description:

Ontos is a C++ based system, offering a C++ client library that serves as the interface between an application program and the persistent database. The Ontos C++ library includes classes for defining collection objects (aggregates) such as sets, lists, arrays and dictionaries and there are iterators for each type of aggregate. All persistent classes must inherit from the Ontos root class Object which includes the Ontos data manipulation constructs such as put_object() and delete_object(). There are also a number of free standing classes containing methods such as OC_commit() and OC_lookup(). Ontos allows programmatic access to the database at a low level – allowing the use of pointers to link objects, and control access to caching optimization and locking, whilst able to hide problems such as the physical location of the data.

From a logical viewpoint, data and method information is encapsulated into a class. However, from a physical viewpoint, only the data component of a class is stored in the database. The functional code resides in the class libraries linked into the application. The DBDesigner can be used to define database schema and subsequently generate the corresponding C++ class definition files for use in the application. The class implementation files form part of the application.

G.3   O₂

Company profile

Name: O$_2$ Technology (formerly called GIP-Altair)

Date formed: September 1991 (original company formed 1986)

Number of employees: 35

Product: O$_2$

Introduced: 1991

Architecture: Multi-client/single-server architecture

The Object Manager creates, stores and maintains objects. The Type Manager creates, stores and maintains type structure descriptions (akin to a schema manager) as well as managing the description of application programs. The Method Manager creates, stores and maintains source and object code of the methods. The Object, Method and Type Managers run on the workstation client. The Server (O_2 run-time) stores the whole database and includes a transaction manager to ensure concurrency control and recovery. The Type, Method and Object Managers together with the O_2 run-time are collectively known as the O_2 Engine.

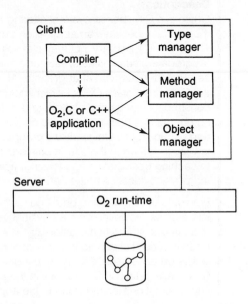

Language interfaces: O_2C, C and C++

DDL: O_2C or C++ via a translator to produce O_2 schema

Hardware/software platforms: Sun-3 and Sun-4 (OS), HP 9000/400

Tool support: O_2LOOK – Toolset for developing GUIs on OSF/MOTIF

O_2TOOLS – This is a graphical programming environment which includes a source manager, an OO debugger, an incremental compiler, plus editing tools for the database and schema

O_2QUERY – An SQL-like query language to manipulate O_2 objects. This can be used interactively on an *ad hoc* basis or from C, C++ or O_2C programs

$O_2LINKC++$ and O_2LINKC – allows programmers to write C++ and C applications which use the O_2 database

Description:
The client/server architecture of O_2 Engine is a page server, so called because the server deals only with pages and does not understand the semantics of objects. This places most of the complexity in the client, leaving the server to perform the tasks that it alone can perform.

O_2C
O_2 is based on C with an object-oriented layer O_2 on top – producing a hybrid language called O_2C. It permits the programmer to declare O_2 objects, send messages to them, and manipulate them. O_2C is also an Object 4GL that includes tools for generating GUIs (via O_2LOOK). The basic construct of the O_2 layer is message passing and for this the Smalltalk syntax of '<receiver><message> (<arguments>)' was followed. Programming in O_2C therefore consists of writing C programs which contain these special primitives for message passing. The precompiler takes O_2C programs, calls the Type and Method Managers to perform type checking, and generates C programs with calls to the Object and Method Managers. These programs can then be compiled using a standard C compiler. The language supports single inheritance and encapsulation. Classes are defined as persistent or not, as the case may be.

C and C++ language interfaces are provided to the database in the form of function and class libraries respectively.

G.4   ObjectStore

Company profile

Name: Object Design Inc.

Date formed: 1988

Number of employees: 45

Product: ObjectStore

Introduced: September 1990

Architecture: Multi-client/multi-server

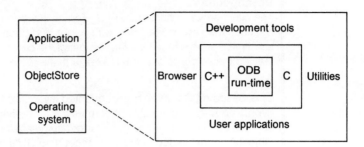

Language interfaces: C and C++

DDL: C++

Hardware/software platforms :   Sun-3 and Sun-4 (OS)
Solbourne (OS/SMP)
IBM RS6000 (AIX)
DECstation (Ultrix)
IBM PC (MS-Windows 3.0)

Tool support :   SchemaDesigner – an interactive graphical schema
designer

Browser – a graphical tool for inspecting an
ObjectStore database

Description:
ObjectStore is based on C++ and provided in the form of a C++ client
library. Final compilation is achieved using a range of third-party C++
compilers/translators.

ObjectStore has three main components: DBMS run-time, application
interfaces and C++ development tools. ObjectStore's DDL uses the same
data structures as C and this provides a low-cost migration path for users
with C applications – C data stored in existing file systems can easily be
converted to use ObjectStore.

ObjectStore supports a high-level query language for objects, which is not
based on SQL. This high-level DML can be pre-processed to C++. Object
design will conform to OSQL when standards emerge.

The server stores and retrieves pages of data in response to requests from
clients. The server has no knowledge of the contents of a page. It simply
passes pages of information to and from the client, and stores them on
disk. Therefore most of the query and DBMS processing is done on the
client side.

G.5 Versant

Company profile

Name: Versant Object Technology Corporation

Date formed: 1988

Number of employees: 40

Product: Versant

Introduced: September 1990

Architecture: Multi-client/multi-server

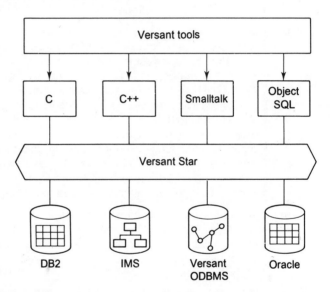

Language interfaces: C
C++
Objectworks\Smalltalk
Smalltalk V/PM

DDL: C++

Hardware/software platforms: Sun-3, Sun-4
IBM RS 6000
HP 9000/400
Silicon Graphics IRIS Series
Intergraph 6000 Series
DECstation
Sequent range
– all UNIX (or Ultrix for the DECstation)

Tool support:	Versant Object Modeller – to define entity-attribute data structures graphically. Can then convert to C, C++, Smalltalk or SQL tables
	Versant Designer – a graphical schema designer
	Versant Repository Builder – allows a DBA to define system metadata contained in a repository
	Versant Screen – to create GUIs
	Versant Report – to create reports
	Versant Object 4GL – enables chaining of actions and objects created using other tools such as Versant Screen

Description:

The Versant architecture is based on a layered approach with the OODBMS at the lowest level. The next layer, Versant Star, consists of a number of products to aid in the process of migration from relational to object-oriented database systems: there are gateways to integrate foreign databases into a range of industry standard languages supported by the Versant system (C, C++, ObjectWorks\Smalltalk, Smalltalk-V/PM and Object SQL); and Versant Star also provides gateways to DB2, Oracle and Ingres. The language interfaces are provided through class libraries which are bound into the application. Versant has developed a flavour of Object SQL, based on extensions to SQL developed by Texas Instruments. As yet, Versant Object SQL cannot be embedded in C++.

At the next level there are a number of toolsets to aid the application developer in constructing and accessing databases by graphically defining data models, setting up and managing distributed databases and developing applications using reusable class libraries for creating forms, reports and queries.

G.6   Objectivity

Company profile

Name: Objectivity Inc.

Date formed: 1988

Number of employees: 50

Product: Objectivity/DB

Introduced: April 1990

Architecture: Fully distributed peer-to-peer

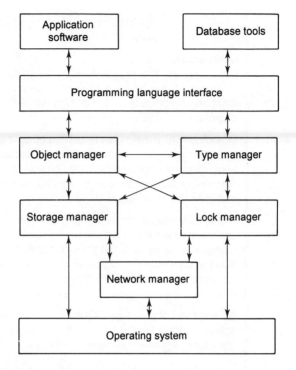

Language interfaces: C
                             C++

DDL: C++

Hardware/software platforms: Sun-3, SPARCstation (Sun OS 4.1)
                                     IBM RS 6000 (AIX 3.1)
                                     HP 9000/300/400/700/800 (HP/UX 7.0)
                                     VAX/Ultrix 4.1
                                     VAX/VMS 5.4
                                     DECstation (Ultrix 4.1)
                                     SONY NEWS (NEW-OS 3.3)
                                     IBM PC (Windows 3.0, Dos 3.3)

Tool support: Database programming interface and DDL

Data Browser – for searching and viewing objects in the database

Type Browser – for viewing database schema types

Debugging Utility – interactive debugging

Dump/Load Utility – to dump/load a logical view of a DB in ASCII

DBA Utilities – suite of DBA tools for administration of physical DB components

Description:

Objectivity Inc. has targeted its OODBMS clearly at engineering environments such as electrical computer-aided design (ECAD), mechanical computer-aided design (MCAD) and computer-aided software engineering (CASE).

Objectivity/DB implements a fully distributed peer-to-peer architecture, based on a layered approach. The architecture supports standalone and networked applications. Data can be fully distributed among heterogeneous machines and operating systems, and location is transparent to user applications.

The Type Manager stores, retrieves and maintains descriptions of all classes defined in the database. The Object Manager keeps track of and manipulates objects within the database. While the Object Manager handles data from the logical view, the Storage Manager handles it from the physical view. The Lock Manager oversees access to objects in the database, managing concurrent access to data.

As with most of the other OODBMSs, encapsulation of data and function is achieved at the logical level. At the physical level, only data is stored. The corresponding functions reside in the application.

Communication between processes is coordinated by the Network Manager, which enables local processes to access data located on remote workstations.

The C and C++ language interfaces are supplied in the form of function and class libraries respectively.

Developing an Objectivity/DB application is a five-step process:

(1) Design DB schema and create a DDL schema file;

(2) Using DDL processor, produce DB schema, schema header file and schema source code file;

(3) Write the source code for the application;

(4) Compile source code and schema header files;

(5) Link application code with Objectivity/DB run-time library and compiled schema code to create the final application program.

Table G.1 summarizes the facilities provided by the six OODBMSs described in this appendix.

Table G.1 Table of features for OODBMSs.

	GemStone	*Ontos*	*O₂*	*ObjectStore*	*Versant*	*Objectivity*
Language interfaces	Smalltalk C C++	C++	O₂C C C++	C C++	Smalltalk C C++	C C++
DDL	OPAL	C++	O₂C	C++	C++	C++ with extensions
High-level query language	No	Ontos-SQL	O₂QUERY	Yes – via a DML	Versant Object SQL	No
4GL	FACETS	Shorthand	O₂C	Yes – DML pre-processed through C ++	Versant Object 4GL	No
Versioning	No	No	No	Yes	Yes	Yes
Inbuilt support for relationships	Inheritance 1:1 1:N N:M Uni-directional	Inheritance only	Inheritance only	Inheritance 1:1 1:N N:M Uni- and bi-directional	Inheritance 1:1 1:N N:M Bi-directional	Inheritance 1:1 1:N N:M Uni- and bi-directional
Methods executed on the database server	YES – OPAL methods	No	No	No	No	No

Vendors

Applied Logic Development Ltd

9 Princeton Court
55 Felsham Road
London SW15 1AZ
England
Tel. +44-81-780-1088
Fax +44-81-780-1941

Contact Caroline Browne

Artefact

Nassaulaan 2a
2628 GH
Delft
The Netherlands
Tel. +31-15-617532
Fax +31-15-618202

**Artificial Intelligence
International Ltd**

The Chapel, Park View House
1 Park View Road
Berkhamsted
Herts. HP4 3EY
England
Tel. +44-442-876722
Fax +44-442-877997

Blaise Computing Inc.

816 Bancroft Way
Berkeley
California CA94710
USA
Tel. +1-415-540 5441

Borland International Inc.

1800 Greenhills Road
Scotts Valley, CA 95066
USA
Tel. +1-408-439-4825

Cadre Europe

Cadre Technologies S.A.
22, rue Juste Olivier
CH-1260 Nyon
Switzerland
Tel. +41-22-62 22 51
Fax +41-22-61 07 85

Cadre Technologies Inc.

Team*work* Division
222 Richmond Street
Providence, RI 02903
USA
Tel. +1-401-351-2273
Fax +1-401-351-7380

CNS Inc.

7090 Shady Oak Road
Eden Prairie, MN 55344
USA
Tel. +1-612-944-0170
Fax +1-612-944-0923

Jim Schwarz – Director of
Software Products

Coopers & Lybrand

SoftPert Systems Division
One Main Street
Cambridge, MA 02142
USA
Tel. +1-617-621-3670
Fax +1-617-621-3671

Data Access Corporation

Miami, Florida
USA

(in the UK –
DataFlex (Information
Management) Services Ltd
DataNet House
114–116 Curtain Road
London EC2A 3AH
England
Tel. +44-71-729 4460
Fax +44-71-739 1247)

Digitalk Inc.

9841 Airport Boulevard
Los Angeles, CA 90045
USA
Tel. +1-213-645-1082
Fax +1-213-645-1306

Enfin Software Corporation

6920 Miramar Road
Suite 106A
San Diego, CA 92121
USA
Tel. +1-619-549-6606

(In the UK – Enfin distributor
is: QA Training
Cecily Hill Castle
Cirencester
Gloucestershire GL7 2EF
England
Tel. +44-285-655888
Fax +44-285-640181)

Free Software Foundation Inc.

675 Massachusetts Avenue
Cambridge, MA 02139
USA
Tel. +1-617-876-3296

Richard M Stallman – President

Genesis

1303 Columbia Drive
Suite 209
Richardson
Texas 75081
USA
Tel. +1-214-644-8559
Fax +1-214-644-4286

Glockenspiel Class Constructors

30 Lower Dominick Street
Dublin 1
Republic of Ireland
Tel. +353 1 733166
Fax +353 1 733034

Peter Maxwell – Product
Manager (Technical)

Guidelines Software Inc.

PO Box 749
Orinda
CA 94563
USA
Tel. +1-415-254-9183

Chandler Vienneau – Sales
Manager

Ingres UK Ltd

Wharfdale Road
Winnersh Triangle
Wokingham
Berks. RG11 5TP
England
Tel. +44-734-496400

Instrumatic UK Ltd

First Avenue
Globe Park
Marlow
Bucks. SL7 1YA
England
Tel. +44-628-476741
Fax +44-628-474440

Interactive Development Environments, Inc.

595 Market Street
12th Floor
San Francisco, CA 94105
USA
Tel. +1-415-543 0900
Fax +1-415-543 3716

in UK:
14–16 Frederick Sanger Road
The Surrey Research Park
Guildford
Surrey, GU2 5YD
England
Tel. +44-483-57900
Fax +44-483-31272

Interactive Software Engineering

270 Storke Road
Suite 7
Goleta, CA 93117
USA
Tel. +1-805-685-1006
Fax +1-805-685-6869

Annie Meyer – Vice President

IPSYS Software plc

Marlborough Court
Pickford Street
Macclesfield
Cheshire SK11 6JD
England
Tel. +44-625-616722
Fax +44-625-616780

Knowledge Systems Corp.

2000 Regency Parkway
Suite 270
Cary, North Carolina 27511-8507
USA
Tel. +1-919-481-4000
Fax +1-919-460-9044

Lund Software House AB

Box 7056
S-220 07 LUND
Sweden
Tel. +46-46-134060
Fax +46-46-131021

Micro Focus Europe Limited

26 West Street
Newbury,
Berkshire RG13 1JT
England
Tel. +44-635-32646

Micro Focus Incorporated

2465 East Bayshore Road
Suite 400
Palo Alto, CA 94303
USA
Tel. +1-800-872-6265

O₂ Technology

7, rue Parc de Clagny
78000 Versailles
France
Tel. +33-1-30 84 77 77
Fax +33-1-30 84 77 90

or

Suite 2200
One Kendall Square
Cambridge, MA 02139
USA
Tel. +1-917-621 7041
Fax +1-617-577 1209

Object Design Inc.

One New England Executive
Park
Burlington, MA 01803
USA
Tel. +1-617-270 9797
Fax +1-617-270 3509

Object International Inc.

9430 Research Boulevard
IV-400
Austin, TX 78759-6535
USA
Tel. +1-512-343-4549
Fax +1-512-343-4569

ObjectCraft

2124 Kittredge Street
Suite 118
Berkley
California 94704
USA
Tel. +1-415-540-4889
Fax +1-415-861-5398

Paul Heidt – Marketing Director

Objective Systems SF AB

Torshamnsgatan 39
S-16440 Kista
Sweden
Tel. +46-8 703 4540
Fax +46-8 751 3096

Objectivity Inc.

800 El Camino Real
Menlo Park, CA 94025
USA
Tel. +1-415-688-8000
Fax +1-415-325-0939

Ontos Inc.

Three Burlington Woods
Burlington, MA 01803
USA
Tel. +1-617-272 7110
Fax +1-617-272 8101

Oregon Software Inc.

6915 S.W. Macadam Avenue
Suite 200
Portland
Oregon 97219-2397
USA
Tel. +1-503-245-2202
Fax +1-503-245-8449

ParcPlace Systems

1550 Plymouth Street
Mountain View, CA 94043
USA
Tel. +1-415-691 6700
Fax +1-415-691-6715

Popkin Software & Systems Inc.

11 Park Place
19th Floor
New York 10007
USA
Tel. +1-212-571 3434

Rational

3320 Scott Boulevard
Santa Clara, CA 95054-3197
USA
Tel. +1-408-496 3600
Fax +1-408-496 3636

Sabre Software Inc. (now called
Centerline Software, Inc.)

Corporate Headquarters
10 Fawcett Street
Cambridge, MA 02138
USA
Tel +1-617-498-3000
Fax +1-617-498-6655

Sapiens Inc.

295 7th Avenue
New York
NY 10001
USA
Tel. +1-212-366 9394

Servio Corporation

1420 Harbor Bay Parkway
Suite 100
Almeda, CA 94501
USA
Tel. +1-415-748 6263

Sequiter Software

#209, 9644
54 Avenue
Edmonton
Alberta
Canada T6E 5V1
Tel. +1-403-448-0313
Fax +1-403-448-0315

SIG Computer GmbH

Zu Den Bettern 4
6333 Braunfels Altenkirchen
Germany
Tel. +49-64 72 20 96
Fax +49-64 72 72 13

Contact Frieder Monninger

Simula a.s.

PO Box 4403 Torshov
N-0402
Oslo
Norway
Tel. +47-2-156710
Fax +47-2-156051

Stepstone Corporation

75 Glen Road
Sandy Hook, CT 06482
USA
Tel. +1-203-426-1875
Fax +1-203-270-0106

Sarah C Bell – Marketing
Representative
Richard Strilowich – Technical
Support

Sun Microsystems Inc.

2550 Garcia Avenue
Mountain View, CA 94043
USA
Tel. +1-415-960 1300
Fax +1-415-336 6536

Systematica Ltd

Systematica House
3–7 Stephens Road
Bournemouth
Dorset BH2 6JL
England
Tel. +44-202-297292
Fax +44-202-291180

Valbecc Ltd

115 Wilmslow Road
Handforth
Wilmslow
Cheshire
SK9 3ER
England
Tel. +44-625 539903
Fax +44-625 539905

Versant Object Technology

4500 Bohannon Drive
Menlo Park, CA 94025
USA
Tel. +1-415-325-2300
Fax +1-415-325-2380

Contact Mike Mooney

Vleermuis Software Research bv

Kantoren Radboudburcht
Stationsplien 161, 3511 ED
Utrecht
PO Box 2584, 3500 GN Utrecht
The Netherlands
Tel. +31-30 32 49 44
Fax +31-30 31 04 26

Whitewater Group

1800 Ridge Avenue
Evanston, IL 60201
USA
Tel. +1-708-328-3800

Winter Partners

London Office:
West Wing, The Hop Exchange
24a Southwark Street
London SE1 1TY
England
Tel. +44-(0)71-357-7292
Fax +44-(0)71-357-6650

Contact Sandy Scott (Marketing Manager)

Zurich Office:
Florastrasse 44
CH-8008 Zurich
Switzerland
Tel. +41-(0)1-386-95 11
Fax +41-(0)1-386-95 00

Zinc Software Inc.

405 South 100 East Suite 201
Pleasant Grove
Utah 84062
USA
Tel. +1-801-785-8900
Fax +1-801-785-8996

Zortech Ltd

58–60 Beresford Street
London SE18 6BG
England
Tel. +44-81-316-7777
Fax +44-81-316-4138

Chris Dodd – Sales Manager

Glossary

Abstract class A category of classes appearing in an inheritance hierarchy which is never instantiated. Abstract classes provide a basis for subclassing to create specializations which are instantiated.

Abstract data type A repository of data through the implementation of an object. An abstract data type hides the physical storage of information from the user but provides a public set of methods that the user may invoke to manipulate the information in the object.

Abstraction The process of analyzing a problem in different levels of detail, according to the level of understanding required or acquired.

Aggregation A specific kind of relationship between classes in which one of the classes forms a component of the other.

Application A complete unit of software capable of being executed. An object-oriented application is composed of a number of interacting objects. Each object contributes to the overall capability of the application to provide services to users (humans or other applications).

Association A general user-defined structural relationship between two or more classes. An association between two classes commonly implies a message-passing relationship between instances of those classes.

Attribute An identified data element within a class. An attribute can be a simple type such as an integer or a string, or a more complex type such as another class.

Behaviour A characteristic functional property of an object. An object's behaviour is defined by the methods within that object.

Binding The association of a message requesting a service with a method providing that service.

Class An abstraction of a set of objects that specifies the common static and behavioural characteristics of the objects, including the public and private nature of the state and behaviour.

Class attribute A data member declared within a class definition.

Class browser A software development tool to help with managing a hierarchy of classes in a library.

Class method A method associated with a class rather than an object. Class methods are typically used to create and define objects. Messages sent to a class method are sent to the class rather than an instance of a class (an object). This implies that the class is an instance of a higher-level form called a *metaclass* (see definition of a *metaclass*).

Client One side of a client/server relationship. The client requests services from the server (see also *Server*).

Cohesion   A term used to describe a characteristic of a design. Cohesion is a qualitative measure of how well the parts of a system 'hold together'. Functional cohesion, where all parts of a module contribute towards the same single purpose, is best. Designs exhibiting sequential cohesion, where the output from one module is used as the input to the next, are almost as good as functionally cohesive designs in terms of maintainability. At the other end of the scale is coincidental cohesion where the components of a module are combined for no good reason.

Concrete class   A class describing a tangible component from the problem domain. Concrete classes represent well understood, stable phenomena – unlikely to change over time.

Container class   The definition of a *container object*.

Container object   An aggregate object. An object used for the express purpose of holding and managing objects of other class types. An object of the class 'company' might be used to hold many objects of the class 'employee'.

Coupling   A term used to describe a characteristic of a design. Coupling measures a module's dependence on others. It identifies the extent and method used in maintaining data connections with other modules. A design which exhibits complex and numerous interconnection between modules is 'tightly coupled' as opposed to a simpler 'weakly coupled' design with few connections. Tightly coupled designs are difficult to maintain because of the heavy interdependence between modules.

Data abstraction   The principle of defining a data type in terms of the operations that apply to objects of the type, with the constraint that the values of such objects can be modified and observed only by the use of the operations.

Data definition language (DDL)   In the context of a database management system, this is the language used to define the database schema.

Data flow diagram   A structured diagramming technique depicting the dynamics of data passing between functions, where the output data is computed from the input data.

Data hiding   (See *encapsulation* and *data abstraction*.)

Data manipulation language (DML)   In the context of a database management system, this is the language used to manipulate data stored within a database.

Dynamic (late) binding   Describes the situation where messages are bound to methods at run-time – normally because the object is declared to be of a generic type such that its actual type cannot be determined until run-time.

Dynamic typing   Describes the case where an object is assigned a generic type at compile-time and the actual type is determined at run-time. For example the use of the 'id' type in Objective-C.

Encapsulation   The process by which abstract data types are created. Encapsulated data is protected from direct outside access by using a clearly defined interface.

Entity relationship diagram   A diagramming technique describing data entities and their structural relationships.

Exception handling A programming concept. A strategy and mechanism for managing erroneous events within an *application*.

Extensibility The ability to extend, add-to, modify the design or implementation of an application.

Garbage collection A mechanism within a programming language, or associated run-time environment, to automatically handle the release of disused system memory back to the operating system.

Generalization An inheritance relationship between two classes where one class (the superclass or parent) supports more generalized qualities, while the other class (the subclass or child) supports more specialized qualities (see *Inheritance*).

Genericity The ability to define parameterised classes; a special form of polymorphism.

Hybrid object-oriented language A programming language which supports both the object-oriented paradigm and structured approaches but does not enforce the use of either.

Hybrid object-oriented life cycle A software development life cycle which includes distinct phases that employ object-oriented techniques and distinct phases that use traditional, structured techniques.

Identifier A label or name used to represent a class- or data-attribute.

Identity The value of an attribute, or set of attributes, which provides a unique tag or label distinguishing one object from another.

Implementation The term used to describe the construction stage in a software development life cycle. The stage after analysis and design, involving the realization of a design in a given programming language. The result of implementation is an executable program.

Incremental development The process of developing software by a short specification–design–implementation phase which is repeated many times to evolve larger systems from small components (also called *'evolutionary development'*).

Information hiding See *encapsulation*.

Inheritance A relationship between classes whereby one class acquires the structure of other classes in a strict hierarchy from either a single (single inheritance) or multiple (multiple inheritance) parents.

Instance Another term for an object (see *Object*).

Interpreter A software tool which facilitates a short edit–run cycle, by removing the compilation stage. Source code is interpreted into a machine-executable form at run-time.

Link A user-defined relationship between two objects (instances).

Message A request for an object to carry out the sequence of actions in one or more of the methods of its class.

Metaclass A higher-order class used to describe other classes (see also *Class method*).

Method A unit of functional logic contained within an object. Methods can be either 'public', where they are accessible to external objects, or 'private', where they can only be used by the owning object. Methods are executed to perform requested services.

Method resolution An object-oriented programming term that refers to the selection of a method to perform a requested operation as the result of a received message. Method resolution can be achieved either at compile-time (static binding) or during run-time (dynamic binding).

Methodology   A collection of procedures, techniques and tools for the development of software.

Name mangling   The term used to describe modifications made to identifier names during some translation process.

Object   An element of a computer system that has a unique identity, state (represented by public and private data), and public and private operations (methods) that represent the behaviour of the object over time. An object is an instance of a class.

OO   Acronym – object-oriented.

OODBMS   Acronym – object-oriented database management system.

OOPL   Acronym – object-oriented programming language.

Operation   A process that is invoked as a result of a received message. An operation is implemented by a method which dictates a behavioural characteristic of an object.

Overloading   A programming term involving the use of multiple specifications of a given method name within a class definition or across several class definitions. Overloading results in a message invoking different behaviour depending on the class of object called or on the number and types of the parameters associated with the message.

Parameterized class (or type)   An object-oriented programming term. Sometimes referred to as genericity. The definition of a general class template. Such templates can operate on different types of objects as specified in the parameter list associated with the class definition.

Persistent object   An object that can survive the process or thread that created it. A persistent object exists until it is explicitly deleted.

Polymorphism   (Means 'many forms'). The ability of an object to assume different forms and thereby potentially to exhibit varying behaviour, depending on the particular form assumed at a specific time.

Property   A conceptual notion. An attribute usually associated with a link defining a relationship between classes.

Pure object-oriented language   A programming language which enforces the object-oriented paradigm. In a pure object-oriented programming language all software executes within units called objects.

Schema   The structure or template of the data in a database. In an object-oriented database this schema may also include methods to access and manipulate data.

Semantic data model   A data model concerned with capturing the usage and meaning of data that can then be used directly for subsequent data structuring.

Server   One side of a client/server relationship. The server responds to requests from the client. (see also *Client*).

Specialization   A class x is a specialization of a class y if x is defined to directly or indirectly inherit from y.

Static (early) binding   Describes the situation where messages are bound to methods at compile-time – normally because all references to methods can be resolved at compile-time. This is the normal situation for a traditional programming language such as C or Pascal.

Static typing   Describes the situation where an identifier is assigned a class type at compile time and retains that type during program execution.

Strong typing   Describes the situation where an identifier is assigned a class type at compile time, but that type may be substituted for any subtype (related through inheritance) during run-time. This enables languages such as C++ and Eiffel to use a restricted form of dynamic binding.

Transient object   A object created during the execution of a thread or process and destroyed either before or upon termination of that process (compare with *persistent object*).

Trigger   The automatic application of an operation to selected objects in a group when the operation is applied to some starting object of that group. Triggers can be stored and executed by the database management system or they may be implemented as private methods within objects.

Unconstrained polymorphism   A form of polymorphism where the typing system of the programming language does not require any type consistency through a class inheritance hierarchy. This behaviour is exhibited by dynamically typed languages such as Smalltalk.

References and further reading

Alabiso B. (1988). Transformation of data flow analysis models to object-oriented design. In *Proc. OOPSLA '88*, pp. 335–53. New York: ACM

Arnold P., Bodoff S., Coleman D., Gilchrist H. and Hayes F. (1991). An evaluation of five object oriented development methods. *Journal of Object Oriented Programming – Focus on Analysis and Design,* SIGS Publication, New York.

Balin S. C. (1989). An object-oriented requirements specification method. *Communications of the ACM*, **32**(5), 608–23.

Batty P. (1991). GIS databases – which way forward? In proceedings of AM/FM European Conference VII, Montreux, September 1991.

Beck K. and Cunningham W. (1989). A laboratory for teaching object-oriented thinking. In *Proc. OOPSLA '89*, New Orleans, October 1–6. New York: ACM Press

Blair G., Malik J., Nicol J. R. and Walpole J. (1990). A synthesis of object-oriented and functional ideas in the design of a distributed software engineering environment. *Software Engineering Journal,* May, pp. 193–204.

Bloor R. (1990). *The Next Generation of Databases.* Daemon, pp. 11–18.

Bobrow D. G., DeMichiel L., Gabriel R. P. *et al.* (1988). *The Common LISP Object System Specification.* ANSI Technical Report 88-002R, X3J13 Standards Committee Document. SIGPLAN Notices, 23

Boehm B. W. (1981). *Software Engineering Economics.* ISBN 0-13-822122-7. Englewood Cliffs, NJ: Prentice-Hall

Booch G. (1991). *Object-Oriented Design with Applications.* Reading, MA: Benjamin/Cummings

Bouldin B. M. (1989). *Agents of Change – Managing the Introduction of Automated Tools.* ISBN 0-13-018508-6. Yourdon Press Computing Series. New York: Yourdon Press

Brown A.D. (1991). *Object-Oriented Databases – Applications in Software Engineering.* Maidenhead: McGraw-Hill

Buhr R. J. A. (1984). *System Design with Ada.* Englewood Cliffs, NJ: Prentice-Hall

Butler G. F. and Corbin M. J. (1989). *Object-Oriented Simulation in Fortran-77.* Royal Aerospace Establishment Working Paper MM 388-89. November

Buxton J. N. and Malcolm R. (1991). Software technology transfer. *Software Engineering Journal,* **6**(1), IEE/BCS Joint Publication

Cattell R. G. G. (1991). What are next-generation database systems? *Communications of the ACM*, **24**(10), October.

Charette R. N. (1990). *Application Strategies for Risk Analysis.* Maidenhead: Intertext/McGraw-Hill

Chen P. P. S. (1976). The entity relationship model: towards a unified view of data. *ACM Trans. on Database Systems,* **1**(1)

Coad P. and Yourdon E. (1990). *Object-Oriented Analysis.* Englewood Cliffs, NJ: Prentice-Hall

Coad P. and Yourdon E. (1991a). *Object-Oriented Analysis,* 2nd edn. Englewood Cliffs, NJ: Prentice-Hall

Coad P. and Yourdon E. (1991b). *Object-Oriented Design.* Englewood Cliffs, NJ: Prentice-Hall

Codd E. F. (1972). Further normalization of the data base relational model. In *Data Base Systems,* Courant Computer Science Symposia Series, Vol. 6. Englewood Cliffs, NJ: Prentice-Hall

Codd E. F. (1974). Recent investigations into relational database systems. In *Proc. IFIP Congress,* Stockholm, Sweden

Codd E. F. (1979). Extending the database relational model to capture more meaning. *ACM Trans. on Database Systems,* **4**(4)

Codd E. F. (1982). Relational database: a practical foundation for productivity. *Communications of the ACM,* **25**(2), 109–17

Colbert E. (1989). The object-oriented software development method: a practical approach to object-oriented development. In *TRI-Ada Proc.,* New York 1989

Constantine L. L. and Yourdon E. (1979). *Structured Design.* Englewood Cliffs, NJ: Prentice-Hall

Cox B. J. (1986). *Object-Oriented Programming: An Evolutionary Approach.* ISBN 0-201-10393-1. Addison-Wesley

Cox B. J. (1990). There is a silver bullet. *BYTE Magazine,* October

Cox B. J. (1992a). What if there is a silver bullet? *Journal of Object-Oriented Programming,* **5**(3), guest editorial

Cox B. J. (1992b). Software industrial revolution. Keynote speech, Object World Conference, San Francisco, CA, July

Crosby P. B. (1979). *Quality is Free.* New York: McGraw-Hill

Dahl O.-J. and Nygaard K. (1966). Simula – an ALGOL-based simulation language. *Communications of the ACM,* **9**, 671–8

Date C. J. (1986). *An Introduction to Database Systems.* Vol. 1, 4th edn. World Student Series. Reading, MA: Addison-Wesley

de Champeaux D. and Faure P. (1992). A comparative study of object-oriented analysis methods. *Journal of Object-Oriented Programming,* **5**(1), March/April

DeMarco T. (1979). *Structured Analysis and System Specification.* Englewood Cliffs, NJ: Prentice-Hall

deNatale R., LaLonde J., Leathers B. and Philips R. (1990). OOP in the real world, Addendum to OOPSLA '90 proceedings, ACM Press, pp. 29–34.

Fishman D. H. (1989). An overview of the IRIS DBMS. In *Object-Oriented Concepts, Databases and Applications* (Kim W. and Lochovsky F. H., eds.), pp. 219–50. Reading, MA: Addison-Wesley

Garfunkel J. (1990). Cobol – the next stage. *Computer World,* July 23, p. 87.

Goldberg A. (1984). *Smalltalk-80: The Interactive Programming Environment.* ISBN 0-201-11372-4. Reading, MA: Addison-Wesley

Goldberg A. and Robson D. (1989). *Smalltalk-80: The Language*. ISBN 0-201-13688-0. Reading, MA: Addison-Wesley

Gossain S. and Anderson B. (1990). An iterative-design model for reusable object-oriented software. ECOOP/OOPSLA '90 Proceedings. In *SIGPLAN Notices*, **25**(10). ACM Press

Henderson-Sellers B. (1991). Hybrid object-oriented/functional decomposition methodologies for the software engineering life cycle. *Hotline on Object-Oriented Technology*, **2**(7), 1–8

Henderson-Sellers B. (1991b). *A Book of Object-Oriented Knowledge*. Brookvale, NSW: Prentice-Hall

Henderson-Sellers B. and Edwards J. M. (1990). The object-oriented systems lifecycle. *Communications of the ACM*, **33**(9).

HOOD Working Group (1989). *Hood Reference Manual* Issue 3.0. WME/89-173/JB. *Hood User Manual* Issue 3.0. WME/89-353/JB. European Space Agency

Humphrey W. S. (1989). *Managing the Software Process*. ISBN 0-201-18095-2. Addison-Wesley

Humphrys M. (1991). *The Objective Evidence – A Real-life Comparison of Procedural and Object-Oriented Programming*. IISL Innovative Solutions Project. IBM Ireland Information Services Ltd (IISL), 2 Burlington Road, Dublin 4, Ireland

Jackson M. S. (1991). Tutorial on object-oriented databases. *Information and Software Technology*, **33**(1), 4–12.

Jacobson I. (1987). Object-oriented development in an industrial environment. OOPSLA '87. In *ACM SIGPLAN*, **22**(12), 183–91

Jacobson I., Christerson M., Jonsson P. and Övergaard G. (1992). *Object-Oriented Software Engineering – A Use Case Driven Approach*. Wokingham: Addison-Wesley

Khoshafian S. and Abnous R. (1990). *Object-Orientation – Concepts, Languages, Databases, User Interfaces*. ISBN 0-471-51801-8. John Wiley.

LaLonde W. R., McGugan J. and Thomas D. (1989). The real advantages of pure object-oriented systems or why object-oriented extensions to C are doomed to fail. In *Proc. 13th Ann. Int. Computer Software and Applications Conf.*, pp. 344–50. Washington DC: IEEE Computer Society Press

Leathers B. (1990). Panel: OOP in the real world. OOPSLA/ECOOP. In *Proc. ACM SIGPLAN Notices, 1990*, **25**(10), pp. 299–302

Lyngbaek P. (1991). *OSQL: A Language for Object Databases:* HP Technical Report HPL-DTD-91-4, January 15.

Maier D. (1986). Why object-oriented databases can succeed where others have failed. In *International Workshop on Object-Oriented Database Systems* (Dittrich K. R. and Dayall U., eds.), p. 227. New York: IEEE Computer Society Press

Maude T. and Willis G. (1991). *Rapid Prototyping: The Management of Software Risk*. London: Pitman Publishing

Mellor S. (1990). Structure analysis and object-oriented analysis. Proc. ECOOP/OOPSLA '90 Conf. In *SIGPLAN Notices*, **25**(10), 135–9. New York: ACM Press

Meyer B. (1988). *Object-Oriented Software Construction*. ISBN 0-13-629031-0. Englewood Cliffs, NJ: Prentice-Hall International

Meyer B. (1991). *Eiffel: The Language.* ISBN 0-13-247925-7. Englewood Cliffs, NJ: Prentice-Hall International

Myers G. J. (1978). *Composite/Structured Design.* New York: Van Nostrand Reinhold

New Science Associates (1989). *Object-Oriented Technology – Commercial Scope and Limits.* New Science Associates, Old Post Road, Southport, Conn. 06490.

New Science Associates (1992). Object *Oriented Analysis and Design Methods – A Comparative Analysis.* New Science Associates, Old Post Road, Southport, Conn. 06490, USA.

Object Design Incorporated (ODI) (1990). *How to evaluate an Object-Oriented Database Management System (ODBMS).* 1 New England Executive Park, Burlington, MA, 01803.

OMG (1992a). *Object Analysis and Design – Working draft version 4.0*, Edited by A. T. F. Hutt, Object Management Group.

OMG (1992b). *Object Analysis and Design,* Volume 1, *Reference Model, Working draft version 7.0*, Edited by A. T. F. Hutt, Object Management Group.

Ould M. A. (1990). *Strategies for Software Engineering: The Management of Risk and Quality.* Chichester: Wiley

Ovum Ltd (1989). *Object-Oriented Systems: The Commercial Benefits* (Jeffcoate J., Hales K. and Downes V., eds.). Ovum Ltd, 7 Rathbone Street, London W1P 1AF

Page-Jones M. (1980). *A Practical Guide to Structured Systems Design.* New York: Yourdon Press

Polilli S. (1991). Object of MIS desire currently not OODPMS. *Software Mag.,* **11**(3), 67–71.

Pressman R. S. (1988). *Making Software Engineering Happen – A Guide for Instituting the Technology.* Englewood Cliffs, NJ: Prentice-Hall

Purchase J. A. and Winder R. L. (1991). Debugging tools for object oriented programming. *Journal of Object Oriented Programming,* **4**(3), June.

Ramackers G. J. and Goedvolk J. G. (1989). OO, a solution to the software crisis? *Journal of Software Research,* Vleermuis Software Research b.v., December 1989.

Reenskaug T. and Skaar A. L. (1989). An environment for literate Smalltalk programming. OOPSLA '89. In *SIGPLAN Notices,* **24**(10), 337–45

Reenskaug T., Andersen E. P., Berre A. J. *et al.* (1992). OORASS: seamless support for the creation and maintenance of object-oriented systems (Taskon A/S, Ganstadalteen 21, N-0371 Oslo 3, Norway). *Journal of Object-Oriented Programming,* **5**(6)

Rumbaugh J., Blaha M., Premerlani W. *et al.* (1991). *Object-Oriented Modeling and Design.* ISBN 0-13-630054-5. Englewood Cliffs, NJ: Prentice-Hall

Schaffert C., Cooper T., Bullis B. *et al.* (1986). An introduction to Trellis/Owl. In *Proc. OOPSLA '86,* pp. 9–16

Schmucker K. J. (1986). *Object-oriented Programming for the Macintosh.* Hasbrouck Heights, NJ: Hayden Book Co.

Shlaer S. and Mellor S. J. (1988). *Object-Oriented Systems Analysis: Modeling the World in Data,* Yourdon Press Computing Series. New York: Yourdon Press

Shlaer S. and Mellor S. J. (1992). *Object Lifetimes: Modeling the World in States.* Yourdon Press Computing Series. New York: Yourdon Press

Shlaer S., Mellor S. J. and Hywari W. (1990). *OODLE: A Language-Independent Notation for Object-Oriented Design.* Project Technology, Inc., 2560 Ninth Street, Suite 214, Berkeley, California 94710, USA

Soley R. M. (1992). *The Object Management Architecture Guide,* edited by R. M. Soley, 2nd ed., OMG TC Document 92.11.1.

Spivey J. M. (1989). *The Z Notation – A Reference Manual.* Englewood Cliffs, NJ: Prentice-Hall

Stonebraker M. and Rowe L. (1986). The design of Postgres. In *Proc. ACM-SIGMOD Int. Conf. Management of Data,* pp. 340–55

Stonebraker M., Kreps P., Wong E. and Held G. (1976). The design and implementation of Ingres. *ACM Trans. Database Syst.,* **1**(3)

Stroustrup B. (1991a). *The C++ Programming Language,* 2nd edn. ISBN 0-201-53992-6. Wokingham: Addison-Wesley

Stroustrup B. (1991b). Notes from European C++ User Group

The Object-Oriented Database System Manifesto: Atkinson M. *et al.* (1989). *The Object-Oriented Database System Manifesto.* Paper presented at the 1st Int. Conf. on Object-Oriented and Deductive Databases, IEEE, Tokyo

Third-Generation Database System Manifesto: Committee for Advanced DBMS Function. *Third-Generation Database System Manifesto.* Memorandum No. UCB/ERL M90/28, 9 April 1990. Electronics Research Laboratory, University of California, Berkeley, CA 94720

Thompson A. K., Madden P. and Angelone E. (1992). *Incremental Approach to Software Quality.* Belfast: The Institute of Software Engineering

Versant Object Technology Corporation (1990). Moving to an OODBMS. *Tutorial Number 3, OOPSLA 1990 Conference.* LOOMIS M.E.S. ACM.

Versant Object Technology Corporation (1991). *OODBMS Product Profile*

Ward P. (1989). How to integrate object orientation with structured analysis and design. *IEEE Software,* March, 74–82

Wasserman A. I., Pircher P. A. and Muller R. J. (1990). The object-oriented software design notation for software design representation. *IEEE Computer,* **23**(3)

Wegner P. (1987). Dimensions of object-based language design. *SIGPLAN Notices,* **22**(12), 168–82. Orlando, FL

Wegner P. (1990). Concepts and paradigms of object-oriented programming – expansion of Oct. 4 OOPSLA-89 Keynote Talk. *OOPS Messenger,* **1**(1), ACM Press.

Whitewater Group (1989). *Actor Language Manual.* The Whitewater Group, Inc., Evanston, Illinois, USA

Wirfs-Brock R. (1990). Lecture notes of NTU Satellite Network broadcast, Fort Collins, CO, USA. Cited in *Journal of Object-Oriented Programming,* March/April 1992, by Dennis de Champeaux in an article comparing methods

Wirfs-Brock R., Wilkerson B. and Wiener L. (1990). *Designing Object-Oriented Software.* Englewood Cliffs, NJ: Prentice-Hall

Yau S. S., Collofello J. S. and MacGregor T. (1978). Ripple effect analysis of software maintenance. In *Proc. COMPSAC '78,* pp. 60–5

Yourdon E. and Constantine L. L. (1975). *Structured Design.* New York: Yourdon Press

Index